Forever England

KU-208-804

Femininity, literature and conservatism between the wars

Alison Light

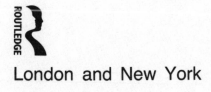

London and New York

First published 1991
by Routledge
11 New Fetter Lane, London EC4P 4EE

Simultaneously published in the USA and Canada
by Routledge
a division of Routledge, Chapman and Hall, Inc.
29 West 35th Street, New York, NY 10001

© Alison Light 1991

Typeset in 10/12pt Garamond by Intype, London
Printed and Great Britain by Clays Ltd, St. Ives plc, Suffolk

All rights reserved. No part of this book may be reprinted
or reproduced or utilised in any form or by any electronic,
mechanical, or other means, now known or hereafter
invented, including photocopying and recording, or in any
information storage or retrieval system, without permission
in writing from the publishers.

British Library Cataloguing in Publication Data
Light, Alison
  Forever England: femininity, literature and conservatism
  between the wars.
  I. Title
  823.912099287

Library of Congress Cataloging in Publication Data
Light, Alison
  Forever England: femininity, literature and conservatism
  between the wars/Alison Light.
      p.   cm.
  Revision of thesis (Ph.D.)—University of Sussex.
  Includes bibliographical references.
  1. English fiction–20th century–History and criticism.
  2. English fiction–Women authors–History and criticism.
  3. Literature and society–England–History–20th century.   4. World
  War, 1914–1918–England–Literature and the war.   5. Women and
  literature–England–History–20th century.   6. National
  characteristics, English, in literature.   7. Conservatism–Great
  Britain–History–20th century.   8. Femininity (Psychology) in
  literature.   I. Title.
  PR888.W6L54   1991
  823'.912099287—dc20 91–587

ISBN 0–415–01661–4
       0–415–01662–2 pbk

for Cora Kaplan

Contents

Preface

This book is neither literary criticism nor cultural studies; literary history nor feminist theory. More devoutly theoreticist readers will search in vain for the exemplification of a particular theory or paradigm; the chapters hover uneasily but, I hope, productively between different modes of analysis; they move unashamedly between the techniques of an older style of literary criticism, with its attention to language and to readerly response, and a critical practice which believes that not only must we look beyond the words on the page for their fuller meaning, but that being different readers, inconstant creatures of time and place, we can never finalise our understanding. If the driving energy behind this project is primarily literary – I am interested in writing and in the forms it takes – it is at the same time fuelled by an historicising passion which wants to see how, and imagine why, such forms, like all that human beings do and make, continue to change.

The inter-war years in Britain ought to provide an exciting focus for literary studies but unlike, perhaps, any other makeshift period in literary history, it has suffered from an inability on the part of its chroniclers to look across the culture as a whole. What comes as second nature to medievalists, as they move from chivalric romances to miracle plays, to students of the eighteenth century, as much at home in the coffee houses as in the court, and even to nineteenth-century literary scholars, expected to have some knowledge of the mechanics of serial publication or of reading aloud, of the contemporary stage as well as journalism, if they are to make full sense of Dickens – the idea that there are many possible literary forms in circulation at any one time and that all of them repay attention and tell us something about each other – is likely still to be felt as heretical by twentieth-century critics.

In part we may wish to blame the shadow cast in the period by the looming presence of literary modernism for narrowing and obscuring our vision. But to do so is to forget that this creature has largely been of our own making, the product of literary critical assumptions and judgements, kept alive and well especially by those who are content to work with a map in which what they call the popular and what they deem the high cultural are seen as poles apart. In fact the natural astigmatism of the literary establishment in Britain seems to be especially pronounced when it turns its half-blind gaze on the post-war years; its obsession with the notion of cultural elites is as obvious in the mesmeric fascination exercised by 'the Auden generation' as by Bloomsbury, in the endless attempts to find a canonical literature rather than in allowing a wider or more generous view of literary pleasures and readerships. It is indeed a curious kind of cultural squint which makes Noel Coward or P. G. Wodehouse of less interest than Stephen Spender or Christopher Isherwood, or which will, at a pinch, allow Noel Coward or P. G. Wodehouse a representative place in the literary past where an Agatha Christie or a Daphne du Maurier merits not even a footnote.

Whilst this book does not pretend to offer a survey of inter-war litera- ture, a sociology of readerships or a history of publishing, one of its primary impulses is to try to avoid reproducing that 'parting of the ways',[1] which literary critics and cultural commentators were themselves so active in creating in this period. Rather than setting 'highbrow' against 'low- brow', the serious against the merely escapist or trashy, I am drawn to look for what is shared and common across these forms in the inter-war years, and to see them all as historically meaningful. In any case, not only are such cultural and literary evaluations dialectical judgements – the labels of 'high' and 'low' only make sense in relation to each other – we need to realise that their provenance is always changing: terms such as 'popular' or 'mass' must open up rather than close down historical enquiry. Those who are queasy about crossing from high to low in either direction will not enjoy this book – for which I make no apologies. I only wish I had been more adventurous and made more of these crossings.

Recent forms of literary theory and practice, especially of a radical persuasion, have made much of treating novels – and all 'texts' – as though they were on trial. They are frequently 'interrogated', grilled for their 'collusion', or, more benignly, analysed like dreams for their gaps and absences. Texts are seen as primarily guilty, of repression at the very least, of wilful misconstruction at the worst. Meanwhile the critic holds the book fastidiously at arm's length (for fear of being found 'complicit') and tries to emerge with clean hands. That has not been my method. It seems to me that given the formative role of novels as a place where our subjectivities, our very ideas of ourselves, are fashioned, any critical prac- tice which does not find fellow-feeling with past readers and writers, however distant they seem from our own conscious projects and beliefs, is as unable to understand the historical meaning of such writing as that which wallows only in the pleasure of the known and familiar and is not interested in anything beyond the safe and local concerns of a comfortable self. Unless we can see how readers were themselves reached and touched, unless we can recognise that we too are bound to our reading by forms of belonging as well as exile, how can we hope to understand the potential for human change and its different historical limits?

It is hardly controversial to suggest that what we call our histories gives us insight as much into our own contemporary preoccupations as those of the past. Those who have taught or learnt English in some form over the last ten years will no doubt recognise how much this book bears some of the traces of the extraordinary shifts and implosions within that subject which have been variously signalled as a buoyant expansion or as internal dissolution, and which have left what was once a solid body of study and practice in a state of deliquescence. This book is as much the product of a resistance to the dispersal of the literary (it is unashamedly about both the English and their reading), as it is a child of that diaspora. It is tempered, I hope, by a distrust of new orthodoxies as well as old.

My own particular route into the crisis in English studies has been via feminist work, and I should like to acknowledge at the outset that this book could not have been written except within the context of the last ten years of feminist debate nor without the experience of the shared sense of intellectual purpose which such work has generated. It was the promise of a brave new world of women's writing which drew me back to university and made it possible for me to imagine a very different kind of literary research, one which could acknowledge other audiences, other pleasures, and indeed give intellectual credence and dignity to some of the reading which had been part of my own past but which never featured in literary critical histories. That energy which went into a cultural revolution – in publishing, in education, in the arts and the media – seems to me to have been the distinctive and lasting achievement of the contemporary Women's Movement. Within the purlieus of the academy, even those who remain sceptical about women's studies or feminist courses (and that includes many feminists) would find it difficult to remain ignorant of the issues which a generation of feminist scholars has raised, about cultural and economic activities, about the writing of history, about the very lineaments and categories of our knowledge.

Feminist literary work has undergone several revolutions, however. It has moved from a reliance on the assumption that novels or plays or poems by women offer universal truths to all women, and that the business of the feminist critic is to find a literature of our own whose triumph over adversity is just cause for celebration, to asking much more awkward and probing questions about any relationship we may wish to see between women and writing. For myself an uneasiness with the idea of 'women's writing', both in its tendency to universalise women's experience and its vision of the transcendent value of literary expression, stemmed from constantly being irritated by its frequent blindness to the categories of class. In the first place I was queasy at the reprinting of feminist 'modern classics' which blithely told us, for example, that Rosamond Lehmann's *Invitation to the Waltz*, published in 1932, 'perfectly captures the emotions of all young girls on the threshold of life'[2] when it was clearly a fascinating fantasy written from inside the insecurities of the English middle class. It bothered me that feminists might praise the 'charm and sensitivity' of Olivia, the heroine, whose encounter with the local sweep's children leads her to compare them to rats, weevils and ants.[3] What was needed was a fuller historical understanding of how the fears of social difference infected the imagination of the female middle classes just as thoroughly as their male counterparts. Not a condemnation of Lehmann, but a placing of her which admitted her conservatisms, the sticking-points of her imagination as well as its flights.

Even that feminism which allied itself with a socialist tradition seemed to have little to say about a sense of class difference in women's lives, not in terms of spending habits, or living arrangements and employment, but of ways of thinking, feeling and imagining – the fences on the inside as well as the outside which have separated and antagonised women. Rather than writing about the working classes – as though class feeling was somehow only their problem and their history – it seemed to me that literary work might do well to look for ways of anthropologising the middle classes, making their assumptions seem a strange and unfamiliar culture rather than the unexamined norm. I was struck by how much those whom Virginia Woolf called 'the daughters of educated men' have been singularly silent about the aetiology of their own class perceptions. Thankfully their novels had been less discreet.

One of the major impetuses behind this book was therefore originally a perverse one. The chapters formed themselves around awkward questions and absences, eventually settling upon those authors who did not seem to invite or want the title 'woman writer', and those (often the same group) whose politics seemed to place them beyond the feminist pale. Like many projects which in the making seem wayward and against the grain, this one has turned out to be of its time, and to be part of a more general shift within feminist writing. It is now harder than ever simply to trumpet the successes of a 'women's history' or a 'women's literature', without recognising that these collectivities at best give the temporary strength of a unity where actually there are dissenting voices and repressed angers, and at worst set up exclusive and hierarchical groupings whose collectivity is maintained at the expense of subordinating others. Women were, and are, internally divided, as individuals and in groups. Such shared concerns and common forms of expression as we discover in any analysis of women's writing are themselves only makeshift: it is often as a defence against the constant instability of forms of belonging that we can best read the fashioning of powerful and mobilising identities in history. This book is therefore about some of the fictions within which women live – what they call their femininity – as well as, in the more narrowly literary sense, the fictions they create.

One must draw the line somewhere in attempting to share the intellectual history of a project with the reader. What means to be informative and contextualising can rapidly become tedious and self-indulgent. In any case such an archaeology, like all excavations, is potentially interminable: the past always has room for more. Acknowledgements are a kind of shorthand for that buried story and remind us how much even the most private labour of writing is indivisibly part of a shared and social life. I remain especially grateful to the welcoming academic community which I found at Sussex University in 1981, and to the many staff and fellow-students who made the potentially solitary business of postgraduate research feel part of a common intellectual endeavour: in particular I benefited hugely from the discussions over four years of the 'Literature Teaching Politics' reading group, and owe much to its members, especially Geoff Bennington, Rachel Bowlby, Jonathan Dollimore, David Forgacs, Frank Gloversmith, Ann Rosalind Jones, Ulrike Meinhof, Marcia Pointon, Alan Sinfield, Peter Stallybrass, and the late Allon White.

This book was originally written as a doctoral thesis and I should like, above all, to thank Cora Kaplan who acted as my supervisor at Sussex before her departure to Rutgers University, and who in many ways made this work possible. My own thinking owes a great deal to her passionate engagement with the question of literary pleasure and to her rigorous and imaginative understanding of a feminist cultural politics (exemplified by her collected essays in the volume *Sea Changes*); I have come to rely upon her intellectual as well as personal generosity. Not least because so many colleagues and students, and not only myself, depended on her inimitable fighting presence in the scholarly as well as political life of Sussex University, and because she is so much missed, am I delighted to dedicate this book to her.

I should also like to thank Geoffrey Hemstedt at Sussex who put me on to Ivy Compton-Burnett and *Mrs. Miniver* when I was still advancing crabwise from the 1950s to the '30s, and who oversaw the final stages of the thesis with genial scholarship and ready wit; his scrupulous proof-reading was beyond the call of duty. And I owe a special debt of friendship to Alex Owen, also a scion of Sussex but now teaching at Harvard University, who gave judicious advice on all the chapters in the midst of her own trans-Atlantic career, communicating an intellectual vitality and a feeling for writing even across the ether. I was greatly spurred on by the example of her research into nineteenth-century spiritualism (published as *The Darkened Room*) and her powerful sense of history as a place which could include the most subterranean currents and the most interior spaces.

Since most of this book was written at a distance from the university which nurtured it, I am all the more beholden to those other friends and colleagues who responded to the work and offered help with it. I would like to thank Frank Gray at Brighton Polytechnic for kindly shouldering the burden of our joint teaching at critical moments in the writing; I owe an apology to Raya Levin for not doing battle with her over her reading of Chapter 1; her distrust of biography strengthened my resolve to include it; I am indebted to John Barrell for his urbane comments on early versions of the introduction and Chapter 2, and am especially grateful to Helen Taylor and Lyndal Roper who read large parts of the manuscript and were unstinting in their affectionate encouragement as well as critical commentary on the work; my warmest thanks to them both.

I have also been more than fortunate in my publishers and want to thank Merrilyn Julian of the erstwhile Methuen Press for setting me on the road to publication, and Janice Price at Routledge whose unfailing enthusiasm for the project has seen it through to completion. She has been, in her own wryly English manner, the most courteous and responsive of editors; her support has been invaluable.

Finally, I have a debt which to acknowledge in full would surely weary or embarrass the reader: I have shared so much of this book with Raphael Samuel that it is hard to imagine having written it without him. My own ideas about national identity gathered strength from his work for *Patriotism* in the History Workshop series, and from his unfashionable fondness for the British between the wars, but the writing also gained immeasurably from his tireless capacity to chisel away at sentences and thoughts, until they assumed reasonable shape. Not everyone would continue to be such a gentle and relentless critic in the teeth of often surly or pugnacious resistance, or put up with my residual tendency to see the middle classes as simply class enemies; thanks to him I came to realise that the subject of this book was conservatism, including my own. In fact I'm inclined to believe that only in our house, and with his companionship, would I have begun to appreciate how much of life is animated by the struggle between the past and the present, between what we feel comfortable and at home with, and what insists that we make things anew.

Alison Light
Spitalfields
February 1991

THE QUIET HOUSE

When we were children old Nurse used to say
    The house was like an auction or a fair
    Until the lot of us were safe in bed.
    It has been quiet as the country-side

    Since Ted and Janey and then Mother died
And Tom crossed Father and was sent away.
After the lawsuit he could not hold up his head,
    Poor Father, and he does not care
    For people here, or to go anywhere.

To get away to Aunt's for that week-end
    Was hard enough; (since then, a year ago,
    He scarcely lets me slip out of his sight –)
At first I did not like my cousin's friend,
    I did not think I should remember him:
    His voice has gone, his face is growing dim
And if I like him now I do not know.
    He frightened me before he smiled –
    He did not ask me if he might –
    He said that he would come one Sunday night,
    He spoke to me as if I were a child.

No year has been like this that has just gone by;
    It may be that what Father says is true,
If things are so it does not matter why:
    But everything has burned, and not quite through.
    The colours of the world have turned
    To flame, the blue, the gold has burned
In what used to be such a leaden sky.
When you are burned quite through you die.

    Red is the strangest pain to bear;
In Spring the leaves on the budding trees;
In Summer the roses are worse than these,
    More terrible than they are sweet:
    A rose can stab you across the street
      Deeper than any knife:
    And the crimson haunts you everywhere –
Thin shafts of sunlight, like the ghosts of reddened swords have struck
              our stair
As if, coming down, you had spilt your life.

    I think that my soul is red
Like the soul of a sword or a scarlet flower:

But when these are dead
        They have had their hour.
I shall have had mine, too,
        For from head to feet,
I am burned and stabbed half through,
        And the pain is deadly sweet.

The things that kill us seem
        Blind to the death they give:
It is only in our dream
        The things that kill us live.

The room is shut where Mother died,
        The other rooms are as they were,
The world goes on the same outside,
        The sparrows fly across the Square,
        The children play as we four did there,
        The trees grow green and brown and bare,
The sun shines on the dead Church spire,
        And nothing lives here but the fire,
While Father watches from his chair
                Day follows day
The same, or now and then, a different grey,
                Till, like his hair,
Which Mother said was wavy once and bright,
        They will all turn white.

        To-night I heard a bell again –
Outside it was the same mist of fine rain,
The lamps just lighted down the long, dim street,
        No one for me –
        I think it is myself I go to meet:
I do not care; some day I *shall* not think; I shall not *be*!

Charlotte Mew (1916)

Introduction

Introductions are usually written last of all and this one is no exception. Their outlook, despite appearances, is retrospective, for whilst they hope to give the reader a taste of what is to come, they are necessarily written with hindsight: they belong to that familiar form of story-telling which starts with 'once upon a time', the sort we can rely on to end. To suggest to readers what they might like to know in order to begin, the author needs already to have covered the ground in advance. Which is why, for the writer of a book like this one, so much of the material for introductions and conclusions seems to be interchangeable; decisions as to what to use as 'signposts' for the reader (an introduction) and which to leave as the clearly marked features of the landscape (the conclusion) involve the same kind of cognitive mapping. Both depend on the artificiality of ordering what was originally discovered or explored only as amorphous possibility. The old teaching adage – 'tell them what you are going to do, tell them when you are doing it, then tell them what you did' – depends on the same reflex which makes a significant sequence out of the random, one which is historical in impulse since it makes a chronology and it gives duration – beginning, middle and end – to what otherwise would be unwritable and unthinkable – an endless present.

Where you decide to start from will itself limit the possibilities of other stories, and other endings, and finding a point of settlement from which to begin ('are you sitting comfortably?' BBC radio used to ask its child-listeners) is always a matter of position. The place from which one writes, but also from which one understands the past, is a matter of perspective and will alter the focus of what can be grasped near to hand, what can only be glimpsed on the horizon. The questions which writing even the humblest introduction raise are therefore not just about the exigencies of literary conventions or even about the process of writing itself, but also about all historical inquiry. They raise in miniature the problems of historicity, of periodisation and its relation to 'lived experience', of positionality,

for writer and reader, and of the demands of form, which are themselves
a kind of placing.

We are perhaps most used to those historical accounts which make what
was actually a mess of immediacy into a narrative; they give us the illusion
of being *in medias res*, of experiencing or knowing a culture first hand
whilst actually shaping it into a form, a generality, a knowability which
depends on a pre-given sense of ending. 'History', in the sense of *all* that
went on, is always in excess of the descriptions we make of it, and if
historians are typically obsessed by the sheer material superabundance of
the past, they are equally aware of its contingency. All historians tell
stories where before, for the people living in those times, *then*, like our
now, there was a heterogeneous present. How much people felt what we
now know to be their future pressing upon them, how far they lived in
expectation or in suspense, reading in the entrails of the present signs of
what was to come, and how far they were moved by the forms of the
past, aware of it as loss, as comfort, or as an invisible force in their lives,
are questions which modern historians ask themselves.

This tension between the retrospective ordering of the past and an
attempt imaginatively to re-enter the moment as it was lived, before, as
it were, we made it history, is central to all historical projects but it is
also at the heart of the novelistic imagination and its excitement. Novels
seem at one and the same time to be always in the thick of things and
yet to hold the world at arm's length; to invite the reader inside a culture,
and yet to insist on listening to its own heart beat. Such a self-examination
can take many forms and need not involve what we might think of as an
authorial diagnosis. All novels, whether they mean to or not, give us a
medley of different voices, languages and positions, and none can sustain
a single 'argument' with the reader. Novels, as Salman Rushdie has written,[1] quarrel with themselves, and it is this quarrelling which seems to
take us right inside a time and place even as it gives us a breathing space
in which to be distant and to reflect. Because novels not only speak from
their cultural moment but take issue with it, imagining new versions of its
problems, exposing, albeit by accident as well as by design, its confusions,
conflicts and irrepressible desires, the study of fiction is an especially
inviting and demanding way into the past.

II

Shall we lay the blame on the war? When the guns fired in August
1914, did the faces of men and women show so plain in each other's
eyes that romance was killed? Certainly it was a shock (to women in
particular with their illusions about education, and so on) to see the
faces of our rulers in the light of shell-fire. So ugly they looked –
German, English, French – so stupid. But lay the blame where one will,

the illusion which inspired Tennyson and Christina Rossetti to sing so passionately about the coming of their loves is far rarer now than then. One has only to read, to look, to listen, to remember. But why say 'blame'? Why, if it was an illusion, not praise the catastrophe, whatever it was, that destroyed illusion and put truth in its place? For truth . . . those dots mark the spot where, in search of truth, I missed the turning up to Fernham. Yes indeed, which was truth and which was illusion? I asked myself.

(Virginia Woolf, A Room of One's Own, 1929)

On the road to her imaginary Fernham (in 'Oxbridge' where, if anywhere, secure knowledge might presumably be found), Virginia Woolf's narrator takes a literary event for an historical one: it strikes her as she hums a verse or two that the lyric voice of Victorian poetry is dead – no more Rossetti, no more joy, no more romance, she says, in her world. Should she explain such a shift by an event, by History with a capital 'h': the war? Surely this was the cause, and the death of romance the effect? But then, she muses, if with this disappearance went too the illusions that men and women had about each other, the false sentiments in which the sexes had disguised and prettified themselves, and that self-deceptive subjective life on which such poetry throve, didn't the event produce more truth? If this unveiling of each other was a revelation of the realities of power, of stark nationalisms, of brute masculinity and of feminine wiles, why feel it was a catastrophe at all? Wasn't the war, that cataclysm universally mourned, from the point of view of male–female relations at least, a good thing?

At this point Woolf's argument from cause and effect breaks down; she carefully loses her way and the thought, which ought to have been a conclusion, disappears into a dotted line. Her refusal to arrive at a final historical judgement, which is also a moral one about the superiority of her own times, is salutary. Once we introduce, as she does, the question of subjectivity, of how the world was lived on the inside, how can we say with confidence that *their* vision of the world was illusion and our own the truth? It was what they lived by, after all, just as we live by our own fictions. However much we might want history to ratify our sense of change, to put *their* present firmly behind *us* and guarantee our own advance into the light, such surety, Woolf suggests by disturbing her own progress, is itself an illusion. It need not stop us arguing for our own beliefs but when we think we have once and for all arrived at the ultimate position of judgement, that is when we have lost our way. History cannot shore up the present and make it safe for us; the past cannot be kept at bay.

Woolf's sense of loss in the poetic feeling of the culture into which she was born, of a literary, liberal class no longer in love with itself, is double-edged: though it might seem that she is exposing their dreams to the harsh light of day, her diffidence betokens at the same time a call for a more capacious and more generous retrospective. It suggests the need for a history which gives due place to these illusions and idealisms, and that an understanding of events which has no room for the romantic and the imaginative is no understanding at all. And once you ask, as Woolf did, about men and women facing each other over the guns of August, you ask about what (or who) makes up the narratives we call history, what matters and is made to matter. Taking the literary into account and making a space for subjectivity is more than just a case of adding feeling or fantasy into a narrative of things and events, cabbages and kings: it must call in question what is seen as history in the first place. In so doing it attacks that opposition of the private and the public which structures and determines the organisation of disciplines and categories of knowledge and which slices them up into manageable portions of fiction and fact, dream and reality, subject and object.

Such a perception has its own history. Even without knowing that this passage was written in the late 1920s we would call it modern. Woolf's journey into history takes her inward; her path is one which leads on to increasingly unsure ground. Her awareness that a history of subjectivity is not simply consonant with external accounts, that wars reach into personal depths as well as public coffers but that the private experience and the public records do not always match; her reticence about moral judgements which repose upon a sense of the rightness of one's own way of being; her ironic deferrals and whimsical understatements – these are all part of the making of a modernity for which the writing finds the appropriate form. Woolf is of her time in citing the war as marking the moment from which it no longer seemed possible to divorce the dramas of the interior life from the mainstream of history: it was what drew her to look for historical truth in other literary forms – biography, real and fictional, elegy, memoir, as well as novels, ways of writing history which could accommodate, amongst other things, the woman's point of view.

For it is not coincidental that the path which takes Virginia Woolf into modernity is a rhetorical search in *A Room of One's Own* for what a feminine relationship to knowledge and the past might be. Her carefully contrived reflections are part of a deliberate ramble around male property: the Oxbridge college where she has just been shooed off the grass is an image in miniature of masculine defensiveness about the territory of learning and also of history itself. Woolf's essay has its polemical edge and it is one which places her as part of a generation of women who saw themselves as trespassing on these male preserves. Woolf's anger at exclusion is none the less tempered by a scepticism about the desirability of petitioning for election to full membership of this society. Her feminism leads her to doubt whether the institutions and the orders of knowledge as they stand are themselves worthy of female admission. On what terms, we might see her as asking, should modern women seek to enter the historical narrative? Now that there was a chance of writing it for themselves, might they not want a different plot altogether?

The search for her own room, for a place which could be both domestic and public, private and professional, suggests how much the act of writing has itself had special meanings for women given their situation both in the house and in history. No one has lived more on the inside than women: indeed, the role of history's insiders might serve as a definition of what we mean by 'bourgeois' when we apply it to the female sex. I shall argue in this book that between the wars a sense of that other history, a history from inside, gained new significance, that the place of private life and what it represented became the subject of new kinds of national and public interest and found new literary forms. To move towards such a history we need to step over the threshold into the most ordinary of houses and least remarkable of lives. Charlotte Mew's poem of 1916, which prefaces this volume, suggests something of what we might find there. In her shifts between the lyrical and the vernacular, her fierce reversal of romantic imagery ('a rose can stab you across the street'), she fashions, like many writers of her generation, a language for the collapse of late-Victorian idealism. But here it is the most purely domestic and familiar world, the only one in which the speaker has a place, the sum of her existence, which is evoked as murderous: family ties, respect for elders, the notion of womanly sacrifice, of home sweet home – Mew writes about a violence being done to an older model of bourgeois propriety as total and as obliterating as that which was taking place on that other Front. Like so many of her male peers, she is a casualty of the end of an era; for her, too, 'everything has burned, and not quite through'. What vision of the future, what hopes for the present rose from the ashes of this past? Whatever we discover when we venture inside that quiet house, we will not be ignoring the history of England but deepening our knowledge of it.

Forever England makes a preliminary inquiry as to what the past might look like once we begin to make histories of the emotions, of the economies which organise what is felt and lived as a personal life but which is always inescapably a social life. If such histories are not divorced from public and collective activity and associations, they cannot be reduced to them: how nearly they are bound up in these other kinds of change and continuity, how much at odds with them, are paths we need to track. I see this work as part of the writing of a feminist history but one which, if we follow in Woolf's footsteps, must sometimes go roundabout. Better to leave ourselves some spaces open, some sentences unfinished and some routes unmapped, than to imagine that it is our job to dot all the 'i's and cross all the 't's in our writing of the past.

III

It was one of the starting-points of this project, therefore, that an understanding of any period might have new things to yield if it acknowledged other perspectives and positions in the culture. However unsatisfactory the idea of 'women's writing' or 'women's history' (for they both have their limits and their pieties), it seemed a reasonable enough way of signalling a desire for something more as well as something other, for a less complacent history, one made on disagreements and disturbances rather than homogeneity and unity. I believed too that this might take us further into the relatively unexamined mainstream of English cultural life amongst the middle classes at home between the wars: a grouping which has been singularly immune to serious inquiry and whose attitudes and practices have so often been taken for granted.

The largest gaps in our histories of British life this century are still those which the careless masculinity of its writers continue to create. It is extraordinary how much the literary history of 'the inter-war years', for example, has been rendered almost exclusively in male terms: whether it be the doings of right-wing aesthetes or the radicalism of the 'Thirties poets', the dying moments of English liberalism, the late flowerings of high modernism, or the making of social documentary and social realism – it has been male authors who are taken to represent the nation as well as those who are disaffiliated from it. This has been at least as true of commentators on the left as on the right: Eliot, Forster, Joyce, Auden, may be supplemented by Lawrence, Orwell, or more daringly by an Edward Upward or an Evelyn Waugh, but in most cases the reading habits of the majority of British people, let alone the women among them, are rarely mentioned.[2]

Indeed 'home' itself, any attachment to indigenous cultures in Britain between the wars, to feelings of belonging rather than exile, are likely to be conspicuously absent in literary histories. It is a legacy of 'modernism' (and its domination of university English), that it turns the gaze elsewhere, to the writings of those for whom marginality was the only desirable place. Paul Fussell, for example, in *Abroad*, gives a riveting account of the rejection of home by male writers and satellites drawn from across the social spectrum but from within a notional high culture, a rejection which he argues took place in Britain between the wars. 'I hate it here', he believes, best summarises their feelings toward a Britain 'safe and smug' and apparently dead from the neck up (if not the waist down). Vividly tracking back to the experience of the frozen miseries of the trenches, Fussell shows these disaffected and disillusioned literati seeking solace and sunshine in exotic experiences or in the challenge of 'abroad'. Against a photograph of Cannes, he sets one of Salford back-to-backs; against the favoured oranges and palm trees, a litany of hate-objects: gasworks, industrial estates, canals, Woolworths, whose repulsive aspect helped fuel the energetic expatriation of 'civilised men'.³

It is easy to read here (though Fussell, who for all his urbane ironisation is largely at one with his spokesmen, resists this line of thought), the hysteria of the dispossessed, the fears of increasing egalitarianism, a reaction to the march of labour and working-class activism imagined as the onslaught of 'barbarians' and vandals. What is striking too – and even less acknowledged than the overtly political dimension of these phobias – is the sense of wounded masculine pride which emanates from these writers. Driven into exile, many modernist prophets and minor *cognoscenti* lament both the proletarianisation and the domestication of national life. Since war, whatever its horrors, is manly, there is something both lower-class and effeminate about peacetime. Whether we encounter it in the fury of a Lawrence (who had suffered bitterly from the xenophobia and class-hatred of his compatriots) and his lambasting of suburban housing as 'little red rat-traps',⁴ in Louis MacNeice's condemnation in his *Autumn Journal* of those who make 'the world my sofa'; in Orwell's George Bowling and his fulminations against 'the wife', or in Evelyn Waugh's fulsome praise of Mussolini's heroic achievements,⁵ Britain is the place where it is no longer possible to be properly male – a country gelded, as Lawrence might have said, and emasculated by the aftermath of war. Domestic life, the emphasis on the world of home and family activity brings down some of the most virulent torrents of abuse: the British Sunday, British cooking, and frequently, British women (foreign maidens are far preferable to awkward English virgins) – these are the outrages which make the British Isles, but especially and usually England, a home unfit for heroes. Indeed Fussell's soldierly imagination is quite right in suggesting that heroes are by definition incapable of domesticity.

The sexual politics of such an account are no less interesting for being familiar. Once one realises just how much sexual prejudice may lurk behind the image of Britain as smothering and defensive, rather than homely and protective, a different kind of assessment is called for. For Fussell, whatever abroad represented, it apparently held no charms for the female sex since 'one' went abroad for 'wine, women and song', if not to escape women altogether and form other kinds of temporary attachment. Abroad was culture, romance and sensuality; home was philistine, prosaic and frigid. 'Home' was also the place where women were, after 1919, in the majority and where women writers were coming into their own. Fussell's account is one of many which suggests in how many different ways aesthetic judgements are intertwined with those about gender. Just as for him truly literary culture and the masculine are inseparable, so the feminine is implicitly associated with the 'middlebrow', a term always bordering on contempt. Thus Freya Stark, Storm Jameson, Rebecca West, all major travel writers of the period, are given short shrift; they fail to conform to, or be interested in, the notions of style which Fussell sees as literary. And most discussions of the period are nowhere near as broad-minded as Fussell's.

Abroad was Fussell's logical sequel to his earlier account, *The Great War and Modern Memory*, a book which for all its generosity of under-standing gauges the trauma of war in terms only of the men who fought and suffered and has little to say about the population at home. Reading that book was a key moment in my own research, however, for what it suggested about the paralysis which struck at the very basis of masculinity and which shook to the core former definitions of sexual difference. Fussell's own later, more romantic search for nomadic heroes, like the outpourings of virulent misogyny in the inter-war years, signals an implicit anxiety about the treacherous instability of former models of masculine power. The decimation of the British male population coincided with (and no doubt contributed to), increased female emancipation, politically, socially, sexually. The flapper and the neurasthenic can be read as shocking reversals of earlier norms and expectations of what women (or rather ladies) and men might be, but these were only the most visible examples of a continual alarm over the meaning of gender differences after the war which found expression in places as apparently disconnected as modern 'sexology' and the desert romance.

I argue in this book that those disturbances on the level of the emotional and ideological understandings of sexuality were more than just a local or minor kind of change. The strongly anti-heroic mood which commentators like Fussell identify as characterising the aftermath of war made a lasting and deep impression right across cultural life and idioms at home. It is my own view that in these years between 1920 and 1940, a revolt against, embarrassment about, and distaste for the romantic languages of national pride produced a realignment of sexual identities which was part of a redefinition of Englishness. What had formerly been held as the virtues of the private sphere of middle-class life take on a new public and national significance. I maintain that the 1920s and '30s saw a move away from formerly heroic and officially masculine public rhetorics of national destiny and from a dynamic and missionary view of the Victorian and Edwardian middle classes in 'Great Britain' to an Englishness at once less imperial and more inward-looking, more domestic and more private – and, in terms of pre-war standards, more 'feminine'. In the ubiquitous appeal of civilian virtues and pleasures, from the picture of 'the little man', the suburban husband pottering in his herbaceous borders, to that of Britain itself as a sporting little country batting away against the Great Dictators, we can discover a considerable sea-change in ideas of the national temperament. A very profound shift of self-image as well as of militarism takes place in the course of these in-between years: the First World War belonged to

Tommy Atkins but the true heroics of the Second were to be found in the actions of 'ordinary people' on 'the Home Front'.

Such changes were potentially democratising in their move away from an aping of the upper classes, and from imperial rhetoric, but they were differently limiting in increasing what might be called the privatisation of national life. The usual view of the middle class in the inter-war period is that it was simply politically and socially conservative – isolationist, inward-looking, indulging in 'the last look round' or 'the long weekend' before the war.[6] For right-wing commentators the 1930s echo the prelapsarian days before the Great War in a kind of dying fall; those on the left are more likely to be impatient for the changes in social mobility which only the late 1950s would bring. The accent on home-ownership and house-building, on domestic consumerism and on the small family would seem to reinforce this picture. It is part of my purpose here to suggest that this is only half the story of the inter-war years; we also need a way of reading forwards into the 1930s from the 1890s, into what was also the continuing process of modernisation.

Nowhere does this become more crucial than when we attempt to write about the experience of women in the period. If Fussell's work prompted me to ask what different kind of topography of the nation we might map if we considered those who stayed at home, this pointed again to the problem of periodisation. Clearly women's history, lived, as it were, in a different place, need not run parallel to that of men, might follow connected but different paths. As the nomenclature suggests, the 'inter-war' years are easily seen, from the masculine point of view, as a kind of hiatus in history, an interval sandwiched between more dramatic, and more historically significant acts. Ironically, feminist studies of the period, with their perspective shaped by the battles for suffrage, have also tended to confirm that view. In the outline of women's history this century, the inter-war years have so far been sketched in as primarily one of feminism's deepest troughs, the era as a whole assumed as having an 'anti-progressive and reactionary character'.[7]

Yet it is hard to reconcile this sombre and depressing depiction of the inter-war years as a slough of feminine despond with the buoyant sense of excitement and release which animates so many of the more broadly cultural activities which different groups of women enjoyed in the period. What new kinds of social and personal opportunity, for example, were offered by the changing cultures of sport and entertainment, from tennis clubs to cinema-going, by new forms of spending which hire-purchase and accessible mortgages made possible, by new patterns of domestic life which included the introduction of the daily servant rather than the live-in maid, new forms of household appliance, new attitudes to housework?[8] How can we write about the idea of female freedom without considering the changing relationship to the female body which surely dominates the post-war years: perhaps the disposable sanitary napkin was in its own way as powerful an event as increasing female education or shifts in the employment market? In other words, we have still much to learn about the modernisation of women's lives, the realignment of public and private behaviours and values, of the norms and expectations of the pre-war years (which could make chaperonage seem antiquated and long hair undesirable), and we need a history which can encompass this kind of narrative as well as the more conventional and self-consciously political forms of emancipation. Compared with the elaborate coiffure of the 1890s, even the softest and least bohemian shingle of 1935 was a species of radical change.

One of my aims in this book is to suggest the need to review these years as marking for many women their entry into modernity, a modernity which was felt and lived in the most interior and private of places. If we assume the inter-war years were in many ways a period of reaction, we have also to make sense of it as a time when older forms of relationship and intimate behaviour were being recast and when even the most traditional of attitudes took new form. If the English middle classes found themselves in retreat after 1919, and the idea of private life received a new enhancement, nevertheless it was not the same old private life – the sphere of domestic relations, and all which it encompassed, had also changed. And even if a new commercial culture of 'home-making' was conservative in assuming this to be a female sphere, it nevertheless put woman and the home, and a whole panoply of connected issues, at the centre of national life.

Indeed, the more I read of writing by women in the post-war years the more I was struck by the sense of something radically other to, and rebelling against, the domestic world pre–1918 which at the same time was quite compatible with deeply defensive urges. If masculinity and ideas of the nation were being 'feminised', one can discover an equally powerful reaction on the part of many women against the ideologies of home and womanliness which belonged to the virtues and ideals of the pre-war world, ideals which had proved so lethal. Even those who would by no means call themselves feminists (and this is true of all the authors I discuss) were linked by a resistance to 'the feminine' as it had been thought of in late-Victorian or Edwardian times. In other words, by exploring the writing of middle-class women at home in the period (a far from stable category in itself) we can go straight to the centre of a contradictory and determining tension in English social life in the period which I have called a conservative modernity: Janus-faced, it could simultaneously look backwards and forwards; it could accommodate the past in the new forms of the present; it was a deferral of modernity and yet it also demanded a different sort of conservatism from that which had gone before. It is the women of an expanding middle class between the wars who were best able to represent Englishness in both its most modern and reactionary forms.

IV

The argument of this book is cumulative; though the chapters may seem to follow different avenues, they nevertheless converge upon that idea of a conservative embracing of modernity, shaped by the experience of dislocation after the First World War and fuelled by essentially pacific rather than aggressive urges. They all try, in different ways, to capture something of the flavour of a cultural compromise with the new and to isolate what I see as the dominant mood between the wars, one which could be conservative in effect and yet was often modern in form; a conservatism itself in revolt against the past, trying to make room for the present. The book thus begins with that revolt against Victorianism, which became so much the hallmark of the modern, as played out in the life and the work of Ivy Compton-Burnett. Compton-Burnett's fiction reminds us that so many of her generation, however much they hated the past, had been reluctantly and forcibly propelled into new ways of living after the war, and that it is this traumatised relation to modernity which produced new kinds of conservative as well as radical response.

This concentration upon what I have called a conservative modernism does not take us into the familiar reaches of an overtly politicised high Toryism with its appeals to ancestral tradition and the superiority of the upper classes, deference to the Church, army and State, or the kind of supremacist glorification of nationhood which had inspired the imperialist endeavour in the late nineteenth century. Rather it asks us to plumb the depths of a more intimate and everyday species of conservatism which caught the public imagination between the wars and could itself recast the imperial, as well as the national idea of Englishness. The readers of Agatha Christie's detective fiction in the period, for example, were invited to identify with a more inward-looking notion of the English as a nice, decent, essentially private people. This was an idiom more about self-effacement and retreat than bombast and expansion, one which could lie both at the heart of a class formation and reach across the classes; it allowed for new kinds of consensus, confidence and power as well as new forms of enjoyment and pleasure. It takes us further toward understanding the meaning of what used to be called a middlebrow culture in the period, one whose apparent artlessness and insistence on its own ordinariness has made it peculiarly resistant to analysis.

In many ways the central chapter of this book, though at the time it seemed a marginal piece of research, is that which explores the journalism of Jan Struther. Struther is not well known but her columns describing the fictional life of 'Mrs. Miniver' in *The Times* became a bestseller and were later transformed by Hollywood into a sentimental film to help the war effort. My instinct (or rather my literary training) prompted me in the first place to see 'Mrs. Miniver's' homespun wisdom as merely unctuous and platitudinous, the most ephemeral and lightweight of writing, too personal and internal to be historically revealing. Gradually I came to reverse that judgement: *Mrs. Miniver* turned out to be the most historically fruitful of all. Above all, Struther's emphasis upon the quiet life, on a celebration of the known and the familiar, brings us up against conservatism in its broadest sense and in its closest relations to the ideas of domesticity in the period: though her writing might seem to occupy the most personal and subjective of spaces, it takes us simultaneously into the most national and public territories of being English between wars.

If the pleasures of home life were at the centre of the national stage in the inter-war years, women writers were amongst the most enthusiastic exponents, as well as critics, of a culture of privacy, and many of them made no bones about preferring the kind of personal life which their own circles of respectability offered even if they felt limited and contained by them. The stress which a writer like Struther laid upon reticence and verbal self-control could also, paradoxically, suggest new positions of power and privilege, new ways of being in charge. Indeed part of the successful appeal of Struther's vision of the ideal domestic life depends upon the emphasis she gives to the idea of the literary itself, to having a writer's mentality and sensitivity, however tiny one's literary empire might be. Most frequently the value attached to the literary was the clearest way of distancing oneself from the experience offered by forms of 'mass' entertainment and leisure. Like those of Daphne du Maurier's readers who were aware of reading a better class of romance when they picked up her novels rather than Barbara Cartland's, the Mrs. Minivers of this world knew themselves to be different from the lower orders because of their rich inner life and literary sensibility.

We cannot assume, however, that what we mean by a 'middle-class' identity in the period, and how it could be asserted, were firm anchors in the social life. Rather I have tried to keep in mind in writing this book a sense of the complex and changing nature of class references in the inter-war period, whose insecurities are dramatised as vividly in Agatha Christie's whodunits as they are in Compton-Burnett's genteel families. The 'middle class' was itself undergoing radical revision between the wars and any use of the term must ideally stretch from the typist to the teacher, include the 'beautician' as well as the civil servant, the florist and the lady doctor, the library assistant and the suburban housewife, and the manifold differences between them. Even though Compton-Burnett and Christie were both daughters of late Victorian villadom, the child of an entrepreneurial homeopath from Hove might have little in common with that of a carefree but bankrupt American man of leisure. And what would they share with Daphne du Maurier, born into a theatrical family of immigrants, or with Jan Struther whose father was a Scottish Liberal MP? I argue that being 'middle-class' in fact depends on an extremely anxious production of endless discriminations between people who are constantly assessing each other's standing. The grocer's wife in Grantham, the female bank clerk in the metropolis, the retired memsahib in Surrey, were far more likely to be aware of their differences than their mutual attitudes. Any study like this has, therefore, to restore the feeling of temporality to class distinctions along with a sense of their fertility.

Just how unquiet the depths were beneath the apparently unruffled surface of sensible and quiescent womanhood in the 1930s can be gauged from the success of Daphne du Maurier's 1938 bestseller, *Rebecca*. The instability of being middle-class, the treacherous and tricky limits to respectability and the awkward insistence of desires which are strictly forbidden, make up the interior landscapes of du Maurier's novels. Her romance with the past uncovers something of the buried passions which always threaten to return and trouble the calm of conservatism's sexual and social economies and suggest at what cost the ideals of femininity and of private life were maintained. Her stories are drawn to depict something of the discontent and restlessness which even the most well-run home cannot outlaw entirely, and are clearly as fascinated as they are repelled by the rebellions on the boundaries of the most secure states. Finally, du Maurier's historical imagination prompts questions too about the connections between a more domestic and isolationist English conservatism between the wars and the more interventionist forms it could eventually take as the nation moved again towards war.

Forever England cannot then be read as a celebration of a literary domestic culture, no matter how cheerfully it has been inhabited by women writers and readers. None of the writers in this book can be made sense of unless we admit that feminist work must deal with the conservative as well as the radical imagination, and that it may have been this which held the hearts and minds of generations of women of all classes and all creeds at different times in the past. Yet until comparatively recently, and until they were confronted by the irony of our first woman Prime Minister belonging to the party which most vociferously opposed woman's suffrage, British feminists have made discussions of conservatism all but anathema. Right-wing women were felt to be another breed, a subject too distasteful or remote to take up time in a movement whose driving energies have been largely spent recovering and reclaiming collective achievements and progressive struggles. Nevertheless anyone who approaches conservatism with feminist sympathies ought to be struck and indeed disturbed by what they have in common.[9]

Above all, the conservative critique of rationalism, its emphasis upon private life and personal feeling, has especial significance for women who

have long been seen as the feeling sex; for feminists, half of the battle
with socialism has been with its inability to recognise the demands of
home and family, the pulls of psychic as well as social structures, all areas
which conservatism certainly takes seriously, and for which it frequently
has a language. Often the most philosophically interesting of political
tendencies, it welcomes discussions of the existential, the religious, and
the subjective, in ways which make it far more appealing than the more
rigorously collective-minded outlook of socialisms. The stress which some
conservatisms lay upon inner resources and moral strength significantly
overlaps with how many women would understand their feminism. For
British schoolgirls Jane Austen's Elizabeth Bennett is as likely to be a
model heroine as Brontë's Jane Eyre, and yet few feminists have explicitly
wished to acknowledge what Marilyn Butler has called 'a Tory women's
tradition, which must also be thought of as proto-feminist'.[10]

On the whole feminists have preferred to believe that feminism and
conservatism are mutually exclusive. Ironically, and as proof of how intertwined these relations actually are, while I was completing this work,
Virago, the major feminist press in Britain, brought out a new edition of
Jane Austen, has republished Struther's *Mrs. Miniver* and has now added
the works of Ivy Compton-Burnett to its list without any apparent sense
of incongruity. All this suggests that a reconsideration of what has been
proto-feminist within conservative philosophies but also what has been
and continues to be conservative within feminism is timely.

V

Central to the writing of this book and the determining of its final shape
and selection of authors was the realisation, then, that I was writing about
conservatism, but that conservatism itself was subject to historical and
social metamorphoses and that its forms were not to be taken for granted.
It would be fair to say that conservatism has become more rather than
less problematic as this work evolved. In the first place anyone who wants
to write about conservatism, both in terms of the Tory party in Britain
and of something broader and more amorphous which may or may not
lead to voting for it, must start from a kind of vacuum.[11] If it is true that
the 'Conservative half of society is still largely awaiting its historians',[12]
we might go further and assert that conservatism, of the lower-case variety,
has been even more unaccounted for; as one of the great unexamined
assumptions of British cultural life its history is all but non-existent.

Such conservatism has perhaps been the greatest blind spot in our
literary and social histories if only because it is the most obvious feature
in the English past. That it wears at all times a cloak of invisibility is part
of its influence and attraction and depends on the persuasive nature of
Conservative political philosophy itself. Those political Conservatives (and

they have been few) who have taken it upon themselves to write about their beliefs, have frequently stressed that Conservatism refuses the status of an ideology. It has been part and parcel of Conservative political thought to be suspicious of the search for utopian blueprints for society and to denigrate the value of political theorisation in the abstract. Rather they have sought to offer a common-sense, pragmatic definition of the role of politics in people's lives: that it is solely the irksome business of politicians and useful only because it frees the rest of us to get on with our lives with the minimum of interference. This was the view expressed by Quintin Hogg in the well-known passages of *The Case for Conservatism* in 1947: the aim of politics is the good life, and the man who puts politics first 'is not fit to be called a civilised being'.[13]

Lord Hailsham was in part reiterating the views of Lord Hugh Cecil, whose *Conservatism* (1912) was the only major exposition of Conservative philosophy and politics in the first half of this century. Both assume that there is a direct link between the conservative temperament – what Cecil calls 'pure or natural conservatism',[14] a tendency of the human mind – and the forging of Conservative political policy. Yet the investigation of the relation between 'Conservatism' as a party politics and 'conservatism' as a set of attitudes and beliefs, or complex of emotional and intellectual responses, has rarely been pursued. Given their dislike of political ideologising, it is not surprising that Conservatives themselves have not usually seen it as part of their political duty to produce such work: what is more surprising is how little their opponents on the left have cared to understand what they are up against. Left-wingers are as likely to write and act as though conservatism needed no explanation and had remained as monolithic and unchanged in time as Conservatives themselves. Indeed, compared to the shelves of analyses of left-wing thought, the sections in libraries or bookshops on any kind of conservative thinking are sparse. Symptomatically, Raymond Williams, the socialist intellectual and thinker, in his dictionary of *Keywords* published in 1976, for example, included entries on 'Labour' and 'Liberal' but nothing under 'Conservative'.

Compared to the 'most thoroughly tilled field'[15] of Labour history, even political histories of Conservatism are few and far between. Where they do exist the tradition of commentary has usually corroborated the definition of politics as views, policies, ideologies passed down from above. Typically accounts will concentrate upon the writings and speeches of public figures and parliamentarians and the enactment of governmental legislation; they chart different versions of a Tory politics in the forward march of Prime Ministers – Peelite Conservatism, Disraelian, the Conservatism of Salisbury and so on, with an emphasis on internal and foreign policy, whether it be arguments over Irish Home Rule or the economic theories of 'the New Right' in the late 1970s.[16] A broader net might stretch to include key thinkers and intellectuals, cast a brief backward glance at

Hooker, Hobbes, or Hume and take the anti-revolutionary reflections of Edmund Burke as the philosophical basis of modern Conservatism.[17] Rarely is the meaning of a conservatism outside the relation to party given space. What is seen as the hard edge of ideology and of practical politics is usually kept firmly apart from the 'softer' questions of psychology and motivation. Rarely has the notion of a 'lived' conservatism received attention from historians: the idea of a conservative cultural or personal life is still novel territory.

On the other hand, when one turns expectantly to social history where the quality of 'everyday life' is taken seriously, the political climate of the inter-war years, for example, is acknowledged but the levels of high policy and of quotidian activity are still all but severed: accounts of changes in the material conditions of people's lives, the new car, the wireless, the vacuum-cleaner, are usually seen as the effects of economic changes or technological developments but rarely explored in terms of the forms of any more interior life. We do not know how such changes worked to create new attitudes, new forms of aspiration and new desires, and were in turn shaped by them. Amongst scholars and academics it is still a relatively maverick suggestion – likely to come from the more innovatory and less academically respectable fields of design history or cultural studies – to propose that a politics of everyday life could be as easily read from the layout of a suburban semi as from the doings of politicians and their ilk. The traffic, as it were, down from Westminster to the man or woman in the street, continues on the whole to be all one way. Political theory and social history, both tend to keep intact the division between public and private life.

By focusing upon the inter-war years, and on a particular version of Englishness, one of the intentions of this work, therefore, is to begin to identify conservatism's shifting appeals, its imaginative purchase as a fertile source of fantasy, inspiration and pleasure which, though it has its discernible constancies, is also continually finding new forms of expression. It is perhaps not surprising that the volatile and disruptive years of the early twentieth century, which found their apotheosis in the Great War, should produce a crisis in conservatisms of all varieties. Since in looking at the literature of the period we are not only exploring fictions *about* conservative mentalities but creations *of* it, one of the effects of such work is to reveal how much political terminologies are themselves historically relative: radicalisms and conservatisms carry different valencies in relation to each other and across time; we cannot rely on their meaning fixing for us permanent and undivided constituencies.[18] Nor can we assume that conservatisms or radicalisms in the period are always consonant with party-political belongings. How far we may wish to tie together the operations of change on the level of high politics with those other kinds of account which deal in shifts in the structure of feeling is beyond my scope in this book, but it would surely be a mistake to try to make these different discourses and processes of development dovetail too neatly. My own primary interest lies in the least articulate level of conservatism, conservatism with a small 'c'.

Conservatives would have us believe that this conservatism, the conservatism of the politically unselfconscious, resists analysis because it comes closest to home: that we are unable or even unwilling to analyse or label it because it seems a peculiarly intimate condition of subjectivity. Its emphasis on the taken-for-granted and its invisibility as a 'natural' part of ourselves has made it especially difficult to give a history to; 'conservatism', if it signals anything as a complex of emotional needs and desires, then draws upon such deeps below deeps in subjective life that it is difficult, even distressing, to disturb the waters. Indeed, the argument might run, such analysis defeats its purpose since conservatism ceases to have the character of hidden resistance, which is partly what we mean by its description, once it is laid bare. Once you prod what lies at the bottom of the pool it is no longer secret and inert.

Yet Conservatives have also been the first to acknowledge (however disingenuously) that conservatism is best understood dialectically: not as a force which is simply 'anti-change' so much as a species of restraint or 'brake' (Lord Cecil's intensely modern analogy comparing the Parliamentary process to the motor-car), holding progress back on the leash of caution but allowing it none the less to advance.[19] The viability of gradualism, the ideal of 'peaceful, smooth and painless'[20] changes, of harmonious or organic changes as opposed to violent revolution or disseverance, is the central intellectual and emotional paradox for Conservatives. But it is one which they themselves have seen as expressing a unity of dialectical opposites. Edmund Burke made plain his own sense of this relationship when he wrote that 'a state without the means of change is without the means of conservatism';[21] this is captured in Cecil's own formulation, 'the two sentiments of desire to advance and fear of the dangers of moving, apparently contradictory, are in fact complementary and mutually necessary', and with characteristic aplomb Quintin Hogg took the thought to its logical limit – if Conservatism meant "no change", clearly the only truly Conservative organism would be a dead one'.[22]

Though we might wish to agree that what constitutes the conservative, or rather what 'conservative' signifies, psychologically, emotionally, personally, has finally to remain hidden, that does not mean that we cannot discover its presence and gauge its power in the dynamics of change as a whole. Its effects can be felt and known, they show through the social fabric and are part of what determines the particular historical forms of change. Although conservatism may itself signal something inarticulate, its unspoken desires are nevertheless articulated in the forms of social and economic production, in the limits of what can be said and written, done or left undone in a culture. The identification of common ideological concerns and transhistorical preoccupations which mark out the boundaries of what we call conservative, sometimes highly politicised, sometimes not – a commitment to family life, to the idea of nationhood, to the notion of necessary authority and so forth – is only the beginning of historical and political analysis as I understand it: the challenge lies in seeing how the expression of these beliefs constantly changes, the capacity of conservatism to alter its shape whilst remaining recognisably the same animal. Not one of its ideological or conceptual anchors has been the property of the Tories alone nor have they been *per se* notions which have always worked against change.

It is bound to be one of my starting-points, therefore, that conservative mentalities, whatever they might be, are not sealed off or separate from other ideological strains or existing apart from other, quite conflicting, even contradictory desires and beliefs. Not only the Tories are conservative but even they themselves suffer from internal contradictions, from the hopes and fears and doubts which leave open that space in which human beings remake themselves and their societies. Those needs which we call conservative must first be recognised and respected if they are to be addressed by new forms of social or political organisation. The political message of this book is therefore, I hope, consistent: unless we understand better the relation between conservatism and Conservatism we are not in a strong position to argue for or against change. Neither can we hope to prevent the worst excesses of a Tory politics – authoritarianism, dogmatic nationalisms, hard and fast prescriptions for sexual relations – from making their appearance under different political rubrics. In my view, those who believe themselves to be partisans drawn to very different political philosophies have a special responsibility to discover not where conservatism seems to us most strange, but, which is harder, to find out where it touches us most nearly – how best to understand the Tory in us all.

'Between the wars' is a convenient and workable fiction but it has its limits. Clearly many of the changes which I discuss, and especially the revolt against Victorianism, can be found much earlier: in fact that revolt is born in the same moment as Victorianism itself. But what we look for as historians and critics when we look for change is something on a much broader scale of cultural self-consciousness which we can see as a generic shift right across society and as – eventually – the making of a new common sense. It seems that the effects of the First World War made visible and precipitated further into the mainstream of English life what might otherwise have remained eccentric, sporadic and minority protests. Thus by the 1930s it was no longer simply bohemians and suffragists who argued for equality in marriage: the idea of 'the companionate partnership' had become a matter of course. Naturally the point at which the formerly radical is adopted into the everyday idiom is also the point at which it loses its urgency and its capacity to disrupt: it becomes conventional.

That dialectic between old and new, between past and present, between holding on and letting go, between conserving and moving on, is a constant one and it is differently felt at different places in the culture. It takes a particularly exciting and intense form in the period between the wars in Britain but it is one of the aims of this study to suggest that given the deep conservatism of British culture the full working out of modernity was bound to be deferred. If we were to place 'between the wars' inside a larger concentric circle, one which we label 1914 – 1956, we can recognise how we might reread that history as one of a single interrupted war. At the same time, it would appear to be a narrative of conservatism constantly revising itself. Placed inside another even larger circle embracing the 1890s to the present day, events between the wars suggest to us that if the 1960s were the truly modernising moment in Britain, that modernisation may now be drawing to its close.

Certainly, as the writing began to take shape, I noticed how prevalent was a farewell tone, and I must wonder why. Is it because we are really at the end of that Englishness, that voice and grammar which drew so much on histories of imperialism and whose modern transformations, which carried such authority between the wars, are now finally exhausted? Is indeed the very idea of an English nationality – of something which, in Rupert Brooke's words, could be for ever England – inevitably tinged with the elegaic? Is it because we are watching the collapse of so many of the sodalities and solidarities which this century has created, and of the epistemological frameworks which gave us collective forms of belonging and belief, that even a history of conservatism must become an epitaph? No doubt, like all historical feelings, it is also personal. I grew up in a city fortified against foreigners; as a child I learnt the names of battles from the war memorials which overshadowed all our sea-front strolls. As someone who once played on bombsites and listened avidly to stories of the Blitz and of 'our finest hour', maybe my own sadness has seeped into the writing: a sort of melancholy recognition that those ways of being English, foolish and even vicious as they often were, were a form of identity and community in which I too was brought up, and whose disappearance, however welcome, is also bound to hurt . . . . But these thoughts are perhaps more fitting to a peroration than a prologue.

Chapter 1

The demon in the house: the novels of I. Compton-Burnett

A WOMAN OUT OF PLACE

> (Angus to his mother): 'You might be a figure in history, corrupted by power. It is what you are, except that you are not in history.'
>
> (*The Last and the First*, p. 87)[1]

'I've read your book', Ivy Compton-Burnett remarked to Rosamund Lehmann on first meeting her at a publishing party for *The Echoing Grove*, 'and I've decided that one of us cannot be a woman.'[2] Nothing could be less feminine than the fictions of 'I. Compton-Burnett', a literary phenomenon whose defiant and contrary voice compelled readers' attention for nearly fifty years. Born in 1884, she published her first novel (which she later disclaimed) in 1911, and went on to write nineteen novels at roughly two-year intervals from *Pastors and Masters* in 1925 until *The Last and the First*, published in 1971, two years after her death. This resilient authorship, which brought her many literary and public honours including a Dameship in 1968, is perhaps less interesting than the one striking fact about the novels themselves: with very minor exceptions they are all pretty much the same. It is as if nearly half a century of social change has not happened, although time does not so much stand still in her work as simply repeat itself. Yet these are not popular fictions, best-sellers whose pleasures reside unashamedly in the formulaic and in the re-evocation of well-loved and savoured certainties of plot and genre. If Compton-Burnett's prose performs a ritual then it is more an exhausting and inward exorcism, a purging of demons who even after all those years continued to possess her.

Her novels really *are* peculiar. The fictions are all but relentlessly uniform in conjuring up the lives of the well-to-do, an imagined petty aristocracy and a propertied but usually impoverished upper middle class in their country places and small mansions, locked into the late Victorian years, the period in which Compton-Burnett herself grew up. Their bizarre quality resides, however, in these doings being rendered primarily as 'sayings': each novel consists entirely of highly-wrought, stylised conversations between family groupings in a mannered Victorianese which is the unchanging vernacular from 1925 to 1969. There are next to no passages of description. Enormous, often criminal events (infants murdered in their cradles, unsuspecting relatives lured into gaping ravines) do happen but they happen in parenthesis, as it were, whilst the minute recording of everyday exchanges between the self-conscious members of the same family constitutes the real dramatic interest. With very little authorial intervention readers are left to make what they can of the sketched-in characters (the shape of whose hands or brows must usually suffice) and to fend for themselves in a narrow echo-chamber of voices. The emotional temperature varies very little from novel to novel: it is always chilly, and for the uninitiated it is possible to wander through whole paragraphs in the dark, beset by 'the tumult of voices'[3] or deciding, as Dame Ivy herself wryly suggested, that 'if you once pick up a Compton-Burnett, it is difficult not to put it down again.'[4]

No doubt it is partly the 'monotonous obstinacy'[5] of Compton-Burnett's novels which has had the power to daunt and disarm her critics. Her work upsets many of literary criticism's dearest discriminations: it does not 'develop'; it awkwardly refuses to belong to any one decade, and stylistically it straddles a no-man's land between the extreme edge of realism and a grotesque, quirky modernism. The literary critical division between novels which document and are 'sociological' and novels of personal sensibility, or between realism and modernism, is never more clearly revealed as a false and unhelpful opposition than in the work of Compton-Burnett, whose novels are obviously neither and yet somehow both.[6] For many it is a project which simply defeats placing and is best relegated to that well-worn category of English eccentricity.[7] Both Compton-Burnett's virtues and failings are taken to be purely idiosyncratic: hers is an 'aggressively original and distinctive talent,'[8] but the accumulative effect of such praise has been to situate the work outside history, beyond the mainstream of English cultural life, in a curious backwater of its own.

This apparent marginality is belied, however, by the monotonous obstinacy of Compton-Burnett's readers here and in North America who keep her reprinted every year. For if not a bestselling author, she seems to have a continuous following with, as one of her biographers remarks, 'ardent followers in every walk of life'.[9] Compton-Burnett appears regularly in Penguin paperback as well as in the more avant-garde lists of Allison & Busby. *Manservant and Maidservant* is one of Oxford University Press's 'Best Novels of Our Time', whilst outside the usual literary circles, she has appealed to enthusiasts as far apart as Nathalie Sarraute (a high priestess of the *nouveau roman*) and Studs Terkel, the Chicago oral historian and radical.[10] A considerable social and cultural presence in her time, holding court to a younger generation which included Elizabeth Taylor, Olivia Manning and Rosamund Lehmann, Compton-Burnett has always been a 'writer's writer' but also one of the very few female authors to get more than a nodding mention in standard critical histories of modern literature.[11]

Nevertheless if Compton-Burnett has become a literary curiosity, she seems hardly less *outré* as a 'woman's novelist' and has indeed proved to be one of the blind spots of feminist literary criticism. This absence of discussion might at first seem surprising given the imaginative centre of her novels, which for all of her long life had the force of a magnificent obsession: the family and domestic existence. Yet she offers us no confessions of a suffering heroine to identify with, indeed no 'I' at all; no consoling narratives of escape from the prisons of home and relationships; no routes either into a private space of feeling or emotionality eschewing, as she does, the novel's special prerogatives of interior monologues and reflective commentary. There are no narratorial words of wisdom to wrap around ourselves nor do the characters connect their lives with a more public sphere or with avowedly social issues. If by 'woman writer' we expect someone who makes 'female experience' and especially heterosexual love the impulse of her narrative, Compton-Burnett is disappointingly uninterested in either courtship or marriage. No one could be less moved by romantic longings, whether personal, sexual or social: the reader, like the writer, does not so much explore as dissect feelings, is encouraged not to be a co-participant in the action so much as a *voyeur*, an observer not an actor in the charades of family life.

In the tentative literary histories so far of British women's writing this century, Compton-Burnett seems a woman out of place. She cannot sensibly be grouped with other inter-war writers, that second generation of suffragists and realists like Vera Brittain or Winifred Holtby, nor with committed experimentalists like Dorothy Richardson and Virginia Woolf; as someone who continued writing into the 1950s and '60s she seems to have even less in common as a literary dowager with a Doris Lessing or a Sylvia Plath. In other words, she cannot be read to illustrate the forward march of women's consciousness or be assimilated to any mapping of feminist or proto-feminist protest in a reading of novels which wants them to be the straightforward social history of our times. Neither is she, on the other hand, a novelist of the inward self, analysing or proposing a proclaimedly feminine subjectivity. Not surprisingly, those critics who have broached her work have again stressed its waywardness: she is a writer who fails to 'fit in'[12] and whose fiction constitutes 'the oddest exhibit which women's literature has to offer'.[13]

Yet it is often the oddest exhibit which tells us most about the museum, its classifications and its processes of selection. It is precisely Compton-Burnett's intractability as a 'woman writer' which might make us reconsider the terms of the definition. If women's writing is a house of many mansions, could it be that we have been reluctant to investigate its darkest corners, to move from its well-lit rooms down into the shadowy cellars?

Compton-Burnett's novels reveal a welter of ugly imaginings about the more perverse and tormented sides of the self, about the capacity to hurt and maim within the 'safe' confines of home. It is a capacity which the novels deem as clearly feminine as any other and which at least one female critic has found 'repellent' and unwomanly.[14] One of her best-loved 'comedies' (for they are also humorous novels), *The Present and the Past*, opens upon a group of children watching a sick hen being pecked to death by its fellows; none of them is for the squeamish and all aim to scrutinise with gimlet eyes 'the below-stairs of family relationships'.[15] For Ivy Compton-Burnett is the most unflinching of guides to what she sees as the misery of a domestic life in which women are as likely to be manipulative and peevish despots as benign chatelaines. Her work forces us to contemplate a full repertoire of feminine desires, of feelings and behaviours we might prefer to disown.

If one of the insights of feminism is to suggest that we can best understand our inward life of thought and emotion as the life too of a particular culture and a particular social life, then it is part of my purpose here to argue that what structures Compton-Burnett's fictional universe can be recognised as social and historical impulses. I begin in this chapter, therefore, with a rereading of her early life so powerfully evoked in Hilary Spurling's imaginative biography,[16] not in order to impress the reader yet again (as even the best biography will do), with its unique nature, but to see where it touches on a common history and representative concerns. Compton-Burnett's life was in many ways typical of that pre-war generation whose needs and anxieties were shaped in the crucible of late Victorian and Edwardian domestic privacy, under – to use the phrase of one of her contemporaries – 'the tyranny of the private house'.[17] Her relation to that past, from which she was abruptly and completely severed after 1918, was to dominate her writing career. I suggest that her fiction needs to be read as a response to a loss which, though it took individual and personal shape, nevertheless was part of a significantly shared experience marked by the social cataclysm of the Great War. Not that the life and the fiction can ever be made to fit (or ought to be so manipulated): Compton-Burnett's novels occupy their own fantastic territory beyond the bounds of the feasible or plausible. This does not mean, however, that their imaginative devices, the contours and the features of their symbolic landscape, are outside time and place, arbitrary or random.

Rather than being outside the mainstream of cultural life, Compton-Burnett was left tragically well-placed in the 1920s to understand something of the traumatic upheavals which were the post-war legacy. Violently evacuated from the pre-war world into a modernity she had not chosen and which in many ways she refused, Compton-Burnett's formation as a writer embodies a complex response to the experience of personal and historical disjuncture, at once holding on to the past and compulsively repeating it, whilst at the same time enjoying a distance from its moral authority and seeking to loosen its emotional grip. I see her fiction as speaking directly to the reshaping of English cultural life after the war, able to confront the explosion of ideals about domestic life and family, sentiments which had been as dramatically undermined by 1918 as the nation's ideals of manhood. It is usual to think of literary modernism as shaped by the experience of exiles, either those who literally put a distance between themselves and their country or who signal imaginatively their sense of being outside any continuous cultural inheritance or stable history of belonging. Such a model is archetypally a masculine one, dependent as it is on certain freedoms of movement, on notions of social mobility and sexual autonomy, as well as on the assumption of economic independence. Compton-Burnett's fiction, on the other hand, suggests another history of modernism, one bound up tightly with the history of femininity. Her novels are also concerned with exile and with modernity but explore their meanings much closer to home, dwelling on an expulsion from childhood, from the values and expectations of the pre-war world, in the most inti- mate spheres of private and subjective life.

A MORBID GROWTH

'We can only hide our heads at home. Home causes the shame, but it also provides a hiding-place for it, and we have to take one thing with another.'
'You would hardly think homes would be so fair,' said Clemence.
(*Two Worlds and Their Ways*, p. 310)

One of the most convincing fabrications Ivy Compton-Burnett ever pro- duced was that of her own family past. Refusing to speak directly about that past – there *was* no biography, she told one friend[18] – the few details which she gave out, 'I was educated with my brothers in the country as a child',[19] were powerfully misleading. One could indeed be forgiven, as Hilary Spurling writes, for believing her 'the daughter of an impoverished squire': many of her nearest friends most certainly did,[20] and new acquaint- ances could be entirely taken in: 'The family, to use her word, was "raised" on an estate, and one appreciated the truth of this in her fiction.'[21] Even if she was unaware of just how unillustrious her forebears actually were (numbering farm labourers, grocers and straw-bonnet makers amongst them), Compton-Burnett was nevertheless quite happy to claim a vague descent from the renowned Bishop Burnet (the seventeenth-century historian) whose portrait graced her walls, and to allow rumours of a family 'place' in the country to circulate, when it is unlikely that she had even so much as visited a country house until she was thirty.

Whilst many of Ivy's readers might assume that she was from the landed classes or at least the genteel poor, she stemmed in fact from the very heartland of the prosperous middle-classes, one generation on from 'trade', with all the virtues and the anxieties of the new suburbs where she grew up, in particular Hove on the South coast, where she spent twenty-four years of her life. With a father who travelled up to 'town', it was 'villa-dom', and not the landed estate, or even the village, which set the social and emotional boundaries of her childhood. Nor is it accidental that in drawing a veil across her immediate origins, Compton-Burnett's denial of her past took the form of social upgrading. Whatever her illusions about her distant ancestry, she surely knew first-hand the tensions surrounding social position within her own family which had made up too the daily life of the late Victorian suburb. Far from being, as Hilary Spurling charitably but rather wilfully maintains, 'uninterested' in class,[22] no writer has been more enthralled by the fictions of English class life, its aspirations and its fears. It is in the light of that selfconsciousness and of its defensive reactions that her own fictions – personal and professional – might be read.

Ivy Compton-Burnett's mother, Katherine Rees, was the beautiful daughter of a former mayor of Dover, an engineer by trade and a man of solid but moderate wealth. They were non-conformist in belief and comfortably well-off, though decidedly not gentry. Katherine had both the fortune and the misfortune to marry a homeopath, James Burnett – a man whose reputation as a healer and as an outspoken critic of the medical profession had gone before him. Though free-thinking in many ways, Burnett was a not inconsiderable entrepreneur; he went early into speculative building, buying land and becoming landlord to row upon row of redbrick villas in Clacton, Portslade and Hove. A mixture of Tory politics and progressive views, he encouraged his children to wear loose clothing, bathe in the sea, eat fruit rather than sweets, and, most importantly, had his daughters educated. An adored husband and father, James Burnett seemed happily to combine his antinomian practices with a more conventional and affectionate paternalism. For his wife, however, it was apparently a cause of continual distress that her husband was never quite to be thought respectable.

In Hove, where the bulk of their married lives were spent, the wife of a homeopath could still be snubbed; if James Burnett throve on his unconventionality, Katherine appears to have borne the consequences for his public salvoes on those decorous seaside avenues. Away for the week in Harley Street, James Burnett enjoyed independence of spirit and body, whilst in Hove Katherine suffered polite ostracism:

Opposite lived a General Basden who, taking umbrage as most people did at having a homeopath for a neighbour, refused to permit his wife to call.[23]

It was Katherine who introduced the notion of the hyphenated surname for her children, no doubt with a view to lending the family some *éclat*. It was an elevation she denied James's children from his first marriage, who also lived with them but whom Katherine considered socially inferior, being the progeny of a chemist's daughter. Both they and he remained plain Burnett all their lives.[24] And it was Ivy's mother who 'for social reasons' took the children to attend the family pew in an Anglican church despite being brought up a sincere Wesleyan herself.

Katherine Compton-Burnett had wanted originally to move from their earlier homes in the new villas of Pinner and Twickenham because they were too rural (and where they only had a three-storey, semi-detached house). She wanted more of a fashionable, metropolitan life, but one which presumably did not, like life in central London, demand a personal pedigree or introduction to 'Society' proper. Hove, and First Avenue where they moved in 1991 when Ivy was seven, ought to have been ideal. A mid-Victorian suburb, its main avenues laid out in the 1860s and '70s, it was a development which grew at a tremendous rate. In 1800 barely one hundred people lived in this small village just outside Brighton; by the 1890s the population was over 26,000. Its housing spanned the entire spectrum of the new respectability, from the three-bedroomed villa to the detached neo-Gothic pile. The Burnetts eventually settled in no. 20, The Drive, a double-fronted detached house on four floors, set back very slightly from the street. This is where Ivy lived from the age of 10 until the break-up of her family in 1915 when she was 31. To walk down that particular avenue is to gain an insight into some of the pretensions and the possibilities of life for Katherine Burnett and her children when she moved there in 1897. But it is also to enter the imaginative territory of the novels of her daughter who later came to disown that past, refused to travel anywhere near Brighton, and detested Hove for the rest of her life.

As one contemporary observer said of The Drive, the stranger 'cannot help being struck with the air of wealth and refinement'.[25] The monumental brick facades demand admiration and comment; they are imposing edifices, advertising the costs of their guarded privacy and trying for all their vernacular materials and styles – tile, redbrick, porches, cottagey eaves – to be 'castles on the ground'.[26] Although they might seem 'sequestered',[27] only a matter of yards separates each house from its neighbour, and even in the 1890s these houses were most vulnerably situated in the busiest part of town, surrounded on all sides by comparable residences eager to assert their degree of social standing. Indeed, what is most likely to strike the passer-by these days is not so much the thirteen-bedroomed no. 20 with its red brick and white facings, so much as the massive frontage of its neighbour, no. 22 – of infinitely superior proportions. A crenellated, turreted concoction, no. 22 makes the Burnetts' home seem positively humble. The whole boulevard seems to embody that competitiveness which so characterises the newly rich and the displaying of those subtle gradations of an anxious 'superiority' always trying to impress: no. 20, in such a context, is a poor relation.

J. M. Richards, in his bold championing of the suburban, sees its essence, even in these earlier forms, to lie in a 'closed-in', self-contained style',[28] a structural impulse which is suggestive of Compton-Burnett's later fictional universe. Yet this enclosure must be seen to be at odds with the participation in the newly created rituals which villadom demanded. Architectural ritual, as Richards argues, is inseparable from the social ritual of the older suburbs. For people 'on the fringe of change' the certainties of 'Society' had to be both refined and maintained with rigour. As the middle-classes widened it became all the more vital that the demarcations between social groups were constantly policed; the castles of villadom had to be defended against both attack from above and onslaughts from below.

Crenellations, turrets, balconies – all these romantic architectural gestures toward patrician grandeur went hand in hand with a fiercely controlling codebook of social niceties aimed at ensuring the careful regulation of this influx of socially mobile *nouveaux riches*. These are precisely not homes so much as 'establishments', not houses from which you can be neighbourly. They are places to be visited in and go out visiting from, with all the rigid formality of cards and precedence which 'etiquette' came to create. Each house tried in its layout to be its own estate; vertical divisions of space – basement, nursery floor, attic – acting as substitutes for the outhouses and lateral dimensions of the gentry. In fact, with everyone living on top of each other, these shut-in households seethed with intimacy; all the more reason for replacing the more relaxed relations of the landed estate with a rigid 'upstairs downstairs' distinction which was meant to minimise all familiarity with servants.[29] Ivy herself could not remember ever having gone 'downstairs'; 'under'-servants to her were all 'squalors' whilst a series of nursemaids, as was a common practice, were given the same name – 'to save trouble'.[30] Yet no amount of aristocratic pretension in styles could disguise the raw newness of the red brick. Its beefiness might hope to conjure up Elizabethan loyalties but it was more likely to suggest new money than patrician stock.

Hove itself aimed to offer what the 'messy vitality'[31] of Brighton, with its sprawl of classes and muddled milieux, could not: spaciousness, uniform and guaranteed gentility, imperial quietness, a limited number of the right people to know and be known by. Its extremes of privacy and extremes of social accountability suggest also the level of constant vigilance necessary for patrolling the boundaries of that social life. Like its similarly divided south coast neighbour, 'Portsmouth and Southsea', the boundaries were as much psychic as physical ones – Hove begins with the mentality which lives there. Yet despite, or rather, because of its marginality, Hove was self-consciously new, a heady mix of the self-made and the snobbish, the almost-Bohemian and the aggressively respectable, capable of producing both the radical businessman, the arch Tory and the high-class murderer.

This mingling of modernity (Ivy never lived in a house more than 30 years old) and of appeals to traditionalism was of the essence of the architectural styles and of the forms of social life in villadom; it was a fertile source of tension. The queasy see-saw between extreme isolation within the most privatised family life and formidable social exposure, characterise all forms of the suburban from the Victorian onward. Yet the precise content of its symbolisation, its expression of needs and desires and fears, differs greatly from one era to another. For Hoveites as for that whole generation of villa dwellers it was fantasies of the aristocratic which caught the imagination and which held the key to the demonstrably superior life. And it was that longing to ape their betters which laid villadom open to charges of vulgarity and pretension and formed the basis of its own self-loathing.

For the sources of villadom's wealth were certainly not from the land but from trade and commerce, and no amount of Society could hide that nagging fear of exposure, of not being quite good enough, of being found out. The new gentlemen's residences were breeding grounds for the refinement of torturing class distinctions – indeed for the notion of 'refinement' itself, the newcomers' substitute for 'stock'.[32] In such circumstances, where visiting could take the form of keeping watch, staying home and becoming ever more inward might appear one way of safeguarding respectability. Unlike the upper classes, whose social networks and obligations were varied and considerable, those villa-dwellers, living, as many were, beyond their means, achieved leisure at the cost of being (as Compton-Burnett saw it), 'immured in an isolated life in a narrow community'.[33] Intense, overcrowded – the Burnetts like many other Victorian households were two families not one – and also secluded, the private suburban house was a unique domestic environment, one which frequently led to 'the rearing of strange family growths'.[34]

Ivy's past is rich in sources of potential unease, the more interesting for their being typical of that newly mobile class of villa-dwellers. Certainly her early childhood seems to have been no more severe than was usual at the time amongst the so-called comfortable classes. Memories of freezing schoolrooms, unheated bedrooms and little food – however traumatising to the modern sensibility – were far from exceptional. Far from eccentric also was the concern with keeping up appearances, the doing things for 'show' which would hide the everyday threadbare regime of 'thrift' and continuing 'retrenchment', the pretence, for example, of dining nightly 'since owning up to high tea would have been unthinkable in fashionable Hove'.[35] What does seem to have been unusual, however, was the extreme

reserve of the family, a family turned in upon itself more and more as
the years passed. Where insularity was taken for granted, they were even
more of a family apart. 'They were', as a contemporary remembered, 'a
funny family. There was a sort of barrier up around them'[36] – and this in
a social milieu where barriers were habitual. Even amongst the frozen
households of Hove, the Burnett family – or 'Compton-Burnetts' – were
'very, very exclusive'.[37] The wife of the homeopath seemed to have lived
the social insecurities of her time in a heightened form. Like many unsure
of the rules she perhaps kept to them with an over-zealous vigour in a
class which could never, by its very nature, be other than parvenu. Indeed
we might say that the family life of the young Ivy Compton-Burnett, like
that she was later to give to her fictional characters, was all but agoraphobic in its impulses.

Until the age of 31 it seems that Ivy Compton-Burnett was a dutiful
daughter of Hove. The strength of the detestation and venom which later
emerges when she mentioned 'that hideous house' could be seen as evidence of how deeply suburban she remained – both in accepting the
judgements of her 'betters' and in the self-hatred which characterised her
class. For if the 'middle class' is itself no one class, but many classes,
divided against and within themselves, then villadom crystallised in its
purest form many of the deepest impulses and properties of the uneasy
betterment which is the essence of being 'middle class'. One of the leit-
motifs of the later fiction, that of the 'façade', might perhaps be read as
a later representation of that earlier unease. Keeping up a front might be
seen as a unifying structure of villadom's interior as well as external life;
it was a way not just of maintaining the outward fictions of social superiority but also of steadying all those inner anchors which secured a sense of
self.

When Ivy Compton-Burnett was 17 her beloved father died. Katherine,
whose husband had been the centre of her life, appears from all accounts
to have visited a wild grief upon her children, lasting until her own death
ten years later. The brunt was borne especially by the eldest son of nearly
16, Guy, and the eldest daughter, Ivy. The household lived from that
moment on in the hushed shadow of death, with even the youngest child,
Topsy, at 5 years old, being called upon to partake in gruesome rites of
remembrance, kissing the dead man's photograph and helping weave daisy
chains on his grave. Suppressed hysteria and deep self-absorption shattered
by outbursts of frenzied weeping – this was the family life from which
Ivy escaped for two and a half years to read Classics at Royal Holloway
College in London, where she was known, not surprisingly, for her very
deep reserve.[38]

Her twenties were to be the scene of worse horrors. Mrs Burnett,
unfashionably in mourning for the rest of her life, became a frail but
relentless domestic tyrant, capricious and self-dramatising, emotionally

blackmailing her children. Guy, Ivy's closest ally in the family and dearest companion, collapsed and died of influenza after four years of trying to take James Burnett's place, worn out as much by the intensity of family grief as by illness. This death, which she could not bear to mention even in later years, forced Ivy to return from college, take charge of an ailing and demanding mother and to teach her younger sisters in a miserable walled-up life of the family. The excess of pent-up feeling which over-charged all, even everyday emotional exchanges, seemed to give the life of the household in those years the quality of melodrama; but for its protagonists this was their ordinary life. The younger daughters found a release of sorts in their passion for music, an outlet which Ivy increasingly condemned. It was in these years, however, that, with the help of her younger brother Noel, she wrote her first novel, *Dolores*.

As the name (from the Latin for 'sorrow') suggests, *Dolores* is a novel heavy with moral feeling, reminiscent of George Eliot both in tone and style. Dolores, a latter-day Dorothea Brooke, discovers her duty in the unhistoric acts (a quotation from the last line of *Middlemarch* which was the original title) through which she is reconciled to her lot: one of constant self-sacrifice. Against Compton-Burnett's early life it is possible to read this fiction as the most desperate kind of wishful thinking, one whose structure of feeling, however overwrought and bleak, must be clung to. Its strictures were increasingly anachronistic (even her own half-sister Olive was a 'New Woman' and had broken free),[39] though in her hibernat-ing family it was still possible to believe that the clock had stopped in 1880. The novel is both a reassurance and a kind of hysterical, unconvinc-ing attempt to give meaning to a life in which 'the desire to be devoted' – the lynchpin of the middle-class family and the foundation of femininity in wives, mothers and daughters – is the only option. Its tone is 'repellently extreme'[40] as Dolores exalts her own mortification, the nobility and neces-sity of self-immolation for the sake of 'service to her kin'. Its fervour is evidently strained. In 1911 Ivy struggled within a 'turgid, overblown naturalistic style'[41] and seems to have exaggerated the idealisms of her girlhood in the hopes of making sense of her inturned life. Once she left Hove, that book, like that early life, was never willingly referred to again. Its rhetoric was to ring particularly hollow after 1918 when so many of her generation had learnt bitterly what sacrifice as a national as well as a feminine ethic could mean. The glorious pain of self-inflicted suffering was a stance which was to lose many of its charms after the carnage of the First World War.

In 1911 Ivy's mother died after a long cancer. With her younger brother, Noel, away at Cambridge, Ivy becomes head of the household, not as a kindly replacement but as its new petty despot. At 27 she tastes the power of the private sphere and becomes an autocrat, arbitrarily organising the lives of 'the girls', her sisters, finally banning their music and locking them further into a kind of death-in-life. Such is their sense of oppression, but so far too have times changed, that all four younger sisters rebel and leave to set up a musical home in London with the pianist Myra Hess.[42] A tyrant without sway, Ivy is forced to sell up and make shift with her brothers' friends; her sisters' will not risk having her visit for longer than tea-time. Then in 1916, on the Somme, Noel is killed and Ivy's last true emotional bond destroyed. She tries to keep his unstable wife, Tertia, from suicide. And in the following year, her two youngest sisters, Topsy and Primrose, are found dead from an overdose of veronal. In 1918, Ivy nearly dies herself from the Spanish 'flu epidemic which claimed so many exhausted relatives in the aftermath of the war. She emerges (as she called it) 'brain dead', in a kind of breakdown, to live a twilight life of recuperation for several years to come.

This is the bare outline of a life which Compton-Burnett later insisted was uneventful and which she would only discuss with extreme reluctance. Indeed in the public sense it was perhaps an ordinary history; she had had what is called a sheltered upbringing. Yet by 1918, the damage was enormous: abandoned, homeless, in an England still licking its wounds, her life was 'quite smashed up'.[43] Without the inner structures of belonging to a family, however unhappy, freedom must have seemed a kind of chaos into which she was plunged. Leaving home had not been the action of a self-willed rebel but the culmination of a process of attrition in which she was stripped of all her emotional and personal ties. In a state of nervous collapse the loss of her personal world matched that of a whole generation – though it took the form at this time not of knowledge but of hopelessness. If Ivy's family had been peculiarly isolated, her brutal evacuation from its bosom left her in a permanent state of exile. She never wanted to go back, but then that world no longer existed. She had no choice and she made the best of it by hating Hove for the rest of her life. It was a matter of survival. After nearly ten years of collapse, Ivy could eventually move on with relief, but nothing which happened later was ever as real as the melodrama of her young womanhood; it was to call her back, again and again in the novels, as if she had never left: that, after all, was home.

If with the Great War, 'the Edwardian Era' – that neat fiction of a later generation's sense of loss – met its end, its stories were still to be written. Not tennis parties and the shoot, a golden age of social harmony and rural idyll, but the violence beneath the stifling respectability of families trapped as her own had been within the walls of their social identities: these are the tales of history from the inside which Ivy Compton-Burnett comes to tell. With hindsight, the miserable existence of Hove could be seen as a Gothic horror and become the object in the novels of a modernist mockery. Dissevered from her former life, Compton-Burnett found relief in a defensive satire which, by compulsively reliving those past traumas, was as likely to keep the wounds open as encourage them to heal.

A CONSERVATIVE MODERNIST

Compton-Burnett's response to having modernity so rudely thrust upon her was both an apparent aversion to her lost past and a writerly obsession with it. From 1918 onwards she 'went into a retrospect'[44] and maintained that only the time before the war held any emotional force for her: 'I do not feel that I have any real or organic knowledge of life later than about 1910.'[45] On the one hand she insisted that her own past life was negligible and refused to speak about it, whilst at the same time it took on extraordinary and all-determining significance. For her the end of an era was also the point at which it was possible to begin writing: private reticence might be the price of public articulation, and what Compton-Burnett managed in her writing was both a liberation from her past and an interminable sojourn there. It is as a backward-looking modernist that Compton-Burnett was able to speak to the heart of English cultural life. She belonged to that regiment of modernisers between the wars who found their future in making anew the past.

It was certainly as a modern that Ivy Compton-Burnett first made her name on the literary scene in the late 1920s – as a slightly avant-garde, even dissident taste, a debunker whose first four novels: *Pastors and Masters* (1925), *Brothers and Sisters* (1929), *Men and Wives* (1931), *More Women Than Men* (1933), derive much energy from breaking Victorian taboos. Compton-Burnett seems simply to be one of those breezy, even exuberant 'Georgians' whom Virginia Woolf saw as mainly being preoccupied with smashing the window-panes in the hot-houses of their childhood values.[46] Iconoclasm was very much the order of the day and wartime experience would have made such sentiments as the following all the more delightfully shocking:

> The sight of duty does make one shiver. . . . The actual doing of it would kill one, I should think.
>
> (*Pastors and Masters*, p. 17)

We have come a long way from the sickly earnestness of *Dolores*: 'the desire to be devoted', so central to pre-war idealism, is thoroughly demolished in these novels with all the recklessness, and some of the heartlessness, of post-war high spirits. The novels revel in their brittle honesty and the relief of letting so many cats out of their bags, as characters invite each other to 'speak with a decent lack of feeling' (*Brothers and Sisters*, p. 108).[47]

Compton-Burnett's early success was part of the tide of revolt against Victorianism which surged in the 1920s with feelings of disillusionment and disgust, as well as relief and gaiety, after the blood-bath of the Great War. It belonged to that great 'change of heart' which Katherine Mansfield believed was transforming English letters, making it impossible to go on in the old ways: 'I feel in the profoundest sense', she wrote, 'that nothing can ever be the same – that . . . we have to . . . find new expressions, new moulds for our new thoughts and feelings.'[48] Like many other writers and artists in post-war England, Compton-Burnett's work makes a virtue of its outspokenness and fearlessly treats of prohibited subjects like homo-sexuality and incest. This was a generation for whom 'wicked' became a delightful compliment, and for whom the Victorian appeared synonomous with the prudish, the repressive and the claustrophobic. Compton-Burnett found favour with readers who thrilled to the malicious jokes, the air of decadence and the smart dialogue.

Yet this breathless modernity of sentiment issued from the most old-fashioned of places. Blazingly frank characters speak out, not, as we might expect, from service flats or metropolitan mews, but from manor houses and landed estates. As her writing found its settled form readers were invited to hob-nob with minor aristocrats in an imaginary rural squire-archy far outside fashionable society. Thus *Brothers and Sisters* has its 'pedigree of farming squires' (p. 5), *More Women Than Men* its desirable Sir Felix, whilst *Men and Wives* opens with Sir Godfrey Haslam surveying his estate of English meadow and moorland; in *A House and Its Head* (1935) we find ourselves in 'the usual dining-room of an eighteenth-century country house' (p. 7) (the knowing assumption of familiarity is by now habitual), and all the fictions which follow are littered with baronets (though not lords) and their ladies whose presence sets the *ton*. The lower classes appear solely as servants whilst the middle-class is confined to the professions (doctors, solicitors, lawyers; certainly not homeopaths or 'trade'). Where solicitors and doctors do appear they are frequently, like Spong in *Men and Wives*, vulgar and foolish; Compton-Burnett draws a firm line between the doings of the gentry who form the main focus of each plot and the commenting chorus of the town's people. Such people too often have ideas above their station; their 'depths of middle-class yearning' (*Men and Wives*, p. 80) are the subject of much mirth.

The transparent snobbery of this literary upgrading is of less interest than its voicing, as a mixture of old and new, a particular way of coping with the losses and changes of inter-war Britain. By 1935 Raymond Morti-mer, in a key review for the *New Statesman*, is able to hail Compton-Burnett as the most modern of modernists, a Cézanne to earlier Monets, but is also alert to her offering readers a kind of *ancien régime*, a 'classical form' which may put the much-needed backbone into flabby English letters.[49] Praising the skeletal rigour of the novels and their lack of subjec-tive analysis – the 'swamp' to which the stream of consciousness can lead – he eulogises their ascetic minimalism, the precise almost stilted dialogue which uncomfortably expresses the age-old themes of domestic tragedy: 'It is like hearing the plots of Aeschylus and Sophocles recounted in the cool detached tone of Miss Austen.' Their formalism, in other words, is anti-romantic and leaves no place for the self-indulgence of individual sensibility; it bespeaks a modernist aesthetic of a kind which echoes the manifestos of writers on both left and right, but one which is arguably conservative since its strictures appeal finally (as Mortimer innocently asserts), to those who like himself are wanting 'a recall to order'.

In the 1920s and '30s Compton-Burnett was part of a chapter in the recasting of notions of English taste, and indeed of 'Englishness' itself, whose legacies are with us still. Her personal restoration to consciousness from the 'brain-death' of 1918 and the tension between past and present in her literary project were inseparable from her friendship with Margaret Jourdain, the furniture expert and consultant, with whom Ivy lived until Margaret's death in 1951. This friendship, which was more than a family tie and as intimate as any erotic one, seems to have offered both women emotional security and freedom whilst moving Compton-Burnett into quite different circles from those of her upbringing. It was in many ways a cross-class romance (if what was staunchly held to be a sexually neutral relationship can be so called) with Jourdain representing the superior partner.[50] Nevertheless, both Jourdain and Compton-Burnett were 'moderns' whose modernity took the form of seeking consolation from a socially elevated fiction of the past.

Jourdain was a pioneer in peddling new notions of the aristocratic for bourgeois consumers. One of a bevy of scholars, dealers and decorators who were busily helping to constitute the new trade in 'antiques' and dressing it in the garb of respectability and 'good taste', her moral mission in her own field of Regency furniture was, like Compton-Burnett's, anti-Victorian.[51] It may be hard for us now, in an age in which Victoriana are a thriving market, to sympathise fully with the excoriation of all such things which so galvanised the post-war generation, firing them to ridicule and censure the trappings of their own pasts. The need to shake off what Leonard Woolf called 'the fogs and fetters'[52] of the Victorian age was nowhere felt more strongly than in the one place which was the distinctive cultural creation of the Victorian middle classes: its version of 'home'. Wallpapers, armchairs, even the pot-plants were impeached, as though the very rooms bore guilty witness to the inhabitants' inner oppression. The 'mounds of plush' and the 'rich, red gloom' of these private houses seemed themselves to be saturated with the stifling emotionality which Virginia Woolf evoked as the atmosphere of her parents' home in the 1890s.[53] Escaping from these interiors was to escape from an unwholesome past into an exhilarating future: for Woolf moving to eighteenth-century Bloomsbury from Bayswater was to enter 'the most beautiful, the most exciting, the most romantic place in the world'.[54]

Jourdain and Compton-Burnett participated in that shift in the fantasy life of English culture which made a virtue of the necessity of the stripped post-war world. The impulse toward imaginative sites which were free of clutter, untrammelled by the baggage of the Victorian, took many forms: the functional 'clean' lines of modernist design or equally the raiding of the past for what was felt to be a more rational aesthetic. Jourdain was part of a group of self-styled *cognoscenti* and mutual admirers who found salvation from Victorian 'bad taste' in a re-invention of the eighteenth century. This revival abandoned the ornamentation and 'knickknackery', the immense crowdedness of nineteenth-century home interiors, for what was believed to be the austerity and moderation of 'classical' design. Where the Bloomsbury bohemians had replaced gloomy wallpapers and plush with pale wash walls and the chintzes of the New English Art Group, Jourdain and Compton-Burnett (under Margaret's instruction) elected to live in unadorned flats with bare walls, lino not carpet, and one or two 'good pieces' of light, 'simple' Sheraton or Chippendale; both were creating spaces which felt physically and psychically free of the past. Both Compton-Burnett and Jourdain, in their different ways, were in the business of redecorating the Victorian interior. Like her companion, Compton-Burnett came to turn out a creditable line of antiques.

Offered as a superior aesthetic, this penchant for the Georgian was actually a new modern fashion. When the Victorians had ushered in an age of new domestic fittings and soft furnishings – a world in which home could be physically experienced as well as mentally recast as a private haven of comfort – they themselves had spurned the public rooms of the eighteenth century as sparse, soulless, and uninviting, a condemnation of 'Georgian stolid ugliness'[55] and an assertion of hospitable, democratic homeliness which lasted well into the new century. 'The Georgian spirit of architecture', declared one Victorian critic, 'was against art' and had produced 'the hideous monstrosities' of eighteenth-century London like Harley Street and Gower Street, as well as 'long rows of unshapen cottages or hovels in the poorer parts'. In his opinion 'gloom and incompetence in matters of art' characterised the Georgian period.[56]

Now just such accusations were levelled at the Victorians. To the Neo-Georgians between the wars Victorian comfort was 'fussiness', its material-ism 'ostentatious' (as though English Palladian was not), and its stress upon interior space, the love of dark coverings indoors and out, smacked too much of the emotional intensity and psychic overload of the private houses in which they might themselves have grown up. Of course the very idea of 'interior decor' was itself a construction dependent on the concepts of privacy and privatisation which the Victorian middle classes had come to enshrine; in returning to the eighteenth century, Jourdain and the Neo-Georgians took with them very bourgeois desires and fears. For they were returning not so much to the eighteenth century as to a mythical *Georgian* period, a tidied-up patrician version of the past, and an historically quite limited understanding of heterogeneous English cultural life.[57] Not surprisingly, for Margaret Jourdain the ideal locus and imaginary paradise of social order and national virtue was the English country house. Jourdain contributed frequently to *Country Life*, elaborating its riches and helping to ensure that the magazine could deem itself 'the keeper of the architectural conscience of the nation'.[58]

Compton-Burnett's choice of settings for her novels might strike us therefore as neither 'curious' nor 'arbitrary'[59] but as personally and culturally appropriate. Besides the pain of revealing her own past there were plenty of good reasons for her make-believe gentrification. The capacity of Margaret and her 'furniture friends' for spite and snubbing seems to have been part of their *raison d'être*: they believed themselves to be, after all, arbiters of taste and scourges of the fake. Whilst Margaret entertained aesthetic young men, Ivy was considered a 'dim woman', governessy and mousey, even 'common'.[60] There was no doubt that she was definitely 'from the wrong drawer' and many assumed later that she was 'Margaret Jourdain's Boswell' and could not possibly have written all those books herself. As Margaret Jourdain's companion she found herself invited to 'great houses', getting second-hand access to the whole mythology of good taste, even learning to speak differently and gradually to build up the persona – which lasted all her life – of a Victorian lady.[61] In any case English literary and artistic circles, both left and right, were united in a contempt for villadom and in a loathing for the only truly modern form of life in the 1930s, which was its descendant, the suburban semi and the bungalow. Revelations about Hove would not have been in order.

In giving herself and her reader an imaginary *entrée* to the class above, Compton-Burnett seems to have been quite unusually clear about the defensive necessity of social fictions: 'I'm all for shams', she said, 'so long as they are good ones.'[62] Her novels are shamming, and they know it – and herein lies the enormous difference between her fiction and the vacuous country house novels to which they bear a family resemblance. The upgradings in the fiction are artificial, stylised and perfunctory, almost laughable like the preposterous names of the characters – 'Hereward', 'Griselda', 'Fulbert', 'Regan' – which capture a mocking sense of aristocratic Englishness and at the same time belong to a self-conscious literariness. We are not led, as in much writing of the time, to dote on the doings of the minor rich or to ogle the interior decoration of the upper classes; there are few thrills here for the *Country Life* voyeur. The settings are blatantly theatrical and take the country house as so much backdrop in order to return to the emotional dramas of a much more humdrum and common past.

The isolation of these country houses, which had by the 1930s begun to be cut off from any real connection to the exercise of power, provides an objective correlative for what Compton-Burnett imagines as the central condition of family life. It is an emotional life only tangentially connected to any historical knowledge of the landed classes. The domestic life which Compton-Burnett explores in these big houses is rather that of the private family and the social upgrading allows her at once to go back to Hove, avoiding the shameful stigma of the suburban and investing its psychic dramas with some spurious dignity. For the specific circumstances of that late-Victorian past to be articulated and universalised, they must be elevated: a reflex which characterises much English fiction and suggests how far its development as a form speaks to the deep unease of the middle classes. Like many novelists, Compton-Burnett escapes her own past by romanticising it: her fictions remind us how central this kind of fantasy is to those who live within a class society.[63]

The opening of her first major success, *Brothers and Sisters* (1929), can be read as symptomatic. It appears to give us the life of the squire, Andrew Stace. 'Andrew's native village of Moreton Edge', we are told,

> lay at the gates of the manor house that was his home; and around lay the lands of the manor of Moreton Edge that was his heritage. The manor house built of mellow, plum-coloured brick had its forecourt severed by a dwarf wall and black-painted railings from the village street. The pediment covering the front of the house was pierced by a circular window like a watching eye; as it might be the eye of Andrew brooding over his world. On the keystone of the arched doorway was cut the date in the reign of Anne, and above it the letters, A.M.S., the initials of the builder of the house and his wife, Andrew and Mary Stace.
>
> (*Brothers and Sisters*, p. 5)

The native village, the Queen Anne house, all imply continuity, stability, and tradition: it is easy to read the signs of wish-fulfilment in this vision of a gentrified existence, the claim to heritage and ancestry which are the Holy Grails of a class which comes from indifferent 'stock' and has no 'breeding'. But this is a house that is 'severed' from the rest of the world, as no manor-house, with its cross-country freemasonries and social network of responsibilities, would be; its narrow ambit belongs much more to The Drive, Hove than to the mellow manor-house. We hear only of the life inside the house and this evocation of the English past imagined as uninterrupted tradition is abruptly truncated as we rush over the space of thirty years between chapters, to pull up sharp at a younger generation who are the novel's main protagonists. Instead of an idealised lost England of pastoral retirement and superior sensibility we confront a confined and inward-looking family, divided from the rest of the world by their private lives which act to keep them apart from society like the low wall and railings at the front of the house. That 'watching eye' dominating the house and unsettling the paragraph forewarns us that this past, like the family itself, has become a 'façade' which it is the main business of the novel to scrutinise. And it is a 'piercing', modern *exposé* which compels the reader and signals the distance which makes such scrutiny possible. We might see in that leap from one generation to the next a figuring of the experience of *dislocation* which those born in the 1890s were likely to have felt. Compton-Burnett represents the signs of the past – 'the mellow manor-house' – as mere gestures in a history imagined not as continuity but as disjuncture, capable of arbitrary breaks and bounds. It is a history become privatised and disconnected, one which reveals Compton-Burnett's modernity as much as it addresses any longing for a different, more settled past.

Able at last to leap into a more aristocratic past, Compton-Burnett's imagination made something modern and radical of it: an indictment of domestic hypocrisy and a frank attack upon the late Victorian family as the place of unhealthy secrets and repression. These were the tensions contained within the four walls of a suburban childhood and the boundaries of family life not as it was lived by the squirearchy but by the inmates of the private house. If the cult of the country house provided their stage, it was nevertheless the dramas of Hove which were re-enacted. In this way 'it seems as if', one of her characters says, 'we are eating our cake and having it.' (*A God and His Gifts*, p. 17) Compton-Burnett revisits the horrors of Hove with the cool eye of hindsight; what she offers the reader is an imaginative return to a family life whose driving energy stems from the same unstinting source: the exercise of power. In Compton-Burnett's fiction all unhappy families are alike; looking back with anger and a sense of relief to that emotionally crowded time, the family itself appeared a definition of unhappiness.

THE DEMON IN THE HOUSE

> It is really too morbid to paint family groups, with a father and a mother and children, and no attempt to leave out anything. After all, why dwell on these things? It does not alter them.
>
> (*Daughters and Sons*, p. 134)

'Home' in Compton-Burnett's fiction is no longer the safe haven in an unheeding world, an idealised place of comfort, privacy and long-standing mutual affections but somewhere where those same ties subject us to the wills of others, the place where we learn our first lessons in submission or tyranny. The family world is a society of captives, bound to each other, capable of daily injustices, and, worse still, of putting up with them. For it is the corruption as much of absolute dependency as of absolute power which Compton-Burnett explores: 'I write of power being destructive, and parents had absolute power over children in those days. One or the other had.'[64] Her families explore the desire to humiliate, reduce and diminish others as it surfaces in its most ordinary form, in the conflict between generations. Autocrats at breakfast, luncheon and dinner, the heady power of parenthood – or grandparenthood – is seen in full sway. Here is Sabine Ponsonby, at 85, lording it over her dependents,

> Who are you, who do you think you are, to be able to speak in such a way of anyone so far above you? What do you think you are? You are raw and ignorant girls and boys, of no use to anyone but yourselves, dependent on others for a roof above your heads, food to put in your mouths, teaching to enable you to associate with the civilised.
>
> (*Daughters and Sons*, p. 176)

Power without check, the power of adults to abuse children, of husbands and wives to terrorise each other, of elders and betters to destroy rather than to protect the younger and the weaker – it is a journey into a heart of darkness, into a collapse of consoling faiths and values every bit as horrifying as Conrad's: it is the imperialism of the grown-ups who, as parents, preceptors, moral judges can be a law unto themselves, colonising their dependents, locking them into their own penal settlement, and imposing their arbitrary rules upon them. Ivy Compton-Burnett's fiction charts the interior subordinations of this small but abiding empire of home, the mentalities of ruthlessness and patronage, self-abasement and self-loathing, which matched and found larger expressions in more public, national exploitations.

The novels offer us the family as an anatomy of authoritarianism. It is a collective experience, seen from the inside, from which no one escapes. There are no heroic individuals who can rise above such a social life or the dominant psychology it produces. As Conrad does through his picture of Kurtz, Compton-Burnett suggests that the temptation to abuse power is irresistible even for the best of people:

> People have a way of not coming out well in a temptation. They generally behave as ill as they can, don't they?[65]

Collective human relations as learnt first in family life are seen as hier- archical, strictly ordered, and demanding slavish obedience. Isolation and leisure, conspicuous privacy and self-advertising wealth, are shown here to be dangerous ideals for the middle classes, a seedbed for authoritarian- ism, for violence and for sadism. And it was, above all, women in the home whose position embodied these ideals.

If, as many of her most devoted readers and critics have asserted, Compton-Burnett makes the family into a prison camp, then it is women who are its most enthusiastic warders. Where her insights differ from those of many of her contemporaries, and remain unpalatable, is in her insistence upon femininity as capable of the worst excesses of domestic cruelty, thrilling to rather than resisting the exercise of power. Her female characters inspire fear and loathing as well as admiration, and are far from being angels in the house. In Compton-Burnett's heightened and intense fictions their behaviour is frequently and typically diabolical. It is as though Victorian femininity is now being arraigned; its softnesses are shown to be smothering; like the velvet and the chenille, the paddings and the quiltings, just so many coverings which drape and disguise the truth. In this stark reckoning femininity becomes pathological and all its dark places are revealed to the light.

As an anti-Victorian Compton-Burnett's accusations are far more discomforting than those which simply charge such homes with being 'patriarchal'. Her fictions unsettle the easy assumption of female victimisation which sees femininity as a passive reaction to male violence; they force us too to contemplate the spectacle of the authoritarian woman, the woman who derives her sense of self not from being an alternative to masculine brutality but from finding forms through which to emulate it. Compton-Burnett gives her women credence for being both intelligent and energetic and in charge of themselves. She destroys the Victorian mythology of femininity as naturally more gentle or more loving as effectively as any committed feminist of the period – like Vera Brittain or Virginia Woolf – and insists upon a private sphere of home which is structured by, rather than remote from, the hierarchies of more public forms of power. Unlike her feminist contemporaries she suggests that these daughters at home are creatures who are just as likely to be attracted to cruelty as to caring, to the satisfactions to be found in hurting rather than helping others. If part of feminist consciousness in the early twentieth century was to vilify the image of the angel in the house, Compton-Burnett's radicalism takes that retaliation to its logical extreme.

Her women tyrants come in all shapes and sizes. From the first novel to the last they reveal a myriad of unwholesome and unwomanly desires. Sophia Stace, in *Brothers and Sisters* (1929), is a selfish and capricious mother 'whose love demanded more than it gave' (p. 26), controlling her children subtly and transforming the ties of family feeling into strings with which to manipulate them. Compton-Burnett's next novel, *Men and Wives*, gives us an even more complex, because more sympathetic, portrait of the domestic martyr: Harriet Haslam, whose sense of duty (that most sacred of Victorian feminine ideals), tortures her and her family. In self-pitying tones she blights both herself and her dependents with her self-sacrifice, employing all the tools of emotional blackmail.

I am a torment to you all, and a burden on your hours that you can never escape! But I am as much of a burden on my own, ten thousand times more of a burden. Griselda, my darling, don't look distressed; don't waste a thought on your harrowing old mother. Don't think of me. Be happy.

(*Men and Wives*, p. 13)

Josephine Napier, the headmistress in *More Women Than Men*, is unscrupulous and self-regarding, jealously in love with her own much younger nephew whose wife she helps to her death – and so the list goes on, right up until the novel Compton-Burnett was writing when she died, posthumously called *The Last and the First*. Eliza Heriot is last but not least of her female dictators, one who

> wielded the power as she thought and meant, wisely and well, but had not escaped its influence. Autocratic by nature, she had become impossibly so, and had come to find criticism a duty, and even an outlet for energy that had no other.
>
> *(The Last and the First*, p. 17)[66]

Wives, mothers, single women (like the atrociously calculating Anna Donne in *Elders and Betters*), widows (the devious Agatha Calkin in *Men and Wives*), aunts, unmarried daughters, grandmothers – all find outlets for their energy which are far from innocent in these claustrophobic homes. Whatever memories of Hove are being exorcised here (and Compton-Burnett herself would say that she believed she worked 'rather low down')[67] it seems clear that these novels are drawn back time and again to fantasies of power; that the image of the woman autocrat is at least as desirable as it is repulsive.

For Ivy Compton-Burnett home is never a place outside the strategies of power and its abuse. Keeping house can mean the invention of inflexible rules and regulations every bit as demoralising and controlling as the regime of the factory of the office. In her novels, slackers are kept in order, mealtimes become ordeals to be got through, and the exchange between generations usually takes the form of a domestic inquisition:

> Did you have a fire in your room last night, Hermia? I saw the ashes in the grate as I passed the door.
>
> *(The Last and the First*, p. 19)

and that most common of intrusions into children's lives: 'What are you doing?' The running of the household, far from being a charmingly feminine task, takes on all the rigid efficiency of a general marshalling his troops. If men can imagine themselves captains of industry, the mistress of the house has her own extensive field of command.

Of course, there are male tyrants. Yet there is something so obvious about their position – they are, as it were, expected to be despotic – that their activities, though brutal, are less frightening. They are not especially devious or cunning, but straightforward, even clumsy oppressors. There is the sexually energetic type like Duncan Edgeworth in *A House and Its Head* or Hereward Egerton in *A God and His Gifts*, or men like Cassius Clare (*The Present and the Past*) and Horace Lamb (*Manservant and Maidservant*), simple, miserly bores, opinionated and ignorant, who use power with 'moderation and cruelty' (*Manservant and Maidservant*, p. 146). It is the female characters who are blessed with lucid self-knowledge; they know their own strength and almost eagerly abandon themselves to self-exploitation:

> How utterly I see through him and yet how utterly necessary he is to me. And how pathetic.
>
> (*Pastors and Masters*, p. 35)

It is the women in the novels whose power is all the more terrible, deriving as it does from the frustrations of the powerless.

For hers is not a moralising view of authoritarianism. Her tyrants are 'built on a large scale . . . powerful for both good and bad' (*More Women Than Men*, p. 178). Harriet Haslam, for example, knowing others better than they do themselves, wishes to save them all by moral bullying. She is tormented by her zealousness, a slave to her ideals, and after attempting suicide is eventually driven mad by 'the burden of mother and father' (*Men and Wives* p. 70). In a rare moment of textual psychologising, she confesses:

> I see my children's faces, and am urged by the hurt of them to go further, and driven on to the worst . . . . May you never know what it is to be tortured by those you love . . . .
>
> (*Men and Wives*, p. 78)

Compton-Burnett's tyrants are often sensitive people, just as her victims, the dependents, the 'children' (and these are homes where one is a child by virtue of being a dependent well into one's twenties) are far from innocent. Whereas there have been plenty of portraits in literature of parental tyranny, Compton-Burnett attacks the whole shared structure of family life. The pattern of generation is itself to blame, and tyranny is not a question of headstrong or heartless individuals but of group complicity. The authoritarian home relies upon obedience as well as fear. As a collective condition it involves a certain amount of consensus. What is clear from these fictional renderings is that the power of the tyrant can be mesmerising even to those whom it is destroying. Many of her victims remain impotent precisely because their fascination with the power of others makes them susceptible to it. They are immobilised by their own sense of awe.

The taste for cruelty and the need to submit are necessarily tied up with the economic inequalities of the family. The systematic ill-treatment of its younger members mostly takes the form of making them 'beholden'; emotional indebtedness must compensate for financial support. Whereas 'the lower classes' have to work in order to survive economically as a unit, these make-believe gentry bolster self-esteem only by appearing leisured. The cost of that 'privilege' is complete vulnerability and accessibility to emotional demands: expressions of guilt, possessiveness, as well as of affection become the normal currency. In these families there is no ready money; wealth, if any, lies untouched in hidden capital. Inexhaustible claims upon feeling seem to take the place of overtly financial transactions. This sense of the family as an *investment* is baldly stated on most pages of the novels: in one breath almost, Sabine Ponsonby tells her emotionally starved grandchildren

You have been lapped in luxury from your birth . . .

and attacks them for being privileged:

Hoses have to be bought and paid for. You seem to think things are to be had for the asking.

(*Daughters and Sons*, pp. 27–8)

Within the bourgeois family this is an elementary form of child abuse: dependents are 'guilty for having to receive' (*The Last and the First*, p. 50).

More disquieting, however, is Compton-Burnett's depiction of child-hood as 'knowing' rather than innocent, of a comradeship between siblings which arises from the shared corruption of humiliating dependency. Child-hood allows a certain distance from the activities of tyrants but it nurtures only precocious powers of observation, not the spirit of rebellion. The novels do not give us childhood as the familiar starting-place of wisdom, the romantic reward for the loss of innocence. Instead behaviour is caught in a constant historic present – it simply *is*, to echo one of her titles, the world and its way. Childhood in the novels, then, is not the place from which we grow but the place in which we stay. Only the very young are still in some sense unassimilated. Like matter out of place, they simply await repression, their anarchy inevitably doomed. We know that the giggling Muriel in *Daughters and Sons* will soon end up as sombrely well-mannered as the rest. To wonder why no one runs away is to miss the point: you cannot escape your childhood, and there is a sense in which none of us ever leaves home.[68]

This is a psychic landscape remarkable for its uniformity. No one in these novels develops, any more than the novels do themselves. Each novel gives us an airless, deeply homogeneous world. Difference is minimalised, and for that reason greatly to be feared. Compton-Burnett insists upon the similarity between boy and girl children, that the bond of joint suffer-ing overrules gender difference. Whilst it was often historically the case that children of the middle classes were kept at home with private tutors until adolescence, the novels imagine a whole series of semi-incestuous unions and celebrate the brother and sister relationship as quasi-marital. They betray not just a sense of continuing childhood solidarity, but also a desire to side-step the sexual and social expectations of being grown-up. The fiction is full of middle-aged brothers and sisters who have elected for celibacy and to live together. It seems an ideal solution to irreconcilable needs, providing a way both of prolonging family life and of avoiding its worst consequences:

'Zillah, we are brother and sister. If we were not, what could we be?'
  'Nothing that was nearer. It stands first among the relations. There is nothing before it, nothing to follow it. It reaches from the beginning to the end.'

(*A God and His Gifts*, p. 49)

Since marriage, like sexual desire itself, disrupts the family order and may bring in outsiders, it is always potentially disastrous. Anything which encourages a sense of individuality at the expense of the group – whether it be romantic love, employment, or simply a different style of dress – must be quashed. As the pairing but differentiating titles of the novels suggest, the family is made up of collective allegiances, oppositions and exclusions, structures which have the ring of eternal sameness about them. Outsiders may question the codes of family life, they can never ultimately destroy them. Like the servants, and the children, they learn to speak the same language or they leave.

Since these are homes in which most activities are regarded as 'vulgar', and speech is constantly restrained, any kind of incident is devastating. It is not just that Compton-Burnett's plots are melodramatic but that in this enervated seclusion *any* plot is melodramatic. All events (and this may include merely going outside for a walk) have the emotional intensity of melodrama. But it is a melodrama which is harnessed to an attack on the family rather than to a shoring up of its values. It is the awfulness of everyday life which is overloaded with emotional and psychic cargo. Plain speaking – when characters manage to break loose from the reining in of their speech – seems strained and theatrical, weighted down with significance of the long suppressed.

The radicalism of these texts lies in their dissolving the distinction between the notion of a public external community and a private inner self. The family is posed not as the opposite of, or different to, the public stream of history but as the place where its meanings are both learnt and shaped. The family is pre-eminently both private and public, intervening between a sense of separate selfhood and the agreed, impersonal structures of a social world. It is the place where we might first learn our difference from others, and our lack of it: recognising oneself as a son or a sister is to acknowledge simultaneously an intimate, unique, and deeply conventional relation. The family is the first place where 'I' must be subordinated to 'them' – an experience of collective life which can itself take many forms. In Compton-Burnett's fiction the family has a life of its own and is much more than the sum of its parts. Its collective regime takes over the individual in purely undemocratic ways; at best the family is a paternalistic empire, at worst a police state. The novels are thus neither the purely personal and bizarre fantasies of a wayward spinster, nor simple cele-brations of a by-gone age; neither confession nor documentary. Instead they remind us forcibly that the limiting social structures within which we live and grow form the breakwaters of the psyche, of the inner world of imagination and feeling.

We are not, however, offered any means of explaining or situating this unhappiness within the novels themselves. The cryptic titles – *The Present and the Past, A Heritage and its History* – express a relational sense of identity, one which is plural not individual and which lives 'history' in a static, improvised present. 'The present and the past' are not made sense of through a narrative of social change, one which involves a notion of a community, however attenuated; nor through a heightened individual sensibility which gives us a relation to it; nor is there any recourse to an order of explanation outside the human (one thinks of the religious lean-ings of many other modernists): there is only a group mentality and there is only the action which unfolds before our eyes. Compton-Burnett's frozen families may remind us of other equally stranded groups in the late realism of the modern novel (D. H. Lawrence's *Women in Love*, or Thomas Mann's *The Magic Mountain*), communities no longer bounded by any positive connection, and whose moral revolt does not lead to a breakthrough into a larger, more generous society. Unlike them, however, her dramas of warring voices refuse to place themselves in a shared exterior world, or a shared history of change.

Nor do the novels deal in a psychology which would explain the inner world. Like Freud's, her stories – 'the beautiful family talk, mean and worried and full of sorrow and spite and excitement' (*A Family and a Fortune*, p. 287) – become their own object, potentially unending. Unlike Freud's, however, they are not talking cures, since their aim is not to treat of or to ameliorate the experience of individual consciousness. Compton-Burnett's fiction is part of an inter-war sensibility which grapples with the breakdown of faith in family life solely within the terrain of the activities of the group. Yet it resists too the idea of a 'group psychology'. It is a project both more total and less liberal than Freud's, for whilst she may suggest the need for a 'psychology', she does not propose one. Her texts give us a chance to recognise the social nature of all subjective life – to see it displayed and to hear it happening, but not to see it change. The scenes have the quality of *tableaux vivants*: the characters seem fixed in an eternal human comedy, their actions unaccountable. This is the fiction of behaviourism not of psychoanalysis.

No aetiology, no genealogy, no psychology, only repetition in an eternal present. These narratives without interpretation allow for no agency and no intervention, and steeped as they are in the precise misery of a social class, they could nevertheless appear, as the years went by, to be proclaiming universal and immovable truths. For ten, twenty, thirty years, the same patterns, the same voice, the same text – something more is at stake here than exorcism. What began as a response to trauma seems to have become a fixation; the act of resistance one of wilful denial. Gradually the private sphere of family and of interior life appears not merely as the legitimate site of history, but as its only site, the only determinant of our lives.

Thus, in an act of removal (characteristically) to Lyme Regis during the Second World War, Compton-Burnett's reading of *Persuasion* led her to conclude

> how much more important in the long run was the twisted ankle of a young girl than all the clamouring of leaders in far off countries.[69]

Perhaps only a well-off Englishwoman could be so blithely insular, but it is surely a misreading of Jane Austen. Austen, writing for an emerging bourgeoisie in the early nineteenth century, was helping to shape a whole new account of personal lives which expressed precisely the interdependency of domestic and social mores. The apparently 'private' activities of her heroines are important not because they have nothing to do with actions on a larger scale but because in private conduct we can read, in small, the larger values and social practices which inform (or ought to inform) 'government' of whatever kind. In the exemplary behaviour of her characters, though their social world be narrow and confined, Jane Austen expected her readers to find the lessons for a community at large: the one is the product and figure of the other.

For Compton-Burnett, on the other hand, the private house has lost that iconic and exemplary place. We are at the end of a long narrative of connection (one of whose key expositions lay in the novel itself), tying together the meanings of the private and the public and interpreting each through the other. Compton-Burnett's project bespeaks a traumatised sense of being and of conduct; an ontology characterised by the refusal to engage with any notion of wider social involvements or place. Yet if the effect of the fictions is the denial of connections between self and modes of historical and social belonging, that sense of disengagement and disavowal could rapidly be made by readers into an enhanced cultural or social position. The very inwardness which originally had the force of a revelation, could so easily become prized, not for what it said about the historical and socially locatable forms of family and of subjectivities brutalised by a class-ridden life, but as a cultural idiom in itself, one which could start to take pleasure in being cut off, and find in feelings of estrangement new and desirable forms of privilege.

THE PLEASURES OF DENIAL

'What makes you talk like that?'
'Excess of feeling and a wish to disguise it.'

A Family and a Fortune, p. 266)

In the 1930s the novels of Ivy Compton-Burnett addressed a special
inwardness in English cultural life. It is possible to read the work as a
literary equivalent of 'Little Englandism' in which its psychic and linguistic
isolation match the demographic and economic self-sufficiency of the
English middle classes between the wars. Compton-Burnett's fiction makes
that inner mapping a kind of evacuation, a de-historicisation which was
representative nevertheless of new ways of making social, cultural and
political identities between the wars. In listening to the attenuated, imaginary conversation of an already self-immolated cultural group, readers could
wreathe themselves in an air of privilege. It was a privilege which depended
upon seeing oneself as cut off from a rightful inheritance and a superior
place, and one whose anti-democratic animus and conservative posturing
put fresh life into much of English culture between the wars. Readers
could see themselves in an embattled and defended relation to the lost
past but also, increasingly, to the urgencies of the present. Such a cultural
identity prided itself on being disenfranchised and dispossessed: a minimalist position which in Compton-Burnett's novels is best articulated, quite
literally, in speech. It was her use of language that readers most admired:
it had at once the appearance of exclusivity and yet, like elocution lessons,
was easily learnt. Like the modulated tones on the new wireless programmes, these voices in the air were modern productions ironically under-
cutting the relation between speaker and knowable social place, turning
communication into the art of mimicry and claims to social status into a
species of ventriloquy. They guaranteed too a kind of elevation whose
snobberies were paradoxically open to all: all one needed to do was to
speak with the right accent, to learn, as Compton-Burnett had done herself, to talk properly.

If readers found these tales from the family crypt harrowing, they also
'howled out loud'[70] and it was her 'extraordinarily subtle humour' which
won hearts.[71] It is the humour which makes what might otherwise be
excruciating bearable, whilst the idea that we are engaged in the exercise
of wit sanctions whatever we overhear or find in the 'family talk'. Over
and again, what would have horrified and demoralised is reiterated with
nonchalance and *savoir faire*. Enormities are greeted with laconic carelessness – incest, for example, simply shrugged off:

So I am Father's sister. Well, I am not troubled about that.

(Brothers and Sisters, p. 178)

The humour provides a licence for the unspeakable to be spoken. Victims and the powerless mutter an ironic commentary; children answer domestic tyrants back with fantastic frankness:

> 'What are you doing, Clare?' said Sabine in her even manner. 'I suppose nothing?'
> 'Why ask a question when you know the answer?'
>
> *(Daughters and Sons, p. 15)*

These humorous asides lift taboos and allow the 'unlovely recesses of the human heart' to be explored in safety.[72] For the reader it is possible to play all the parts, to be both innocent and experienced. This excessive outspokeness gives us an opportunity at last to have the say we were denied in childhood. At the same time we can play at tyranny; the deplorable statements of her domestic despots are simultaneously condemned and admired; we can have the naughty pleasure of finding them secretly funny precisely because of their awfulness:

> 'I seldom like what is natural; it is usually so unlikeable. People should be civilised. Mrs Duff [the cook] has a good home and every consideration. What more can she want?'
> 'Put yourself in her place, Mater, and answer the question.'
> 'I should not think of it. It would not be fitting. The place is hers, not mine. We don't move people about, even in thought.'
>
> *(The Last and the First, p. 111)*

At the level of individual quip, verbal enjoyment rests in a constant wrenching of proverbial wisdom out of joint, inverting platitudes, and inventing what Kingsley Amis scathingly called 'cliché-critique':[73]

> With me nothing fails like success.
>
> *(Daughters and Sons, p. 74)*

> To know all is to forgive all, and that would spoil everything.
>
> *(ibid., p. 82)*

> 'Be patient with me, my dear. I shall be older and wiser presently.'
> 'You will be older and not wiser. At our age people get less wise.'
>
> *(Pastors and Masters, p. 33)*

In fact *all* the speech in the novels aspires towards aphorism; all the grammar exists in a curious state of truncation. If brevity is the soul of wit, Compton-Burnett's dialogue compresses the most mundane sentence so that it seems like a one-liner. The abruptly chopped syntax and the frequent end-stopping of conversation with the use of 'that', gives even the most banal remark the air of repartee. The characters converse in a kind of verbal shorthand, so abbreviated and pared down that all exchanges seem to be droll badinage. Uttered *sotto voce*, they also smack of wisdom:

'I had very little education myself, and I have seldom found the want of it.'

'Other people have done that,' said Chilton to France.

(*Daughters and Sons*, p. 57)

'Well, Mater or not, I am no tyrant', said Eliza. 'People are not afraid of me. Sometimes, I think, too little.'

'That is not likely,' said Hermia. 'Fear goes a long way.'

(*The Last and the First*, p. 29)

It is this rigid staccato rhythm which renders the speech impressive; the cryptic appears sybilline: the prosaic oracular. The epigrammatic gives the conversation an air of deliberate quotation; mere talk is translated (in one of Compton-Burnett's favourite formulations) into 'utterance', and what is overheard bears the appearance of profundity.[74] It is not surprising that Compton-Burnett should be accused of being a cult author. But it is more true to say that *every* reader is admitted to the charmed circle of the *cognoscenti*. If the humour works by flattery and by complicity – we too can be as witty as the characters – it offers us all the lure of joining the world of the 'knowing', the pleasure of being an insider, a licensed eavesdropper listening to 'public secrets'.[75] Mutual admiration at our own cleverness can be – as it is in these houses – a stand-in for family feeling. We belong at last to that special band of talkers. The in-jokes and the tight linguistic demands of the text work to create a glamorous esotericism which seduces us into thinking that once we have cracked the verbal code, we have arrived.

If, as Freud suggests in his own account of verbal humour, all jokes are dominated by 'a tendency to compression, or rather to saving',[76] then Compton-Burnett's wit is surely one of the most parsimonious. It draws upon a long tradition of English satire – of humour in the service of moral and psychic economies of restraint. Her frugal household backchat is impelled by a thrift taken to the point of extreme meanness. Nothing can be allowed to be thrown away. Like the actual penny-pinching of those homes, the humour is a kind of psychic and emotional retrenchment. It alleviates with the minimum of expenditure. That great skill of the English middle classes – economising – is here dignified as highbrow, and given all the authority of a very fine art.

On a psychological level these stenographic exchanges are meant to convey to the reader the effects of pressure, of the emotional damming up and rigorous self-control demanded by such straitened lives. Yet there is a way in which Compton-Burnett's insistence on an exclusive and stylised manner could be seen to elevate the quotidian conversation and shameful seclusion of these families as surely as their location in imaginary country houses upgrades their social position. The linguistic dressing-up is of a piece with the fears and obsessions of the novels. The labyrinthine dialogue is another way of keeping up a façade, of avoiding exposure, whilst at the same time offering the reader the pleasures of nasty gossip. Narrowly inward-looking, the humour of the novels compulsively covers its tracks, protecting itself from invasion and intrusion. It is a form of containment which seals off the writing, from the syncopated sentence to the fictional world itself, and reminds us of the impulses behind that 'self-enclosed world which is the essence of suburban style'. But whereas in Hove or Croydon, or South Ken', being talked about could in fact be your ruin, this polite malice never rocks the boat too hard, and never makes an exhibition of itself.

Not surprisingly, in these chronicles of the emotional and linguistic constipation of respectable English life, verbal 'laxity' frequently implies either moral or social 'looseness', and usually both: Dulcia Bode in *A House and Its Head* is immediately recognisable as foolish and 'fake' as soon as she utters a colloquialism. Within this retentive economy any kind of generosity is bound to be suspiciously extravagant or even to suggest 'incontinence': 'It's wrong to waste, but what's worse, it's vulgar.'[77] Any exposure of feeling is a kind of squandering and is demeaning: the most verbose are likely 'to give themselves away' and only the most costive of communications is deemed proper. Indeed it is impossible for Compton-Burnett to imagine a more relaxed organisation of social or personal life. Servants, for example, all speak as their employers do in her novels, even though their social pretension is laughable. In any case, those who speak differently are to be feared: their social values may also be different. Linguistic and social chaos are only words apart. The ramrodding of speech in the novels, and its enforced homogeneity, is perhaps analogous to the creation of the 'cut-glass accent' in the 1920s and '30s, a measure of both the assumed superiority and the brittle defensiveness with which being 'a better class of person' was asserted.[78]

At its crudest, Compton-Burnett's wit is little more than a snubbing which takes the 'vulgarity' of others as an easy target, a kind of literary one-up-manship whose surface of smart sayings barely covers the most familiar prejudices of respectability. Typically, the body and the passions cannot be referred to except as a source of shame and embarrassment; there are no jokes about sexuality, very few laughs – and then only from children – about physical experience; only governesses or servants or those without social status are aware of their 'bodily functions'. Where other forms of comedy relish physical excess – slapstick, for example (a term which originally signified a literal and tangible comic device), or a comedy which involves 'knock-about' and generates 'belly-laughter' – this humour denigrates the body as animalistic and terrifying, a sign of the socially inferior. Naturally, sexual desire always creates havoc in these homes.

Above all, though, it is the 'talk' itself which is seen as a measure of one's social standing; its very cleverness sets one apart from the *hoi polloi*.

Fortunately, clever talk is one of the few luxuries within reach of the relatively impecunious; no wonder, then, that Compton-Burnett offers it as the true measure of a 'civilised' life, presided over by the twin goddesses of isolation and leisure. Or, as she put it in an interview, 'People in civilised life don't do much, do they?'[79] Whilst, by inference, those who *do* do things (and do not talk like 'us') are not civilised:

'Now why should people have this aversion to manual employment?' asked Roseberry, looking round . . . .
'It is because it is seen as requiring a low intelligence, and because it does require it. And because it is dull and unrewarding in itself.'
(*Mother and Son*, p. 15)

In these novels, inactivity and emotional disengagement are not just a chosen option, they are the best option:

'You don't feel that marriage would mean a fuller life?'
'I don't want the things it would be full of . . . .'
(*A God and His Gifts*, p. 5)

On the surface such refusals seem anti-bourgeois, a denial of agency and of that engagement with public life and institutions which could be seen as the lifeblood of a middle-class existence in the nineteenth century. Yet it is precisely this kind of retreat from their own history which between the wars came to be established as the mark of true propriety and which need not interfere with other more familiar structures of bourgeois economy. (In Compton-Burnett's own life we might see her denial of her past as in part the successful attempt to turn into cultural kudos that awkwardly material pile of capital which had been accumulating and accruing to her as a result of her father's entrepreneurial activity, and which made it possible for her to lead a life of leisure in the first place. What is interesting, however, is that she saw more propriety in being hard-up than in being wealthy.)

It is ultimately the pleasures as much as the pains of an estranged and repressive privacy that Compton-Burnett's fiction gives us. Despite the modern dislocation of her characters' world, Compton-Burnett's investment in a traditional view of social place and hierarchy remains intact. This is amusement not anarchy: pain may be momentarily alleviated but its causes remain untouched. Her fiction, for all its attacks upon the stifling standards of a bourgeois past, remains mewed up within its limits. The bitter jokes made by the tormented inmates of these dreadful houses perversely harp upon those injuries.[80] The jokes can never become a means of collective enfranchisement, only of further bondage. Family discourse can be laughed with but not at. What passes for plain speaking simply displaces rather than dislodges the sources of anxiety from which the humour springs. In the long term of forty years of novels, what is at work is not de-repression, the exhumation of those old buried horrors, but what Herbert Marcuse called 'repressive desublimation': the creation of new sources of fear and anxiety. As one of the 'brilliant refrigerators of family utterance',[81] her chilling travesties of English family life never condemn its strictures as either absurd, unnecessary or replaceable. That it is not a comedy which seeks to celebrate or transform the world is quite clear. 'Really it is all tragedy', one of her characters maintains. 'Comedy is a wicked way of looking at it, when it is not our own' (*Mother and Son*, p. 44). This humour leaves in place what it appears to destabilise. Even Compton-Burnett's last novel, *The Last and the First* (published after her death), was revealingly circular in structure, with the boldly outspoken Hermia leaving a home ruled by her peevish stepmother, only in order to return willingly to its appalling constraints, this time as the keeper of the keys. Hilary Spurling reads this as a genial restoration of harmony by a writer in her autumnal wisdom; it could equally well be read as pathological conservatism.[82] Compton-Burnett's homes may be prisons but, after all, their enclosure is a safe one, sheltering the traumatised sensibility as well as producing it.

Where other contemporary humorists wrote narratives (as different as *This Happy Breed* and *Decline and Fall*), charting the pathos as well as the bitter ironies of loss, Compton-Burnett's are not in that sense narratives at all.[83] Rather they are modes of *hanging on*, and the humour, far from offering, as comedy can, glimpses of alternative, freer worlds, is busy running fast in order, like Alice, to stand still. Compton-Burnett claimed Chekhov as a progenitor, sharing with him a sense of stasis as a collective class condition, of an agnostic universe in which isolation and leisure pre-empt any chance of emotional release and stifle the opportunities for either tragic romances or heroic individualism. Where she shows herself to be of a later generation, and of a later class formation, is that for Compton-Burnett stasis has become desirable. (When she went to the theatre in later years it was Samuel Beckett's comedies of inertia she most enjoyed.)[84]

Nothing could be further from the 'genial, laughter-loving sense of life and its enjoyable intercourse'[85] of Oscar Wilde, with whom Compton-Burnett, as a humorist, has most often been compared.[86] Not only is Compton-Burnett not an 'apostle of pleasure',[87] her novels remain in the end bounded by the very social hypocrisy and rules of conformity which Wilde attempted to turn upside-down. They lack Wilde's capacity to call in question the whole restricting pretentiousness not just of social classes (Jack Worthing spawned in a handbag), but of the social order itself. For Wilde is most unlike Compton-Burnett in being at his most searching and serious as a social critic when he is also a libertarian. His work frequently attacks 'the many prisons of life – prisons of stone, prisons of passion, prisons of intellect, prisons of morality'.[88] For him 'all life is limitation'; whereas for Compton-Burnett, all limitation is life. Her aphoristic wit works as much to deflate and chasten as to exhilarate; for all her revelations about private life, no one would call her irresponsible, let alone indecent.

Compton-Burnett became a hit in the 1940s. With *Parents and Children* at the beginning of the war her sales began to rise; in 1944 *Elders and Betters*, one of the most bitter of her volumes (Vita Sackville-West declared it was like sucking a lemon)[89] sold out eventually at 6,000 copies, and the publication of *Manservant and Maidservant* in 1946 marked a new high in her reputation both here and in the United States.[90] The novels may well have appealed particularly to wartime audiences because of their atmosphere of austerity and latent violence: 'the moral economy of Ivy's books had always been organised on a war footing.'[91] They also chimed in with a growing mood of alienation and disenchantment amongst English writers and intellectuals at the end of the war, and their recoil from the cross-class camaradie which the new Labour government seemed likely to encourage.[92] Typically, Elizabeth Bowen saw the novels as capturing the 'icy sharpness' of London after a blitz;[93] her own *The Heat of the Day* (1949) imagined a London deserted and ghostlike, unpeopled (by those of her own ilk) – a class fantasy which was a million miles from a Home Front where people were smiling through and mucking in. L. P. Hartley, himself engaged in fashioning new dreams of the Edwardian era, claimed that Compton-Burnett's writing seemed 'nearer to reality than that of any living novelist'.[94]

In the aftermath of fascism critics saw parallels between Compton-Burnett's authoritarian families and the passions which 'have recently devastated continents'.[95] Edward Sackville-West called her novels 'rook-enchanted concentration camps'; there was, he asseverated, 'no feature of the totalitarian regime which has not its counterpart in the atrocious families' they portrayed.[96] Nowhere does the actual incongruity of this marriage between a comedy of manners and the drama of the family *Lagers* strike anyone as worthy of comment. The peculiar, even shocking pleasures which readers might derive from these ghastly farces are left unquestioned. In later years Angus Wilson combined praise for her as one of the most unflinching of realists, 'in the age of the concentration camp', with a comparison with 'the wit of Wilde at its best, or Congreve . . . or Meredith'.[97] It is as a writer who is 'madly comic' and 'richly entertaining' that Compton-Burnett's *univers concentrationaire* continues to receive lavish praise.[98]

Certainly her most devoted fans found in this comedy of reserve an argument for a more disciplined Englishness, a bracing experience to be appreciated by those for whom stoicism was the highest good and 'relief the keenest form of joy'.[99] In the 1940s Compton-Burnett was applauded as a standard bearer by those who believed that England and English had fallen into disarray. (This, after all, was the decade of *Scrutiny*,) The purity of her prose, shorn of all ornamentation and devoid of colloquialisms, appealed as exemplary; she was the formidable taskmaster or governess who would keep us all from slipping. Edward Sackville-West, writing in 1949, savours 'the intense satisfaction that arises from submitting oneself to Miss Compton-Burnett's regime' with an almost masochistic pleasure.[100] A fantasy of obedience and the pleasure of English puritanism meet in the moral assumptions of literary criticism: the novels may look easy but they are not. Their very difficulty becomes the guarantor of Compton-Burnett's and the reader's 'maturity' and reading becomes its own reward.

Thus Robert Liddell in the first major study of Compton-Burnett in 1947 introduces a tone of admonishment. Her work 'is not always read as it should be', and this is because standards (suitably ineffable) have crumbled, and these are 'bad times' (presumably in the new Labour Britain). Happily confusing moral standards with speech idioms, he claims that Compton-Burnett wrote before 'English' was destroyed. The rigour of her prose appeals to him, like a brisk walk in a sharp wind. It helps us – almost literally – keep a stiff upper lip.[101] In 1965 Charles Burkhart is still using these terms to praise Compton-Burnett's diction for 'modern readers who have not been totally dulled and deadened by a language overused', and Cicely Greig, with rather less subtlety, opines that she 'demands a certain level of education from her readers'.[102] A note of self-congratulation even crept into the *Times* obituarist who declared that she 'was an uncompromisingly highbrow writer who made no concession to her readers' laziness'.[103] Such appreciation made little sense of her as a modernist; modernism, associated with a levelling down, was now something to attack: her work is rather 'one of the things we live by . . . (in spite of our shortcomings and backslidings)' and the evil which it wards off is 'the sentimentality and the language of Wardour Street'.[104]

In the 1920s Compton-Burnett had been hailed as a scourge of the Victorian; by the 1950s she is increasingly being seen as a champion of its values. The duration of her writing career saw what was once brand-new take on the patina of tradition; the former parvenus, like her own family, become the old guard, and late Victorian villadom, so hated in its day, celebrated fifty years on by a newly insecure middle class who were too busy attacking another generation of suburbanites to notice the irony.[105] Did she smile to see those once vulgar brick slabs and ostentatious piles of Hove and Bayswater become by the 1950s and '60s the home of all that was sacred in the conservative imagination, and laugh that the brash values of an *arriviste* class could now seem the backbone of the nation? Apparently not. Rather it seems as if she decided to 'retrench' further, retreat ever inwards from the world until she found herself trapped behind the Victorian–Edwardian façade she had helped to create.

HOUSEBOUND

I have found how impossible it is to undo the past. It is odd that people should ever think it possible.

(More Women than Men, p. 180)

In the post-war world Ivy Compton-Burnett came gradually to fit the fictions she had invented. She 'looked and dressed all her life like a Victorian maiden lady',[106] shaking hands, 'like royalty', with limp fingers curled – 'quite unlike our more vulgar and modern gripping and shaking habits'.[107] According to her oldest friends she learnt finally to talk just like her characters in a stilted manner which newer acquaintances believed to be old-fashioned 'proper English'.[108] To Anthony Powell hers was 'a quite unmodified pre–1914 personality';[109] her voice entirely 'an Edwardian lady's voice';[110] a 'period piece', she treated her typist, Cicely Greig, with the lofty courtesy one showed to someone 'obliged to earn her living, poor thing'.[111] Once Cicely Greig was content to be 'of the governess class', all was well. Yet both of them enjoyed relating examples of servants who tried to speak like their superiors in a 'burlesque of "refined" speech', like Compton-Burnett's own 'factotum', Mary, an Irishwoman, who was rather 'simple', and all but worshipped her 'Dame'.[112]

Compton-Burnett pleaded genteel poverty all her life, and now in the levelling years of post-war democracy insisted that she was one of the new poor. Bemoaning the hardships of the Welfare State (the horrors of 'government doctors and dentists'),[113] she frequently impressed friends with her impecuniosity, allowing them to save her taxi-fares, and prompting one, when Compton-Burnett seemed pathetically hard-up, to approach the Royal Literary Fund which granted her £500. Friends were outraged when, later, she herself wrote for more funds and was refused, and when an application for a Civil List pension was also rejected.[114] In fact, they had been completely taken in by her inability to touch the considerable capital which had been salted away over the years from the rents on her father's properties and the sales of her own work. The same friends were shocked to discover that Compton-Burnett died a wealthy woman, leaving an estate worth £86,000. It was a deception worthy of one of the least lovable of her fictional characters.[115]

Compton-Burnett's post-war years are interesting not simply for the familiar but fascinating spectacle of an ageing writer moving further into conservatism but for the ways in which that move was shaped by a cultural re-imagining of the Edwardian. The 1950s and '60s saw Compton-Burnett's work taken up by a younger generation many of whom were busily working out their own relation to the Edwardian, of which perhaps L. P. Hartley's *The Go-Between* has been the most popular example. On the other side of the ideological fence, the fiction might be scorned but its appeal still felt; Jimmy Porter might be looking back with anger but even he is susceptible to the lure of that Indian summer:

> The old Edwardian brigade do make their brief little world look pretty tempting. All home-made cakes and croquet, bright ideas, bright uniforms. Always the same picture: high summer, the long days in the sun, slim volumes of verse, crisp linen, the smell of starch. What a romantic picture. Phoney too, of course. It must have rained sometimes. Still, even I regret it somehow, phoney or not. If you've no world of your own, it's rather pleasant to regret the passing of someone else's.
>
> (John Osborne, *Look Back in Anger*, p. 17)

Both versions agree upon a notion of the Edwardian as a time of settlement whether as an object of attack or of desire. For many of Compton-Burnett's fans, despite the horrors she reveals in family life, 'the Edwardian era' is recast as a Golden Age; a prelapsarian moment in English history, with its myth of harmony and social cohesion to be perpetuated as though that imperial, *rentier* class still lived in the same way. It becomes a desirable universe which can be inhabited by those whose actual knowledge is vestigial but who are defending their own social positions against the prospect of egalitarianism. As the rigid hierarchies of the house on five floors or the country place become less and less the place of actual social experience, they appeal more and more as an imaginative locus, one which is clung to with increasing defensiveness as it appears on the point of total dissolution. Compton-Burnett seemed to these readers as much elegaic as iconoclastic. Although the novels themselves are without nostalgia, they spoke to a mood of loss and to those readers who mourned the 'tragic' disappearance of what they took to be an essentially nobler past.[116]

The 1950s and '60s were in many ways good years for Compton-Burnett, even though she had lost her companion (Margaret Jourdain died in 1951), for she was now free enough and confident enough to enjoy her social and literary position. Her selective amnesia about her past, and her own 'inscrutability', ensured that she could keep its dark secrets to herself. Who, after all, was now likely to gainsay her? Kay Dick, a new young fan whom Ivy reminded of a 'patrician step-aunt', seems to have been completely duped by the accounts Compton-Burnett gave of her childhood which featured the 'descent' from Bishop Burnet but also elevated her father from being a homeopath to a 'neurologist' who had studied under Freud in Vienna. As Kay Dick subsequently realised, Freud would have been 9 years old when James Burnett visited Vienna in 1865. These deceptions were merely, Dick then suggests to her readers, 'grandiose fantasies' intended 'to disconcert her listener', though they obviously did not strike her at the time as either implausible or disconcerting.[117] Interestingly, Dick acknowledges Compton-Burnett's snobbery but excuses it as a natural part of her upbringing in 'that solid pre-First World War social order in which certain groups were "kept in their place" [Compton-Burnett's words]': it was 'fear of the unknown rather than innate snobbery'[118] which produced her reactionary views. Rather, we might argue, knowing what we do of Compton-Burnett's social origins and the traumas of her past, that it was precisely fear of the known, and the need to defend fragile rather than secure class divisions which led her to fabricate all these lies.

In the 'bad times' of social egalitarianism, this imaginary past could serve as an escape from, and indictment of, an alarming present. 'How I loathe the age of affluence', she told her friends, many of whom were becoming increasingly splenetic and unbridled in their Toryism.[119] As the 1950s drew to a close, the South Kensington dowager, like the Bournemouth hotel resident so beloved of Terence Rattigan, began to feel more and more like a hunted species: 'These are hard days and we are a doomed class.'[120] Upset by 'falling standards', many of her intimates with remaining private incomes took themselves abroad, feeling more and more hounded at home, more and more threatened by a future in which England is given over not just to the philistine 'lower orders' but to 'foreigners': 'A nice thing if an English woman is to be turned out by Poles to make room for South Americans.'[121]

In the 1960s fear and anger harden into real phobias. Inwardness becomes agoraphobic. The interior becomes the enclosure; cabined and confined in the end to the ever-diminishing space of an imagined superiority. The unrelieved psychic geography of the novels becomes the only space for an increasingly disengaged personality:

There is nothing one would want to write about in the scene today. Oh, nothing![122]

'Out there' in the London streets are the hated objects – the 'uneducated English masses'[123] who stand to gain at her own expense. She is only 'a stone's throw from three of London's busiest thoroughfares' but in May 1968 is imprisoned 'by her own will' in her flat; by age and by illness too, but also by an imagination that was housebound long before she was.[124] Afraid as ever of the wind, which is increasingly felt to be a harsh wind of change, of a world populated by people like Keith Waterhouse's Jubb, so unpleasant and uncivilised that 'one ceased to regard him as a human being',[125] a world of 'pure squalor'.[126] Retrenchment becomes almost paranoiac. Because her world never existed in its ideal form, and because this new world offers only a precarious tenancy, it has to be fought for tooth and nail against *them*: the masses, the vulgar, the new writers like Waterhouse, but also the Snows, the 'coloured', 'the youth', but also cinema-goers, thriller readers, those who live in suburbs like Hampstead, buy shop flowers or shop cakes, or put the milk in the cup first – the demonisation is as creative as it is exhausting.[127] Given such exclusivity there is only one logical response to the world: 'Oh, *no* . . . no . . . I don't go out.'[128]

It is hard to imagine the kind of internal pressures which could make any writer undertake such a sweeping disavowal of the world outside; Compton-Burnett seems to have made a life's work out of turning her face to the wall. Yet whatever her private opinions, the novelistic imagination was not, unlike that of many of her younger readers, expressive of a grandiloquent kind of Toryism but was of a far less aggressive and confident conservatism. It indulged in neither Brideshead elegy nor religious consolation; it depended rather upon retreat and denial, and a carefully constructed subterfuge. Whilst it may be true that beneath the steely dissection of the private house there was always the dangerous seam of loss which readers could turn into yearning or a felt longing to preserve its forms, and that ultimately it seems as though the security of that tyranny was preferable to an insecure future, nevertheless it is ironic that these accounts of the misery at the heart of the English middle classes could be taken as offering readers a walk-on part in a superior lifestyle, that the scandalous deformation of spirit which the novels re-enact could seem preferable to a more 'squalid' present, that what had struck readers in the 1930s as an heretical exposé of child abuse could ever be read as establishing, rather than demolishing, the myth of the English middle-class home as a privileged form of existence.

Yet to call such an imagination 'conservative' is to say very little unless that definition can also recognise that Compton-Burnett's alienation from 'normal' family life gave her an oblique relation to sexual conventions which, though it dated from the 1920s, remained with her to the end. Compton-Burnett strongly advocated the liberalisation of censorship laws and was outspoken amongst her friends in her support of the Wolfenden report in 1957, and its recommendations for de-criminalising homosexuality.[129] In her seventies and eighties she kept up open and enduring friendships with lesbians – though romantic overtures were apparently all rebuffed – and her closest male companion (especially intimate after Margaret died), was Herman Shrijver, who was both Jewish and homosexual, and whose gossip and many kindnesses sustained her for over forty years.[130] Sexually progressive views were by no means incompatible with a reactionary class politics: we would need to read both as part of that traumatised femininity formed in the wake of the Great War.

I have argued in this chapter that Compton-Burnett's life and work are eloquent testimony to the poverty which can lie at the heart of respectability and which makes the English middle class in its different historical forms a truly deprived class. Compton-Burnett's personal retreat is itself evidence of the damage done in that earlier social life, a world in which, as one of her characters says, 'atonement is not possible' (*Manservant and Maidservant*, p. 229). In claiming Compton-Burnett for English literature or for 'women's writing' we are therefore also claiming the cruelty and brutality of forms of Englishness, whose ideal of monied leisure can be seen as the seat of selfishness, and whose powers of self-control can so easily turn into tyranny. In 1988 Prime Minister Margaret Thatcher told the Conservative Women's Association (in almost Ivyish tones) that the family was indeed 'the building block of society',

> It fashions our beliefs. It is the preparation for the rest of our life. And women run it.[131]

Reading Compton-Burnett reminds us that the most 'superior' forms of English family life, far from being places of 'refuge and rest',[132] are historical nightmares from which some never wake up.

I have argued too that the work is testimony to a conservatism which was fuelled, in the first place, by a modernist rather than a traditionalist impulse between the wars. It manifested itself in a language of reticence and understatement which could provide different and new kinds of protective camouflage, and which made Compton-Burnett's representations of social life modern performances despite their backwards glance. It is this tension which needs more exploration and we might take our cue from the American critic, Mary McCarthy, who inadvertently alerted us to this contradiction in an essay on Compton-Burnett in 1967.[133] Her inventions, she wrote, are a 'reliable make', 'production is steady' and the 'specifications for the current model' much the same as for 'the original patent'. The fictions bear a 'trademark' stressing the '*sameness* of the formula: senior service'. McCarthy sees this simply as an extreme form of English insularity and traditionalism. What might strike now is McCarthy's language of commodification – 'she produces Compton-Burnetts, as someone might produce ball-bearings.' The Englishness which might seem to McCarthy to suggest features of an enduring and unchanging landscape have been clearly manufactured; the past, like the country house in the novels, because it is cut off from social and historical continuities, has become something to play with and enjoy. Her fictions are 'curios' as McCarthy suggests, but we might add that like 'antiques' they are a modern phenomenon. Compton-Burnett's mechanical reproduction of her fictional world over the years argues the modernity of their conservatism, one whose character needs further investigation. Nor is it a coincidence that when McCarthy looks for a literary bedfellow for Compton-Burnett it is to the new commercial fiction between the wars that she turns and to the queen of formula crime:

> A Compton-Burnett is a reliable make, as typical of British Isles workmanship as a tweed or Tiptree or an Agatha Christie.[134]

As a clue to the modern retailing of old-fashioned Englishness there is more to this comparison than we might at first expect. Again it take us indoors, inside those apparently quiet houses and the lives of their respectable residents.

Chapter 2

Agatha Christie and conservative modernity

THE STRANGE DISAPPEARANCE OF AGATHA CHRISTIE

No two writers might seem at first a more unlikely couple than Ivy Compton-Burnett and Agatha Christie; the one a highbrow's delight and the other at the top of the league-table of the world's bestsellers. Yet Compton-Burnett's critics have left us with some suggestive clues about her writing which might encourage us to cross the high-walled barriers with which English literature fences off its different territories. Like Christie, Compton-Burnett has been seen as the producer of 'a wholly original species of puzzle' whose cryptic plots, we are told, appeal to readers' 'detective commonsense';[1] her tortuous narratives have been compared to 'tales of suspense and detection' and even Margaret Jourdain, her close companion, noted the thread of snobbery with violence which runs through the work when she cheerfully relegated her friend's fiction to the realms of 'Mayfair murders'.[2] Given Compton-Burnett's own conviction that the satisfaction of curiosity is 'the only thing that is as good as it promises to be', it is perhaps not surprising to learn that she herself looked favourably upon that other literary Dame: 'think of the pleasure she must give – think of the pleasure' was her own admiring comment.[3] (Some of her devotees have not been so generous: Robert Liddell, Compton-Burnett's chief literary lieutenant, eagerly protested that her superior criminology had nothing to do with 'the crime club attitude'.)[4]

It seems to me, however, that Compton-Burnett and Christie have much deeper historical affinities than a merely accidental likeness. Indeed they might even be literary sisters under the skin. In this chapter I shall argue that they have in common a modernist spirit: each in her own way is an iconoclast whose monitoring of the plots of family life aims to upset the Victorian image of home, sweet home. It not coincidental that both deal in domestic inquisitions and share a compulsive focus on family secrets, reworking the conventional forms of Victorian transgression – the inheritance drama, mistaken identities, hidden madness – in the concentrated form of 'family talk'. Christie, like Compton-Burnett, offers a modern sense of the unstable limits of respectability; like her she portrays a society of strangers whose social exchanges have become theatrical and dissevered from a sense of place. Both share a modernist irony, a strict formalism of technique, and employ a language of reticence which was able to articulate a conservative Englishness but in a modern form.

Like Compton-Burnett's fiction, Christie's writing seems fixed in a mythic time, 'a golden age' apparently outside history, familiarly evoked as 'that unforgettable never-never land of chintz and country houses'.[5] The assumption, so common now as to be almost unassailable, is that Christie's fiction is that of a 'natural' Tory, with Christie herself a kind of jolly and bucolic lady rather like the Miss Marple which Margaret Rutherford gave us in the MGM films of the 1960s.[6] Her settings are assumed to be inherently backward-looking, her social attitudes simply snobbish, and her imaginary milieux an idealised picture of 'the long summers' of the English upper middle class in a tightly class-bound society.[7] It is a view which has become even more entrenched in recent years as Christie has been elevated to something like a national institution, seen as a particularly home-grown variety of writer, 'as English as Buckingham Palace, the House of Commons and the Tower of London'.[8]

An Agatha Christie television bonanza in the 1980s set the final seal upon this image.[9] Whether it was the roaring twenties, the genteel thirties or the village settings of the 1950s, the name of Christie became synonymous with lavish and painstaking reconstructions of 'period'. Watching any of the recent dramatisations featuring 'Miss Marple' on television, one could be forgiven for believing Agatha Christie to be the high priestess of nostalgia rather than the 'Queen of Crime'. Nemesis, for example, gave us a story set sometime in the 1950s and with the minimum of ostentation made the most of the period look: unobtrusive but gleaming vintage cars, tailored suits and permanent waves, the faded floral prints of servants and the Brylcreemed hair of the stray ton-up boy, or of the dour Inspector Slack (the policeman-cum-wide-boy who frequently crosses swords with Miss Marple on TV) – a number of loving touches conjured up for us the tranquil and hidebound English life of the Home Counties. Miss Marple seemed indeed to live in 'Mayhem Parva', a village sealed in aspic, intent on keeping modernity at bay.[10]

What the television series offered its viewers was Agatha Christie as part of the 'English heritage'. As the climax of Nemesis approached, the stirring strains of a chamber orchestra could be heard accompanying the camera up an overgrown drive to a noble edifice, an eighteenth-century mansion, its venerable columns shrouded with moss and fallen into disrepair. In the grand finale the shy and twittering spinster sleuth was shown achieving her object of restoring a misjudged heir, cleared of the suspicion of murdering his fiancée, to his rightful country seat. The prodigal son, reinstated in patrician splendour, had been transported, in one fell swoop,

from sleeping rough on the Thames Embankment to lording it in a miniature Blenheim. Tory dreams are made, it would seem, on such stuff.

Yet even a cursory glance at the original novel suggests how much this
vision was a lively concoction on the part of the television producers and
owed as much to a Toryism of the 1980s as it did to any conservatism
on Christie's part. Written in 1971, *Nemesis* shows little sign of caring
about the English past. 'Rafiel House' – the imaginative centre of the
televisation – is all but entirely absent from the text and, although Miss
Marple does find herself on a coach tour of the stately homes of England
it is merely a subterfuge to provide, as with all Christies, a closed environment in which the suspects can meet and plausibly spend their time in
the talking which makes up the bulk of the book. There is no lingering
over the dilapidated glories of classical architecture as we were treated to
in the television interpretation (which thereby no doubt increased the
export value of the series); no descriptions of buildings or their interiors;
no pregnant pauses in which to contemplate England's grandeur, lost or
otherwise: typically the second murder, which the TV company took as
an opportunity to wander round an eighteenth-century library, takes place
on a blowy cliff-top.

In fact the only 'beautifully proportioned' house in the novel is the
home of the mentally askew, and this crumbling Queen Anne house,
covered with vines and ivies, is far from being the object of authorial
drooling on the bounties of the past. It is a pathological place, an image
of repressed desires and unhealthy loves which comes closer to the Gothi-
cism of Mrs Radcliffe than to the classical imagination of Pope or Austen.
The prodigal son is a shadowy figure in the novel, a 'jailbird' who is a
far from romantic character, having already assaulted several girls; he is
vindicated in the closing pages only to be left doubtfully contemplating
the job market. Miss Marple's reward is not the heir's patronage but a
hefty fee from his millionaire father, and her side-kick in the investigation
is not Inspector Slack (who has been developed almost entirely for the
series as 'evidence' of Christie's class snobbery), but another old-age pen-
sioner.[11] The novel is not simply an encomium in praise of social stability,
but a much darker assertion of the destructive capacity of love:

> Love *is* a very terrible thing. It is alive to evil, it can be one of the
> most evil things . . . .
>
> (Nemesis, p. 186)

If this is conservatism, then it needs a more capacious kind of understanding than the 1980s heritage versions brought to bear on it.[12]

These latest renderings of Agatha Christie's writing have certainly fed
the animus of a literary establishment which in any case has always
given 'the popular' short drift. There is something about Agatha Christie,
however, which seems to mark her out for an especially cold shoulder

and the particularly gratuitous insult. It may be respectable to write about Conan Doyle or even Raymond Chandler but Christie remains beyond the pale, the producer of harmless drivel, an unsuitable case for a critic. It is an extraordinary fact, given the centrality of her work to British cultural life, that no self-respecting British critic has ever written at decent length about her, or felt impelled to look more closely at what that work might speak to.[13] It is an absence which the growth of 'genre' studies of popular fiction has yet to address. With their emphasis on structural and narratival features shared across long periods of time, generic studies of Christie's work naturally tell us little about her relation to her own contemporaries; the emergence of her work from out of a set of shared, historical concerns continues to lie buried.[14] Ironically too, such studies often reinforce the already iron distinction between what counts as 'high' or 'low' culture: crime fiction becomes a tradition in a vacuum, not one form chosen from amongst many.[15]

Critics of all political hues are likely to pass Christie by. Marxists, who have been amongst the most enthusiastic historians of crime fiction, have little patience as a whole with the inter-war period, and have been the least inclined to go beyond the clichés which surround Christie's writing; she merely takes her place alongside Allingham or Sayers as a writer of 'drawing room fiction' offering 'fictional reassurance for the bourgeoisie'.[16] Recent feminist interest in crime writing has also tended to hear the voice of the English middle class as an unchanging monotone.[17] Whilst drawing our attention to the claiming of the genre by a plethora of women writers between the wars, it has been the Miss Marple books which have provided the critical perspective on Christie, despite their being largely the creation of her later and least popular years.[18]

Rather than homogenising half a century of novels into a timeless mulch which serves us as inadequately as a means of national celebration as it does for an object of attack, I propose to take Christie's conservatism as an unknown rather than a given, and to assume that its provenance, like that of the middle classes or ideas of femininity, is historically contingent. Ironically, what is now peddled as 'Olde England' appeared in a form originally seen as cheapskate, felt to be as new and as intrusive as the loudspeaker, wireless or film. Christie's kind of detective story began life as one of many new varieties of a commercial culture whose expendability and temporality (such novels could be read at one sitting) offended those who preferred nineteenth-century forms. It is this Christie, whom I see as a popular modernist, who has gone missing. It is her part in the imaginative recasting of what I call a conservative modernity that I wish to explore. In rediscovering the Christie of the inter-wars years, I shall argue that the fiction speaks to very different kind of conservatism from the kind with which she is usually associated, one which went straight to the heart of new kinds of anxiety about English social life and new ideas of the English. And that it is the Poirot years rather than those of Miss Marple which help us best to understand the relationship between the feminisation of the genre, modern recasting of ideas about the sexes and the politics of the form. It may be precisely because she is not the comfortable high Tory for whom she has so often been mistaken, but a representative of a conservatism much closer to the bone of English life, that she has remained both a literary embarrassment and continuously popular.

MODERNIST MURDER: A LITERATURE OF CONVALESCENCE

Everyone, fans and detractors alike, agrees that Agatha Christie is primarily a constructor of puzzles. Historians of the genre usually cite *The Murder of Roger Ackroyd*, published in 1926, as the first novel in which Christie proved her skill at that literary sleight of hand for which she was to become famous for over half a century.[19] *Ackroyd* is a perfect example of the crime puzzle: the detective story as a kind of conundrum whose pleasure derives from trying to guess the murderer, and which sacrifices characterisation and plausibility to the exigencies of suspenseful plotting. Detective fiction of this kind became enormously successful between the wars and had a wide and heterodox appeal; writers were drawn from across the political spectrum, including the socialists G. D. H. and Margaret Cole, Christopher Caudwell, Cecil Day-Lewis, children of the liberal intelligentsia like Romilly and Dorelia John, and those of quite different political persuasion like G. K. Chesterton and Dorothy L. Sayers. By 1939 one-quarter of all fiction published was detective fiction and it was established as the majority reading of the 'coffee break and commuter classes'.[20]

The appearance of the 'whodunit' as a recognisable and distinctive kind of detective story, differentiated from those thrillers and mysteries with which stories about crime had formerly overlapped, was a modern event in literary and cultural history well worth considering.[21] Many of the most popular writers of the inter-war period had, of course, made their names before the war and continued to offer the usual fare to their readers – the clubland heroes of Dornford Yates, 'Edwardian in their security, their serenity and their courtesies',[22] the melodramatic thrillers of William Le Queux or Phillips Oppenheim were still selling well, and the continued popularity of John Buchan and 'Sapper' suggests how misleading it would be to imagine sudden or clearcut breaks with past literary forms and ethics. Even Conan Doyle published Sherlock Holmes stories until 1927. Yet whilst it is clearly the case that not everyone opted for 'hard hearts and shrewd little heads',[23] the emotional and intellectual universe of the whodunit seems to have been something recognisably new, a post-war phenomenon which developed out of a desire to modernise the crime fiction of the past.

Even those afficionados who praise the ingenuity and the skilful plotting of the puzzlers have had little to say about the social and psychological significance of the form except as evidence of English insularity. The emotional detachment and blithe self-preoccupation of the whodunit is read as a reflection of the exceptional arrogance of the middle classes between the wars, their lack of interest in political events (the strike of 1926 is the most usual antithesis to the doings of Poirot or Lord Peter Wimsey), or of the complacency of the nation as a whole: 'Britain between the wars was such a safe country in which to live.'[24] What might strike us most, however, about those who decry the 'superficiality' of such fiction, its 'puppets and cardboard lovers and papier mâché villains',[25] and its hollowness as far as moral or social truth is concerned, is that they are reacting as much to the modernist aspects of the form as to its conservatism.

Once we consider the whodunit as a form of popular modernism, these apparent failings, the emptying of moral and social effect, the evacuating of notions of 'character', the transparency of the prose ('a surface so wooden and dead')[26] appear in a different light. What has come to seem to us the epitome of the old-fashioned and the genteel, arguably began life as a modernising, de-sacramentalising form, emancipating itself from the literary lumber of the past. In popular fiction as much as in high culture, older models were to be broken up, self-consciously redeployed, parodied, pastiched, pilloried. We might expect the literature of crime in particular, which had formerly been the place of violence and of male heroics, to be particularly traumatised by the war. Christie begins writing at the very point when 'light reading' was looking for new forms in which to couch majority sentiments and detective writers sought to make crime entertaining 'after the trauma'.[27]

The signs of Christie's own modernity are clearest in her uneasy dabbling in available popular forms throughout the 1920s, and the ironised use of earlier literary conventions. Few but devoted fans, or literary historians, can read the entire mixed bag of thrillers, short stories and whodunits which Christie produced in the 1920s with unadulterated pleasure (I defy anyone now to enjoy The Big Four), but the awkward playfulness of the fiction is symptomatic of a search for different and more appropriate forms. Certainly the debts are there, and a dialogue with the Victorian and Edwardian forms of popular literature continues in her work well into the 1930s. In the detective stories it is naturally the Sherlock Holmes stories which stand in for an Edwardian past.[28]

Christie's first novel, The Mysterious Affair at Styles (1920), is in many ways a stilted book, casually relying upon earlier narratorial shorthands. There is, as Christie later admitted, almost an embarrassment of riches.[29]

All the paraphernalia of an already well-worked genre are somewhat dutifully displayed – a map of the house, missing poison, disguises; the subplot
of foreign espionage is singularly unoriginal, and belongs to a Phillips
Oppenheim or to John Buchan. Captain Hastings, our narrator, speaks in
the pre-war language of romance; he enthuses about the smallness and
whiteness of a lady's hands in a way which would befit a Baroness Orczy
hero, and the love interest between the characters is Edwardian novelettish.
In a plot overloaded with material clues – fingerprints, threads of cloth,
a torn scrap of writing – Hercule Poirot's first display of his technique is
reminiscent of Holmes but it already feels a touch fustian, like the old-
fashioned plodding of more painstaking and dogged contemporaries,
Inspector French (of Freeman Wills Crofts's novels), and Doctor
Thorndyke (of Austin Freeman's), both of whom began life before the
Great War.

Yet even here Christie sounds a modern note, and it is an ironic,
debunking one. The relationship between Hastings and Poirot, though
copying that of Watson and Holmes, suggests a mocking relationship to
the past. When Sherlock Holmes chaffed his assistant with the words –
'You are a British jury, Watson!', there was respect as well as gentle teasing
in his cry; the sentiments Watson espoused might be rather orthodox and
unimaginative but they were probably the reader's own. Hastings, on the
other hand, is more of a stooge than a helpmeet, and as a representative
of the pre-war world he seems a casualty of history as well as of the
Front, born, as it were, middle-aged. His moral rectitude is a kind of
prelapsarian innocence, his attitudes 'dated', closer to buffoonery than
pathos.[30]

Whilst there is little in the criminology of *Styles* to disturb a Conan
Doyle (the murderers are adulterers and punished for transgressing conventional sexual morality), Christie's conservatism is less noticeable than the
lack of emotional charge attached to any of the moral and social values
which underpin the plot. Whilst 'Styles' is a country house, it is not a
hallowed place disturbed by the horror of crime. Christie's image of family
falls far short of any sanctification, but it also fails to shock the reader.
Instead we are asked to take for granted that members of a family will
be at each other's throats, squabbling and often petty, and that the mistress
who is murdered is neither likeable nor admirable but a foolish, domineering snob. This is a world of interlopers where the family mingles with a
VAD, a landgirl and homeless refugees (like Poirot); it is the era of the
'temporary gentleman' in which no one can be sure of each other and
'well balanced English beef and brawn' (p. 109) is likely to mask the
culprit. Old retainers are the most suspect; husbands and wives naturally
do not respect the marriage bond. For the reader of Conan Doyle these
transgressions, though thrilling, would ultimately be deemed contemptible.
In Christie's world nothing is sacred. Crime makes not for tragedy, nor

even for the shudders of melodrama, but oddly and startlingly, for a laugh.[31]

The Holmesian world surfaces in Christie's early fiction as a kind of repeat performance, in a series of literary comebacks, openly theatrical in guise and comic in effect. Christie's first collection of short stories, *Poirot Investigates* (1925) borrows freely from Conan Doyle (Poirot has adventures and writes a casebook), whilst at the same time attempting to send up the past. The first story mocks the idea of the Great Detective (a motif taken to unfortunate extremes in the mishmash of stories she later strung together to make *The Big Four*).[32] The Edwardian plots appear mechanical, like so many empty gestures – jewel thefts, inheritance dramas and county families jostling alongside film stars and flashy Americans drinking martinis in a kaleidoscopic collage. The short-story form itself has become ill-fitting, no longer at one with the positivistic faith in solutions which gave Holmes a moral as well as narratival force; it seems instead hackneyed and truncated. Many of the twists of the plots serve deliberately to expose the expectations of Edwardian readers and to reverse them: the wily Chinaman, who might so easily have been villainous, turns out to be an American actor; even the toffs are simply playing parts. The keynote in all these stories is that of the fake: not the fake as morally reprehensible but as a source of enjoyment in modern life. This is the world of farce, not melodrama.[33]

Linguistically readers plunge into a similar *mêlée*; older forms of expression and new forms of the vernacular make up a cocktail mix of Edwardian ponderousness and up-to-the-minute slang (one cannot imagine Watson getting 'fed up' as Hasting does). Christie seems to have decided early on to follow the advice she was given by her friend, the Devon novelist Eden Philpotts, to whom she sent an early effort, and 'stick to gay, natural dialogue'.[34] The remorseless jollity of her 'lighthearted thrillers', *The Secret Adversary* (1922), *The Man in the Brown Suit* (1924), *The Secret of Chimneys* (1925), *The Big Four* (1927) and *The Seven Dials Mystery* (1929), might now irritate us with their knowing but girlish heroines ('Tuppence', but also 'Bundle' and 'Frankie') and their facetious mixture of deflating humour and weary sophistication; they remind us of the breathless juvenility of a Freddy Lonsdale or a *Salad Days*. It is an archness one hears again and again in the period – in Wooster, in Wimsey, but also in Waugh and Huxley, and in the essays of Virginia Woolf – a refusal of seriousness, of the cumbrous and weighty, as well as of the moral sententiousness of the older generation. Christie's dialogue is minimalist; the conversation between her young people aims, like Coward's, at a 'delightful silliness';[35] like his, her conversation pieces perfect the art of the throw-away remark, the topical and perishable. Volubility stresses the ephemeral as though meaningfulness itself had been thrown into the melting-pot.[36]

If we associate Sherlock Holmes with the fog and reek of a London alley, the sun has definitely got his hat on for Tommy and Tuppence Beresford, Christie's 'Partners in Crime', whom the cover of the Crime Club edition described as 'Blunt's Delicious Detectives'. Theirs is a world in which policemen can be 'jaunty' and 'dapper', and its glib repartee has much more in common with the effervescent young things of the West End theatre than with the bone-chillers of the Victorian stage. Christie's thrillers certainly creak under the heavy load of older typologies of villainy, but they are at least as interested in the 'essentially modern-looking couple' (*The Secret Adversary*, p. 8) who play the detectives. Both are war survivors ('Tuppence' has been a VAD like Christie), without a 'bean', and sit having tea in Lyons, eager not to return to the world of their Victorian childhood. Indeed the dedication of *The Secret Adversary*, offering the 'delights and dangers of adventure' to those with monotonous lives, suggests that modern restlessness and fear of boredom, which as the new slang implied was the worst horror (it could be 'crashing', 'devastating'), fuelled the desire to write.

The very idea of 'light' reading to 'kill time' might be seen as a modernist alternative to the virtuous qualities of nineteenth-century realism, its notions of durability and fixity; what was popular was like art deco, deliberately jokey, temporary, as evanescent as the 'bubbly' with which the wealthy youngsters replaced their elders' 'vintage' port. Pleasures were to be improvised like the drinks, and brazenly daytime like matinées. Noel Coward's manifesto, voiced by Elyot in *Private Lives*, 'Let's be superficial', was a rallying cry for all who wanted to sound a contemporary note, and detective fiction was no exception. A horror of being 'stuffy', that word which conjures up both the horse-hair sofas and the moral airlessness of that late Victorian world, was to be countered by an 'airy' manner. Breeziness characterises Christie's early work as much as it does Compton-Burnett's. But unlike Compton-Burnett, the 30-year-old Agatha Christie seems to align herself with 'the young idea'. Youthfulness was for many the measure of modernity, a carelessness and vitality of being which could be cultivated, with varying degrees of pose, by the older generation too. If nothing else, what marks Christie's work, for all time, as of the post-war generation is its brightness of tone and the premium placed on youth, that elixir with healing powers which had been so wantonly wasted. Christie's fiction seems to set its face firmly to the future, to address all those who identified with a younger generation stifled first by their elders and then silenced by the tragedies of the war.[37]

It is as a literature of convalescence that we might understand something of the sea-change which came over detective fiction after the war. For what is most noticeable about the appearance of the whodunit, and most paradoxical, is the removal of the threat of violence. The crime story was the one place where the reader might reasonably expect violence, but what had formerly been enjoyed as one of the most aggressive of literatures, became distinctly pacific in its retreat from old-fashioned notions of the heroic. The universe of these novels, secular, largely amoral and anti-sentimental, marked a shift in the self-perception of the respectable reading public away from the notions of mastery and destiny which had so gover-ned the idea of English character and with such disastrous consequences. Naturally the dominance of women writers in the inter-war years and their reworking of what had formerly been a largely masculine genre must give us pause, but both male and female writers in the period found a kind of modernity in making fun of heroes.

Where early crime fiction had drawn on the linguistic and emotional universe of a Maria Marten or a Sweeney Todd, this new fiction marked a break with that literary inheritance and worked to remove the sensations from sensation literature. Gone are the lingering Gothicisms even of Conan Doyle – 'Mr Holmes, they were the footsteps of a gigantic Hound!' – a world which for all of Holmes's rational deductions and scientific positiv-ism still thrilled at the 'horrid' and drew upon the lurid accounts of crime, the scandal-mongering broadsheets, the 'shilling shockers' and 'penny dreadfuls' which had catered to an audience for whom public executions had been an enjoyable spectacle. Despite his own disavowals, Conan Doyle's writing smacks of the Victorian pornography of death, the linger-ing over the ghastly physicality of dead bodies, the gruesome detail like the message scrawled in blood in the aptly named 'Study in Scarlet'.[38] Though popular entertainment was 'slow to shed its emotional colour-ing',[39] it seems that this graphic depiction of mortality was to lose some of its savour for many after 1914. Like the soldiers in Wilfred Owen's 'Insensibility', the luckiest had seen 'too much red' and were rid of its hurt for ever; the rest longed for an anaesthetic.

By contrast, the whodunit between the wars came rapidly to be as insensible to violence as it could be. As a literature of convalescence it developed a strongly meditative framework, relying upon a kind of inturned and internal ratiocination rather than on what would stir or shake the reader. As many critics have noted (usually dismissively) it is the lack of emotional engagement in the detective fiction between the wars which matters. Writers like Lynn Brock or John Dickson Carr stuffed their books with red herrings, far-fetched motives and teasing clues, or set their mysteries in locked rooms, their plot contrivances reaching new peaks of artificiality. Whereas in Conan Doyle the detective is the only one without feeling, whodunit readers were encouraged into dispassion, as though the audience consisted of neurasthenics. The plot and the characters may be one-dimensional but they are lacking roundness in the way that a cubist painting is. Fleshiness, either figuratively or literally, was perhaps in gross bad taste after the butchery many had witnessed. Violence is literally bad form.

The revulsion against violence went together with a loss of appetite for melodrama which made detective fiction one of the primary sites for the exploration of newly secular mores. The non-heroic and the de-consecrated tend to go hand in hand. It is hard to imagine, for example, a murder in a vicarage in 1850, or even 1880, as an object of entertainment for the respectable reading public. Crime in Christie's novels comes less and less to be a matter of outrage; the fiction lacks a sense of awe or of the violation of the sacral. As the critic Edmund Wilson complained, we don't particularly care what happens to either victims or murderers.[40] Thus Malcolm Warren in C. H. B. Kitchin's *Death of My Aunt* (1929) can decide that he's not sure murder is a sin, Gladys Mitchell's detective in *Speedy Death* (1929) does the job herself, in Anthony Berkeley's *Dead Mrs Stratton* (1933) the murderer gets away with it, whilst Romilly and Katherine John's *Death By Request* (1933) actually makes the murderer a provincial (megalomaniac) vicar. The moral universe of the novels has been largely dislocated from its aesthetic one, and moral feeling carries little charge when compared with the pleasures of the form.

These are not cathartic novels, stimulating and releasing deep feeling. Rather their effect is preoccupying, the mental equivalent of pottering, which works more to relieve generalised anxiety than to generate strong emotion. One enthusiast saw detective stories as a 'sedative for the nerves',[41] a literary 'Happy Hour' for those for whom boredom and having to think was one of the worst fears – what Margaret Cole, herself a devotee of crime, saw as the fate of the 'preaematuri':[42] those who had already lived too much, and who suffered from 'that mental St Vitus'[43] which was the legacy of the nerve-wracked. Whodunits could be just the answer to that lack of capacity for concentrated thinking which plagued the returned soldier, a balm to stave off the apathy which so many seemed to dread. The nerves of those who had undergone the privations of war at home – rationing, black-out, cold, the influenza epidemic, bereavement, and the long, long hours of waiting to hear the worst – were equally jarred. Pitting their wits in a struggle that was cerebral without involving strain, this was the generation who made the crossword the national pastime of the middle classes.[44] As restorative as the new nerve tonics on the market or the 'healthy' beverages like Ovaltine and Horlicks which became so popular, whodunits were perhaps the literature of emotional invalids, shock-absorbing and rehabilitating, like playing endless rounds of clock patience.[45]

It took at least ten years for most people to bear to read about the war, and even though some writing, like Wilfred Owen's poems printed by Sassoon in 1921, had appeared immediately afterwards, such horrors took the general public a long time to face. The year 1928 saw the appearance of many of the most well known and widely read of the war memoirs: Blunden's *Undertones of War*, Robert Graves's *Goodbye to All That*,

Remarque's *All Quiet on the Western Front*, Sassoon's own *Memoirs of a Fox Hunting Man*, and not until 1933 Vera Brittain's *Testament of Youth*. R. C. Sheriff's play *Journey's End*, a grim and ironic commentary on public school heroism, was a West End sell-out in 1928 with an extraordinary run of 594 performances at the Savoy.[46] During that time-lag, one can speculate that detective fiction provided one form of recuperation and fulfilled something of the need to abandon the heroic mode.

Paul Fussell maintains that there were two kinds of unique literary product from the war, the memoirs themselves and literary attacks, often satirical and ironic, by a new generation of young men like Waugh and Isherwood, upon their elders and betters.[47] We might wish to add the crime puzzle as a third place where many of these post-war attitudes and tones were aired for the first time and became stylised. Many writers like Berkeley, Kitchin, Lewis and Cole had themselves seen action, or waited in frozen trenches for it. The detective puzzle relied upon the anti-sentimental, and established the effect of confirming an attitude of detachment and dispassion in the reader which a writer such as Somerset Maugham was to turn to bitter account in his *Ashenden* (also published in 1928), giving us the first modern, because de-romanticised, secret agent. The same protective irony which might be used as a necessary distance from pain, could also be turned into hilarity, the kind of debunking spirit which informs that other war memoir of sorts, written by another two ex-servicemen: *1066 And All That* by Sellar and Yeatman. Their irreverent account of British history was deliberately anti-heroic, and anti-chauvinist, mocking the British sense of themselves as 'top nation' and viewing the past as a public school exam gone mad. As the last page declares, history, in the sense of 'deeds' and glory, meaningful and dramatic acts, had stopped. There was only 'nowadays'.[48] It is a message which carries over from much crime fiction too.

'No one talked heroics now', complain the returned soldiers in one of Vera Brittain's poems[49] and the fiction of formal violence was one place where heroics seemed out of place. Sherlock Holmes, despite his drugs and violin playing, bore a direct relationship to that brotherhood of boy's own adventurers whose public school ethics and optimism of will took them all the way to the Somme. Whatever the traces of *fin de siècle* decadence, readers had been able to assume that Holmes could be a man of action when he chose, an English patriot with a firm knowledge of the Queensbury rules.[50] The post-war world, however, had made the notion of the conquering detective unpalatable to some, and it needed to give way to a more modest, sometimes agonised sense of English manliness. Most writers solved the problem of embarrassment at aggressive virility by the age-old recourse of reinstating the clever foppishness of the aristocrat. Dorothy L. Sayers's Wimsey is a descendant of the Scarlet Pimpernel, but it is specifically his war experiences and his neurasthenia which make for some of his nervy asininity.[51] Many of the sleuths of the 1920s and '30s were self-deprecating amateurs, like Allingham's Albert Campion or Berkeley's Roger Sherringham, men who resort to physical violence only *in extremis*, and whose personal characteristics are likely to include fastidiousness, a narcissistic delicacy, inane giggling and even laziness. Where Holmes was given to cryptic and sybilline utterances, the new detectives of the 1920s were likely to be garrulous and full of badinage and banalities. Despite his passion for the freakish, the scientific Holmes would never have listed criminology, as Lord Peter Wimsey does, under 'recreations'.[52]

In his own small way Agatha Christie's Poirot was part of that quest for a bearable masculinity which could make what had previously seemed even effeminate preferable to the bulldog virtues of 1914. Christie, like Sayers, recognised the impossibility of creating a confident, British middle-class hero in the old mould. Poirot embodied a compromise between the present and the past, one which offered readers some of the hopefulness of modernity without its anxieties. For although Poirot is a relic from the late nineteenth century in appearance and manners he is also a committed modernist. He evinces a penchant for pure form, and for the minimalist rejection of the florid and ornate. Living in a block of newly built service flats (decidedly not 'mansion' flats), 'ultra-modern, very abstract, all squares and cubes' (*Hallowe'en Party*, p. 144), with chrome furniture and geometric designs, even a square toaster, Poirot revels in being the *dernier cri*, fashionable in a way which Sherlock Holmes would have found despicable. He is as likely to solve crime in seedy nightclubs and mews apartments as in rural settings, and his social milieu is far more mixed (imagine Holmes embarking on the 'Adventure of the Cheap Flat'). A cosmopolitan as well as metropolitan, Poirot is clearly a creature of the Jazz Age as much as he is a left-over from the Edwardian riviera. Fittingly it was in the *Sketch*, that gossip paper of the younger generation, where the Poirot stories first took off; the same paper also featured Mrs Christie in 1925 at her new house in the suburbs (appropriately named 'Styles') and received its modish imprimatur with photographs of Mr Noel Coward breakfasting in bed in his dressing-gown.

Readers need not feel their own manliness impugned by Poirot since, as a foreigner, he is forgiveably cissy. He is too old and too unfit to be heroic (his tight patent shoes prevent him from walking too far, let alone taking a lunge at an assailant).[53] From the start his function is parodic: where Holmes is clean-shaven, hatchet-faced and lean, Poirot displays his carefully groomed moustaches and is an egg-shaped five feet four. Hastings tells us on his first encounter with Poirot that 'a speck of dust would have caused him more pain that a bullet wound',[54] a neat travesty of conventional British masculinity. Naturally his figure puts disguise out of the question. Above all, Poirot is theatrical, more of a Falstaff than a soldier hero, who enjoys playing to the gallery and being mistaken for a mountebank. He plays the part of the detective as blithely as he does that of the foolish outsider. We admire his panache but we also find him farcical. As the mockery of his name suggests, a pear-shaped Hercules is nobody's idea of a classical hero or a contemporary tough guy.

Poirot could afford his readers some necessary relief from those lantern-jawed fellows who bludgeon their way out of innumerable tight spots in the more backward-looking fiction of the period. His refugee status is usefully ambivalent. On the one hand he can be the object of English charity and condescension – 'we' were the saviours of 'gallant little Belgium'; on the other, being Belgian is an oddly unspecific kind of foreignness, and as Colin Watson points out, the British, surprisingly, have no terms of abuse for Belgians.[55] Poirot was thus the best of both worlds, a dispossessed modern, belonging nowhere in particular, and a comic upholder of the values of the past. Like so much else in Christie's fiction he could offer her readers the pleasures of modernity without its pains.

From the beginning the whodunit was a self-conscious form given to self-parody. By the end of the decade, it had already become so well-worked that Monsignor Ronald Knox was able to draw up a list of its mock rules in 1928, a decalogue to be jealously observed by the Detection Club founded two years later. Authors were already proclaiming themselves bored and exasperated by the search for novelty, and convalescence was growing irksome.[56] Christie, however, stayed with the form and was consistent in her rejection of the heroic. All of the detectives with whom she experiments in her early years are anti-romantic in essence: the unsentimental Beresfords, or youthful amateurs like Bobby and 'Frankie' (*Why Didn't They Ask Evans*, 1934), the dried-up solicitor, Mr Satherwaite, Parker Pyne (*Parker Pyne Investigates*, 1934), as well as Miss Marple (penned as early as 1928 and appearing first in *The Thirteen Problems* in 1932).[57] One cannot, even now, imagine a convincing cult of their personalities of the sort that has led to innumerable Sherlockiana and the deerstalker profile at the Baker Street Tube.[58] In her retreat from pre-war mores Christie's fiction increasingly emphasised the idea of private lives, and spoke to the new home-centred pleasures of her expanding readership, of which the whodunit was one.[59]

It might seem more than churlish, then, to complain, as many have done, of the 'gutting' of characters, their insulation from life and the bloodlessness of crime between the wars, when that anaemia can be seen as a revolt against the sanguinary rhetoric of 1914, and as part of the haemorrhaging of national languages of romantic self-esteem. The idea that murder 'has to do with human emotion and deserves serious treatment'[60] was hardly the angle on slaughter which post-war readers would find revelatory. Nor were they likely to confuse literary fantasy with the real thing. It is in this light that we might assess those who preferred acrostics to aggression.

It is the disavowal of a romantic masculinity and its heroic performance in the public world of action which seems even now to annoy critics. We can surely detect a faint misogyny in reaction against 'the feminisation' of the genre and its 'spreading hips of cosiness'; wounded male pride in the mockery of the fiction which takes it as 'emotionally emasculated'.[61] This was the tone first set by Raymond Chandler in 1944 (himself a Dulwich schoolboy turned San Francisco tough guy), for whom the rejection of Englishness between the wars seems to have been a manly necessity. His attack on the inter-war whodunit clearly equated the domestic emphasis of the fiction with the suburban, and the suburban with the feminine. It resembled, he wrote, 'a cup of lukewarm consommé at a spinsterish tea-room', where what was really needed was 'a sharp, aggressive attitude to life'. Such virility was only to be found in the adventures of the modern American hero, leaving England no doubt to 'the flustered old ladies – of both sexes (or no sex) and almost all ages.'[62]

For Chandler the only 'reality' discoverable in writers like Christie was 'the conversational accent of Surbiton and Bognor Regis', but in his eagerness to condemn its conservatism he failed to see how much of a modern speaking voice this could be, one which in giving pride of place to domestic culture could be differently emancipating and provide new images of Englishness. Certainly in the early 1930s the 'surburban idiom'[63] of the whodunit was found offensively modern in its taking liberties with the pieties and forms of the past. If Agatha Christie is to be understood not as the *doyenne* of country house fiction but as queen of the 'middlebrows', then we need to remind ourselves just how modern a conservative creature the middlebrow was.

MURDER IN THE LOUNGE

Nothing could be less like a 'Study in Scarlet' than *The Murder of Roger Ackroyd* in which the nefarious doings of a Home Counties village are etched almost entirely in shades of grey. The deadpan style of the narration matches the muted and unobtrusive presence of the doctor who relates the tale – a fact which gives the story its special twist. But what is more remarkable than her prestidigitation is the obvious pleasure which Christie takes in 'the local geography' (p. 11) of her imaginary village. Dr Sheppard, our narrator, may be mildly satiric in his observation of human nature (as in the 'Mah Jong' chapter where he laconically comments on the gossipy hypocrisy of village life) but Christie resists all temptation to score off her characters or to be clever at the expense of her readers; she preserves a neutrality which is always easy-going in portraying middle-class manners. In fact she seems to relish the unpretentious: 'I'm a perfectly normal matter of fact individual' declares Nurse Leatheran, the narrator of *Murder in Mesopotamia* (p. 143), and Christie leaves it at that.

What is striking about Christie's fiction between the wars is not its snobbishness but its comparative freedom from much of the rancour and discontent about an expanding middle class which motivates her fellow writers. By contrast her writing seems to be entirely at peace with the idea of addressing a more heterogeneous kind of readership, and even when it takes place in gentrified surroundings the reader in the suburbs could feel equally at home. There might be a body in the drawing-room but there is nothing to offend or intimidate the reader in the lounge. It was much more usual to sneer at the ordinary or suburban, or to elevate it in some way, create special individuals and dress up one's authorial voice. Always a tendency in English fiction, self-aggrandisement seems to have become an almost universal habit between the wars.[64] Christie, however, found a voice in which to cultivate the ordinary and the informal and to mount an unsnobbish defence of its pleasures. Rather than writing 'butler-baronet' fiction, she captured the accents of a rapidly developing social life which was happy to be inward-looking and domestically-minded. Though it might take a conservative form, it was nevertheless a modern Englishness which sought to shrug off some of the snobberies of the past.

Read alongside Dorothy L. Sayers or Edgar Wallace, Christie's novels appear remarkably open-minded about that whole variety of lives which began to fall under the provenance of an expanding middle class. Whilst her cast lists do include the proverbial retired colonels and vicar's ladies, they also feature secretaries, commercial salesmen, shopkeepers, receptionists, shop-girls, nurses, solicitors, housewives, doctors and dentists, like Norman Gale, the romantic hero of *Death in the Clouds*. Her presentation of the commonplace is unalloyed by any authorial cleverness; rather she is able to enter sympathetically into lives presumably beyond her ken, like that of the hairdresser's assistant irritated by her client's snobbery, and able, due to a sweepstake win, to go to the South of France herself:

> so many of her ladies had been going to Le Pinet or just come back from Le Pinet. Jane, her clever fingers patting and manipulating the waves, her tongue uttering mechanically the usual clichés, 'Let me see, how long is it since you had your perm, Madam?.' 'Your hair's such an uncommon colour, Madam.' 'What a wonderful summer it has been, hasn't it, Madam?' had thought to herself, 'Why the devil can't *I* go to Le Pinet?' Well, now she could.
>
> (*Death in the Clouds*, p. 14)

Christie's sympathy is always with what she sees to be the ordinary; her prose tries hard not to antagonise the reader and makes few assumptions about their class position:

Life, thought Victoria, life at last! Sitting in her seat at Airways Terminal there had come the magic moment when the words, 'Passengers for Cairo, Baghdad and Tehran, take your places in the bus, please' had been uttered.

Magic names, magic words . . . to Victoria they were a marvellous change from the oft-repeated phrases, 'Take down, please, Miss Jones.' 'This letter's full of mistakes, you'll have to type it again, Miss Jones.' 'The kettle's boiling, ducks, just make the tea, will you?'

(*They Came to Baghdad*, p. 46)

Few authors are capable of writing 'down' rather than 'up' without patronising or ingratiating themselves with their readership. Christie shared that unfrightened sense of respect for her audience which prompted Noel Coward's advice to his juniors: 'Consider the public. Treat it with tact and courtesy. Never fear or despise it.'[65]

Poirot, for instance, differs hugely from other sleuths of the day in being a comparatively unsnobbish creation. Most commonly, detectives were 'professional amateurs' or private individuals, usually men about town, full of undergraduate cleverness, perhaps collectors of fine china or connoisseurs of wines. Their eccentricity was most often used in the service of a class ideal, as members of the gilded aristocracy. Though Lord Peter Wimsey or Roger Sherringham may disparage their own ability as men of action, they are not above a spot of fisticuffs. They can still be figures of romance whose apparent fatuity or self-deprecation is the privilege of wealth or birth. Wimsey – 'all nerve and nose'[66] – is the sort of person who gets tired 'of breakfasting every morning before his view over the Green Park' (*Clouds of Witness*, p. 9) and his confident assumption of effortless social superiority is meant to send a thrill of envy and reverence through the reader. Very few writers seem to have been immune to the glamour of Mayfair flats and manservants or gentlemen's clubs, which litter the pages of detective fiction from writers as politically different as Edgar Wallace and G. D. H. and Margaret Cole. Even the Coles felt obliged to give their detective – 'the Hon. Everard Blatchington' – patrician status.[67]

The untitled detective was most commonly a public school and an Oxford man, like Nigel (a class name if ever there was one) Strangeways, the creation of Cecil Day-Lewis ('Nicholas Blake'), who has been endearingly sent down for answering exam papers in limericks. His manner, though less bumptious than the persiflage of a Peter Wimsey, nevertheless serves, with its scattering of literary quotation, as a constant reminder of his 'first class education'. Anthony Berkeley, himself a graduate of London University, was typical in upgrading his detective's *alma mater*, making him an Oxford blue.[68] The adoration which was afforded to all things Oxford between the wars suggests that Christie's two major detectives, neither of whom was varsity, may have come as a welcome relief. With a complete absence of undergraduate humour and mannerism, Christie never risked condescending to or intimidating the reader; not herself a graduate, she seems to have been respectful of learning but uninterested in the airs and graces which attach to academe; she is not drawn as so many others are to base any of her whodunits in the scholastic world.[69]

As a foreigner, Poirot cannot be a gentleman. He is, however, a bourgeois and proud of it. Not only does he eschew physical action and become more and more of a purely armchair detective, relying on his 'leetle grey cells', he is one of the few elderly male detectives in fiction, a retired professional man, who has seen, like many of his readers, enough action to last a lifetime.[70] Like so many of the anti-heroes of the period, Poirot is 'a little man'. Under stress he builds houses of cards or when the going gets really rough orders a special *tisane*. The address of his Whitehaven (or sometimes Whitefriars) flat is precisely not a matter of *cachet*; he is not an Old Boy and he has no club. His tastes are not expensive but homely: he likes eating and is not averse to rustling up an omelette or two. He is a happy tourist, feeling as much at home in a guest house on the English riviera as on the Orient Express: neither Sherlock Holmes nor Peter Wimsey would share that enthusiasm. In her creation of Poirot, Christie stimulates neither class envy nor deference. Poirot is forward-looking and democratic in his appeal: it is ultimately civilian, domestic pleasures which he celebrates.

Both Sayers and Christie might have readers who lived on new housing estates but it is Sayers who asks them to identify with sentiments like those of Lord Peter Wimsey when he presses an invitation to his family seat:

> Harriet, will you come with me one day to Denver and see the place before the new civilisation grows in on it like the jungle?
>
> (*Gaudy Night*, p. 298)

Christie is neither horrified by the new when it falls within the realm of the respectable nor concerned with proving her disdain for the 'vulgar'. She envinces little sense of dismay at the trespassing on class preserves or territories, those 'invasion fears' which disfigure so much literature of the inter-war years with excesses of vitriol or paranoia, as in Betjeman's famous attack on Slough, or Orwell's *Coming Up For Air*. For many of her peers the contemporary is a threat and social mobility undermining; *The ABC Murders* (1936), however, which deals impartially with three households, lower-, middle- and upper-class, has none of that hysteria about middle-class expansion. This remains the case even when Christie describes the spread of building in her own part of the country, Devon:

> Churston, lying as it does between Brixham on the one side and

Paignton and Torquay on the other, occupies a position about half-way round the curve of Torbay. Until about ten years ago it was merely a golf links and below the links a green sweep of countryside dropping down to the sea with only a farmhouse or two in the way of human occupation. But of late years there have been big building developments between Churston and Paignton and the coastline is now dotted with small houses and bungalows, new roads, etc.

(*The ABC Murders*, p. 82)[71]

Apart from this carefully distanced report (imagine what other verbs besides 'dotted' a Betjeman or an Orwell would have chosen), we hear only that Combeside, belonging to Sir Carmichael Clarke, is a modern house, not large, 'a white rectangle, that was not unpleasing to the eye'. In *The Body in the Library* even that ultimate object of inter-war derision – the bungalow – is seen through the eyes of a police inspector as a charming and decent home, as indeed for many of her readers it would be: 'Neat little villa. . . . The sort of place that had been built fairly freely all over the countryside in the last twenty years' (p. 113). No diatribes here against speculative building but a much more compassionate sense of the newly respectable.

Christie's interest in the domestic life of the middle classes is ecumenical. Her 'big houses' can easily include a gabled Tudorbethan house in a stockbroker belt or new suburb (*The Crooked House, Pocket Full of Rye*) and very little narrative energy or pleasure is drawn from anger at social pretension. She is not spiteful in the manner of a Francis Iles (Anthony Berkeley) satirising the suburban middle classes in *Malice Aforethought*, nor does she waste many words on that most hounded of inter-war beings – the upstart.[72] Up at the big house is likely to be a parvenu, like Roger Ackroyd, clearly one of the *nouveaux riches*, but who is treated amiably; where others may have subjected him to a withering snub, he is merely a comic figure, like

> one of the red-faced sportsmen who always appeared early in the first act of an old-fashioned musical comedy, the setting being the village green . . . . Of course, Ackroyd is not really a country squire. He is an immensely successful manufacturer of (I think) wagon wheels. He is a man of nearly fifty years of age, rubicund of face and genial of manner. . . . He is, in fact, the life and soul of our peaceful village of King's Abbot.
>
> (*The Murder of Roger Ackroyd*, p. 12)

Whilst later characters are unlikely to have made their fortunes from horsedrawn vehicles, nevertheless nearly all of them are self-made men – businessmen, financiers or retired servicemen – all *arrivistes*.[73]

Christie usually gives the most snobbish comments to their likeliest espousers. In *Towards Zero* the obvious suspect, as Inspector Battle comments, is Neville Strange's dubious second wife, Kay, who is definitely 'not a lady', has 'known nothing but hotel life' and comes 'from bad stock' (p. 310). These put-downs are uttered by Lady Tressilian, an arrogant aristocrat dispensable enough to be murdered early on. In fact the narrative suspense demands that the reader's sympathies be equally divided between Kay and the first wife, Audrey, who *is* a real lady, but also nervy and introspective, and quite possibly mad. Kay and her caddish lover Ted (described by a splenetic Major as having 'a touch of the dago') are given untramelled space in which to express their own dislike of the stuffiness of middle-class mores, and in the end they are vindicated.

It is hard, then, to understand the damning of Christie as a writer of country house fiction and a breed of backward-looking Tory. Her novels are largely indifferent to the doings of the upper classes and she is certainly not in love with a Lord. (In fact she thought *The Mystery on the Blue Train*, the only one of her books with an aristocratic hero, positively her weakest.)[74] Her aristocrats are often an unsavoury bunch, like the sadistic Lord Edgware and the repressed Duke of Merton, much less desirable and likeable than the film stars in *Lord Edgware Dies*. Writers like Margery Allingham and Dorothy L. Sayers try to dazzle their readers with mesmeric titles, flattering them with a sense of intimacy with the 'great' and enthusing sycophantically over patrician taste,

> [Inspector] Parker . . . sank luxuriously into a corner of the chesterfield. . . . A leaping wood fire was merrily reflected in the spotless surface of the black baby grand; the mellow calf bindings of Lord Peter's rare editions glowed softly against the black and primrose walls; the vases were filled with tawny chrysanthemums; the latest editions of all the papers were on the table. . . .
>
> (*Clouds of Witness*, p. 114)

Christie makes no such move to idolise, in the manner of a Ngaio Marsh, for example, who lingers on the munificence of the London season (in *Death in a White Tie*), where 'Sir Herbert Carrados' surveys proudly the two hundred bottles of 'Heidsieck '28' consumed during their champagne supper (p. 44). The reader will search in vain for similarly lavish details in Christie's texts – hardly a line describes the luxury of the Orient Express in the novel which features it. It is not as society hangers-on that Christie's readers are encouraged to imagine themselves.

If country houses evoke ancestry, settled traditions and kinship, Christie's, when they do feature, fail on all counts, seeming mainly to interest the writer at the point at which they are no longer inhabited by aristocrats but are modernised by the middle classes. Christie's presentation of such changes can be caught in the description of 'End House', which has been in the Buckley family for years, and which is a clear candidate as Poirot suggests for being a 'dark, mysterious mansion, haunted by a family curse' (p. 14). Yet far from investing it with the Gothic, Christie is at pains, through Hastings' prosaic description, to dispel any sense of horror about the house:

> The house itself was large and rather dreary looking. It was shut in by trees, the branches of which actually touched the roof. It was clearly in bad repair.

Inside, however, it is the contemporary which has the upper hand:

> There was no mournful note here. The room gave on to the sea and was full of sunshine. It was shabby and betrayed conflicting styles – ultra modern of a cheap variety superimposed on solid Victorian. The curtains were of faded brocade, but the covers were new and gay and the cushions positively hectic. On the walls were hung family portraits. Some of them, I thought, looked remarkably good. There was a gramophone and there were some records lying idly about. There were a portable wireless, practically no books, and one newspaper flung open on the end of the sofa.
>
> (*Peril at End House*, p. 27)

End House is hardly a symbol of patrician largesse and authority but of modern domestication; it offers a new image of bourgeois pleasures, one which depends upon the consumption of a commercialised culture: the gramophone, the wireless, journalism. What interests Christie is this mixing of old and new and the possibilities it creates for different kinds of desires, new species of deception.

In the same spirit the country house is cheerfully updated over the years: into an hotel in *Evil under the Sun*, a home for juvenile offenders in *They Do It with Mirrors*, a boarding school in *Cat among the Pigeons*, a nursing home in *By the Pricking of My Thumbs*; even Styles itself, to which Poirot returns in his last case, *Curtain*, has been revamped as a guest-house. There are few if any bitter asides on the winds of change or wistful passages of farewell. Even if change is not positively welcomed (there is a slight tone of disapproval in Hastings's stiff account), the nostalgic is avoided. Whatever their appeal, it is not to invite the reader to linger in what Raymond Chandler called 'Cheesecake Manor.'[75]

In her detective fiction, Agatha Christie has no Brideshead and there is more flirtation with the idea of the landed gentry as the 'civilised' class in Virginia Woolf or D. H. Lawrence than in her work. The whodunits are not excuses for bemoaning the decline and fall of the big house, and the death-throes of liberal culture. Where she does use big houses, they are seldom described as repositories of national character or a lost civility; it is their character as private homes which appeals to her. Hers is not a romantic conservatism, cleaving to the aristocratic as a mark of a better past or a model for the good life. Rather she speaks to a readership

reconciled to the present, unfrightened by change and confidently domestic. In fact Christie is as likely to be fascinated by 'new money' as she
is by new homes: both offer different possibilities for economies of desire,
for exploring the tensions which lie within any domestic life.

The only moments of pathos in her prose come as a response to the
shabby and the sadly respectable. In *The ABC Murders* the lonely travelling salesman (another modern wanderer) living in a seedy guest-house
and suspected of murder, is an object of far more intense interest than his
upper-class counterpart. Christie's description of the effects belonging to
a murdered shopkeeper is again typical not only of her authorial neutrality
but her sure sense of the dignities of private life as expressed in the
domesticating of an environment, however impoverished:

> From the parlour a stair led to two upstairs rooms. One was empty
> and unfurnished, the other had evidently been the dead woman's bed-
> room. After being searched by the police it had been left as it was. A
> couple of old worn blankets on the bed – a little stock of well-darned
> underwear in a drawer – cookery recipes in another – a paper-backed
> novel entitled *The Green Oasis* – a pair of new stockings – pathetic in
> their cheap shininess – a couple of china ornaments – a Dresden
> shepherd much broken, and a blue and yellow spotted dog – a black
> raincoat and a woolly jumper hanging on pegs – such were the wordly
> possessions of the late Alice Ascher.
>
> (*The ABC Murders*, p. 33)

The list in which a crucial clue is buried is, of course, a standard whodunit
device, but Christie's eye for touching detail suggests how much her
sympathy was with any kind of attempt at domestic culture. Poirot's
only murmured comment is '*pauvre femme*'; one can imagine what Peter
Wimsey's would have been.

What interests Christie is this range of respectability and those who
have no such culture do not exist for her as subjects: they have, as it
were, no interior. It is rare for Christie's plots to be excited or fuelled by
cross-class animus in the way in which, for example, Sayers's *Gaudy Night*
is. There is certainly no sense of the lower orders as having crawled out
of an unfathomable abyss such as we might find in *The Coat of Arms*
(1931), for example, where Edgar Wallace's put-downs of menials are of
a violence no less chilling for being casual – 'a snub-nosed country girl
who has never done anything more intellectual in her life than wash dishes'
(p. 203). Frequently Wallace's own narration merges with that of his
detective, who lets off steam at the waiter whom he has already introduced
to the reader as 'a dull, criminal type':

> He is part of the world's waste, the dirt that is swept behind walls at
> irregular intervals
>
> (p. 200)[76]

There were plenty in the 1930s only too willing to do the sweeping. The ideological universe which Christie offered readers is of a different hue from the Brownshirt mentality of the day: it is not interested in demonisation, or in action.

Christie's novels tend to play down any fraternisation across ranks. Where the public in 1935 might be salaciously or self-righteously drawn to real-life crimes, like the Rattenbury case which disturbed the proprieties of both sexual and social behaviour, Christie sidesteps such volatile material.[77] This may be both cowardly and generous: in her fictions one cannot predict the murderer by caste, except in being able to assume that it will not be the working-class person. The lower orders are those who are 'feckless' or shifty, ungrateful and surly, essentially undomesticated. Her maidservants are proverbially adenoidal but not homicidal and whilst stage rustics pepper the pages with dropped 'h's they are never a foil to more incendiary and pathological hatreds. Like the aristocracy they may be seen as ignorant and self-regarding, but above all, uninteresting: their appearances are minimal and carry little narrative weight. Real life lies elsewhere for Christie, inside the homes of the middle class of whatever variety, and in their feelings for each other.

The same ambiguous kind of moderation can be found in the relative absence of nationalistic sentiment in Christie's fiction of the 1930s, and of the more virulent expressions of imperialistic fervour. Despite the bloodbath of the First World War, it was 1921, rather than 1914, which saw a crescendo of jingoism in Britain, and much popular fiction continued its glorification of the English gentleman well into the 1930s. Plenty of Christie's contemporaries continued to look east for their villains, to the 'lower races' of the Empire, but also the unregenerate Chinese who had shown themselves immune to Victorian missionary zeal and could be indiscriminately mixed with Russian anarchists and Bolshevists, the Mafia, Jews and trade unionists in an unholy alliance of Tory phobias. 'Dr. Fu Manchu' created by Sax Rohmer in 1913, fed contemporary fears about the 'yellow races' for thirty years; 'Sapper' was another who kept alive the pugilistic national spirit and satiated the demand for conspiracy tales in his 'Bulldog Drummond' stories. 'Thirties readers could still enjoy a novel like *The Black Gang* (first published in 1921 but into its 38th edition by 1935), where, in the opening chapter, the strong and silent hero, a quintessentially decent Englishman, has his enemies bested thus:

'What are these two Hebrews?' A man from behind . . . came up to the leader [Drummond] and whispered in his ear.

'. . . My friend and I do not like your trade, you swine. It is well that we have come provided with the necessary implement for such a case. Fetch the cat'. . . . As his full meaning came home to the two Jews, they flung themselves grovelling on the floor, screaming for mercy.

'Gag them.... The cat for cases of this sort is used legally,' he remarked. 'We merely anticipate the law.'

With a fresh outburst of moans the two Jews watched the door open and the inexorable black figure come in, holding in his hand a short stick from which nine lashes hung down.... 'Flog them to within an inch of their lives,' said the deep voice.

(*The Black Gang*, p. 18)[78]

Authoritarian Englishness is equally approved of when Lord Peter Wimsey attacks 'dagoes': as a gentleman he is naturally a member of the master race. Others continued to peddle in exotica simply when a vicarious thrill was required: Lord Arranways in Wallace's *The Coat of Arms* is killed with 'the sword of the Aba Khan', which just happens to be handy in an English inn.

If the thriller was the obvious place for letting rip the more melodramatic and defensive elements of the Tory imagination, then it is interesting that Christie, who had tried her hand at these, wrote none in the 1930s.[79] She seems to have been unable to sustain either the necessary passion or paranoia: her treatment of nationalistic sentiment is circumspect and at least as evasive as the treatment of class. Whilst she does not challenge the xenophobic statements of her characters neither does she endorse them either as narrator or in the construction of plots. The most offensive remarks are given to the most likely candidates, and Christie handles English prejudice adroitly, sitting rather firmly on the fence. In *Cards on the Table* (1936), Mr Shaitana, a figure of Mephistophelean evil and unspecified parentage, inspires instant dislike:

Every healthy Englishman who saw him longed earnestly and fervently to kick him! They said, with a singular lack of originality, 'There's that damned Dago, Shaitana!' ... Whether Mr. Shaitana was an Argentine, or a Portuguese, or a Greek, or some other nationality rightly despised by the insular Briton, nobody knew.

(p.10)

As Colin Watson argues, it was quite possible that readers might miss the irony in Christie's choice of phrases ('singular lack of originality', 'rightly despised') but the implied distance from English rectitude is there.[80]

It is interesting also to speculate that some of the popularity of Poirot – for the 1930s and '40s were his years – depended upon some sense that overt displays of national superiority might be mildly embarrassing. Though frequently mistaken for a Frenchman (about whom there is always something fishy), Poirot functions in the stories to point up as well as indulge English prejudices about foreigners – that they are vain, excitable, eat funny food. Poirot frequently mocks, with the reader's implied agreement, the shortsightedness of English insularity. In *Three Act Tragedy* (1935) he admits cunningly to turning the tables on English jeering:

to speak the broken English is an enormous asset. It leads people to despise you. They say – a foreigner – he can't even speak English properly. It is not my policy to terrify people – instead I invite their gentle ridicule. . . . And so, you see, I put people off their guard.

(p. 191)

The surprise twist of *The ABC Murders* depends on exposing the overweening self-love of an English xenophobe.

In 1930 Christie published her first 'straight' novel, *Giant's Bread*, under the name of Mary Westmacott, keeping her identity secret for another fifteen years.[81] Far more directly personal and loosely structured it is amongst other things a well-meaning attempt to get to grips with racial disgust, and shows her struggling against her own prejudices to be fair-minded about Jews. Her portrait of the Levinne family whose son becomes the hero's best friend, reproduces many contemporary assumptions, no less shocking for being conventional, but is also unexpectedly outspoken in attacking the hypocrisy of her own class:

'Oh, of course – *Jews!* But perhaps it's absurd of one to be prejudiced. Some very good people have been Jews.'
  It was rumoured that the Vicar had said: 'Including Jesus Christ', in answer. But nobody really believed that . . . nobody believed that he would have said anything really sacrilegious.

(p. 72)

Certainly in the 1930s, Christie seems to tone down the stridency of earlier anti-Semitic sentiment: in *Peril at End House*, Jim Lazarus (described by Hastings as having 'a rather fleshy nose') is treated with comparative goodwill, and allowed to marry one of the heroines; even more rehabilitated is Oliver Manders in *Three Act Tragedy* who marries the heroine, 'Egg' Lytton Gore. In Christie's autobiography, written of course with hindsight, she describes herself as typical of 'ordinary people in 1932 or 1933' in her 'complete lack of foreknowledge' as far as the consequences of anti-Semitism were concerned.[82]

Moderation, neutrality, impartiality – small gains perhaps, but in a climate of escalating fascism not entirely negligible ones. Where many other authors might effectively have whipped up class feeling or stirred patriotic strings, Christie's writing is part of that retreat within the middle classes from the more gung-ho expressions of national confidence. Christie invites the reader to be both less demonstrative and more lenient. Her popularity suggests a readership who liked to think of themselves as more pacifically minded, tolerant and happy-go-lucky. Such mildness may have been born in part out of reticence, by default, as it were, and from a sense that older and more aggressive expressions of class feeling were in bad taste; it may indeed be a cowardly kind of tolerance which doesn't want the boat to rock ever again, and certainly there is a sense of lullaby about Christie's calm world. Any softening toward foreigners may well have been partly self-protective (like the admission of India to test cricket in 1932) and was far from indicating a wide-sweeping liberalisation.[83] For many the absence of nationalistic sentiment was evidence of nothing more than a desire to put one's head as far as it would go into the sand.

It might also be born, however, from a growing confidence about the rightness of a different kind of middle-class life, one which was more profoundly domesticated and more unashamedly inward-looking. Poirot's readers, in imagination at least, longed to be in the class of luxury cruisers, rather than empire builders or missionaries. In Christie's hands convalescence turned into relaxation; Christie's is the literature of the easy chair and of the lounge and it belongs to a social life apparently indifferent to power and centred upon leisure. Her stories suggest an inter-war imagination in which the middle classes are the modern class, less sentimental, more unbuttoned than their pre–1914 versions (literally when one thinks of fashions), steering a course 'between old-fashioned courtesy and new-fashioned informality'.[84] Yet they were also more preoccupied with their own concerns. Her fictions might be more democratic in their range of reference but they were also more solipsistic; they spoke to a much wider and more heterodox middle-class readership but mainly of themselves.

The paradoxical nature of that loosening up of social mores between the wars is neatly caught by Christie herself in a passage of her autobiography. Reflecting on the snobbish attitudes of her Edwardian youth, she remarks on the increasing openness of middle-class life, as it moved away from a fixed notion of social acceptability based purely upon kinship and connection:

> Three phases have succeeded each other during the span of my life. In the first the questions would be: 'But who *is* she, dear? Who are her *people*? Is she one of the *Yorkshire* Twiddledos? Of course, they are badly off, very badly off, but *she* was a *Wilmot*.' This was to be succeeded in due course by: 'Oh yes, of course, they *are* pretty dreadful, but then they are terribly *rich*.' 'Have the people who have taken The Larches got money?' 'Oh well, then we'd better call.' The third phase was different again: 'Well, dear, but are they *amusing*?' 'Yes, well of course they are not well off, and nobody knows where they came from, but they are *very* amusing.'
>
> (*An Autobiography*, p. 124)

Yet what is as likely to strike the reader, especially anyone who is not English, at least as much as a sense of the slackening of class rules, is the consistency of the questions themselves, the underlying obsession with the need to 'place' people as groups or individuals, and the setting up of desirables and undesirables which is so much the bedrock of English social life: 'Who is this person?' inexorably linked to 'are they *worth* knowing?'; a sense of difference automatically expressed as social evaluation, whereby even being 'amusing' is yet another version of social qualification, of entry to some imagined community of the acceptable, of becoming 'one of us'.

Christie's achievement in the inter-war years was to find a form which could playfully head off and defuse potential nervousness about modernity and make light of the fears of an expanding middle class, turning into 'mere entertainment' and making enjoyable what in others took more rabid and vindictive expression. It did not testify, however, to the disappearance of those fears but to their continuing presence in new forms. The very idea of 'respectable crime' avidly consumed by such a variety of readers, available at every bookstall and library and established as public entertainment, was not without its contradictions. It meant bringing to the surface and promiscuously flaunting those private needs and desires which had usually been represented or explored in the more 'proper' and accredited forms of high culture. Ironically, Christie's domestication of crime was bound to turn the spotlight even more harshly upon the bourgeois interior and expose for all to see what might constitute a class mentality: we can read her novels as one huge advertisement of the murderousness of English social life and of the desperate need to convert to pleasure all those anxieties which an existence like that of the post-war middle classes could produce.

A SOCIETY OF STRANGERS

In one of the few passages in her autobiography which deal with the darker side of her life, Christie in old age vividly recalls a recurring childhood nightmare which involved the repeated appearance of a soldier in uniform – 'the Gunman'. Her terror at this figure was not, she believed, connected to either the gun he carried or the idea of shooting. Rather it was his presence, not always in costume, in amongst ordinary events – a tea-party or a walk with people she knew – which frightened her. She would be sitting happily in the company of relatives and friends but when 'the pale blue eyes in the familiar face' turned to meet her – '*It was really the Gunman*'. Equally terrifying was a game the young Agatha played with her sister Madge, who would pretend quite unannounced to be 'the Elder Sister', indistinguishable from her in appearance but who was mad and only occasionally came to the house. Suddenly adopting a soft, oily voice, Madge would ask, 'You know who I am, don't you, dear? I'm your sister, Madge. You don't think I'm anyone else, do you? You wouldn't think *that*?' What was extraordinary, Christie remembers, was that it was always at Agatha's special invitation that her sister played this game: she wanted to be pleasurably terrified.[85]

At the heart of Agatha Christie's writing, productive of both its reassuring comedy and of its narrative grip, is just such a game of make-believe which plays deliberately with the metamorphosis of the everyday and the comfortable into the unfamiliar and the sinister. Many of Christie's titles remind us of both the terrors and the magic of the nursery: *Hickory Dickory Dock*, *Five Little Pigs*, *One, Two, Buckle My Shoe*, *Crooked House*, *A Pocketful of Rye*, *Three Blind Mice* (the original form of *The Mousetrap*) – all use the suspense that lies in the nursery rhyme, and remind us of how the mounting excitement of their repetition depends on that unsteady boundary between the homely and the malevolent.[86] Christie saw her own childhood fantasies as a rebellion against safety, a kind of playing with fire that only the well-insulated, both in personal and social terms, could allow herself. We might suggest that in her detective stories a calculated taking of risks and a comic collectivising of social unease take a form which would especially delight and engross the 'comfortable classes' of inter-war Britain.[87]

Both the nightmare of the Gunman and the 'game' of the Elder Sister express the child's fear of the unexpected violence which manifests itself first in that most apparently secure of places, family life. A similar anxiety troubles her whodunits which compulsively reiterate the same question, one which has the character of both fascination and fear: is this person what they seem? asks character after character of each other. What lies behind the calm façade which is their outward appearance? As a primary anxiety, it takes a peculiarly modern form since it suggests a level of disturbance which is not, and cannot be, easily quelled by moral reassurances: these are questions which put in doubt not just the security of one's social position, but also the possibility of social exchange and meaningful community itself. It is this sense of a safe, known world thrown out of kilter which Christie's fictions share with many modernist writers.

The instabilities which these popular murders set in motion bear a direct relationship to the existential crises which torment the writers of high culture: the obsession with unstable identities, the ultimate unknowability of others, the sense of guilt which accompanies civilisation, and the concomitant effects which such destabilisation has upon the certainties of realist narrative – all find their modified parallel in Christie. We trust her narrators (as close as any to Stephen Daedalus's ideal author, paring his fingernails, as far removed from the text as possible), at our peril; our desire to find solace or approval in identification with others is stymied both by the characters' lack of emotional depth and our uncertainty over their moral nature, an ambivalence upon which the plot depends. The exigencies of the puzzle-form draw attention above all to the contrivance of the writing whilst its minimalist economy poses a kind of challenge to the reader: our awareness of how many pages we have to go makes reading a whodunit a particularly physical experience of writing, a precursor, perhaps, of the antics of the *nouveau roman*.

Yet what could become painful existential questions are in Christie's fiction playful ones; for modernist writers such duplicities can become pure trauma and occasions for despair, locking both reader and writer into the waste land of an alienated and often isolated subjectivity. Christie, however, comically transmutes such anxieties into a new kind of community: what could be corrosive and fragmenting doubts about the moral and social fabric and the meaningfulness of individual life, are turned magically and ritually into a new kind of reassuringly collective experience. Murder, which for three-quarters of the novel is the agent of disintegration, becomes a means of social integration, and by the end of the novel enables the setting up of a new society. As a modern, however, Christie can only create a society of strangers, but she makes it a society none the less.

The 1930s were Christie's most prolific period; she produced twenty-four books in the decade with sometimes up to four publications in one year. Yet if the enclosed environment of a Home Counties village is usually assumed to be her typical milieu, it is an interesting paradox that only about a quarter of her entire output has actual village settings and that the majority of these books appear after 1945.[88] In fact it is the pleasures of travel which dominate her plots in the 1930s. Hercule Poirot may rely on armchair methods, but he certainly gads about, visiting Egypt, Jordan, Syria and Turkey. In the 1930s there is hardly a novel which does not bear some mark of 'abroad': we have *The Mystery on the Blue Train* (written in the Canaries in 1928), *Murder on the Orient Express* (1934), *Death in the Clouds* (1935) (set on a plane between Croydon airport and France), *Murder in Mesopotamia* (1936), *Death on the Nile* (1937), (dedicated to SB 'who also loves wandering about the world'), *Appointment with Death* (1938), set in Petra, as well as the number of European watering-places – Monte Carlo, Corsica, Cannes, the Riviera and exotic cities like Baghdad which feature in the collections of short stories.[89]

No doubt Christie was of her age in sharing the contemporary passion for trains, boats and planes.[90] As travel between the wars became more regulated (passports were introduced in 1924) it was also more accessible to the majority. Ironically, the war left a surplus of transportation which saw former destroyers turned into luxury liners and cruisers, and made possible the growth of air travel. Tour companies expanded as did scheduled flights, but more importantly the whole ethos of travel changed. Abroad need no longer be only the glamorous playground of the rich or the place for the more highbrow romance of literary travellers. Christie captures a middlebrow world of burgeoning tourism which at its most expensive could include Nile cruises and journeys on the Orient Express, but less luxurious forms of holiday-making and sightseeing too; her plots bristle with boarding- and guest-houses, local hotels, like the one on the English riviera in which Poirot is staying in *Peril at End House* or the venue in Devon for *Towards Zero* where the characters are suffering from the 'tropical' heat of 70 degrees Fahrenheit.[91]

Even so, it is relatively unimportant whether Christie's readers enjoyed such excursions in the flesh. Travel books are not like travel guides intended for *bona fide* travellers – rather they are armchair romances for the stay-at-homes. Christie's detective fiction, itself reading for leisure, must have been doubly appropriate as holiday reading. In fantasy, if not in fact, travel abroad could now be something imaginable and desirable for its own sake, as a pleasurable activity like the outdoor pastimes which became so much part of inter-war years, tennis, gardening, and hiking. These were not journeys of adventure or conquest, which depended upon independent initiative and individual prowess. Rather it was the domesticated and managed aspect of tourism which appealed to people; the idea of going in a group. From being a place known only as part of the Empire, 'abroad' is amorphously exotic whilst at the same time being reassuringly familiarised. In Christie's novels it is the game-hunter and the Safari which conjure up Empire between the wars, and not the administrator or the missionary. Abroad was being imagined as a place for consumption and leisure, a home from home.[92]

In Christie's stories it is the journey, the voyage, the pleasure of moving from one place to another, and the disruptions it may bring with it, as a way of passing the time, which engross the reader rather than the engagement with actually being abroad. It is the journey that offers the best metaphor for the disruptive process inaugurated by a murder and for the founding of a society of strangers who come together as its result. The train journey in particular, 'running along conventional tracks' but taking the traveller into unknown territory, 'predictable and unexpected',[93] can mediate between the public world outside and the private interior, and was an ideal place for strangers to become a temporary community, safely enclosed and yet being carried into the unfamiliar.[94] Apparently random groupings are transformed by the murder in their midst, like the suspects in *Death in the Clouds* or the passengers assembled on the Orient Express:

> . . . people, of all classes, of all nationalities, of all ages. For three days these people, these strangers to one another, are brought together. They sleep and eat under one roof, they cannot get away from each other. At the end of three days they part, they go their several ways, never, perhaps, to see each other again.
>
> (*Murder on the Orient Express*, p. 21)

By the end of the story they are revealed not just to share the characteristics of a household, cooped up together, but actually to be one.

Christie's crimes are always 'closed' even when at first they seem public and open.[95] Murder socialises and familiarises, and far from propelling terrified individuals into private and isolated nightmares or into the arms of an entirely impersonal process – the Law (the scenario for Kafka's *The Trial*) – murder creates a 'circle', a shared intimacy like that of home. Every murder explored by Poirot, as a private investigator, 'from the inside', by an examination of personal or familial relations given in private conversations, establishes how much the suspects have in common as potential murderers – how similar, despite differences, their lot is. They are all, often literally, in the same boat. Christie uses abroad as a more effective means of concentrating her plots and isolating her characters so that their local anxieties and indigenous behaviours are thrown into relief. Her characters take their domestic outlook with them, like so much bottled water, and murder simply works to reinforce the sense of privacy which has been invaded. It is not surprising, therefore, to find that for Agatha Christie murder can even be a kind of marriage bureau, uniting couple after couple of suspects through the experience of a corpse.[96]

Like Nurse Leatheran in *Murder in Mesopotamia*, reading *Murder in the Nursing Home* as her own patient is murdered, Christie's travel settings produce a Chinese box effect: readers are given back a mirror image of their own concerns and the peripatetic settings enhance, rather than dimin- ish, the social and psychological inwardness of the plots. If the voyage out from home is a metaphor of desire, and the journey an ancient symbol of the process toward death, then Agatha Christie's travellers make a circular and not a linear progression. The end of all their travelling (to adapt T. S. Eliot), is to arrive where they started from and know the place for the first time. And in this sense the peculiarly unprogressive drive of the detective story is reinforced. For crime produces the plot, linking characters, causing a new 'train' of events. Yet this kind of crime fiction works, as G. C. Ramsey points out, by being told backwards, with the full forward narration of events only coming in retrospect in the closing chapters.[97] Much of our time as readers is spent 'back-tracking', a point which Christie most clearly expresses in the shape of *Towards Zero*. As one character says:

> I like a good detective story, but, you know, they begin in the wrong place! They begin with the murder. But the murder is the *end*. The story begins long before that . . . .
>
> (*Towards Zero*, p. 9)

We might go further and say that if literary modernism, as many critics have argued, is more drawn to spatial than to temporal forms, the crime puzzle can be seen as a compromise between the two; like the jig-saw (itself an inter-war craze) this is a narrative whose break-up of linear development and continuities is only a temporary fragmentation, the pieces deliberately scattered for the express pleasure of putting them back together again.

The ABC Murders, published at Christie's peak in 1935, shows how fierce is her desire to circumscribe crime, drawing a domestic circle around it. It opens with a discussion between Hastings and Poirot as to their ideal murders. Hasting prefers the exotic, melodramatic Edwardian style whilst Poirot argues instead for:

> A very simple crime. A crime with no complications. A crime of quiet domestic life . . . very unimpassioned – very *intime*.
>
> (*The ABC Murders*, p. 18)

By contrast the first murder in *The ABC Murders* seems to fit neither of their requirements. It is (in Hastings's words) the 'sordid and uninteresting' killing of 'an old woman of the name of Ascher who keeps a little tobacco and newspaper shop' (p. 19). There then follows a series of murders linked only by the alphabetical sequence of the 'ABC' railway guides – Alice Ascher in Andover, Betty Barnard in Bexhill, Sir Carmichael Clarke in Churston. Apparently unconnected by any factor like age, sex or class, the killings seem to have been the work of a homicidal maniac, public crimes at random, comparatively motiveless.[98]

Yet the entire work of the plot is to reverse this expectation. In the course of investigation, the murders are presented in their domestic context, as 'three dramas of family life' (p. 115); each one becomes an intimate story of its own. Then the victims and relatives are encouraged to join together, to hunt the criminal, until the denouement reveals that he is not the psychopath who has been arrested but one of them, and the apparently public nature of the crimes has merely disguised a domestic murder after all. What appeared to be meaningless and arbitrary has been brought under control and now 'makes sense'.[99]

Just as murder can connect the lives and hopes of strangers, so too can it equally estrange the apparently connected and disaggregate the united fronts of family or household. In the process of a murder inquiry every member of the family can be found guilty of having it in for someone else, of being at heart a potential murderer. Blood is certainly thinner than water. Christie's rural settings, which so many have seen as hermetically sealed, provide an especially empty security, apparently representing order and harmony but quickly revealed as a 'cover' for its opposite. It is not just the metropolis which can signify displaced and anonymous humanity; by the 1930s it is possible to imagine the 'Home' Counties, that place which conservative ideology was construing as the heart of England, as the reverse of homely. The village in her novels is a community whose members ought to know each other but don't. Thus one character speaks of village life:

'That's the worst of a place like this. Everybody knows everything about everybody else'

and the hero corrects her,

'Oh, no,' said Luke . . . 'No one human being knows the full truth about another human being . . . Not even one's nearest and dearest.'

(*Murder is Easy*, p. 78)

It is a sentiment which can equally dominate a closeted Egyptian household in 2000 BC, where people are viewed by Christie's *Ka* priest as having false doors like tombs,

They create a false door – to deceive. If they are conscious of weakness, or inefficiency, they make an imposing door of self-assertion, of bluster, of overwhelming authority – and, after a time, they get to believe in it themselves. They think, and everybody else thinks, that they *are* like that. But behind that door . . . is bare rock . . . .

(*Death Comes as the End*, p. 78)

'No one', he later reiterates, 'knows anyone else' (p. 132). Whether in Mesopotamia or St Mary Mead, society is a society of strangers.

Not for nothing is Christie's most usual character a tenant. Her villages are full, not of residents since time immemorial, but of birds of passage taking up their weekend cottages and summer lets: 'Sittaford House' in *The Sittaford Mystery* (1931) is rented by a mother and daughter from goodness knows where, and even *The Mousetrap*, which has come to stand for immovable English country life, takes place in one room of a guesthouse. It is an essentially rootless and unsettled world she invents in which people have very shallow lineages. In her most narrowly rural settings this is a country life dissevered from long genealogies of aristocratic connection, many of whose village inhabitants are only one-generation dwellers. The point about a retired major is that he has retired from somewhere else: he is as much a newcomer as a commuter is. Christie seems to be playing with the fear that must haunt many a refugee from the city: that far from being the ideal refuge from the city, secure and unchanging, the country might turn out to be no different after all.[100]

In *The Murder of Roger Ackroyd* not only do we find that Ackroyd is playing at being a country squire, the Ferrars, local noteworthies settled at Fernly Park, came only a year ago, and even the maid is a lady in disguise: 'You can't tell who are ladies and who aren't nowadays' (p. 129), wails one character. The pukka Colonel Carter with his military slang and barrack room stories has never been in the Shanghai Club in his life; the next-door neighbour at 'The Larches' isn't quite the horticulturally minded retired gentleman we are led to expect – Hercule Poirot cultivating his marrows is all part of the world turned upside down. Such villages, like the new dormitory towns and growing suburbs, where neighbours may only just have arrived, are a seed bed for mistaken or double identities. Exactly what social position is occupied becomes less important than the possible bogusness of it.

Christie modernises the detective story by domesticating it, bringing it firmly inside the respectable classes. For Conan Doyle and many of Christie's own contemporaries the criminal by definition could only be 'one of them'; for Christie, as her characters must always realise with alarm, the criminal is first of all 'one of us', someone who for nine-tenths of the novel must carry on seeming successfully to be just that. The gaze is turned inward to 'all the things one had read a hundred times – things that happen to other people, not to oneself' (*Styles*, p. 102). It is people 'one' knows who are potentially murderous, the most obvious 'types'. And it is not physical disguise so much as psychological disguise which is potentially pathological. The most innocent (the least likely) person may turn out to be the criminal, the obvious deviant and the degenerate are frequently red herrings: the criminal classes are not the ones to fear. It is within the charmed circle of *insiders* that the criminal must be sought; the cuckoo in the nest, not the alien from outside.

Christie's domestication of weaponry exhibits the same juxtaposition (one is reminded of her nightmares again) of the macabre and the familiar. Although she does employ poison almost obsessively (though always in its domestic varieties – arsenic for dosing the dog, cyanide for wasp nests stolen from the garden shed) there is clearly a morbid pleasure in choosing the banal impedimenta of home life and wreaking havoc with them: the kitchen pestle, the meat skewer, the golf club, a paperweight wrapped in a sock – all make an appearance in a repertoire of everyday things to kill with. (Herbert Read commented upon Christie's 'butcher-like indifference to life', observing that her novels exhibit 'a housewifely neatness in the slaughterhouse'.)[101] Death may come from septicaemia caused by the pus from a cat's wounded ear, or the substitution of hat-paint for cough linctus (*Murder is Easy*), from a corn knife (used to stab two victims in *Lord Edgware Dies*), or from the new leisure culture imagined lethally: sunbathing plays its part in *Evil Under the Sun*, and more gruesomely lawn tennis (with a racket concealing the steel ball from a bedstead in its handle) in *Toward Zero*. With only a slight shift of emphasis such an imagination might be thought paranoid. Indeed, it is hard to envisage Hitchcock or Highsmith without Agatha Christie.

What was more remarkable than the fuss a few people made about the 'trick' ending of *Roger Ackroyd*[102] was the much larger number of readers who made no fuss at all but took the idea of entering the mind of a respectable murderer for entertainment merrily in their stride. Unlike many of her contemporaries Christie seems to have been uniquely audacious in always being prepared to make respectability itself suspect. Early on in each novel the normality and conventionality of all the suspects is insisted upon: everyone seems 'eminently sane, respectable and completely ordinary' (*Murder is Easy*, p. 58). Yet it is part of the whodunit's suspense that, as Inspector Battle announces in the same novel, 'anyone may be a criminal' (p. 188). This is a level of anxiety both inclusive of, and larger than, anxieties about class.

In Sayers or Allingham it is often quite clear from page one who are the really nice people who will never turn out to be murderers, yet it is precisely the nice people in Christie who make the cleverest killers – *Peril at End House*, *Murder is Easy* and *Curtain* all provide examples. In *Towards Zero* 'Neville' is exactly the kind of English gentleman whom Kenneth Tynan would later lambaste as a resident of 'Loamshire', that mythical home county where loose-limbed young people in flannels and frocks were forever bounding through French windows and asking, 'Anyone for tennis?'[103] A crack cricketer and a tennis pro, 'good at sport, modest, goodlooking' and 'always the little pukka sahib', but it is he who has been terrorising his wife and tries to get her hanged. In *The Mystery on the Blue Train*, even the wounded war hero (that ultimate object of sanctification) is a dubious character.

In fact niceness can itself provide a motive: 'the passion for respectability is strong' observes one resident of her neighbours in *Mrs McGinty's Dead*. 'These are not artists or Bohemians . . . nice people like to preserve their niceness' (p. 109). Gentility is certainly not a reliable guide to moral character and is frequently the reverse. The sweet old lady in the old people's home may be a hardened killer, old and trusted friends of the family are slowly bumping them off, and the retired military gentleman may brutally bash his oldest friend's head in just because he was jealous of his expertise in acrostics. Christie's murderers include young mothers and a 12-year-old girl; even victims can be guilty of murder. Thus any notion of Christie's 'sanitising' crime has to take into account her largely unsacramental approach to respectability. It is at least arguable that the idea of one's own husband as a murderer, or the woman next door, is potentially as disturbing as locating the pathological 'out there' on the mean streets. Only the clergy don't murder (though they are not above suspicion), a scruple which suggests a more old-fashioned kind of con- servatism than one which thrives on social snubs.

Hence the significant ambivalence of the role of types or 'cardboard' characters in her work, for which Christie has been much attacked.[104] As types they ought to represent known and fixed qualities, in the manner, as Christie's second husband Max Mallowan believed, of a 'modern version of mediaeval morality plays'.[105] Her stories are indeed peopled with instantly recognisable types – the 'acidulated' spinster, the mild-mannered doctor, the dyspeptic colonel – but they are not embodiments of unchang- ing virtue or villainy. They no longer carry any reliable moral cargo but signify the possible untrustworthiness of values rather than their security. Christie is here as clearly 'post-realist' as any other modernist, deliberately playing with the assumptions of an earlier literary form, and working in pastiche:

> I had thought Mr Coleman's manner rather more like a P. G. Wode-house book than like a real live man. Had he really been playing a part all the time?
>
> (*Murder in Mesopotamia*, p. 89)

She cheerfully acknowledges her own self-conscious use of the cliché in the preface to *The Body in the Library*, self-deprecatingly comparing it to cookery, the concoction of a new recipe from familiar ingredients.[106]

Social life is always a kind of impersonation in Christie's novels; it is openly seen to be theatrical, a matter of convincing your audience by a clear repertoire of gestures and speech mannerisms. The idea of the social mask is, of course, much older than class societies, but in the whodunit it is robbed of emotional and moral force, retaining only a sense that theatre, however artificial, is a surviving form of collectivity. When Christie searches for a metaphor for the man who isn't all he seems, she evokes not any felt register of moral iniquity but a lighthearted language of theatricality. Class behaviour has become a kind of play-acting, and the murderer is the consummate actor (sometimes literally so). Hence *Three Act Tragedy* is arranged as a West End play with the first act entitled 'Suspicion' and its solution based upon Poirot's realisation that he has been looking 'not at reality but at an artfully painted bit of scenery' (p. 181). The illusionism of the stage is crucial to *Lord Edgware Dies* and *They Do It with Mirrors*, and characters are frequently described as Dr Leidner is in *Murder in Mesopotamia* as a man 'playing the part of himself' (p. 187). Her novels always adapted well to the theatre because, like Noel Coward, Christie was able to make entertaining a sense of the staginess of contemporary class life which, though it was largely play-acting, was performed, none the less, in deadly earnest:

> It's all a question of masks, really; brittle, painted masks. We all wear them as a form of protection; modern life forces us to.
>
> (*Design for Living*, p. 102)[107]

Whodunits belong to those 'designs for living' which became available across the social classes between the wars, those new and modern productions of English social life which 'theatricalised' it. Like film and radio and cut-price fashion, the whodunit offered a representation of English behaviour and character which could be copied by anyone who took the trouble to learn the right lines or surround themselves with the right props. Bearing, posture, appearance and the 'proper' intonation of voice became a matter of careful reproduction, and whilst the image itself might be a conservative one its reproducibility was modern and was forever undermining any notion of its authenticity. As René Cutforth writes, reflecting upon the 'calculating' quality of life between the wars,

> there was a Thirties face, a Thirties expression . . . in the Thirties you were on stage the whole time and tense with the effort of playing the part of a thoroughly relaxed and secure individual.[108]

Class life in England has long been a species of guessing game, and who but the respectable classes could have invented charades? Assuming social superiority, or inferiority for that matter, is always a kind of shamming, in which you pass yourself off as employer or servant, mistress or maid, as though this were itself the sum of your subjective life. In one sense what is immoral about Christie's murderers is not that they believe themselves to be better than other people but that they get caught in the act. Her plots speak to the heart of the universal preoccupation of respectable society, the exposure of the fraud or the swiz, the confidence trickster, the person who leads you up the garden path, the wolf in sheep's clothing, the con-man. It was a game of assessment and judgement which reached almost manic proportions between the wars.

Misleading, then, to take the fiction at face value, and imagine that Agatha Christie never addresses any sense of social disturbance: on one level her writing speaks to nothing else. Far from suggesting a world in which every person knows their place, and in which values are firm and fixed, the fiction explores the difficulty of social belonging in a modern world in which the very idea of social status has something theatrical and impermanent about it. If they are ultimately defensive fictions, looking for an insider on whom to blame the apparent uncertainty of social life, then that same refusal to look beyond the Home Counties and their inhabitants for her psychic swindlers could surely open up for Christie's readers the unsettling implication that 'it is the middle classes who are the murdering classes',[109] and their victims are their own selves. The fiction may work in the end to offer 'reassurance' but since her communities always thrive on suspicion their insecurities can never be resolved. Perhaps it is this contradiction which makes these fictions for many such compulsive reading and turns readers into addicts, hooked on 'crime'.

Should we not read the flood of whodunits between the wars not so much as a sign of the fixity of class assumptions but as symptomatic of their instability? The middle-classes, as many commentators argue, had lost after the First World War many of the markers by which they had formerly known themselves. With most of the upper class decimated in the war, and increasingly 'relegated like Red Indians to reservations (mostly in Scotland)',[110] the middle classes were both cut adrift and left to take up the reins. Older distinctions between gentry, clergy and the professions became less and less serviceable in a class which included financiers, businessmen, growing service industries, the entertainments world and a pattern of social life which saw commuting as more and more of a norm, and where people of moderate incomes were less and less likely to remain in the place in which they had been born. The decline in domestic service, the growth of public and motorised transport (removing the older distinction of 'carriage folk'), the entry of single women into the labour market – one could find all kinds of economic and historical shifts which might contribute to an argument for the inter-war middle class as a profoundly restless and heterodox grouping, whose amorphousness made the proliferation and rigidities of class distinctions all the more competitive.[111] Christie's fiction certainly suggests that the middle class between the wars was not one coherent grouping with a shared set of values and complacencies but continually fragmented factions, ill at ease and suspicious of each other, endlessly divided against themselves.

If one were looking for a text which offered a symbolic landscape for the fears and desires of respectable England in 1939, *Ten Little Niggers* ought to appear alongside those more usually selected.[112] An apparently random group of strangers is gathered on an island by a mysterious host who has inveigled each of them there by playing on their own selfish desires. 'Nice' people, they are shown, through their own thoughts, to be primarily interested in enjoying themselves and in getting what they can out of this free holiday. The island seems at first to represent the ultimate dream of private wealth and luxury, to be an almost magical place – 'the mere word suggested fantasy' (p. 26) – a world of its own away from the pressures of ordinary life. But its privacy soon begins to pall, as one after the other, the guests begin to die. Beneath the layer of respectability each is clothed in a fatal self-centredness and they are murdered because each in turn, from doctor to child's nanny, from elderly caretaker to carefree young man, is revealed to be a murderer. Their security on the island rapidly becomes claustrophobic and imprisoning, the comfort meaningless, as they must fend for themselves, and any chance of mutual liking is destroyed by fear and suspicion; what seemed philanthropic on the part of the absent host is turned into its opposite – a misanthropic judgement; what little society the guests manage to establish is eventually eroded until no one is left alive on the island.

Ten Little Niggers is the most inward, least comic of Christie's fictions, relentless in taking the logic of her own fears about the social fabric to its extreme conclusion: every person is both a potential murderer and victim. As a metaphor for the corruptions of insularity, it can be read on many levels, not least as an image of the mental universe of the British middle classes in the late 1930s, shut in and clannish, and increasingly marooned. *Ten Little Niggers* can be read as a veiled warning that those who live on an island must beware of becoming cut off. But there are other resonances too and we cannot see it as merely arbitrary that Christie's setting, however unconsciously chosen, is 'Nigger Island', a place 'just off the coast' of England, belonging to it and yet wildly different from it. For her readers such a name could be relied upon automatically to conjure up a thrilling 'otherness', a place where revelations about the 'dark side' of the English would be appropriate. Whilst this imagination is clearly consonant with an earlier imperialist literature and its imaginings of racial differences – with Conrad's representation of Africa as the *Heart of Darkness*, for example – Christie's location is both more domesticated and privatised, taking for granted the construction of racial fears woven into psychic life as early as the nursery. If her story suggests how easy it is to play upon such fears, it is also a reminder of how intimately tied they are to sources of pleasure and enjoyment.

Perhaps only a writer who was as peripatetic as Agatha Christie could have understood both the appeal and the dangers of security, and only someone with a comparatively weak and disinterested sense of the English class system could have evoked so many of the shared anxieties which the differently respectable could feel about social belonging. However mythologised Christie later became as the quintessence of traditional Englishness, her life was far from straightforwardly conventional. Christie came from that *couche* of the English middle class which managed to be badly off but confidently so. Her happy villa childhood in Torquay (one of the most popular of Edwardian pleasure spots) seems to have been unusually free and easy, with an American father who lived a life of leisure quite agreeably on his dwindling independent income, taking the family abroad whenever finances grew unsteady. Christie had a far from stay-at-home girlhood, much of which was spent in France and the Channel Islands until – again for pecuniary reasons – she 'came out', not in London but Egypt, during a season in Cairo.

A passionate traveller all her life, Christie's first marriage included a year going round the world on an Empire tour, and her instinct when that marriage collapsed in 1928 was to leave her little daughter and go to the Middle East on her own, eventually winding up at an archaeological dig where she met her second husband. Divorced, marrying again at 40 a man 15 years younger than herself (and a Catholic to boot), Christie's life was to be fairly itinerant for the next twenty years. Max Mallowan's own archaeological expeditions began in the first year of their marriage, 1930, and Agatha Christie stayed with him for a large part of every year between 1930 and 1938, so that during her most creative period her inventions of Englishness are nearly all written on the hoof. And when she comes to start her autobiography in 1950, she finds it easiest to remember her Devon childhood gazing at the snow-topped mountains of Kurdistan.[113]

Maybe it was the fact that she was able periodically to live abroad which allowed Agatha Christie's writing to express an affectionate sense of the English middle classes: such a regard is often best felt at a distance.

Agatha's husband certainly compared her pleasure in writing to that of travel – both were equally forms of escape, which perhaps made it easier for her, back in England, to be a passionate homemaker.[114] It is this dynamic which is embodied in the detective stories, the desire to stay snugly within known limits and the necessary urge to upset that tranquillity and test those boundaries. If there is little nostalgia (in the sense we now use it of sentimental retrospect) in her inter-war writing, then Christie's novels are nevertheless profoundly nostalgic in the original sense of the word: in their deep longing for that safe and unchanged home, from which we are all exiled by adulthood and culture, but to which we can dream of returning at the end of the narrative, even though we know that were we to find it, such permanence might be as soul-destroying as continual restlessness.

In order to gauge what nostalgia in the work of Agatha Christie really means one needs to imagine her a stout woman in her forties, in a hot tent or on a dusty verandah, looking across the desert, and settling down to write about murder in the vicarage.

AGATHA CHRISTIE'S CONSERVATISM

The thrills and spills of Agatha Christie's fiction are a kind of licensed terror like those of the funfare ride, staying firmly on the rails and never going over the edge. What H. R. F. Keating calls the 'hawser-tug'[115] of the story always draws us to the safe anchorage at the end of the tale and to the place where the apparent disarray is reformed into order. The conservatism of the stories may appear to lie both in their summoning up a fear of moral and social anarchy and in their feeding the desire that people have to live in an ordered universe: no detail is left unexplained, no past incident allowed to be ambivalent or left open in the interpretation of events. Yet despite appearances to the contrary Christie's is a far from rational universe.

The philosophy which sustains Christie's conservatism and with which she resolves many of her textual dilemmas rests on an age-old belief in fallen and flawed humanity and an almost mystical faith in the co-equality of evil with good. On the deepest level crime is never rational or rationalisable; it is never finally explained since the manifestations of good and evil are ultimately a mystery, random but indisputable. We may know why a crime was committed, but not, in the end, why it was *that* person and not another – this, we are told, is due simply to 'evil', whose origin, if it has one, is God. Evil is a category in the fiction which transcends insanity and even immorality, and whose mysterious emotiveness can be effectively employed to pull the reader back from the more modern, relativising and secular implications of Christie's plots.

Christie's novels are only interesting for their espousal of a conservative theology in so far as it always sits uneasily with an enlightened and modern outlook, and may have been representative of readers' own ambivalence in the mid–1930s: the addictive nature of the reading depends in part on just this disjuncture between conservatism and modernity. The language of good and evil in the fiction feels 'trumped up' and reads like a mere reflex, the echoes of a more proselytising religiosity heard faintly through a mild Anglicanism. Usually the imposition of moral absolutes and the introduction of this older vocabulary seems arbitrary and produces odd, unconvincing moments when the novels lurch toward melodrama without having worked up the excessive emotion which melodrama needs. Once the ordinary person has been discovered 'evil', their difference must manifest itself (even though it has been hidden so far) in order to distance them from the rest of us: thus we have a strained recognition in which tragedy moves rapidly through melodrama into farce. The murderer undergoes a Jekyll and Hyde-like transformation:

> the handsome vigorous young man turned into a rat-like creature with furtive eyes.

> *(Death in the Clouds*, p. 249)

Or the discovery of the effects of 'evil' are ludicrously understated:

> You lived for eight years with a criminal lunatic – that's enough to sap any woman's nerves.

> *(Towards Zero*, p. 188)

Since the effect of the plots has been to divorce moral and aesthetic feeling and to discourage identification, we can hardly feel terror or relief on behalf of the characters. Ironically, Christie's attempts as a twentieth-century Manichean to shore up these moral fictions serves only to underline their lack of serious application.

If she is a conservative, then, Christie's conservatism is not one which likes to dwell upon the processes of the law; she is much more likely to play down both retribution and punishment (the majority of her murderers commit suicide or remove themselves conveniently) and she evinces little interest in the judiciary. Poirot frequently feels sympathy for the murderer and may even turn a blind eye, most startlingly in *Murder on the Orient Express* where the crime goes unpunished. The most that Poirot will say is that, as a bourgeois, he 'disapproves' of murder but this hardly carries the passion of a hanging judge (who incidentally is made the equivalent of a mass murderer in *Ten Little Niggers*). Rather, Christie's conservatism is a species of compromise and withdrawal: it contrasts starkly with the grim eschatology and fever for retribution which can be found in the treatment of 'real life' crime in the press between the wars.

The family too is a similarly weak mainstay in the novels. Christie is clearly post-Victorian in her view of the large close-knit family as a

UNIVERSITY OF WALES LIBRARY SWANSEA

breeding ground for thwarted desires – 'inside the family one is apt to get too intense' (*Appointment with Death*, p. 33). The narratives always work to relieve rather than to stoke up feelings, and like the lonely mansions, sites of sensational fiction in the 1860s, which turn up modernised and spring-cleaned in Christie's fiction, the past becomes something to laugh at or shrug off (the Gothic house in *They Do It with Mirrors* is mockingly described as being 'best Victorian Lavatory period'). Part of the appealing fantasy of the whodunit lies not so much in the desire to murder one's relatives but in its being done for you with the minimum of pain and loss. Murder cheerfully rids the individual or the family once and for all of the burden of its past (what in *The Body in the Library* is called 'the yoke of perpetual remembrance' (p. 132), which families themselves impose). Murder is in many ways the nicest thing that can happen to a family, being, as Christie's second husband argued (without any trace of irony), a no-nonsense business without any 'degrading features'.[116] The fiction is particularly keen to despatch patriarchs and matriarchs (Mrs Boynton in *Appointment with Death*, Simeon Lee in *Hercule Poirot's Christmas*, Aristide Leonides in *Crooked House*); her families are usually replaced at the close by the modern couple, an ideal relationship, more instrumental, de-sentimentalised, and without fuss.[117]

It is the modern discourse of popular psychology with provides an appropriate language for Christie's version of conservatism, robbing her novels of their melodrama and lending a humanising, common touch to moral judgements. In the novels of the 1930s psychological explanation of crime and motivation is taken for granted and direct references to psychoanalysis are not unusual.[118] Both *The ABC Murders* and *Appointment with Death* feature an 'alienist' whose psychoanalytic assessment of the crime runs in parallel with Poirot's own speculations. Christie self-consciously describes the activity of the detective as similar to that of the analyst, looking for buried evidence in personality, for motivation in the hidden springs of character:

> We must look within and not without for the truth. We must say to ourselves – each one of us – what do *I* know about the murderer?
>
> (*The ABC Murders*, p. 121)

His job, like the analyst's, is to listen, as the reader does, to oral testimony, the story that each suspect gives of the past, in order to spot its gaps and absences. The crime is solved by the uncovering of a series of hidden relationships and past connections to which we are given clues in language:

> Speech, so a wise old Frenchman said to me once, is an invention of man's to prevent him from thinking. It is also an infallible means of discovering that which he wishes to hide.... A lie ... and by it I shall know the truth.
>
> (p. 164)

On the face of it Christie is modernist enough to recognise the force of unconscious desires: 'If we only knew what it is we know' sighs Poirot, or as the psychologist in *Appointment with Death* puts it,

> Below the decencies and conventions of everyday life, there lies a vast reservoir of strange things.

> (p. 62)

Much is made of the scientific language of psychology, reference to complexes, paranoia and fixation, and the reader is offered a clearly laid-out pathology of family life in *Appointment with Death*, in which a son is unable to leave his possessive mother, who is called a sadist and has formerly been a prison warder. Both the murder and the crime of family life are to be solved by talking. Yet the true criminal is never sick and always sane in the stories. In *The ABC Murders* the real murderer, like the man suspected of the crime, turns out to have an inferiority complex and conforms to the alienist's psychological profile; unlike him, the murderer 'knew what he was doing', is as sane as the next person and therefore able to be ostracised and punished. Christie's psychologising of crime is well-meaning, intended to broaden the reader's understanding of behaviour, but offers little resistance to a more conservative view of human nature.

For Christie in the mid–1930s psychological explanation appears as a form of common sense, a kind of secular morality with new claims to certainty and continuity which help us to form reliable judgements about the nature of human beings.[119] Psychological assumptions are commonplace in Christie's fictions – 'knowing just what makes the wheels go round' becomes a series of learnable axioms, whose effect is not to open up the Pandora's box of subjectivity but to limit and contain disorder, making the world knowable, manageable, liveable in. In all of Christie's fictions, as we listen to people's talk, there is only one correct interpretation of their stories, only one way of making sense and not, as psychoanalysis suggests, a labyrinth of interminable possibilities. Although Christie's psychologising of crime seems to take us further into the interior of modern life, we end up keeping our distance, armchair psychologists just as we are armchair sleuths.

Where Christie seems able to tie psychoanalytic insight back into a firmly conservative ideology is in her view of the unconscious as something wholly negative:

> There are strange things buried down in the unconscious. A lust for power – a lust for cruelty – a savage desire to tear and rend – all the inheritance of our past racial memories. . . . We shut the door on them and deny them conscious life, but sometimes they are too strong.

> (*Appointment with Death*, p. 29)

The unconscious is seen in an almost Darwinian light as the repository for purely anti-social desires of an unambiguously destructive kind, which represent traces of 'savagery' in the individual, a racial and social past which must be overcome and survived. This is a Freudian view without any of Freud's radical potential, without his notion of an organising drive to pleasure, or of desires apart from vicious ones, nothing erotic and nothing contradictory – only a bleak landscape of necessary repression, in which all instincts are to be denied.

Nevertheless in the context of the late 1930s even such a view could be marshalled as an argument against the excesses of fascism which comes in turn to be rejected as an outbreak of 'barbarism'. The same passage continues in a strong vein of declamation, rare in Christie's work:

> We see it all round us to-day – in political creeds, in the conduct of nations. A reaction from humanitarianism – from pity – from brotherly good-will. The creeds sound well sometimes – a wise regime – a beneficent government – but imposed by *force* – resting on a basis of cruelty and fear. They are opening the door, these apostles of violence, they are letting up the old savagery, the old delight in cruelty *for its own sake*! Oh, it is difficult – Man is an animal very delicately balanced. He has one prime necessity – to survive. To advance too quickly is as fatal as to lag behind. He must survive! He must, perhaps retain some of the old savagery, but he must not – no definitely he must not – *deify* it!
>
> (p. 29; Christie's emphasis)

Christie represented that breed of conservatism which preferred 'gradual progress on a loose rein'[120] and her work gives us an idea of how worried British conservatives sought to mark their difference from Nazism. For someone of Christie's mould fascism was a kind of hubris and its antidote was humility, the Christian 'contentment with lowly place' (p. 31), and an ideal of the balanced life. It is a message which she repeats two years later in *One, Two, Buckle My Shoe* (in America *The Patriotic Murders*), in which the stalwart and traditional conservative turns out to be power-mad dictator and where the obvious suspects, a younger generation, anarchists all and fanatical in their hatred of the past, are eventually left with the future in their hands. Christie's solution to the moral chaos of modernity is certainly not to call for strong leadership: she is closer to the mood of 'appeasement' in Britain in the late 1930s than to any warlike stance.

In the writing of the post-war years such quietism offered little resistance to the cruder expressions of social determinism which Christie discovered in genetic theory and the new 'science' of socio-biology. With her 'sweet, placid, spinsterish face, and a mind that has plumbed the depths of human iniquity' (*The Body in the Library*, p. 89), Miss Marple's feminine skills rest firmly on a belief in an unalterable human nature which is 'much the same wherever you find it'. Whilst she might seem democratic in her comparison of a Scotland yard chief to the local gardener, the occasional tetchy note creeps in.[121] Miss Marple is given to sharing her thoughts with the reader in a way that the Poirot of the inter-war years never did. This admission of a more subjective dimension gives the last few novels an unwonted Gothic tinge, at its most convincing in *Endless Night* (1967), an interior monologue which reads like a more paranoid *Roger Ackroyd*; *By the Pricking of My Thumbs* (1968) has a dead child walled up, and *Nemesis* (1971) uncovers the murder of a young girl who has lain buried for years in an overgrown garden. Consequently too, in this more alarming universe, the elevation of the importance of law and justice over compassion is more strongly asserted.

Nevertheless, what is most striking about these later novels is how little support Christie gives to the idea of a more authentic, proper past or to a reassertion of an older way of life. *At Bertram's Hotel* (1965) for example, takes the form of Miss Marple's literally revisiting that past in the shape of a decorous London hotel which appears not to have changed since Edwardian times. The hotel, an embodiment of an older and more gracious England, turns out to be a modern façade, a cover-up, in which the past has been staged as 'so much *mise en scène*' (p. 15), an ambiguous symbol for those who would like to cling to former glories, suggesting how much the invention of tradition always assumes new and modern forms. Christie may not entirely like the post-war world, but she is surely behind Miss Marple when the latter opines

> I learned (what I suppose I really knew already) that one can never go back, that one should not ever try to go back – that the essence of life is going forward. Life is really a One Way Street, isn't it?
>
> (p. 183)

Indeed the 'hidebound' Miss Marple spends part of her remaining years on a holiday in the Caribbean (another of Christie's island stories) and on a round-Britain coach tour.

The strongest conservative feeling in Christie's fiction lies not in an idealisation of the past, and certainly not in a planning of utopias, but in the desire to stay put in the present. In her later life that present could take place in a variety of modern settings: the world of the student hostel in *Hickory Dickory Dock* (1955), Chelsea bohemia in *The Pale Horse* (1961), or the drug scene in *Third Girl* (1966), but her emphasis is always upon continuities. Braving the terrors of the new housing development which has sprung up around St Mary Mead in *The Mirror Crack'd from Side to Side* (1962), Miss Marple soon loses her anxiety about 'the trousered young women, the rather sinister-looking young men and boys, the exuberant bosoms of the fifteen year old girls':

The new world was the same as the old. The houses were different, the streets were called Closes, the clothes were different, the voices were different, but the human beings were the same as they always had been.

(p. 19)

In the same vein, Tommy and Tuppence Beresford can put in periodic appearances throughout Christie's life and be emblematic not of the idea of social change, but of an essentially unchanging domestic ideal:

they liked themselves and each other and day succeeded day in a quiet and enjoyable fashion.

(*By the Pricking of My Thumbs*, p. 17)

Christie's conservatism is not romantic and individualist but matter of fact and conforming; not backward-looking, but inward-looking. Her dream is not of a grander, nobler existence but of a quiet life. Her characters are not the large and sweeping aristocrats of the literary imagination but little people, whose worst faults are to be too pleased with themselves in believing, as most of us do, that our own concerns are the only really legitimate ones. Her characters may be lovably absurd or mildly eccentric but the best of them are always better than they seem at first, and if she writes with an apologetic sense of the possible complacency of such a mentality, she is a supreme creator of it:

We are stupid, perhaps, and unimaginative – but not malicious. I myself am conventional and, superficially, I dare say, what you call smug. But really, you know, I'm quite human inside.

(*Towards Zero*, p. 89)

Agatha Christie's was one distinctly anonymous voice which helped to create and ratify the new accents of the British middlebrow between the wars and to shape that idea of a nation of benign crossword puzzlers and home owners, enjoying privacy and moderation and domestic consumption, and indifferent to Politics at large. It was a conservatism whose emotional pull was by no means confined to Tory voters and which found expression in a recasting of the British as a commonsensical, level-headed but reticent – 'retiring' – people, for whom the pleasures of domestic life were not merely a complementary alternative to those of the public sphere but infinitely superior: home, indoors, could provide proper values and behaviours which were not simply meant as an antidote to the pressures of work but which could become a model for a better public life. Such an ideal is there across inter-war culture in surprising places like the language of the Highway Code for example, first published in 1931, which turns the modern experience of driving into a hymn to safety and good manners; in the Reithian BBC; in the changing attitudes to royalty – summed up in the popular response to the death in 1936 of King George

Vth, 'that most home-loving of monarchs'[122] – 'He was a good little man and we'll miss him.'[123] It is there too in Beaverbrook's *Daily Express*, the paper with the largest circulation and growth between the wars, which had serialised *The ABC Murders*, and which best captured the tenor of that popular conservatism.[124] For Beaverbrook's readers there was nothing much wrong with the country and the paper carried on giving out cheerful bulletins right up until the outbreak of war. Like Rupert Bear arriving for tea by aeroplane, the new could simply make itself at home without threatening or changing the old.[125]

There are other ways in which we might seek to frame this story of adaptation to modernity, but in the end we might look for the special powers of Christie's conservatism not in any overt references to political ideologies or moral fictions but in her command of a language of domestication and privatisation, one whose casual self-effacement we can now recognise as a historical and social style: 'a peculiarly British inarticulacy'.[126]

Presently we had to cross the river, which we did on the craziest ferryboat you can imagine. To my surprise it was a mercy we ever got across, but everyone seemed to think it was quite usual.

It took us about four hours to get to Hassanieh, which, to my surprise, was quite a big place. Very pretty it looked, too . . . Dr Reilly was just as nice as ever, and his house was nice too, with a bathroom and everything spick and span. I had a nice bath, and by the time I got back into my uniform and came down I was feeling fine.

(Murder in Mesopotamia, p. 17)

For all its candid friendliness and unpretentious colloquialism such speech is as much about reserve as it is about expressivity: 'nice' is both chatty and impersonal, revealing nothing. It is an idiom which refuses to be clever, colourful or literary, but whose relaxed rhythms, despite being 'light and agreeable', nevertheless have the effect of warding off intimacy. With its stock modifiers and well-worn expressions, there is nothing arresting or memorable about this language except its incapacity to distinguish the individual; it is the linguistic equivalent of a 'blind' – in the fiction its very transparency is suspect. It can be a false, put-on *bonhomie* providing protective colouring for the speaker, and like an accent, tell us nothing about a person and everything about the social group with which they wish to be identified. In fact Christie 'spoke' much of her writing on to a dictaphone, aiming to catch the inflections of 'plain everyday conversational English'[127] through a very modern and mechanical means of reproduction.[128] What appeared to be random and informal was actually studied and controlled.

Nor is it coincidental that Christie's mouthpiece is one of those brisk and competent women who supply the likeable females of her whodunits.

If we see Christie as part of that reconstruction of the British middle classes after the war as an anti-romantic and home-oriented nation, we might notice how the formerly masculine qualities of reserve (the 'stiff upper lip') come to be claimed as a new kind of femininity. We might see in this retreat into hearty reticence a rejection of the intensity of feeling and uncontrolled expressivity with which the feminine had formerly been associated. For Christie it was by denying the feminine (in its late Victorian and Edwardian dress) and by ventriloquising what had been the male part, cheerily domesticated, that she could find ways of speaking as a modern woman. Reticence could be a form of conservative self-protection but also of new-found power.

We can recognise Christie's idiom as historically representative of that generation of respectable women who seemed to be incapable of speaking the language of romance after the trauma of war. It is as though reticence was one way of breaking that connection between femininity and the private world of feeling and spirituality, a femininity which had been the disastrous complement to that heroic masculinity destroyed in the war: without the one, the other made little sense; worse still, it might be accompanied by feelings of guilt, embarrassment and grief. Better to play down any signalling of sexual difference altogether. You did not need to be a feminist to declare, as one of Christie's characters does: 'I hate this differentiation of the sexes!' (*Appointment with Death*, p. 54).Christie's favourite women are 'nice' girls, like the plain Jane Grey in *Death in the Clouds* or Katherine Grey in *The Mystery of the Blue Train*, sensible and unassuming, whose sexuality is muted and lies in their quality of reserve. Like the owlish and mild-mannered heroes, they sacrifice the romantic in favour of the domestic. Self-reliant and quietly efficient, they are the antithesis of the fluttering female and have replaced that Edwardian sense of the feminine as symbolising 'higher things' with an even-tempered common sense and competence. Taken up by the cinema in the 1930s and '40s such an image could constitute a respectable eroticism of the kind represented by a Margaret Lockwood or Deborah Kerr.

Christie's own discretion was nowhere at its more blithely tight-lipped than in the autobiographical mode. She did write about her own life, in *Come, Tell Me How You Live* (1939), an account of time spent on archaeological digs with her second husband in the Middle East, and in *An Autobiography*, begun in 1950 and published posthumously in 1977, but both are masterpieces (and I use the word advisedly) of self-conceal-ment. Like the photographs she reproduces, her attempts at autobiography are painstakingly conventional portraits, and the reader searches in vain for shared confidences or divulged secrets, troubled self-criticism, worried heart-searchings. In fact the most fraught time of Christie's life – her disappearance after the discovery of her first husband's infidelity, and her consequent breakdown – is simply skipped between chapters. Intensely shy in public life, Christie's autobiography suggests not only that her private person was no different but that the taking over of a public voice about the self was a particularly anxious business for her generation of women.[129]

In her own life Christie's refusal of introspection seems to have enabled a positive self-image in direct contrast with the idea of womanliness prevalent in her youth. Her feminine ideal in middle age is of a humorous, unsentimental, level-headed companion, not the vulnerable, physically weak, ladylike woman whose life revolved around what she felt, and who was so beloved of romantic novelists. With her first husband, Archie Christie, it is as though she played out a more idealistic and vulnerable pre-war femininity; her second husband was apparently attracted to her by her sensible outlook, her warm good humour and her 'zest', a capacity to enjoy life without a hint of martyrdom or complaint. Her aim as a wife seems to have been to be 'agreeable', a word she uses most often of her father, and to cultivate 'a naturally happy frame of mind'.[130] Christie became a very large, robust woman, 'of irrepressible bounce' (the opposite of a frail flower), able to make jokes about her size and not afraid of appearing undignified: 'all things make her laugh' and the object of life becomes not sacrifice or service but harmless enjoyment.[131]

> You can enjoy almost everything. There are few things more desirable than to be an acceptor and an enjoyer.
>
> (*An Autobiography*, p. 135)

Christie's preferred self is profoundly anti-romantic and cannot resist puncturing every stirring moment with a sense of the ridiculous. The climax of *Come, Tell Me How You Live* is a potentially lyrical farewell to Syria as she looks across from the rail of the boat to the mountains of Lebanon, dim and blue against the sky. 'One feels poetical, almost sentimental' (p. 190) until in the next paragraph a crane drops a cargo of lavatory seats into the sea. Such bathos is a complex baulking of emotion: if it suggests a shying away from feeling, at the same time it allows a modern ironising which Christie clearly found liberating; it permits her a more capable and assertive sense of self. That refusal to explore or probe feelings also seems emancipating in giving Christie room in which to side-step much lass feeling: she does not present herself as a 'lady'. Although her social world includes the titled and famous, there is little attempt at exclusivity in the writing (her friends in the inter-war years appear not to belong to any coterie or cultural group but to the cross-class worlds of theatre and journalism); she is equally irreverent about, though respectful of, 'culture'; few bestselling authors can have been as eager to claim the role of philistine:

> This is not a profound book. . . . It is in fact, small beer – a very little book, full of everyday doings and happenings.
>
> (*Come, Tell Me How You Live*, p. 13)

Christie's autobiographical self is always a creature of the daylight. Her writing takes place as though lived in a permanent present and the prose has a childlike immediacy to it – 'Here we go! We are off!' – that reminds us of those rousing adventure stories for girls which became popular between the wars. Yet a schoolgirl is likely to be struggling toward a vocabulary of selfhood which includes all kinds of disturbing desires and Christie's is an adult resistance to such disturbance. Her girlish passions, 'the dog, bowls of Devonshire cream, apples, bathing' (ibid., p. 103) are not a pose but a felt identity – one maintained with such consistency over the years that such a refusal of the 'deadweight of interiority'[132] has to be seen as more than simply 'a lack of depth'.[133] Like her own chatty characters, Christie maintains a strict separation between a feeling, perhaps tortured private self and a cheerful public demeanour. Sexuality, unhappiness and despair – anything 'upsetting' has to be kept out of the public eye. The only acceptable face of independent modern femininity is that of the 'coper', usually the domestic manager, making the most of the little things in life.

Christie's autobiography is not written, as one might expect, around moments of deep feeling and psychic crisis or growth, but is organised by a celebration of the pleasurably routine and the familiar. What she likes best are the quiet moments of everyday life, not the highly dramatic ones. In her travels in the Middle East, Christie was able to find a correlative for her brand of conservatism in a version of Islam, which she believed to promote an acceptance of life and a desire to live fully in the present as well as to embody a rejection of romantic individualism. Her husband's archaeology, that most far-seeing of historical researches, seemed to reinforce this emphasis on the slowness of change and the continuity of human societies and to contradict, as she felt Islam did, the western view of history as a linear progress. Surely the closest Christie ever came to a conservative manifesto was in the thoughts she gave to her heroine in *They Came to Baghdad*? On an archaeological dig 'Victoria Jones' stops to muse on some prehistoric finds and to argue that 'Life's all the same really, isn't it – then or now?':

> those *were* the things that mattered – the little everyday things, the family to be cooked for, the four walls that enclosed the home, the one or two cherished possessions. All the thousands of ordinary people on the earth, minding their own business, and tilling that earth, and making pots and bringing up families and laughing and crying, and getting up in the morning and going to bed at night. *They* were the people who mattered.

(p. 167)

Of such small beer has a whole national consciousness been made.

For Christie the desert seems to have provided the necessary space from which to contemplate Englishness but it was also the place where she made herself at home. In an extraordinary passage reflecting on the women she had seen in Syria, Christie wrote:

> it must be nice to have your face veiled. It must make you feel very private, very secret . . . Only your eyes look out on the world – you see it, but it does not see you. . . .
>
> ((*Come, Tell Me How You Live*, p. 172; Christie's ellipses)

It is as though she envied Muslim women their *chador* as a kind of welcome camouflage and imagined it a source of private power. We might see it as both bold and unthinking of her to equate their experience with her own worship of privacy, though she certainly expresses a kind of cultural respect in not assuming the simple victimisation of those other women and in recognising something of their autonomy. For Christie there seems to be some special relief too at the idea of being de-sexualised in public, of a femininity no longer on display, which betrays the anxieties of her own age and class. Perhaps we should see a kind of protective veiling in the cheerful reserve of the Englishwoman between the wars and also, in the end, question its desirability as a form of power.

We might tell ourselves another story altogether about Christie's 'naturally happy frame of mind', and the limits of that Englishness, by looking at the work of her *alter ego* as a writer, 'Mary Westmacott'. Certainly *that* Christie seems to have been aware that the feminine qualities she values could easily become a straitjacket; that the kind of life she celebrates borders (at best) on the dangerously complacent, and that what passes for easy-going English diffidence could be another way of being powerful. In 1944 she published 'the book she had always wanted to write',[134] *Absent in the Spring*, written at white heat over one week during the war, whose middle-aged heroine, Joan Scudamore, is a woman remarkably like herself. Conventional, provincial, mildly Christian, Joan believes herself to be broadminded, generous and not given to histrionics. Returning from a visit to her daughter in Syria she finds herself stranded in the desert, left to wait for a vague train connection with no company except the houseboy (who does not count), nothing to read and nowhere to walk, except into the desert itself. Without the trappings of her social life she is forced to look inward and this epitome of the 'balanced *bien élevée* bourgeoise'[135] gradually goes to pieces as she contemplates the kind of woman she has become. Christie ruthlessly removes each plank of Joan's personality, revealing the selfishness and repressiveness which underlies each apparent virtue: Joan, who believes herself brisk and gay, is shown to be bossy and emotionally controlling, to be incapable of 'letting herself go' and to be sexually cold; instead of seeing her as a good wife and mother, she realises with horror that her family loathe and pity her. She goes back to England chastened, full of good intentions, only to pick up where she left off and remain exactly the same.

Absent in the Spring is an impressive novel by any standard, a *tour de force* of very concentrated power which as a bleak and economical study of self-deception points to a level of self-knowledge and indeed of self-hatred in Christie we might not suspect from reading her autobiography. Joan's story, however, ends with the coming of war and the novel is written with a hindsight which suggests that by 1944 that image of the coping, bright and emotionally reticent woman had met with a crisis of confidence. What had seemed desirable in 1938 or 1939 now seemed to be self-deluding and limiting. Although she may have had herself in mind, Agatha Christie would not have had to look very far for an image of British womanhood which caught the tone of well-bred conservatism in 1938. Joan Scudamore, the object of Agatha Christie's contempt in 1944, might be seen as a latter-day version of 'Mrs. Miniver' whose life and times are the subject of my next chapter.

Chapter 3

'Peace in our time': *Mrs. Miniver*

A NATIONAL HEROINE

Anyone who now encounters 'Mrs. Miniver', either in her original mani-
festation in the pages of *The Times* at the end of the 1930s, or translated
into the Hollywood heroine played by Greer Garson in the MGM film
of 1942, will be tempted to sneer at her. It is hard enough to believe that
the genteel musings of an upper-middle-class lady charting her life could
have seized the national imagination of British readers, let alone inspired
a film which won two Oscars as the motion picture of the year and was
hailed as 'one of the greatest films ever made'.[1] In its day the collected
book form of *The Times* columns was a bestseller, especially in the US
where it was Book of the Month. Roosevelt was to tell 'Jan Struther', its
author, that *Mrs. Miniver* had helped bring the Americans into the war
and Churchill maintained it did more for the Allied cause than a flotilla
of battleships.[2] Nowadays, the very mention of Mrs. Miniver or the
exploits of her family – husband Clem, children Vin, Judy and Toby – is
liable to summon up a snigger: surely the interest in such patriotic slush
has had its day?

For if the name now conjures up anything, then it is probably as a
byword for Britishness during the war that Mrs. Miniver stays in popular
memory. Greer Garson gamely seeing her family through the bombing
and her husband off to play his part at Dunkirk was for cinema audiences
around the world the epitome of the wartime spirit of England: a 'tribute
to the courage and character of ordinary people attacked by a force they
are determined to resist'.[3] The film, celebrated as 'one of the most effective
pieces of propaganda for Great Britain since the war began',[4] was also a
'woman's weepie' and Hollywood cheerfully went on to exploit Garson's
portrayal of the plucky housewife by giving her an incurable disease in
the mawkish 1950 sequel, *The Miniver Story*, and having her die bravely
in her rose-covered cottage. (One magazine in 1945 nominated her as
the archetypal 'womanly woman'.)[5] It was to commemorate the fiftieth
anniversary of the outbreak of the Second World War that the feminist

press, Virago, recently reprinted Jan Struther's book, with a Garson look-alike and V2s boldly on the cover.[6]

What then is one to make of the fact that the original *Mrs. Miniver* did not even have the glamour of wartime dangers to justify its sentiments? Struther's occasional columns first appeared in *The Times* in October 1937 and actually ceased in 1939, during the 'phoney' war: her Mrs. Miniver never even so much as smells a bomb. No Battle of Britain, no Blitz, no D-Day – it is the months of the Munich crisis which are the real setting for Mrs. Miniver's reflections on the quality of life. This is the Britain which expected and dreaded that the next war would be like the last, and which dutifully tried on its gas-masks in October 1938, only to put them away again a week later. Jan Struther's sketches are a personification, not of the spirit of the 1940s but of respectable England in the 1930s as it approached the war. Not wartime camaraderie but the mood of those many members of the Great British Public who favoured 'appeasement', hoping against hope that a peaceful agreement with Hitler would be possible and who refused to admit the inevitability of war. Nor is it a coincidence that Mrs. Miniver appeared in the paper most in agreement with the government's policy during the period: far from being an exemplary tale of the 'suffering and courage of civilians in all-out warfare', *Mrs. Miniver* is a feminine hymn to 'peace in our time'.[7]

But to see her as a Neville Chamberlain in petticoats is to descend into caricature again.[8] For there can be no doubt that *Mrs. Miniver*, even in her more pacific version, had already touched a chord. Over the two years in which the columns regularly appeared at the rate of never more than two or three a month, *Mrs. Miniver* became a minor cult, the columns signposted as 'special articles' in *The Times*' contents list unless more serious events overshadowed them.[9] She and her family were the subject of two fourth or 'light' leaders on the editorial page, cropped up in crossword clues and called forth a series of fan letters debating the domestic details of her life (what was her first name? how old was her eldest son? which route did she take on her holiday drive to Scotland?).[10] Letter writers stressed their identification with her (like her fondness for the sign pointing to 'the North' on the Finchley Road in London), and missed her presence when the sketches began to fall off after the outbreak of war:

Sir, – We, the undersigned sister and brother, believing ourselves to be as representative a pair of Miniver fans of opposite sexes as this country can produce, unite in the hope that the reactions of Mrs. Miniver to the war will from time to time be made public. We feel that in the present circumstances her peculiar brand of commonsense idealism, her search for the golden mean which provides the only true content, would be more than ever comforting. We should also be assured on seeing her name in the headlines that we were to be neither harrowed, lectured, exhorted, nor repressed. Most of what is written to-day has one object or the other, and a great deal has all of them, properly and necessarily, but the mind needs relief.

One of us recently overheard in the train the remark that life would be more bearable and moral [*sic*] would rise if only the 'Pools' would restart. Delightful as the suggestion sounds, it would not raise our moral, because we neither of us take part in the 'Pools'. Our desire is more modest and more easily met: we want Mrs. Miniver to restart.

We are, Sir, your obedient servants,

DOROTHY VINCENT.

CYRIL FALLS.[11]

What was that magical relief which Mrs. Miniver offered, and how did it become possible for the meditations of a middle-aged, middle-class, middlebrow woman to speak for the nation? And what, exactly, did she have to say?

NOT A 'PROVINCIAL LADY'

Jan Struther had already contributed one or two 'fourth or light leaders' to *The Times* when the editor, Peter Flemming, asked her to write a regular contribution aimed at cheering up the Court page. Usually given over to charting the appointments and arrangements of the royal family, the page consisted mostly of lists: 'The Season's List', 'Hunt and County Balls', marriages and memorials, honours, wills and bequests, who was who at the opening day at Goodwood or Ascot, ecclesiastical news and charity appeals. Actual journalism might branch out as far as meteorological or zoological titbits – The Popularity of the Canary', 'Tame Pheasants as Pets' – or readers might be tempted by scholastic miscellanea on antiquities like 'Early Coptic Sculpture'.[12] Apart from the bridge column, 'Mrs. Miniver' was to be one of the few more informal items and an innovation both in style and social register: Peter Flemming made the rather bold suggestion that Struther should perhaps write a diary of 'an ordinary sort of woman who leads a life rather like yourself'.[13]

In the first few sketches we learn that Mrs. Miniver leads the comfortable life of the professional middle class: like Jan Struther herself, she has a house in a Chelsea square, and a second home – 'Starlings' – in Kent, a professional husband, Clem, (a domestic architect with an office in Westminster) and three children, who exactly match in age Struther's own two boys and girl: Vin, Judy and Toby.[14] Unlike Struther, however, Mrs. Miniver is not a writer, even part-time: she has no job, but revolves around her home and her family, and her running of a small but efficient household of resident nanny, parlourmaid and cook. The sketches, which appeared at irregular intervals, take the form of accounts in the third person of Mrs. Miniver's daily life, though they usually centre upon her interior thoughts and reflections upon it.

There had already been a precedent for this kind of journalism with E. M. Delafield's *Diary of a Provincial Lady*, which appeared in the weekly *Time and Tide* in 1929 and reached a wider readership with its successful publication in book form in 1930.[15] *Time and Tide* was launched in 1920 as a child of the suffrage movement, aiming to keep up the momentum of feminist campaigns after the war. It was edited by the redoubtable Lady Rhondda and attracted such notable feminist contributors as Vera Brittain, Winifred Holtby, Cicely Hamilton and Rebecca West.[16] The contrasts between Delafield's *Provincial Lady* and *Mrs. Miniver* are instructive: to move from one to the other is not just to traverse a social register – Delafield's heroine is definitely nearer the top drawer – but also to encounter some of the contradictory shifts in outlook which those ten years had made with regard to ideals of femininity and of feminism itself. *Mrs. Miniver* is both a continuation of, and a reply to Delafield's proto-feminist account of domestic life, but where one of the effects of reading *A Provincial Lady* is to raise at least a gentle protest in her reader, Mrs. Miniver's journal of a housewife aims to reassure her.

On the face of it the provincial lady has a lot in common with Mrs. Miniver, facing similar dilemmas of the well-heeled domestic life, but for the former the trials of domestic life are mainly the matter for comedy. Delafield's heroine is stoically funny about the limitations of her lot, and expresses a rueful but hilarious sense of her own social inadequacies:

November 12th: Home yesterday and am struck, as so often before, by immense accumulation of domestic disasters that always await one after any absence. Trouble with kitchen range has resulted in no hot water, also Cook says the mutton has *gone*, and will I speak to the butcher, there being no excuse weather like this. Vicky's cold, unlike the mutton, hasn't gone. Mademoiselle says, '*Ah, cette petite! Elle ne sera peut-être pas longtemps pour ce bas monde, madame.*' Hope that this is only her Latin way of dramatizing the situation.

Robert reads *The Times* after dinner, and goes to sleep.

(p.5)

The aristocracy, in the daunting figure of the odious 'Lady Boxe' puts in a daily appearance, and much pleasure is derived from the heroine's secret exposé of her patronage.

December 16th: Very stormy weather, floods out and many trees prostrated at inconvenient angles. Call from Lady Boxe, who says she is off to the South of France next week, as she Must have Sunshine. She asks Why I do not go there too, and likens me to piece of chewed string, which I feel to be entirely inappropriate and rather offensive figure of speech, though perhaps kindly meant.

Why not just pop into the train, enquires Lady B., pop across France, and pop into Blue Sky, Blue Sea, and Summer Sun? Could make perfectly comprehensive reply to this, but do not do so, question of expense having evidently not crossed Lady B.'s horizon. . . .

Reply to Lady B. with insincere profession of liking England very much even in the Winter. She begs me not to let myself become parochially-minded.

(p. 16)

Delafield's browbeaten heroine is both an embodiment of, and a rebellion against pre-war expectations for women of her class, groomed solely for marriage and motherhood and to be 'an emotional serf'.[17] That she is one of many who found themselves 'poor managers and domestically inept',[18] does not lessen the hold which home duties have over her, even if it does add a humorous twist to the situation. Self-mockery is a ready but dubious form of feminine fortitude. Nevertheless the effect of the heroine's wry monologues on her own weaknesses are to turn her life into a triumph against adversity. As readers we are allowed to be a little superior to the provincial lady and her frailties as she guys herself, and whilst nothing in Delafield's writing actually challenges the status quo, the satire suggests some distance from its conventions, and provides some food for thought for those who wish to go further and complain outright about the narrowness of a woman's (or rather a lady's) lot.

By contrast, Mrs. Miniver is frankly celebratory of domestic life. Coming home from 'Starlings' to her London home, in the very first entry of 1937, no domestic disasters await her, only domestic peace:

Tea was already laid: there were honey sandwiches, brandy-snaps and small ratafia biscuits; and there would, she knew, be crumpets. Three new library books lay virginally on the fender-stool, their bright paper wrapper unsullied by subscriber's hand.

(p. 3)

She greets her familiar indoor life with mingled affection and some relief:

Her normal life pleased her so well that she was half afraid to step out of its frame in case one day she should find herself unable to get back. The spell might break, the atmosphere be impossible to recapture.

(p. 1)

The complete absence of irony or satire, or self-mockery in Jan Struther's pages suggests how much, at least in fantasy, a confidence about the pleasures rather than the pains of domesticity seemed appropriate to *The Times* reader in the late 1930s. It is a mark too of the new importance that the domestic and private life had come to assume in national life, that the daily thoughts of a woman at home could be seen as fit reading for a majority newspaper, rather than for a woman's magazine, or a specialist weekly like *Time and Tide*. Even *The Times* was becoming a 'family newspaper'.[19]

If behind Delafield's writing there is a buried sense of protest, any sense of coercion is missing altogether from *Mrs. Miniver*. If the fantasy within the provincial lady's life is to be free of her daily round (which she eventually manages in part by becoming a successful writer just like Delafield herself and buying a *pied à terre* in London), we should not conclude that such was the only compelling fantasy about home. It is not the fantasy of escape but of happily staying put which Mrs. Miniver invites her readers to share. The popularity of Mrs. Miniver's fictional mentality suggests how contradictory are the desires which an emphasis upon a home-centred femininity can call up in women. It is never simply a question of women 'colluding with' or being forced into accepting subordinating images of themselves, but rather of the complex and often conflicting ways in which the internalisation of such images manifests itself. The stress which was laid in the 1930s especially upon the primacy of home and motherhood in women's lives was by no means simply confining and could be re-imagined positively. In *Mrs. Miniver* 'being at home' is seen as offering new and different kinds of pleasure. Indeed the problem for many feminists, then as now, has been that the images of satisfied motherhood and comfortable home, far from being repugnant, are infinitely appealing.[20]

Mrs. Miniver's confident femininity partly expresses itself as a refusal of a sense of social inferiority and incompetence. Mrs. Miniver must have come as a breath of fresh air: she is content with herself and her appearance, enjoys being in her forties (she never seems to fret, as the provincial lady does, about her greying hair – and her husband has kept his good looks), and she seems to be in control of her life. She doesn't need feminism, being sensible, articulate and self-possessed. She is always unobtrusively right ('Well, no, thought Mrs. Miniver, not quite'). Not for her the anxieties of mixing socially, anxieties which Lady Una Troubridge neatly summed up in her book on modern etiquette: 'What will people say about me?' 'Will they think I'm dressed right?'[21] Time and again Mrs. Miniver successfully avoids collision with the Scylla and Charybdis of respectable life: she is never guilty of either social or sartorial solecism. In fact, quite the reverse: her personal appearance and behaviour are impeccable, her social aplomb unshakable: 'She never experienced shyness. She got on well with strangers' (p. 38).

Her 'crisp commonsense' sees her through most tricky situations, from negotiating the swing doors of a department store with her arms full, to dealing with a heated discussion at the dinner table. Confronted by a violent disagreement on blood sports and called upon to adjudicate (exactly the kind of delicate situation to paralyse an *ingénue*), Mrs. Miniver has just the right remark to hand:

> 'I think they are indefensible, but irresistible,' she answered. She had found through long experience that this remark usually closed the subject pretty quickly. It left very little to be said. Besides, she meant it.
>
> (p. 13)

Equally at home with spluttering colonels, ardent left-wingers and bellicose reactionaries, she is invariably used as a buffer at dinner parties. Her own conversation is always to the point; she is intelligent but does not try to be witty; she never utters 'bromides'.[22]

Like the provincial lady, however, she is not immune to being snubbed. Patronised on another occasion by someone of the Lady Boxe ilk, who vaunts the superiority of large places in Gloucestershire over small places in Kent, Mrs. Miniver is neither exasperated à la Delafield nor nonplussed by such insensitivity; she is sanguine and quietly amused, storing up the lady's rudeness as a tale to tell her husband: 'she said nothing: she did not want to interrupt what promised to be an enjoyable turn' (p. 87). Unrattled, she doesn't mind being thought 'ordinary' (she is a lady without being 'ladylike'), and is happy to stay in the wings, observing others' failings without protest, rather than demanding the limelight for herself. Her main role is that of peacemaker, always being tactful and tolerant, pouring oil on troubled waters in the family or amongst friends. She never *interferes*.

Etiquette amongst one's peers was one thing, but how to 'handle' the lower orders was at least as preoccupying for the middle-class woman as the fear of making a gaffe or committing a social blunder. After the war fewer and fewer working-class women, especially younger ones, were prepared to go into service, or did so only under pressure.[23] A note of muffled outrage starts to creep into many of the writings of well-to-do women, confronted by such 'desertion' and feeling concomitantly the security of their own positions undermined:

> There is no freedom with unwilling service, ill performed, higher wages demanded than can be paid, principles of cleanliness and orderliness violated, appearances having to be kept up and rigid rules adhered to for fear 'the girl will give notice'. It is tyranny,

was one view.[24] Whilst more self-assertion on the part of working women (and the possibility of jobs elsewhere) did no doubt play its part in eroding older codes of deference, the excessive frequency with which the idea of servants ruling the roost comes to feature in writing between the wars suggests how uneasy the upper-middle classes actually were about their own privileges. It was as much a compensating and reassuring fantasy on the part of well-off women in the period to believe that it was they who were at the mercy of the servant class and not vice versa. The psychic stress of 'managing' the servants which many bourgeois women must always have felt, no doubt became particularly nerve-wracking once the structures which shored up those differences were less emotionally convincing. 'Do you inwardly quail at the thought of a necessary "talking to" which has to be given to employees?' asked Lady Una.[25]

How comforting, then, to see yourself as well-meaning victim of working-class intransigence, as the provincial lady does, your lost command the fault of the mutinous crew behind the green baize door:

> *June 27th*: Cook says that unless I am willing to let her have the Sweep, she cannot possibly be responsible for the stove. I say that of course she can have the Sweep. If not, Cook returns, totally disregarding this, she really can't say what won't happen. I reiterate my complete readiness to send the Sweep a summons on the instant, and Cook continues to look away from me and to repeat that unless I *will* agree to having the Sweep in, there's no knowing.
>
> This dialogue – cannot say why – upsets me for the remainder of the day.
>
> (*A Provincial Lady*, p. 80)

Mrs. Miniver's life, on the other hand, is far less emotionally taxing, her household being much smaller and relatively free from some of the fraught emotional load of the Edwardian home. Hers is an ideal half-way house between those encumbered establishments and the servantless home. She is not overly conscious of being the mistress and her relations with her employees are rarely discussed. Nor is she entirely dependent on resident staff to meet her every need; when necessary she briskly buys extra help in. One cannot imagine Delafield's heroine actually going 'in search of a charwoman' to do for one of her dinner-parties, and knocking on her door at her home in a 'red-brick jungle' of municipal dwellings. Mrs. Miniver makes a virtue of necessity, tackling such tasks in the spirit of adventure and chatting amiably to 'Mrs. Burchett', 'a large, neat, cheerful woman'. Mrs. Burchett is as much a figment of the imagination as the tyrant in the basement, a 'capable pearl' who 'beams reliably' and leaps at the chance to wash Mrs. Miniver's dishes, even though she doesn't need the money:

> 'To tell you the truth,' she added with gusto, 'I was just wishing summing like this would turn up. Not that I need to do cleaning at present, really, Burchett and the boys all being in work. . . . Of course, charing . . . I suppose it's only like clearing up somebody else's mess instead of your own, but it does make a change . . . .'
>
> (p. 30)

What is striking about this encounter, however, is not its wishful thinking, but that Mrs. Miniver goes on to reflect how much Mrs. Burchett has in common with her best friends – a zest for life – which makes them either 'merry, or wise or comforting or revealing'. Mrs. Burchett is of this temper, and for a moment at least, Jan Struther's one-dimensional portrait goes beyond that of the cheerful Cockney, if not quite managing to give her a life and personality of her own.

For readers of *The Times* the idea of cultivating friendly relations with servants might still be a revolutionary one. Nevertheless Jan Struther's columns do give us a sense that more than one reader might be feeling emancipated by the changes in class relations, and buoyed up by the possibility of more cross-class 'fraternisation'. A coming to terms with 'the cook in and out of the dining room to borrow the *Daily Herald*' which caused many less forward-thinking householders both bewilderment and anger, had its gains, not least the relief which those like Virginia Woolf felt at not having to worry constantly 'about the question of Nellie'.[26] Paradoxically, as more and more of the burden not just of home management, but even housework, fell upon the middle-class housewife and less could be delegated to a household of servants, some new emotional freedoms as well as new limitations emerged. Rather than seeing the identification of respectable women with homemaking in the 1930s as purely negative in its effect, and a mere repetition of the 'incarceration in the private sphere' of the Victorian home, we might reflect upon just how different these 'private spheres' were.

Domesticity for Mrs. Miniver may be a bore but it is not a prison. The well-off woman of the 1930s could indeed be far freer than her Victorian grandmother, wrestling with the Angel in the House, or her daughter in the 1950s suburb, servantless. Mrs. Miniver is certainly not confined to the house. With 'help' in the kitchen and nursery, she need never be child-ridden: she and her husband go away alone as often as they please. She can drive the car and make her own expeditions wherever she wishes, have lunch with a woman-friend or even a 'man-friend' (provided he is suitably unattractive, as no doubt 'Badger', the absent-minded professor she keeps in tow, is). With both the running of the house and of her children pretty much left to others, being a married woman was itself in the process of being redefined.

The married state, for women of Mrs. Miniver's class, had long been the only way of being truly grown-up. It was the only way of being taken seriously by society at large, of 'joining in', as Penelope Mortimer describes her own sense of the independence she sought through her marriage in 1938[27] Being a married woman implied and even allowed some knowledge of sexual matters; it meant you gained a place and status and avoided the dreadful dependencies and stigma of an extended girlhood: 'an inferior state from which escape was desirable at any cost', as E. M.

Delafield put it in one of her harsher novels, *Thank Heaven Fasting* (1932).[28] As a girl growing up before the war, Monica, the repressed and polite heroine,

> would not have been encouraged to read the newspaper, even had she wished to do so, and it would have been bad manners to read a book unless her mother had also been doing the same.
>
> (p. 65)

Ruled over by her domineering mother, Monica finally escapes to marriage with a pompous, ineffectual man and such a fate seems infinitely preferable to her than spinsterdom, as the bleak closing lines convey:

> she was safe for ever. There was no need to be afraid, or ashamed or anxious, any more.
>
> (*Thank Heaven Fasting*, p. 222)

In this novel, Delafield comes much closer to exploring uncomfortable truths about the women of her circle than in *A Provincial Lady*, representing as she does through the character of the sheepish Monica those legions of women for whom it was the vulgarity associated with the idea of working for a living which made marriage the only option, as much as any exclusion by men from the ranks of employment. To become a married woman was to gain power, not least over your inferiors, but also to remove 'the reproach amongst women'[29] and to be no longer in the twilight world of the 'young people'. It is then only a half-truth to argue that 'the search for freedom and independence would be brought to a halt by marriage',[30] since for many middle-class women, marriage gave them the only freedom they had known. One of the problems which feminists continue to face, then as now, in arguing against 'the slavery' of the married state, is that for many women it brings a huge improvement in the quality of their lives: for the middle-class woman it could actually mean she was now in a position to give orders.

Though she is attempting to capture the attitudes of earlier times, Delafield's novel is very much of its own time in dissecting the role of marriage in women's lives. Perhaps the gradual shifting of emotional intensity and expectation away from relationships with servants may have contributed to a sharper focusing of attention upon sexual relations within marriage: what might be expected of husbands becomes a frequent topic of debate, for feminists and anti-feminists alike, within women's magazines and more mainstream discussion, in a way which would have been unthinkable before the war.[31] Interestingly, we hear nothing of Mrs. Miniver's growing up or of her romantic longings. There are no scenes of courtship to interrupt her thoughts or even passages of sentiment between her and Clem. She never looks back to the heyday of her youth but is firmly and happily in the present. Life after the wedding is what interests her most, and such magic moments as she shares with her husband are those which involve a degree of reflection on the married state itself: marriage is the subject of energetic analysis in ways which would have baffled and shocked the Victorian or even Edwardian matron. *Mrs. Miniver* is typical in assuming that a woman's thoughts on being married could be suitable for public consumption and discussion.

Mrs. Miniver's marriage is modern in being semi-detached, spacious and companionate: its pleasures are mutual. For her

> the most important thing about marriage was not a home or children or a remedy against sin, but simply there being always an eye to catch.
>
> (p. 13)

When they are not exchanging glances, she and 'Clem' save up the daily incidents of their lives to tell each other in the evening:

> This was the cream of marriage, this nightly turning out of the day's pocketful of memories, this deft habitual sharing of two pairs of eyes, two pairs of ears.
>
> (p. 86)

She and her husband, Mrs. Miniver muses affectionately, are like two circles in a Venn diagram, overlapping, but not too much. Theirs is a 'partnership', a careful balancing of the books, which involves both addition and subtraction, within a limited company. If the metaphors from accountancy seem rather calculating, the fiscal analogies do at least imply contractual responsibilities, and those in turn promise some independent rights – and is there a hint of buried romanticism in the final image?

> She saw every relationship as a pair of intersecting circles. The more they intersected, it would seem at first glance, the better the relationship; but this is not so. Beyond a certain point the law of diminishing returns set in, and there aren't enough private resources left on either side to enrich the life that is shared. Probably perfection is reached when the area of the two outer crescents, added together, is exactly equal to that of the leaf-shaped piece in the middle.
>
> (p. 40)

Here in sum is the 'equal but different' view of the sexes which was espoused by inter-war feminists like Vera Brittain, a modern reworking of the philosophy of 'separate spheres' of activity and personality for women and men, which, though it clung to certain rather fixed notions of what was feminine and masculine (child-rearing, for example, was always assumed to be the woman's business), nevertheless allowed for some idea of female autonomy.

In another disquisition upon marriage, Mrs. Miniver daringly welcomed those couples who are happy to be invited to dinner without their partners.

'To avoid turning into Siamese twins had been one of their private marriage vows' (p. 47), and any loss of romantic oneness which such formulations imply has to be weighed against the gains in independence. In the image of the companionate marriage we have come a long way from the child-wife of the patriarchal Victorian marriage in which the woman remained dependent upon, and protected by, her father-husband.

Mrs. Miniver's idea of partnership may not be exciting, but neither is it brutal or degrading. As a reaction against earlier cultural views of femininity which had relentlessly eroticised all aspects of women's appearance and behaviour, the 1930s often appear passionless. Yet no doubt there was much to be said for the introduction of separate beds, a new feature of respectable married life in the period. Usually cited as testimony to the prudishness of the middle-class wife, it perhaps had the advantage of making sexual relations potentially a matter of choice rather than conjugal right. Similarly, life with the colourless suburban husband, an image of gentle masculinity much reproduced and pilloried in the period, could allow women infinitely more breathing space than life with the masterful male. If it lacked romantic thrills, it also lacked emotional thraldom.

Motherhood too has little sentimentalism attached to it, and even fewer of the pleasures of self-sacrifice: Mrs. Miniver wouldn't dream of doting upon, or losing herself entirely in, her children. It is certainly not the centre of her femininity as it may have been for her mother or for her daughters in the 1950s. The Minivers only spend one weekend in the month purely upon activities with the children; other times are spent away with one's companion, without the brood. This is not the motherhood of Bowlby, Winnicott or Spock, though it bears some relation to the more free-thinking fresh air regimes of Dr Truby King in which 'baby' is encouraged into independence and separation from the earliest moments.[32] Certainly one can imagine Mrs. Miniver approving of Truby King's no-nonsense tones; her own lack of gush and sentiment about her children puts her firmly at a distance from them. Such a distance could indeed seem cold but it was meant, in theory, and at best, to be thoughtful and respectful. Over and again one has the sense of Jan Struther's generation reversing the patterns of their pre-war youth and doing all they can to avoid the emotional hothouse atmosphere of their own childhoods.

With a less romantic sense of childhood, with relatively little by way of child-oriented consumerism, and as yet no languages of 'teenage' or 'adolescence', it is adulthood which in the 1930s is at a premium for children and grown-ups alike. Though she may tend to see her offspring in rather a self-satisfied way as miniature versions of herself, Mrs. Miniver respects in them their own need for independence. Putting words into her daughter's mouth, one exchange suggests how much approval is given to not fussing over, or 'molly-coddling' children:

'Why don't you like Marigold's mother? asked Mrs. Miniver. 'She's always very kind to you. And she's frightfully fond of children.'

'Oh, I know. She told me so. But you see, when people are frightfully fond of children you never know whether they really like *you* or not, do you?' . . .

'And besides,' Judy went on, 'she makes such a Thing about everything, if you know what I mean.'

Mrs. Miniver knew only too well. She had been at school with Marigold's mother.

'And do you happen to know,' she asked, 'what Marigold thinks of me?'

'Oh, she likes you,' said Judy. 'She says you leave people alone.'

(p. 80)

Perhaps only the English middle classes between the wars managed to construe the undemonstrative mother as paradoxically the most loving.

As a modern mother, Mrs. Miniver tries to reason with her children, treating them as thinking persons. Remembering how she was 'told to run and play in the garden' in 1914, and how she had then been plunged into a mindless 'orgy' of jingoism – 'of boycotting Grimm and Struwwelpeter, of looking askance at their cousins' old Fraulein' – she determines to behave differently with her own children:

this time, at any rate, children of Vin's and Judy's age had been told beforehand what it was all about, had heard both sides, and had discussed it themselves with a touching and astonishing maturity.

(p. 61)[33]

Her children are indeed paragons of sturdy independence, always busy and co-operative little bees in the holidays, intent on making things or playing word games; their adventures are of the 'Swallows and Amazons' variety, wholesome and educative, and marvellously enterprising:

their main occupation had been fitting up one of the outhouses like the cabin of a ship, with built-in bunks, straw palliasses, and a locker full of imaginary charts. (Vin drew the charts, Judy painted them and Toby put in the casual dolphins.) But they had also made a brick-kiln in the kitchen garden and baked in it at least a dozen quite satisfactory bricks . . . enough to give them the feeling that if they were ever wrecked on a desert island they would soon be able to run up a house or two.

(p. 26)

For Mrs. Miniver family feeling is 'an invisible network of affectionate understanding' (p. 19) between separate and separable persons. Whilst she acknowledges the miseries of motherhood, 'the morning sickness; the quite astonishing pain', she has no wish to dwell on either its troughs or its peaks. So semi-detached a mother did Mrs. Miniver appear to be that a fourth leader in *The Times* felt obliged to reprimand her for not being more able to come down to her children's level: 'Mrs. Miniver, we know, was an eldest child and perhaps she was early led into the way of holding rather aloof from the little ones.'[34] More than a slight shade of disapproval crept into the description of the way in which she 'sat and watched and savoured' her children's activities without attempting to join in them. Nor was *The Times* entirely happy with Mrs. Miniver's views on marriage, and another jocular leader was devoted to speculations about Clem, and his need to be seen as more than 'an apanage or emanation of his brilliant wife'.[35] Though its tone was lighthearted, one senses an unease and a ruffled male pride which even in such trivial matters needed some soothing. A slightly nasty edge was applied to descriptions of Clem's 'fastidious' and 'critical lady', as though the discovery that women were capable of assessing both their husbands and their marriages suggested they were taking too much on themselves.

Far from seeing the inter-war period as one in which women simply went 'back to home and duty', we need to ask ourselves how their conception of both had changed. If Mrs. Miniver was a kind of ideal, then by the standards of earlier times it is an extremely self-centred woman who emerges. Such an effect is strengthened further by the interesting lack of familial commitments and obligations in her life: most notably of all, she has no parents, and especially no mother or mother-in-law to contend with. Gone is the pre-war generation with their old-fashioned views, and except for an eccentric and suitably unthreatening aunt Hetty ('glorious woman'), her nearest relatives (brother and sister-in-law) live conveniently in Scotland. Mrs. Miniver is her own role model, only accountable to her peers. What's more she has no biography, no past and no future.

It seems then that whatever the actual familial pressures which women were expected to cope with, they were by no means acceptable duties. The modernism of many women writers in the period, whether feminist or no, took the form, in particular, of exploring or rejecting the tortured feelings between mother and daughter. Works like May Sinclair's experimental *Mary Olivier* (1919) and Radclyffe Hall's *The Unlit Lamp* (1924) broke new ground in probing the psychological toils of the mother–daughter relationship and especially the predicament of the unmarried daughter left at home, whilst a novel like *Thank Heaven Fasting* was outspoken in its condemnation of the possessive mother who drives Monica into matrimony.[36] There is a sense in which both feminism and new ideas of femininity in the 1930s, even where they tied women to the home, were inspired by not wanting to be like mother, whose image was always one of confinement. *Mrs. Miniver* is both liberated and cowardly in side-stepping the issue altogether.

What *Mrs. Miniver* offered readers was a utopian distance from marriage, motherhood and home. For if, as the ideal modern woman, neither husband, children nor housewifery dominate her life, the search for privacy does. Mrs. Miniver's musings are one long celebration of its joys, of that retreat into self-containment which has often been a woman's vision of paradise. Mrs. Miniver has whole days of the solitude in which to think her own thoughts. Far from domesticity being imagined as the end of the middle-class woman's independence it can be recast in the inter-war years as the very source of her private and expressive consciousness. From *Mrs. Miniver* we gain some sense of why privacy comes to be such a valued part of the middle-class woman's life.

Privacy does indeed afford some liberties. In a culture where women are expected to be available and accessible, and indeed accountable, the privilege of time to oneself can be the most primary form of autonomy; withdrawal from the needs of others, even where it seems passionless, the route to self-determination. The episodes of *Mrs. Miniver*, like all journal keeping, are efforts perhaps at such self-ownership, exercises in claiming a private space. For what might now strike us, looking again at that home-coming, is just how unpeopled it is:

> She rearranged the fire a little, mostly for the pleasure of handling the fluted steel poker, and then sat down by it. Tea was already laid: there were honey sandwiches, brandy snaps and small ratafia biscuits; and there would, she knew, be crumpets. Three new library books lay virginally on the fender-stool, their bright paper wrappers unsullied by subscriber's hand. The clock on the mantlepiece chimed, very softly and precisely, five times. A tug hooted from the river. A sudden breeze brought the sharp tang of a bonfire in at the window. The jigsaw was almost complete but there was still one piece missing. And then, from the other end of the square, came the familiar sound of the Wednesday barrel-organ, playing, with a hundred apocryphal trills and arpeggios, the 'Blue Danube' waltz. And Mrs. Miniver, with a little sigh of content-ment, rang for tea.
>
> (p. 7)

If this is a private sphere, it is a remarkably solitary one. There are no obtrusive servants, but also no husband, no children, no friends or neigh-bours to complete a welcome round the hearth. Instead each one of Mrs. Miniver's senses – touch, taste, sight, smell and hearing in turn – is catered for in splendid isolation. The home has been arranged all for her: it is her 'space' and no one else's. And importantly it has become the place where she alone can be perceptive and aware. *Mrs. Miniver* suggests how far in the late 1930s it was possible to come from the attack on home as the place where the quest for selfhood was stifled by familial and collective duties: instead we have a new kind of ideal in which the home is seen by the woman herself to be the making of her. It is not just the protection of privacy which enables Mrs. Miniver to remain Panglossian – never bored or depressed, never irritable or martyrish but full of a positive attitude toward life – it is her confidence that home is where she can be most expressive of her 'self'.

MIDDLE-CLASS WITHOUT TEARS

It would be tempting to see Mrs. Miniver's appeal as simply one of social snobbery – even for a member of the comfortable classes, she leads a privileged life. Mrs. Miniver has very good connections. Her home may be in the 'raffish'[37] Chelsea rather than the more salubrious Mayfair, but there are enough of the traces of 'society' and the season in the calendar of her days to suggest that if the Minivers are not actually from the top drawer, they are not too much below it. The Minivers spend three out of four weekends away, sometimes at their own place in Kent (where they buy an adjoining cottage just for fun) or on country house visits:

> Every year without fail Mrs. Miniver received an invitation written in a sloping Victorian hand on lavishly stout cream-laid. . . . The letter began with old Lady Chervil's unvarying formula:
>
> > My dear Mrs. Miniver,
> >   Chervil and I shall be delighted if you and your Husband will stay with us from Friday 19th to Monday 22nd November.
>
> Mrs. Miniver tossed the letter over to Clem. . . . They always went to Chervil.
>
> (p. 28)

Mrs. Miniver's husband (the impossibility of calling him Mr. Miniver suggests how much his wife takes precedence) receives shooting invitations and they go to Scotland for the open season, where a brother-in-law is McQuern of Quern. Their eldest son, following in his father's footsteps, is at Eton (as a casual reference to 'Long Leave' reveals); eccentric spinster aunts have houses within boating distance of the school and think nothing of fetching the silver teapot out for tea in the strawberry beds; and nieces are finished in Switzerland. Meanwhile London life is a busy social round of dinner parties (where one might discover an ageing colonel who knew one's uncle – Torquil Piggott – in Singapore), sherry parties, chamber concerts, dress shows; a stylish existence with friends whose improbable but impressive appellations include a few handles – 'old Lady J' (p. 46) – and a sprinkling of the double-barrelled (the Lane-Pontifexes, for one). Even Mrs. Miniver's dentist uses 'rather good shaving soap' (p. 82).

Clearly Struther made her heroine a cut above many *Times* readers, adding, no doubt, to her attraction. The average member of the inter-war middle classes was much more likely to be pottering in an herbaceous border in the suburbs or gazing down the gravel drive in one of the dormitory towns, than strolling regularly to Hyde Park. Social life might be expected to revolve around occasional bridge parties and making the special trip up to town for a linen sale, or a new hat, rather than lunching regularly with tame aristocrats in the metropolis. Mrs. Miniver may not have a chauffeur but she is not a provincial homemaker; early on we see her at pains to dissociate herself from the more humdrum kind of middle class. When she ritually buys an engagements book, (itself a sign of a certain standard of living) she rejects the plain, serviceable one for a green lizard extravagance at a 'fabulous price' (p. 22). (Naturally the 'cheap leatherette', which would make one's life look squalid, doesn't get a look in.) Not wanting her activities to be 'soberly confined' to a 'pleasant', 'sturdy', 'honest' little brown calf volume, hers is not the life of the stolid middle class, with its Victorian virtues and work ethic. Instead she chooses one with 'flair'. As a member of the professional middle class she is eager to avoid the taint of 'trade'.[38] One can only imagine the agonies of those less affluent readers for whom Mrs. Miniver was probably an unspoken guide to etiquette, as they tried to tread that thin line between the sensible and the dull, the stylish and the frivolous.

Yet Mrs. Miniver is a past mistress at avoiding the snobberies of her kind. Her son, we learn, hasn't been made at all grand by his public school; she has no debutante daughter so we never know whether she could have afforded the season. Material success means little to her for we hear next to nothing of the usual status symbols, the furnishings of her house, what make of car she has, what food she eats. She clearly distances herself, too, from those matrons of Kensington and Brompton, who like their children's perambulators are 'well-built, well-sprung, well-upholstered'. She is not guilty in her pages of a single put-down. Above all, Mrs. Miniver is not a socialite, her diary is not a gossip column record of the rich and famous. Her concerns and worries are personal and general: trips to the dentist, buying a child's doll, Christmas shopping, – none of them needs any special *entrée*. She may sprinkle her appointments book with titles but her attitude towards the aristocracy appears to be far from fawning. It is cleverly not deferential but gently mocking 'how unpleasing, musically, is the sound of a pack of upper-class English voices in full cry'; though one numbers them amongst one's friends, the aristocracy are 'museum pieces' who live their lives 'in inverted commas' (p. 11) and shiver in badly heated, barnlike, homes. Mrs. Miniver's patronage of the nobility must have been pure pleasure to her readers.

Not only is she quite unapologetic about the norms and decencies of her world (her own standards of comfort are almost reprehensibly high, she tells us complacently), more than that, she is positively proud of them. Her place on the Court page was a fitting one, suggesting as it did that there was nothing amiss in 'reading about what the King was doing for lunch' and 'what Mrs. Miniver was doing for tea',[39] and when the Queen mother is at Sandringham and Mr Chamberlain in Edinburgh, Mrs. Miniver is watching a Scots blacksmith remove his trousers and toss the caber only a few miles away. We cannot all make Ascot, Mrs. Miniver implies, but we do lead equally full and rewarding lives. *Mrs. Miniver* is a measure of how far the ideal good life could now, in the late 1930s, be a middling sort of life.

For less privileged readers it was possible to ignore her upstairs drawing-room and her patrician friends, and merely revel in being one of a happy breed. *Mrs. Miniver* offered her readers a species of solidarity: ours, she seems to say, is the modern class, no longer wanting to ape the aristocracy but confident of its own way of doing things. Ours is the good life. It is the Mrs. Minivers of the inter-war world who could be imagined as the backbone of the nation and Jan Struther writes with an immense confidence in, and sense of the rightness of the values she offers, such as perhaps was only really possible in the late 1930s. There is nothing of that hectoring or complaining note which comes to be associated with so many upper-middle-class voices after the war; hers is not yet the voice of the 'Establishment', being modern not old-fashioned, neither starchy nor condescending.

Naturally such a charmed life was a gift to the satirically minded. The complete lack of discomfort in Struther's writing made it an easy target for accusations of self-satisfaction. What the parodies of *Mrs. Miniver* revealed, however, were the kinds of anxiety and defensiveness Struther's heroine tries to rise above. One of the *Times* leader writers (a stable which included Struther herself) could not resist a little clubmanship and attempted to pull her down a peg or two further, hinting at her being *nouveau riche*: her house, 'Starlings', it suggested, was probably a 'conversion'. It might even contain (most unlikely given the appointments of her London home) those horrors, 'a lounge hall and a loggia'. Although we hear absolutely nothing of Mrs. Miniver's appearance or dress, *The Times* insists that she is 'a little lady', 'exquisitely feminine', 'at once dainty and cosy and rather grand'.[40] (Even if she is a bit stand-offish with her children.) It is as though the very idea of being happy, middle-class and female is offensive in itself: Mrs. Miniver, with her chronicles of middle-class content, seems to have inspired the same kind of spiteful fascination as Jilly Cooper was to, writing in *The Sunday Times* forty years later. One hilariously violent letter writer to *The Times* who admitted to being an avid reader, expressed both his social and sexual loathing in hoping that a bomb would drop on her and Clem run off with another woman.[41]

Even as reputable a literary gentleman as E. M. Forster felt obliged to expose her to a protracted snub, in a piece which revealed more about his own social snobberies than Jan Struther's. For Forster the problem with

Mrs. Miniver was exactly what made her appealing, the fact that she was neither truly patrician nor healthily plebian, and had none of the largesse or devil-may-care gaiety which Forster nostalgically ascribed to those who have everything or nothing. She came instead from the class 'to which most of us belong', evocatively described as 'the class which slaughtered the aristocracy and has been haunted ever since by the ghost of its victim'.[42] Such a view might be a fair summary of his own class feelings, and of the romantic Toryism of an older, pre-war generation (it is incidentally a précis of the plot of Du Maurier's *Rebecca*), but Forster wholly misjudged Mrs. Miniver. Far from being haunted by the aristocracy, Mrs. Miniver is relatively uninterested in them, and one suspects that it is this faith in her own sort that is the hidden cause of Forster's anger. Where Forster has no choice but to look backwards to the days (1850? 1890? 1914?) when the three classes were properly arranged – 'there was a harmony in the fabric of England which has now been lost' – Mrs. Miniver is not trying to copy the past, and would surely have felt no sympathy with Forster's belief that 'our minds still hanker after the feudal stronghold which we condemned as uninhabitable'. Perhaps that is why Forster's essay ends with what seems an arbitary and almost incoherent dismissal of her in the face of the levelling effects of political movements in the world. Far from her belonging to a museum of inconsequential national types, Forster has an inkling that hers might be the sort that inherits the earth, and this is the prospect which alarms him. In his distaste for Mrs. Miniver, it is hard not to see a distaste too for a more democratic and egalitarian society.

How much more acceptable to the middle classes is the literature of their own anxieties! What Jan Struther's critics found unbearable was her airing of their clean linen in public: her outrageous suggestion that a comfortable life had a lot to be said for it, and that the middle classes, however they are fraught with social conscience and pricked with self-hatreds, do also have a good time. Far from bemoaning her lot, envying or resenting others, or seeing herself as having fallen on hard times, Mrs. Miniver expressed only the positive side of life: hers was a life without the troublings of destructive fears and unruly desires: she offered her readers the pleasures of peace of mind. In her magical transformation of daily life the middle was always a safe, and not a slippery place to be, a comfortable and not an awkward position. It was a fantastic, fictional resolution of anxiety – no one's daily life could be quite so wrinkle-free – but it bore a direct relation to the fact of bourgeois contentment, which many readers both had as a social ideal and were intermittently able to achieve. The life of a Mrs. Miniver was a good life, even if you could only get it occasionally. Indeed the 1930s were actually propitious and prosperous years for many within the very broad band of the middle class.

In their refusal to have anything in common with her, those who carped at Mrs. Miniver remind us unwittingly of exactly why she was so popular. So much energy within the middle classes was devoted to disavowing each other, and to disowning their own 'middle classness', that Mrs. Miniver's blithe spirit made a welcome change. When one considers how absolutely essential to the nature of their social life are the competitive divisions between and within the middle classes, and how much more this establishing of caste and of minor aristocracies of taste matter, one can see why Mrs. Miniver afforded considerable relief. If there is no stable middle-class identity, only different variations of unsurenesses and self-assertions, and different membership qualifications, how reassuring are those who insist that their comfortable houses are built on rock and not on shifting sands.

Nor was Jan Struther's version of 'commonsense idealism' and the search for the golden mean an entirely ignominious way of going about life. In her close identification with her heroine, Struther offered the standards of 'making the best of life', 'putting your best foot forward', and a celebration of the enjoyment of living which are now unfashionable, even embarrassing attitudes. They certainly seem to have spoken to many in the 1930s, and to have offered, in some sort, a kind of secular spirituality.[43] Benevolence and a celebration of life's pleasures may not be sufficient as a philosophy of life, but it is at least as honest as a bad-tempered denial of their existence. Jan Struther, as a private person, seems to have lived happily enough within her own bubble of optimism: it would be churlish to try to puncture it. And if Mrs. Miniver seems never to suffer from her unconscious, so be it. She lives in the world of faery. As for the Jan Struthers of this world, who can say? Maybe they too found a way of being middle-class without tears.

ETERNITY FRAMED IN DOMESTICITY: THE MAKING OF A LADY WRITER

Jan Struther belonged to that tribe of professional writers and literati who occupy that vast and ill-defined middle ground between the dedicated artist and the full-time journalist. A frequent contributor to *Punch* and the *Spectator*, she had already published two volumes of poetry, some children's verse, had edited R. L. Stevenson's *Kidnapped*, and a collection of her articles, *Try Anything Twice*, appeared in 1938.[44] In style and content these short pieces match the tenor of *Mrs. Miniver* and confirm that Struther's forte lay in working up some incident of everyday life, or examining some turn of common speech, as an occasion for a secular homily or humorous observation. Their titles – 'On not reading the papers', 'Feather brooms', 'Weather collecting' – with their mix of trenchant commonsense and a self-consciously literary sensibility brought to bear, sometimes whimsically, sometimes sonorously, upon the trivia or miscellanea of life, place her in a long line of popular English essayists. Though less mannered and far less fanciful, 'Mrs. Miniver', is a distant relation of Charles Lamb's 'Elia', who through 'an affected array of antique modes and phrases', could make the humdrum – whether it be 'Old China' (i.e. crockery), 'A dissertation upon roast pig' or 'The praise of chimney-sweepers' – the object of civilised and educated reflection.[45]

Displaying such a reverence for the literary and such a desire for a 'polished' style as usually earns the highbrow's contempt, 'occasional' pieces of this sort derive their humour and their energy from the deliberate juxtaposition of the ornate and the homely, the highflown and the every-day, the learned and the intimate. Mrs. Miniver, though not a diarist proper, manages just that combination of the apparently random and the highly wrought. Unlike a diary, her confessions never reflect badly on their author, and where diaries capture a sense of the immediate, the undigested, and unfinished (an effect Delafield manages to convey with her abbreviated and breathless style), Mrs. Miniver's raw material is well-cooked and liberally garnished. Although the subject matter appears arbitrary and unpredictable, it is carefully and lovingly fashioned into a literary form.

The literary impulse which shapes all the episodes is caught in one scene which sees her looking back over her past year, as it is etched in 'the skeleton map' of an old engagements book. Its detail, 'Meet Clem, 2.27', 'Pike-fishing with Vin', 'Lunch Bucklands', 'Bridget for week-end', may be 'bare and laconic', but such appearances disguise a rich inner life which makes each day 'crammed, like all other days, with feelings, ideas and discoveries' (p. 23). All these apparently commonplace days furnish material for anecdote, reflection and narrative, like 'Bridget's fascinating story about her cousin, the three-penny bit, and the deaf chimney sweep' (p. 24). A queue of cars brings an opportunity to reflect on traffic lights and the possible symbolism of their colours; a boring wait in a friend's office becomes a time for meditation on the meaning of life. When Mrs. Miniver greets Clem at home in the evening, it isn't to talk about her bargains or how the butcher's boy behaved, but to tell him her day's thoughts, to exchange a collection of funny stories and to share the overheard snippets of speech from taxi-drivers and duchesses (she and Clem collect 'haws and ahems'). In 'spinning our straw into gold', as *The Times* somewhat dryly implied, Mrs. Miniver is a Rumpelstiltskin of the choice phrase.[46]

It was as a literary stylist that Mrs. Miniver made much of her appeal. Her 'delicate sentiment' and 'cultured' life, the fact that she 'could be trusted to find the technical phrase for the latest ballet', were what delighted her readership, her scrupulous cherishing of words.[47] It was its cultivated tone which drew delighted responses like that of the American poet and author, Stephen Vincent Benet (he who wrote the line 'Bury my heart at Wounded Knee') who was moved to praise the skilfulness of the writing: 'every word is in place, like the flowers in a beautifully tended garden'.⁴⁸ In fact, one of the happy confusions of the sketches is somehow to make Mrs. Miniver seem their author. After all, the writing implies, why shouldn't every woman at home see herself as a budding columnist through the exercise of a literary temperament?

Clearly Mrs. Miniver has a range of writerly techniques at her fingertips: the carefully chosen, slightly archaic or poeticised words which remind one of literary or classical education: a car becomes a 'tumbril', a pet 'prognathous'; cheek-lines are 'delible', arguments (or 'duels') are 'eupeptic'. Novel similes and witty comparisons abound (often drawn from homely observation): traffic lights are 'a tin hollyhock' (p. 16), pavements are 'seal-sleek' (p. 14); 'the air was knife-keen and fresh as lettuce' (p. 48), the 'buds like a baby's fist' (p. 90). She has a preference for the epigrammatic: 'love is no actuary' (p. 36), 'a day without a chunk or two of solitude in it is like a cocktail without ice' and 'swans looked as though they were reading their own fan-mail' (p. 39). Words are rolled off the tongue simply for their own pleasure: 'summer was bathos, *dégringolade*' (p. 97), as though domestic life were one huge Thesaurus: 'the worst of gardening', she says, 'is that it's so full of metaphors' (p. 89).

For Struther/Miniver the arts are a constant companion and source of inspiration: spring is like a stage show, or like Wedgewood – 'with white clouds delicately modelled in relief against a sky of pale pure blue' (p. 32); landscapes resemble tapestries, the cottage gardens are 'little glowing squares of rich embroidery' (p. 39); Hyde Park is a theatrical set, a car is part of 'one's *mise en scène*' (p. 5) whilst the pond at Hampstead Heath 'would have made an admirable opening for a ballet' (p. 83). Even the luggage piled up by Clem on the back seat of the car resembles a 'cubist cornucopia (p. 58). A love of literature is one of her ruling passions: 'Mrs. Miniver', as one critic artlessly assures us, 'is sustained, as always, by poetry.'⁴⁹ When the family are letting off fireworks, Mrs. Miniver's mind moves from the 'reckless extravagance' of bonfire night rockets to a line, 'Brightness falls from the air', and then a verse, from Nash. This, though having 'nothing to do with fireworks at all', gives rise to a few thoughts on the transience of things, and then by analogy becomes a comment on the activity of writing itself:

> she knew that it was just what she had needed to round off the scene for her and to make its memory enduring. Words were the only net to catch a mood, the only weapon against oblivion.

(p. 24)

The art of writing is always uppermost in her mind. Lying in the dentist's chair she imagines the fun which John Donne would have describing the electric drill:

With what delight he would have seized upon it, with what harsh jostling and grinding of consonants he would have worked out metaphor after   metaphor. . . .

(p. 83)

By finding the apt quotation or the *mot juste*, Mrs. Miniver enhances her own experience, but she is not above being a critic of other people's efforts. When she reads an article on marriage in the paper we get an inkling of the kind of thing she likes: 'good of its kind . . . with more restraint and a lighter touch than most' (p. 45). Unfortunately it is also full of 'three-quarter truths'. The scene (which involves her discussing with Clem the inviting of married couples to a dinner party) then affords her the chance to offer her own thoughts on marriage *en passant*; Jan Struther thus revealing how much lighter and more restrained her own 'touch' could be.

Passages are lovingly punctuated (Mrs. Miniver's prose never puts a hyphen wrong) and the grammar unobtrusively correct. This was a class of reader for whom a love of 'style' was a matter, not of 'lifestyle' – of the display of character or position through food, or dress, or interior decoration – but of a connoisseurship of words, whose physical properties, oddities and talismanic powers made them almost collector's items.[50] Mrs. Miniver is far less likely to assert her social superiority through the trappings of wealth or birth, than through her capacity to wield words. She suggests a reader who takes a pride in being cultured and who sees the avoidance of all cliché and tired phrases as part of being an interesting individual with a unique sensibility.

In a contretemps with her housekeeper (the flatly named 'Mrs. Downce'), it is Mrs. Miniver's command of English that has her entirely routed, rather than an obviously *haut en bas* manner:

'Is everything all right?' she asked in a casual voice, pulling off her gloves.

'Well, no, madam, I'm afraid I couldn't hardly say that.' Mrs. Downce paused ominously.

'(*Oh, come on, you old fool, don't keep me on tenterhooks like this – which of them is it? Toby? Judy? Vin?*) I'm sorry to hear that. What's happened?'

'Well, madam, there's nothing what you could call happened, it's just there's a norrible smell.'

Mrs. Miniver nearly laughed out loud with relief.

'Smell? Where?'

'Everywhere, madam. All over the back part of the house, that is. A *norrible* smell.'

Mrs. Miniver crossed the hall, opened the door which led to the kitchen premises, and shut it again very quickly.

'Good heavens!' she said. 'It's unspeakable.'

Mrs. Downce's face bore the triumphant look peculiar to those who, suspected of hyperbole, are found to have been employing meiosis.

'Downce thinks it's the drains. His mother died of typhoid.'

(p. 43)

Mrs. Downce, with her double negatives, faulty pronunciation, and obsession with the insanitary doesn't stand a chance against 'Madam's' knowledge of Greek rhetoric. And even her being right about the smell associates her even more firmly with the 'back part' of the house, and seems simply to increase a sense of the working classes making melodramas out of the sordid (and going so far as dying of typhoid). The episode continues with the soldierly Clem demonstrating his leadership qualities ('why on earth didn't you get a plumber?'); the Downces are revealed as utterly dependent on their betters; the Minivers stride in, trace the smell to its source – lingering fishbait from the eldest boy – and the domestic comedy comes to an end. Even without the complicity implied by the parenthetical abuse, the reader is invited to make a simple but loaded choice: on the one hand you can opt for ignorance, bad speech, smells, on the other, erudition, action and improvement.[51]

When Clem is being clever about the servant problem and about parlour-maids who keep moving on, he jests that it may be due to the 'incurably trochaic' nature of their names ('Norah', 'Jessie', 'Gladys', 'Ellen'): 'next time, go for a dactyl' (p. 126).[52] It is not the working classes who will appreciate the joke. Far more energy is directed in the writing toward distinguishing oneself, not from the lower orders (a game hardly worth the candle) but from other members of the middle class who are less literary and less civilised. It is for the benefit of her own class that Mrs. Miniver's dearest possessions ('of the sort we all have') are carefully listed as she is faced with packing when the war approaches:

> small objects one could send to the country – a picture or two, the second edition of Donne, the little antelope made of burnt jade . . . .

(p. 65)

Discreetly valuable, not flashy or ostentatious, these are the belongings, so we are expected to feel, of a special individual, someone with taste. She is the kind of woman who never visits the cinema or wiles away time with the wireless (unless it's to hear a good concert or a controversial talk) and whose friends, like herself,

> hate sitting long over meals; walk quickly or not at all; enjoy arguments, jokes, and silences, but detest making conversation.

(p. 39)

She loathes 'small talk'. Mrs. Miniver has her own brand of reticence.

From the popularity of *Mrs. Miniver* we gain a sense of how much a love of the literary and of words (even if it was only a matter of completing *The Times* crossword) is one of the many ways in which the middle class divides itself into vying coteries, each trying to convince the others that they and their friends are the truly interesting people. If one is tempted to call this outlook 'middlebrow', then such a slur is merely in keeping with the frame of mind which sees a knowledge of 'the arts' as 'symbolic' capital, as a means of achieving prestige and displaying position: the middlebrow is impossible in a culture that has no highbrow. Such small vanities as the likes of those who enjoyed *Mrs. Miniver* may have indulged in, seem far less culpable than the larger snobberies which operate, for example, around the cult novelist whose work can only be read by her peers. Mrs. Miniver's literary enthusiasms are at least open to be shared.

If *Mrs. Miniver* is evidence that being literary between the wars could be a middlebrow activity, the literary elevation of the homely had a special and different significance for female readers and writers. In the 1920s and '30s the meaning of domesticity is itself up for public debate: what it is, how much it costs, how women live and cope at home in their different social groups, all are the subject of intense and widespread concern and argument. With the introduction of new technology and domestic consumer markets, and especially in reaction to the decline in willing domestic service, the idea of how the home is, or could be, run became a matter of almost feverish national interest. In addition, the need for new homes and discussions of housing policy (one of the main political issues in the period), housing design, and the growth of welfarism brought the working-class home into political life as never before. That such questions as household budgeting and family nutrition might be a matter of political and not just private intervention was evidenced by the number of government and official enquiries into these areas.[53] Housing and home life, maternity and childcare were also taken up by 'new' feminists in the period, like Eleanor Rathbone, and by the Labour Party and trade union movement (as never before or since). Although they may seem at first to have little in common with *Mrs. Miniver*, the work of Margery Spring Rice (whose *Working-Class Wives* appeared in 1939) or the earlier collection of letters from working women edited by Margaret Llewelyn Davies in 1930, *Life As We Have Known It*, are all evidence of growing public interest in the internal workings of domestic life as suitable material for public and national reflection. (Jan Struther is typical of her time in making Mrs. Miniver also a committee woman discussing slum clearance in Shoreditch.)

Particularly in the fiction by women in the period we can see an increased consciousness of the materiality of domestic life, of home as the place of things, as well as of social relations, of things which need buying, cleaning, moving, maintaining. In many of these novels home takes on almost an independent character, often a negative one, and becomes a protagonist often warring with the heroine and intruding on her hopes and dreams. The physicality of home and its paraphernalia are described, listed, anatomised with what might sometimes seem an obsessive amount of detail. Frequently the woman at home feels herself to be a kind of sorcerer's apprentice desperately fighting to keep control of the things which make up a home. Even Mrs. Miniver, whose domestic worries are largely those of an employer, shows a knowledge of 'the mechanics' of the household which would have ill-befitted the Victorian or Edwardian lady:

> Everything went wrong at once: chimneys smoked, pipes burst, vacuum cleaners fused, china and glass fell to pieces, net curtains disintegrated in the wash. Nannie sprained her ankle, the cook got tonsilitis, the house-parlourmaid left to be married, and the butterfly-nut off the mincing-machine was nowhere to be found.
>
> (p. 93)

Jan Struther was one of many comfortably-off women who began to perceive the fabric of everyday life as a fit subject for writing. The literary avant-garde and populists alike, with different degrees of self-conscious assertion, aimed to shrug off the 'disgrace' of writing purely from inside domestic life and to claim that its ups and downs were suitable, if not superior, material for literary alchemy. More adventurous or bohemian writers made the actual physical experiences of womanhood a subject for novelistic exploration, giving sometimes graphic descriptions of birth, breast-feeding, contraception, and even menstruation.[54] For others it was revelatory enough to focus upon the material processes of housekeeping: domestic routines, shopping and the preparation of meals, but also actual physical settings: furniture, crockery, the layout of homes and rooms all receive the imprimatur of literary consciousness.

In their new sense of 'a mind full of ghosts of saucepans and primus stoves',[55] the daughters of educated men were not just responding to the burden of housework as it began to fall more and more on their shoulders instead of their servants'; their consciousness was a concomitant too of the revolt which many had made against the domesticity of their own childhood homes, represented by their mothers, and which aimed to revise that idea of domesticity and its pleasures. Many of the formal adaptations and experiments in novelistic techniques (diarising, internal monologue, 'stream of consciousness') which try to express and construct notions of a purely feminine subjectivity, are ways into analysing, exploring and revising 'the kind of knowledge the domestic woman might be expected to have'.[56] The use, for example, of 'a day in the life of a woman' became a familiar literary trope, from its appearance as modernist experimentation in Woolf's *Mrs. Dalloway* (1925) to more popular and social realist forms of writing like Lettice Cooper's *The New House* (1936).[57]

Woolf's and Richardson's interest in the possibility of a woman's sentence or of a recognisably feminine aesthetic, found a more mainstream correlative in the less technically ambitious practices of the middlebrow novel – like E. H. Young's *The Curate's Wife* (1934), or E. M. Delafield's *The Way Things Are* (1927) – which take as their subject *the consciousness* of what it is like to be married, to be at home, but above all to 'be a woman'. In the often laborious and exhausting attention to the fluctuation of feeling and thought inside their female protagonists, such writers share a commitment, not just, in Dorothy Richardson's terms, to making 'an art of life', but also a fascination with the identification of femininity with forms of interiority, and of inner space. Far from reading the writing of the period as a retreat from real life into modernist reverie or self-absorbed introspection, one of the often fraught successes of much writing by women in the inter-war period is to bring to public awareness some of the costs at which a culture of domesticity is maintained.[58]

The recognition that domesticity is 'a feminine achievement' and even 'a feminine idea'[59] becomes a troubled awareness in the inter-war period right across the cultural board, and not just amongst feminists. A sense of the painful contradictions which women's own attachment to domestic ideals and practices can create in women surfaces in many of the novels. Having to represent 'insideness' – intimacy, deep and rooted emotionalities, privacy – the conflicting pulls of the set of emotions which domesticity itself implies, and which the home is meant to harbour, it is this that makes the house one of the dominant metaphors and physical settings in the novels. A novel like Cooper's *The New House* is typical in the descriptions it gives of the old and new objects encountered in the homes which are central to its plot (the substantial Victorian villa, the new labour-saving house): they are used not only as the 'conventional notation for pointing to social changes',[60] but also as a measure of how far feminine subjectivity has been identified with the inside of the house. Moving house in the novel becomes a metaphor for changing femininities and for exploring the irreconcilable conflicts of fear and desire which emerge from such changes: for Rhoda, the heroine, it becomes literally a matter of leaving her mother.

Naturally the 'woman's novel' and that 'unmistakably female tone of voice'[61] are class voices. To see them as universal is to miss the fact that many writers were themselves making 'class consciousness' a new element in their novels. E. M. Delafield's ironically titled *The Way Things Are*, in which Laura, a married woman and a mother, takes a lover and is faced with her own incapacity to choose passion above 'home', rewrites the narrative of social confidence with which so many nineteenth-century novelists chose marriage as the culmination and celebration of bourgeois values. Where a Jane Eyre or a Dorothea Brooke are reconciled by marriage both to their class and their sex, the novels of the 1920s and '30s demonstrate how far women of the middle classes felt hemmed in precisely by the norms and social assumptions which they had internalised: the need of the heroine for comfort and status, as much as any masculine tyranny (Laura's husband is a typically mild-mannered man) is frankly exposed at the end of the novel. We cannot admire Laura when she returns to the fold, but we are meant to understand that it is her own inability to imagine life outside her class which keeps her tied:

> The children, her marriage vows, the house, the ordering of meals, the servants, the making of a laundry list every Monday – in a word, the things of respectability – kept one respectable. . . .
>   It dawned upon her dimly that only by envisaging and accepting her own limitations, could she endure the limitations of her surroundings.[62]

In its own way, *Mrs. Miniver* is a commentary on the new kinds of domestic pressure which *Times* readers might be feeling. She too experiences an invasion of domestic chores from time to time when:

> Every morning you awake to the kind of list which begins: *Sink-plug. Ruffle-tape. X-hooks. Glue* . . . and ends: – *Ring plumber. Get sweep. Curse laundry.* Your horizon contracts, your mind's eye is focused upon a small circle of exasperating detail. Sterility sets in; the hatches of your mind are battened down. Your thoughts, once darling companions, turn into club bores, from which only sleep can bring release.

> (p. 93)

Although her worries are mostly managerial ('Ring plumber. Get sweep. Curse laundry.') there is enough recognition of the repetitive nature of housework and its dissipating tasks to form the beginnings of a protest. What Mrs. Miniver wants, however, is more space for thought. Her advice is to 'put on spiritual dungarees' (not cloth ones) and cope by maintaining a philosophical distance from the sordid side of domestic work. With a vaguely Shakespearian note to her soliloquy, she decides that 'this dusty and tedious little patch of time' will pass and in any case (she is staring at a Turkish carpet at the time) it's all part of life's rich tapestry. Worse than the odd passage of wearisome domestic responsibility is the disorder which might ensue without her shouldering its stresses. Thus what begins as a mild objection to her lot easily slides into acceptance of it, since without the 'allotments and rubbish tips, the gasworks . . . and . . . dilapidated hoardings' how would one appreciate 'civic splendour and country peace'? The encroaching of housework merely serves to heighten Mrs. Miniver's awareness of the compensating pleasures of her own superior consciousness.

In a period which saw women increasingly bombarded with images of themselves as shoppers and managers of 'the household budget', *Mrs. Miniver* is clearly antipathetic to the idea of the middle classes as the materialist classes. As one of many innovatory pieces clearly written by women journalists, *Mrs. Miniver* would frequently appear alongside the 'Round the Shops' column in *The Times* and next to articles expatiating on 'efficient housekeeping', 'the problem of the small flat', or 'recipes for small households' – advice which suggests how far the middle-class woman was expected to make home her 'workshop'. In such a context *Mrs. Miniver* acted as an antiphon, a reflective, meditative voice gently persuading readers that the woman at home need not be swamped by the material world of things but could use her position for more sensitive perceptions.

In fact, Mrs. Miniver rises above the conventionally material aspects of feminine existence; we never know whether she uses cosmetics or what kind of hat she wears; she never gets a ladder or a smut; more tellingly, we never see her confiding in a woman friend. When she goes shopping, it is for luxuries not necessities (a Christmas or birthday present), and she brings back not purchases, but experiences. She may visit department stores, but even her spending isn't sordid: shopping is pure pleasure for her, an extension of ego and autonomy which bears no resemblance to the daily round,

> To do it cold-bloodedly, in a half-empty shop, without difficulty or competition, is as joyless as a *marriage de convenance*.
>
> (p. 15)[63]

We never hear her ordering the mutton. No doubt the readers of *Mrs. Miniver* could have the best of both worlds as they strayed from her musings back to the advertisements for new tailor-mades at Debenhams and the latest Deretta fashions. They could share in Mrs. Miniver's sense of her specialness without having to be either arty or Bohemian.

The main object of Mrs. Miniver's literary impulses is to keep physicality at arm's length. Household matters should 'be a low, unobtrusive humming in the background of consciousness' (p. 92), analogous perhaps to the ideal place of servants who represent the material world of 'domestic labour' (a term which covered both the work and the people who did it). The physical presence of children (and servants) ranks firmly on 'the debit side of parenthood':

> the morning sickness, and the quite astonishing pain; the pram in the passage, the cold, mulish glint in the cook's eye; the holiday nurse who had been in the best families; the pungent white mice, the shrivelled caterpillars; the plasticine on the door handles, the face-flannels in the bathroom, the nameless horrors down the crevices of armchairs; the alarms and emergencies, the swallowed button, the inexplicable earache, the ominous rash appearing on the eve of a journey . . .
>
> (p. 19)

What makes it all worthwhile on Christmas morning is to contemplate

her children's pleasure from a distance (without 'dramatics')and to derive
a wise self-possession from the scene. It is this idea of the getting of
domestic wisdom which Jan Struther captures in the closing sentences
of the passage as Mrs. Miniver looks at the dawn sky caught between the
curtains of 'cherry-pink chintz':

> Eternity framed in domesticity. Never mind. One had to frame it in
> something, to see it all.
>
> (p. 20)

Whilst that 'never mind' hides a sense of constraint, it is as a frame for
'finer feeling' that the limitations of domesticity can be borne. And it is
perhaps the implied nobility of the woman who suffers such tedium which
makes the confession seem smug.

Mrs. Miniver actually conveys no felt sense of domesticity as a fragmenting experience of the sort which her lists of scattered energies and random
demands imply: her ego remains intact and her vision whole. Surely, the
writing tells us, a woman who can see symbolism in a traffic light is no
mere housewife! At times the literary framework can engender pathos and
poignancy, as when she is depicted taking her small children to be fitted
for gasmasks (during the months of the Munich crisis) and is forced to
recognise that her maternal concern with hygiene is futile in view of a
coming war:

> Finally, in another room, there were the masks themselves, stacked
> close, covering the floor like a growth of black fungus. They took what
> had been ordered for them – four medium size, two small – and filed
> out into the street.
>
> It was for this, thought Mrs. Miniver as they walked towards the car,
> that one had boiled the milk for their bottles, and washed their hands
> before lunch, and not let them eat with a spoon which had been dropped
> on the floor.
>
> (p. 63)

But even then, lest any too painful emotion creep in, the passage shifts
abruptly into a 'comic incident' provided by 'a fat woman . . . with a fatter
husband': ' "You did look a fright," she said. "I 'ad to laugh." ' 'One
had to laugh' is Mrs. Miniver's final word – keeping a careful pronoun
between herself and her feelings.

No doubt readers encountered such passages with the light of grateful
recognition in their eyes – here was motherhood dignified – and it would
be heartening to see Jan Struther's columns as examples of 'liberal (and
liberated)' values, as at least one critic does.[64] Yet *Mrs. Miniver*'s reliance
on the idea of a kind of Ur-wisdom which women find in domestic
contemplation need offer little challenge to the most conservative views
of femininity. What Jan Struther gives us as Mrs. Miniver's literary men-

tality can be read as a variation on the theme of feminine intuitiveness: Mrs. Miniver is 'a fool about inanimate objects' (p. 5) and listens carefully to windscreen wipers in order to work out what they say ('Beef tea', apparently). Where husband Clem is strong and silent, 'words, for her, clarified feelings' (p. 39) and though she may wax lyrical about spring days and country drives in private, the reader is at liberty to find her charming effusions entirely in keeping with a view of woman as an essentially emotional creature. What is more, the woman who, far from being depressed or dispirited by days spent largely in her own company, is able to keep a weather eye on the storms of life and become a natural philosopher hardly needs to expand her horizons.

In the context of fascism in Europe any privileging of the domestic wisdom of women was likely to be an emotionally loaded topic for more politically aware writers in the late 1930s.[65] Nor were women necessarily resistant to fascist doctrine. In less restrained hands, the myth of domestic wisdom could take on a proto-fascist feel, as it does in Enid Bagnold's *The Squire*, published in 1938.[66] Jan Struther's own conservatism is less heroic and much more beguiling. Her literary translation of the everyday has none of the overt romanticisation of motherhood which a more reactionary politics could make use of, and equally little of the more despairing sense of domestic invasion which lies beneath the surface of more feminist accounts. Her use of the literary is always to play it safe, never aiming to unsettle but to keep the reader on an even keel.

When Virginia Woolf writes in her diary that 'one gains a certain hold on sausage and haddock by writing them down', it is with a sense of her own boldness that she mentions such mundanities.[67] We can also read a social history and a history of class into that sentence. Woolf cooking dinner in the half-darkness of Rodmell, without a resident servant, is a prototype of a new kind of middle-class woman who is not above knocking herself up an omelette or even – in years to come – cooking a Sunday lunch. Making such matters a subject for diarising is also a recognition that 'sausage' and 'haddock' are words for human perceptions, which gain a kind of acknowledgement by being written down. Once 'literary', the contexts they belong to, like cooking, become capable of different meanings, different interpretations. In Woolf's anticipation – 'And now with some pleasure I find that it's seven; and must cook dinner. Haddock and sausage meat', a romantic might want to glimpse a utopian vision in which cooking and writing could enhance each other as human activities; maybe women writers have been in a special position to perceive that neither need rate above the other.

But it is also clear from the tone of Woolf's entry ('I intend no introspection. I mark Henry James' sentence: observe perpetually. Observe the oncome of age. Observe greed. Observe my own despondency'), that if sausage and haddock are material pleasures, a connecting hold on physical life, then they are far from safe anchors. And domestic harmony is for any woman a precarious metaphor of the self. After all, there is something depressing too about such unadulterated fare; it is resolutely proletarian cuisine, a sadly comic as well as an emancipated meal to prepare. Any image of unity or equilibrium is surely disturbed by Woolf's own knowledge, which has to be dealt with, mocked, flaunted if you like, but cannot be ignored, that lady writers become domestics when they cook themselves tea. Even, or especially, without Nellie, Woolf is still the employer and making haddock and sausage can only be for her a matter of some occasion, and for which she expects credit.

Both the actual pleasures of domestic labour and the deeper reaches of self-consciousness are beyond Jan Struther's Mrs. Miniver, who would have been as incapable of writing about sausage and haddock as she is about despondency. The framing of domesticity was for her the creation of an essentially still life: if the woman of the 1920s had been typically 'distrait', then Mrs. Miniver's fantasy was that of the utterly composed woman.[68]

PEACE IN OUR TIME

At the core of Mrs. Miniver's philosophy of life is a desire to hold on to the liberties of the known and the familiar; she is a loving and a careful annotator of the pleasures of 'invariable custom' (p. 50). Even holidays become an extension of domestic life rather than a letting oneself 'go'. Country house visits to one's friends are best when they make you feel at home. (No world turned upside down for Mrs. Miniver.) In one of her rare moments of fallibility, arriving somewhere new for the weekend, Mrs. Miniver admits to feeling

> a form of claustrophobia – a dread of exchanging the freedom of her own, self-imposed routine for the inescapable burden of somebody else's.
>
> (p. 39)

She even confesses to having bought 'a really grand dressing gown' to bolster her ego.

'Every summer for fifteen years' the Minivers drive to Scotland and their pleasure resides not only in the fact of this repetition ('they always started at seven'), but in a ceremonial rediscovery every year of their favourite stopping-places en route as they contemplate 'the number of little memory flags with which, on their minds' map, the road was studded' (p. 49). Each corner turned invites a mutually agreeable stroll down Memory Lane, and far from the habitual becoming mechanical or monotonous, it becomes a small patterning of life, a measure of its sense. In this mental universe old favourites (like the car which Mrs. Miniver is loth to part with) are always preferable to the new-fangled, and well-worn paths more appealing than any wandering off the beaten track.

The passion for continuity which Mrs. Miniver expresses is not, however, a hymn to national or public rituals (there is never any mention of royalty or the church in these pages) but rather a display of the more intimate pageantry of subjective experience. She is always chronologising her life, making a consistent and meaningful story from the random detail and disconnected events which go to make up her past. A family archivist, Mrs. Miniver is motivated constantly by a desire to preserve and retain: there is nothing she wants to throw out or lose, whether it be old Christmas lists and diaries, the crooked pane of glass in the dining-room window, or the notches on the door-post against which she measured her growing children. Rather than being a source of disturbing or contradictory impulses, the past is a personal comfort:

> it had never occurred to her before that you cannot successfully navigate the future unless you keep always framed beside it a small, clear image of the past.

> (p. 120)

For the readership of *The Times*, *Mrs. Miniver* was perhaps itself such a rudder: as a species of social history *Mrs. Miniver* suggested that it was private life that constituted the real and important life of the nation. And it is a private life whose benefits and deepest pleasures can be found in affectionate and particular details.

Such an appetite for the privatising of the present and the past was not unique to her column in *The Times*. Patience Strong in the *Daily Mirror* was running a daily 'Quiet Corner' with verses expounding sentiments similar to Mrs. Miniver's. Though there was more religiosity and sentimentality in Patience Strong's offerings, her emphasis also fell on the centrality to personal and spiritual well-being of home life, on the power of meditation and on material domestic pleasures ('I love to see a pair of slippers on the fireside mat.') And although the word 'cosy' would never have passed Mrs. Miniver's lips the tone of 'life's like that', the conviction that life is a jigsaw to be fitted together over the years of private reflection, and the note of moral uplift are all familiar. Published as a little anthology *Quiet Corner* sold 80,000 copies; *Quiet Thoughts*, published in 1937, reached a fifth edition and 45,000 copies by 1941.[69]

So much a national style had the penchant for homely and becalming advice become that the short-lived new weekly, *Night and Day*, launched in 1937, ran a lampooning 'Contentment Column' which collected 'Encouraging and Inspiring Items from the Press, a Corrective to Scare Headlines and Private Worries', like the comfortable words of the Dean of Durham under the heading of 'ZEAL', 'it can do us no harm now and then to consider what good we are in fact accomplishing', or the cheering news (under SHOCK TACTICS) that

> A cinema film depicting Miss Margaret Baker giving a lecture on 'Milk versus Beer' was made at the recent Temperance Summer School at Westhill, and copies are available for Temperance societies and other organisations possessing a projecting apparatus.[70]

In the same satirical vein, the first issue had carried a mocking piece 'In defence of home' by Rose Macaulay which pronounced that *Night and Day* would 'stand by the Sanctities (by day and night) of the Home' and exhorted readers:

> By all means let us retain our homes, their comforts, their sweet lethargy, their sanctity. My own flat is full of sanctity and lethargy, and I will not have it undermined. The home, where selfishness begins and charity ends, where we recline in one commodious chair and place the feet on another, moving not at the call of telephone or door-bell – we will admit no violation of this exquisite convenience. The little flats of England, how beautiful they stand! Why not stay in them?

Such satire was a sign of how far the domestication of the British had been popularly elevated to the status of national character.

Like 'Patience Strong', Mrs. Miniver fortified her readers. Her humble sketches, with their resemblance to both more lofty 'pensées' and sermons, offered a source of collective wisdom consonant with an overriding 'faith in an essentially optimistic universe'.[71] Each vignette has an ameliorative aim, and invariably ends on an upbeat and a note of balanced common sense. Obviously a child of the enlightenment, Mrs. Miniver's dependability as moral and social guide was crucial ('we can trust Mrs. Miniver'); her capacity to look on the bright side was at least as popular as 'the charming *aperçus* of her mind'.[72] Indeed fifty years after the outbreak of the Second World War it was Mrs. Miniver's unwearying optimism which most impressed Jan Struther's granddaughter: 'You genuinely do feel rather nicer than you did when you started.'[73]

In 1938 such a pacific outlook had a special resonance as newspaper headlines got scarier and scarier. Certainly there is nothing in Jan Struther's columns during the months of the 'Munich crisis' to disturb the keynote of 'temperate optimism'[74] which *The Times* sounded on its pages of international and national news during the build-up to war. A belief in conciliation between Britain and Nazi Germany as the best policy was given unequivocal support by the newspaper which declared the gratitude of 'the great bulk of the public which realises that dictatorships and democracies must live side by side'.[75] Prime Minister Neville Chamberlain and his 'constructive effort' toward 'a stable peace' were lavishly praised, and various letters published after his return from parleying with Hitler suggested the setting up of national monuments, the dedication of hospital beds, and a 'thanksgiving' fund in his honour.[76] The political manoeuvrings and historical events of the Munich crisis have been well documented and debated, but if we wish to understand the mentality of 'appeasement', we need to see it not as a simple, single attitude of mind but as a structure of feeling drawing upon a number of different emotional sources. What *Mrs. Miniver* testifies to is both how emotionally decisive were the months of the Munich crisis and how short-lived that moment of appeasement was. If *Mrs. Miniver* captures something of the mood of those people who were able to see 'Mr Chamberlain's wonderful work' as a guarantee of a rosy future for Britain, if not for the whole globe, the columns also suggest the shifts in public opinion and the stresses and strains such optimism attempted to cover.[77]

Mrs. Miniver gauges the temperature of much national feeling in the almost imperceptible shifts it charts in attitudes to war itself. Like many of her generation, Jan Struther writes in the shadow of the first war, and at least two of the pieces in *Try Anything Twice* are denunciations of militarism. In the 'Phenomenon of the militarist's sister' (she whose honour had always to be defended against the enemy), she satirised the bellicose views of those who will not give up their aggressive beliefs

for the sake of humanity or of civilisation, or to prevent a few thousand more children choking to death in the not too distant future.

(p. 269)

Elsewhere she argued in quite unbuttoned fashion against the giving of war toys to children:

It is a short step from dropping a wooden bomb on a regiment of leaden Italians to calling old Giuseppe, the barrel organ man, to whom they have given a penny every Friday for years, a dirty wop.

('The toys of war', p. 262)

Although she was not able to be quite as bold in the guise of Mrs. Miniver, a clearly anti-militaristic thread runs through the early pieces up to October 1938. In November 1937 we hear her declaring the abolition of blood sports as a low priority compared to the desire to be rid of war,

it seemed to her that to abolish shooting before you had abolished war was like flicking a speck of mud off the top of a midden.

(p. 12)

And on 31 March 1938 when *Times* readers could turn over the page to pictures of Hitler's 'triumphal return' and 'hero's welcome' in Vienna after the Austrian *Anschluss*, Jan Struther captures again that part of public opinion which was still against war at any price. Placing Mrs. Miniver on Hampstead Heath, she encounters two street orators, one left-wing, the other right, and their highflown rhetorics, 'shot through and through with the steely tinsel of war' (p. 37), seem to her to be interchangeable with their language of sacrifice and self-immolation (by implication horribly reminiscent of the Great War). The column finishes with an ironic parody of war-mongering in a Punch and Judy show. Those who advocate the necessity of war are seen simply as brutal extremists.

At the beginning of September 1938 'with the threat of war hanging like a leaden nimbus in the air', politics is kept at bay with the reassuring message (and one to be often repeated), as Mrs. Miniver watches her children intent on their holiday games, that the important things in life don't change:

> international tempers might flame or cool; the turning kaleidoscope of time might throw mankind's little coloured scraps of belief into new patterns, new ideologies
>
> (p. 60)

but a child will still play for hours with a home-made toy. Part of the attitude of appeasement was just this desire to cling on to the virtues of a stable civilian life, though by the next entry (28 September) the Minivers are acquiring their gasmasks and with the outbreak of hostilities imminent, anti-war feeling could begin to shift into anti-fascist sentiment. For the Mrs. Minivers amongst the readers of *The Times* war could only be contemplated if could be morally and politically differentiated from the emotional and social conditions of 1914:

> If the worst came to the worst (it was funny how one still shied away from saying, 'If there's a war', and fell back on euphemisms) – if the worst came to the worst, these children would at least know that we were fighting against an idea, and not against a nation.
>
> (p. 62)

Women's job in such circumstances is to fight against jingoism, the 'slow, yellow, drifting corruption of the mind', against which there is no protection.

'Back to Normal', the slightly ironic headline for Mrs. Miniver's column of 6 October (and which, with an indirect reference to 'the Crisis', is also subtitled 'The Afterthoughts of Mrs. Miniver') conveys the conflicting emotions of those who had wanted to avoid war and who gratefully imagined that it had been averted. On the one hand there is a sense of how far family and civilian life could never just go back to normal: not only had gasmasks and the digging of trenches in central London (with their ominous echo of the Great War) physically brought war home; the call for volunteers and moves for 'passive defence' of the nation all made it impossible for civilians to go on ignoring the possibility of war. At this point Mrs. Miniver herself signs up as an ambulance driver, 'Clem' disappears off to an Anti-Aircraft Battery and her children's schools are evacuated. Jan Struther, in an unwonted expression of emotion, captures something too of the enormous strain which even the most optimistic members of the public felt themselves to have been living through:

> seven years in as many days; and Mrs. Miniver, at any rate, felt as though she had been wrung out and put through a mangle. She was tired to the marrow of her mind and heart.

(p. 65)

On the other hand, cheerfulness is still the order of the day and Mrs. Miniver could almost have written the fourth leader which *The Times* had run on 1 October after the signing of the Munich agreement, which claimed that the experience of a 'false alarm' had allowed them to 'skim the cream of war' and live in a heightened atmosphere of 'high endeavour' with a 'kind of stardust' in the air.[78] Mrs. Miniver too sees living under the shadow of war as an occasion for personal and national improvement and a privileged chance to enjoy an enhanced sense of life's bounties, in particular a reassertion of the pleasures of the humdrum and the everyday:

> nothing in the world seemed more desirable than a long wet afternoon at a country vicarage with a rather boring aunt.

(p. 66)

If she had been thoroughly exhausted by the last few months, the consoling message of Mrs. Miniver was that far from being unnerved by her experience, she could make something positive of it. Though meant as a sign of how far she had come since her appearance in the autumn of 1937, Mrs. Miniver's assurance that 'this time it wasn't chrysanthemums she was rearranging, but values', seems to underline her composure.

Those who had managed to turn a blind eye to the meaning of fascism in Europe or who had trusted to the efficacy of appeasement were very rapidly disenchanted. Only a month later, in November, the escalation of Nazi violence against the Jews in Germany and Austria during the infamous *Kristallnacht*, and the passing of new laws which fully excluded them from national life, expropriated their means of survival, and placed them in effect outside the protection of the law, forced many people to realise that the idea of 'peace in our time' was an illusion. The growth of anti-fascist feeling found a stimulus in the flourishing popular magazine *Picture Post* which had itself been launched in October on the crest of 'the general feeling of relief'.[79] On 26 November it ran a hard-hitting spread entitled 'Back to the Middle Ages' which depicted in graphic detail the persecution of the Jews and the savagery of Nazi policy. In a far milder vein but as evidence too of the swift move away from appeasement even amongst the more conservative sectors of the population, was Jan Struther's piece of the same week in *The Times*.

Boldly confronting Mrs. Miniver with a placard saying 'JEWS', Struther uses her heroine to attack readers' apathy and the ever-present desire to ignore 'the Jewish question':

> However long the horror continued, one must not get to the stage of refusing to think about it. . . . Money, food, clothing, shelter – people could give all these and still it would not be enough: it would not absolve them . . . .
>
> (p. 72)

As one of 'the fortunate ones' Mrs. Miniver feels herself to be amongst the 'unwilling *tricoteuses*' forced to watch an execution from the front seat.

> The least they could do was not to turn away their eyes; for with such a picture stamped on the retina of their memory they would not be able to lie easy until they had done their best to ensure that it could never happen again.
>
> (pp. 73–4)

Such a moral stand could easily seem self-righteous, especially as her sentiments are framed by a reflection on the universality of evil (including in one breath Guy Fawkes, Hallowe'en and the Wicked Queen from *Snow White*) and certainly the imagery stresses her powerlessness rather than a call to arms or the need for international intervention. And it ends (as ever) on what must now seem a ridiculously hopeful note – 'in an hour or so the tide would turn'. Nevertheless it was a brave piece in its context and many *Times* readers clearly took offence, writing to 'Mrs. Miniver', and prompting Jan Struther to publish an open letter as Mrs. Miniver again, urging readers to contribute to the fund for Jewish refugees.[80]

After the emotional roller-coaster of these months, it is not perhaps surprising that a sense of calmness pervades the actual run-up to September 1939. It is as though the Munich crisis had provided a kind of dress rehearsal which had exhausted the emotions meant for the proper performance. Interestingly, the period immediately before war is announced seems to Mrs. Miniver to be almost entirely rewarding:

> That is the one great compensation for the fantastic way in which the events of our time are forcing us to live. The structure of our life – based as it is on the ever-present contingency of war – is lamentably wrong; but its texture, oddly enough, is pleasant . . . and this is largely because almost everybody you meet is busy learning something.
>
> (p. 111)

The prospect of war is actually seen as instructive, often literally so – for the working classes in particular it will be a kind of adult education. One episode sees her teaching a hapless victim on a park bench the art of the reef-knot ('I do get so muddled up with them knots'), and musing on the fact that at least the war would mean there would be no one left in England without such handy skills: 'And that's always something' (p. 110). But any prospect of reform is balanced by Mrs. Miniver's natural caution. Reflecting on the benefits of evacuation for 'slum children', which Mrs. Miniver sees as a purely welcome measure, her desire for civic improvement is offset by a reluctance to set too much change in motion. 'With luck', muses Mrs. Miniver, 'they would one day see cows.'

> But not otherwise. Unless, of course, a miracle happened; unless the structure could be changed without altering the texture, and the people of England, even after the necessity for it had been averted, remembered how to tie a reef-knot.

How to alter the structure without altering the texture of English life, much exercises Mrs. Miniver in the summer of 1939. Though she refuses to choose between left and right wing (always preferring, in her words, 'the wishbone'), and is worried by ideas that haven't yet had time to take root ('the fault, no doubt, of the times we live in. Things happen too quickly, crisis follows crisis, the soil of our minds is perpetually disturbed', p. 100), she is scornful of those 'who have nothing more precious to lose than a sense of material security':

> good heavens, has it been such a grand world up till now (except for a few lucky ones like ourselves) that one should try to keep it unchanged?
>
> (p. 140)

Such a radical outlook is entirely compatible with a view of society as a delicate organism which needs gentle and not violent adjusting and with a bedrock of emotional conservatism: the consolation Mrs. Miniver is able to offer less enthusiastic *Times* readers is the constant and unchanging nature of personal life – 'everything that really matters always does go on being the same . . . love and courage and kindness and integrity and the quite astonishing resilience of the human spirit.' It is a message likely to appeal across classes and political allegiances.

In a piece called 'Mrs. Miniver on Europe', written in August 1939, it is clear how far an organic view of society and of the social classes could be quite consonant with firm anti-nationalism. Returning from 'abroad' (where a niece has been 'finished') Mrs. Miniver speculates upon the similarities between people of different nations. How much stronger, she argues, 'the links are between people of the same calling than people of the same race'. 'Calling', implying as it does that one is born to sweep streets or run businesses, and that social position is simply a matter of vocation, avoids both the inequality and structural discontent of 'class'. Ironically, however, her sense of these divisions is as potentially internationalist as those of communism and gives a sense of how the nation might subsume political differences in its fight against fascism:

> A man who works with wood, a man who works with iron, a man who works with test-tubes, is more akin to a joiner, a smith, a research chemist from the other end of the earth than to a clerk or a shopkeeper in his own town.
>
> (p. 116)

Observing a Swiss boy playing with her son – and pointedly quoting in German – she sees them as 'one nation'. Like the old and the blind they share 'the same relentless country' regardless of nationality. Her refusal to de-humanise other nations surfaces in her insistence on their familial resemblances to the British; it was a way of resisting, perhaps, the romantic and effacing language of 'the foe', so popular in 1914.

The outbreak of war in September 1939 is the one moment of anti-climax in the columns. Mrs. Miniver's contributions begin to fall off, except for a few open 'letters' to her sister-in-law, written between September and Christmas, a form which allows Struther a more personal and more immediate style.[81] Even so it is a fully composed Mrs. Miniver who looks forward to the war as giving the country a good shake-up: war appears as a necessary evil for a country 'needing danger'. The conflict, which is still in the future, will invigorate us all like a national tonic, restoring our morale:

> it oughtn't to *need* a war to make a nation paint its kerbstones white, carry rear-lamps on its bicycles, and give all its slum children a holiday in the country. And it oughtn't to need a war to make us talk to each other in buses, and invent our own amusements in the evenings, and live simply, and eat sparingly, and recover the use of our legs, and get up early enough to see the sun rise. However, it *has* needed one: which is about the severest criticism our civilisation could have.
>
> (p. 123)

We might peevishly observe that many of these puritan pleasures would only be new to her own class; certainly the bright tone reminds us how much Jan Struther evidently had no imaginative conception yet of what war would mean. There is pathos as well as a touch of smugness in her cheerfulness, however. We might wonder how much it was just this sense of municipal and civic responsibility that laid the foundation for 'the spirit of the Blitz', and whether Mrs. Miniver might have been one of the thousands of middle-class people who enjoyed their 'fraternisation' with the lower orders during the war and helped Labour to a landslide victory in 1945.

In true writerly fashion, and confirming her sense of the doings of ordinary people as the nation's real history, Mrs. Miniver signs off urging her sister-in-law to keep all their letters, as a record for the future of 'this tragic, marvellous and eye-opening time'. We leave her no doubt girding up her 'spiritual dungarees' and (only half-jokingly) pitying Hitler ('poor, misguided man') for not realising that the English were only dangerous as a nation when bored. Surely George Orwell had the Mrs. Minivers in mind when he suggested that the best weapon the British had in their fight against fascism was their colossal ignorance? Yet few of Struther's readers could have glimpsed the chasm opening up before them which their proverbial wisdom would be quite unable to span. With hindsight, should we laugh or cry?[82]

Nothing dates like contentment, and there is nothing new, of course, in the conservatism which attaches its strongest feeling to the preservation of home life. Nor are its pleasures and its limitations especially the prerogative of the politically right wing or the socially well-off. As keepers of the shrine of custom, contrivers of the place of rest, it has been both women's fortune and their misery to be bound to sustaining the dream of a world made safe from the cold outside:

> what mattered was that here at least was one small roomful of warmth and happiness, shut in by frail window-panes from a freezing, harsh and inexplicable world.

(p. 72)

If only Jan Struther had let just a little draught of self-criticism disturb that tidy psyche or allowed stronger winds to ruffle that thick wrap of contentment. In retrospect Struther's breezy optimism reads like self-delusion and Mrs. Miniver's homespun philosophy, which was meant to reassure her readers that all was right with their world, now seems numbingly complacent. Her anchorage in safe thoughts soon gets claustrophobic, like the oppressive, stuffy calm before a storm. And quite a storm was brewing in 1939.[83]

When Hollywood took up the story in 1942, that calm optimism had already been tried and tested by the Blitz and the Battle of Britain. *The Times* thought it brave of the Americans to make a story of Jan Struther's prose which already looked, after four years of war, somewhat naïve and precious. They also had to admit that the movie makers had no idea of English class life. No doubt with a view to democratising the potentially snobby, smart metropolitan setting of the book, they opted instead for a village, complete with local aristocrat and vicar, in which Caroline Miniver becomes 'Kay' Miniver – 'a British suburban homemaker'.[84] The film could thus conjure up a notion of English rural tradition entirely absent from the original sketches, even as it aimed to move viewers with the sense of a war effort which depended on ordinary folk going about their daily lives. The American version seized especially upon the idea of ongoing family life, and dramatised a Britishness embodied by its civilian population with their idealised virtues of common sense and everyday fortitude.[85]

It was also more conservative in its view of the sexes, with Mrs. Miniver starting the film as a frivolous shopper and finishing it (having encountered meanwhile a Nazi pilot in her kitchen, and coped with her prospective daughter-in-law being bombed to death in her car) a paragon of maternal and womanly strength, sacrificing all for her children and husband (the soldierly Clem who goes off to do his bit at Dunkirk). Though the centrality given to the female character as she manages on the Home Front makes this a woman's film, there is little of Struther's independent and witty consciousness, only Greer Garson's knowing looks and dulcet tones underlined by a highly emotive musical score. What's more, a vigorous sense of the loyalties of church, army and state runs through the film, with the final scene giving us the gathered family in their bombed parish church and pulling out all the patriotic stops.

Neither the film nor the book form of *Mrs. Miniver* has worn well, and on the face of it they might seem to have little in common. The film belongs as clearly to the more romantic Toryism of the Churchillian mood as the original does to the less resounding conservatisms of 'appeasement'. Yet under the impress of war it seems that it was easy for the one to build upon and transform the other; those same retiring virtues of 1938 could themselves, in a larger theatre, paradoxically come to seem the stuff of a nation in arms. The war inflated and magnified Jan Struther's domestic sentiments into something far grander, and provided a new heroic stage for a British people seen, not as a race of empire builders or natural warriors, but rather as an essentially unassuming nation, peaceable by temperament, who wanted nothing better than a quiet life. At the heart of it was a powerful and new sense of national history, not as the doings of the great and the good, but as that which was made by the little, ordinary people at home, 'muddling through'.[86] Well before the bombing began, a patriotism of private life was being felt and expressed. When Mrs. Miniver comes home after the holidays, the kettle on the fender, the fire glowing and the barrel organ's strains drifting on the wind in the street outside, this is already a little England, best characterised by a love of privacy and home comforts. It is that same mood of quietude and intimacy which was caught in Vera Lynn's rendition of 'There'll Always Be An England', a popular song of 1939; its evocation of national spirit – 'If England means as much to you as England means to me' – as understated and personal as that of 'Rule Britannia' was loud and bombastic.

With a shift of key and in more starkly dramatising times, that same cheerful enjoyment of life could become stoic; that sense of independence one of standing alone, that reticence a necessary suffering in silence.

Perhaps inside every Mrs. Miniver was a national heroine, struggling to get out.

Chapter 4

Daphne du Maurier's romance with the past

> This other self knew that life need not be bitter, nor worthless, nor bounded by a narrow casement, but could be limitless, infinite ...
>
> (*Frenchman's Creek*, p. 15)

To enter the world of Daphne du Maurier's fiction is to breathe an entirely different air, away from the shuttered interiors of Compton-Burnett, the closed circles of Christie's fiction, and the safe domestic confines of a Mrs. Miniver. It is the wide open spaces of hill and sea which dominate her novels: the howling winds around *Jamaica Inn*, starkly isolate on Bodmin moor, the crashing Cornish breakers and precipitate cliffs of *Rebecca*, all conjure up a familiar literary romanticism, a reworking of that repertoire of images which the nineteenth century evoked as a landscape of desire. With the atmospheric opening of *Jamaica Inn*, 'a granite sky' and a 'lashing, pitiless rain', we know straightaway that we are in the place of 'pathetic fallacy', and the land of longing, and that Mary Yellan, travelling alone across the deserted country into the dark night, is journeying into a storm teeming with narrative excitement, whose emotional elements will be as fierce as those which pound on the door of her coach. Making our way, like her, into the story, we expect to weather tempests of feeling as frequently as those of gales and rain.

Pastness in all its forms, personal, familial, biographical and national captured her imagination and there is much in du Maurier's writing to suggest hers is a romantic Toryism, one which invokes the past as a nobler, loftier place where it was possible to live a more expansive and exciting life. The old-fashioned grandeur of Manderley in *Rebecca*, the Cornish residence of Maximilian de Winter, with its retinue of servants and splendid breakfasts, Dona St Columb in *Frenchman's Creek*, a plucky heroine and lady of substantial wealth, who like Honor Harris in *The King's General* captivates the strongest and proudest of males, high-class intrigues amongst the gentry – here surely are the themes dear to the Tory imagination in its vision of a lost past to be contrasted with a lack-lustre present. Add to this the image of du Maurier herself as the wife of a general who in later years was privy to the royal household,[1] enjoying 'the life of a fairytale princess in a mansion in Cornwall', and the picture seems complete.[2]

Yet such a view would slew out of all recognition those images which most fasten on the mind of the du Maurier reader. It is not for her polemical or hortatory powers that her books are remembered, nor even for her re-creation of a convincing past; the pedagogic, but also the antiquarian's, impulse is weak in her historical fiction, and she is not much interested in evoking 'period' detail or in teaching the reader the gracious habits of a former age. Rather it is exactly the unruly and the ungovernable, those objects of official distrust and fear, which she captures with most energy and which dominate her novels, almost against her better judgement, as it were. It is a dialectic she made explicit in *Jamaica Inn* where the selfsame anarchy which assumes a debased and terrifying form in Joss Merlyn, landlord of the hostelry and leader of the wreckers, exerts a fascinated pull on the heroine in the person of his brother Jem. What is sickening lawlessness in Joss can be a desirable recklessness in Jem: both are 'the colour of a gypsy', both break the law, but the one revolts and the other excites, as Mary Yellan feels when she contemplates Jem's hands:

> they had the same strength, the same grace, as his brother's. These attracted her; the others repelled her. She realized for the first time that aversion and attraction ran side by side; that the boundary-line was thin between them.
>
> (p. 126)

Du Maurier's heroes are not only soldiers but pirates and gypsies, those miscreants who form the mob. And the true villain of *Jamaica Inn* is not the drunken Joss Merlyn but the sober and respectable, and quietly psychopathic priest, who is the vicar of Altarnun.

It is the same boundary-line between the abhorrent and the desirable that is explored in her most powerful creation, a female character who has substance only in the fantasies of others, Rebecca. The narrator of the novel, a good bourgeois heroine, selfless and modest, remains nameless but gives up the title-role in the book to that Other Woman, fearless, wild and immoral, the epitome of female licentiousness, 'vicious, damnable, rotten through and through'. Though the novel does its best to convince us of her vileness – 'Rebecca was incapable of love, of tenderness, of decency' (p. 283) – it merely increases her imaginative hold. Du Maurier herself seems to have found her scarlet woman irresistible: Rebecca, who 'did what she liked' and 'lived as she liked', who 'cared for nothing and no one',

> Rebecca seizing life with her two hands; Rebecca triumphant, leaning down from the minstrel's gallery with a smile on her lips.
>
> (p. 284)

Even after the grimmest of fictional comeuppances, it is Rebecca who haunts both writer and narrator, who won't stay dead but keeps on coming back.

If du Maurier's is a romantic imagination then it is one always drawn to play with fire, to linger on the boundary-lines of her beliefs. Her novels are deeply contradictory: pressing the reader to escape bounds whilst at the same time urging an acceptance of how things are and clinging, safe, to familiar pieties. Both these desires are played out in different kinds of opposition, and in the choice of different genres and forms of writing, throughout du Maurier's long career, from the preoccupation with the limits of sexual freedom in her novels of the 1930s and '40s, to her later concern with the boundaries of the body and the possibility of the 'supernatural'. Although she may seem to dwell on irreconcilable opposites, du Maurier's fiction suggests how much those disparate longings are in fact the two sides of the same coin: only an imagination which sets such store by moral, sexual, social, even physical controls, can find the idea of unbridled release both dangerous and desirable. Du Maurier's writing is not powerful because it successfully conveys a conservative vision but because of the pleasure it takes in undermining its own beliefs. Du Maurier's writing suggests that conservatism has its own divisions, its own buried desires, that it has its own unconscious, its cravings which cannot be satisfied and its conflicts which cannot be resolved.

A BETTER CLASS OF ROMANCE: GENDER AND GENRE

> There is no such thing as romantic love.
> (*The Rebecca Notebook and Other Memories*, p. 99)

Romance, as Ivy Compton-Burnett might have said, has gone through all its stages for the reader of today. To be hailed nowadays as a popular romantic novelist or even 'the last of the great romantic writers'[3] is an ambiguous tribute, especially for the woman writer, bringing with it the suggestion of a 'genre', the bestselling 'formula' fiction of the 'boy-meets-girl' variety, epitomised in Britain by the industrial output of Mills & Boon. Daphne du Maurier is perhaps thought of, popularly, as 'a woman's novelist', read mainly for her love-stories. Yet what sense does it make to call *Rebecca*, as one Mills & Boon author has, 'the archetypal romantic novel'[4] when it ends not with conjugal bliss but middle-aged resignation and exile? Not one of her 'love-stories' has a happy ending: *Jamaica Inn* begins with a romance (that between Mary Yellan's aunt and uncle) which has gone sour and warns us that when Mary decides to go with Jem at the end of the novel, it is a path leading to her own misery and disillusionment; *Frenchman's Creek*, the most frivolous of her novels, is even more uncompromising in returning its heroine to a marriage she is bored with, and there is no romantic fulfilment either for Honor Harris in *The King's General* who remains ultimately separated from her lover. Du Maurier is noticeably short on wedding bells.

Even more disarming, perhaps, for those who wish to see her as a typical woman's novelist, is the propensity she had, throughout her life, to adopt the masculine persona. *I'll Never Be Young Again* (1933), *My Cousin Rachel* (1952), *The Scapegoat* (1957), *The Flight of the Falcon*, (1965) and *The House on the Strand* (1969), are all written in the first person singular, masculine gender; in many of her short stories, and amongst them the best-known, 'The Birds' (1952) and 'Don't Look Now' (1970), she takes the male part. This kind of impersonation could be read as a form of pseudonym, like those adopted by nineteenth-century women authors, allowing protective covering and giving the writer a space in which to be taken seriously in a culture which has long thought disparagingly of 'authoresses'. It is more than a question of reception, however. Du Maurier is drawn in the fiction itself to cross those boundaries which for the last century at least had made certain kinds of writing a matter of writing like a man:

> Joss Merlyn marked his assailant with his second shot, spattering him in mid-stomach, and while the fellow doubled up in the mud amongst his companions, mortally wounded and screaming like a hare, Harry the pedlar caught another in the throat, the bullet ripping the windpipe, the blood spouting jets like a fountain.
>
> (*Jamaica Inn*, p. 169)

Clearly whatever 'romance' meant for Daphne du Maurier, it involved a reinterpretation of the idea of the woman's novel.

Du Maurier herself disliked being thought of as a romantic writer: she wanted to be 'read straight',[5] and certainly her work must be a nightmare for the eager compiler of 'genre studies' compendia, containing as it does (according to one authority) the already blurred categories of 'gothics, romances and family sagas',[6] to which we might cheerfully add 'mysteries', science fiction and ghost stories (leaving aside her 'non-fiction'). Accepting the Mystery Writers Award for *My Cousin Rachel* in 1952, du Maurier was adamant that it was no more a mystery than it was a romance: like *Rebecca* before it, she maintained, it was a study in jealousy.[7] Is *The House on the Strand*, which takes the reader back and forth between medieval and modern Cornwall, science fiction, a crime story (for the narrator investigates a murder), or a historical novel? To call her a romantic writer in the case of a story like 'The Birds', in which a householder and his family barricade themselves in against the unnatural and inexplicable savagery of the bird population, only makes sense in the broadest and oldest use of the word – as a tale of extravagant and unlikely happenings.

The question of 'genre' is a useful one to raise, however. In the first

place it reminds us of the modernity of many of these critical adjudi-
cations; in the second, of the modernity of many of the forms themselves,
and finally, that the shaping of bestselling forms of fiction into a recognisable typology, which took significantly new commercial impetus in the
period between the wars, altered the conditions for all writers. Once it
became possible for readers to ask for a 'detective story' or a 'romance',
'an Edgar Wallace' or 'a Georgette Heyer', and to know what to expect,
any writer, and especially those aiming at a broad readership, was up
against the question of genre and could expect to be measured in some way
against those categories. Moreover, they were categories which frequently
confirmed the expectation that particular forms of writing spoke especially
to women or to men.

The meanings of romance and of 'romantic' as terms of literary description became more narrowly specialised between the wars, coming to
signify only those love-stories, aimed ostensibly at a wholly female
readership, which deal primarily with the trials and tribulations of heterosexual desire, and end happily in marriage. At the same time, there is a
sense in which, as part of the creation of this 'genre', romance went
downmarket as it was boosted by the growth in forms of 'mass entertainment' in the period and its commercialisation made it a bestselling form
for a much larger group of readers. Cheaper paperback editions and a
plethora of new fiction weeklies for working women and girls (or 'books'
as they called them), including *Peg's Paper* (1919), *Red Star* (1929), *Secrets*
(1932) and *Oracle* (1933), offered them a staple of 'really grand stories',
especially romances, 'that will make you eager to draw up your chair to
the fire and have a real good read'.[8] Whereas before the war 'leisure' might
be seen as primarily the property of the 'leisured', that is, wealthy, classes,
a new market of 'leisure consumers' amongst the working classes was in
the process of being created. Those women's magazines wishing to dissociate themselves from this cheap entertainment, laid their stress not on
fiction (which was a mere sideline) but on 'services' to readers (the range of
'experts' to deal with readers' problems which the new *Good Housekeeping*
introduced, for example), on household management and 'constructive'
uses of free time.[9]

Film, and especially Hollywood cinema, together with the spate of film
magazines which became a craze in the late 1920s and '30s, made romance
even more visible as the major form for a more heterogeneous class of
audience.[10] And for many critics of the new forms of mass entertainment,
it was romance which provided the model of all that was meretricious
about the popular cultural forms of modernity: the creation of a reader
or viewer whose individuality is effaced as they abandon themselves to
the screen or to the 'tide of cheap, easy fiction', 'waiting passively to be
stimulated'.[11] What might strike the reader now examining these criticisms
is how much the descriptions echo traditional views of feminine sexuality

as a whole, and can be readily collapsed into a vocabulary of distaste for the lower-class woman in particular. It is as though these new audiences and readerships can only be forgiven if they are seen as experiencing a kind of moral and intellectual violation against their will; if they enjoy it, they must be, like the fictions, 'cheap and easy'. The language in which F. R. Leavis condemns the experience of cinema in his attack on mass culture conjures up again a debased, because feminine, position:

> [Films] provide now the main form of recreation in the civilised world; and they involve surrender, under conditions of hypnotic receptivity, to the cheapest of emotional appeals.[12]

Progressive bourgeois women writers, and university women, were in the van of the attack on this lower class of fiction, of which Q. D. Leavis's pioneering study of 1932, *Fiction and the Reading Public*, is only the best-known example. Rebecca West deplored 'Marie Corelli's incurably commonplace mind' (whilst generously admitting that if 'she had a mind like a milliner's apprentice', she was nevertheless 'something more than a milliner's apprentice').[13] In her review of Ethel M. Dell's *Charles Rex*, West advised the critic who was trying to understand the appeal of best-sellers to remember that

> whistles can be made sounding certain notes which are clearly audible to dogs and other of the lower animals, though man is incapable of hearing them.[14]

Storm Jameson (an admirer of the Leavises and an English graduate herself) lamented a fiction 'infected with film technique' and feeding 'herd prejudice', in which

> Deep calls to deep, and the writer's thought is sucked into the immense vacuum created in women's minds by a civilisation in which they have either nothing much to do or too much (too much machine-minding).[15]

The inclusion of that last sympathetic parenthesis suggests how far 'empty' leisure was no longer the sign of the aristocratic or idle, wealthy woman but of the worker; increasingly a new pressure is felt to differentiate the cultural pleasures of women who might count themselves in the middle classes, not just from the excesses of the class above, but from the reading and viewing of those below.

When Virginia Woolf in 1929 looked forward to the day when women's writing 'would no longer be the dumping ground for the personal emotions',[16] her version of feminism was in keeping with a horror of 'gush' or 'tosh', of the emotionality with which the pre-war bourgeois woman had been burdened, and whose rejection was now *de rigeur*. Many writers of fiction adopted a tone of irony toward the emotions which would have caused consternation to their mothers. E. M. Delafield, for example, was typical of her flippant generation in wryly asking the rhetorical question of her readers which presupposed their own disavowal of such things:

> Imagination, emotionalism, sensationalism, what woman is not the victim of these insidious and fatally unpractical emotions?'
>
> (*The Way Things Are*, p. 336)

The revelation of inner desires and emotional depths was traumatic not just for 'severely political' or public women,[17] however, but for all those aiming at a modern female respectability, different both from the image of bourgeois femininity in the past and from a contemporary sexuality displayed across more proletarian forms. We might speculate that the modern bourgeois woman between the wars retreats from the visibly erotic or from displays of femininity, as the working classes become more publicly sexualised. Certainly, with intensity of feeling and expressivity such thorough bad taste, many writers left romance well alone or found ways of writing from a less 'feminine' position in the culture.[18]

Crime fiction, for example, was one place within the more popular literatures that 'middlebrow' and 'highbrow' could meet, and where both men and women of the middle classes could be united in despising romantic literature. No 'shopgirl, factory girl, skivvy or housewife'[19] was likely to read Christie, but if she did, it was surely with a sense of its superiority to Bertha Ruck, *Peg's Paper* or Mills & Boon, if only because it did not advertise its femininity. Regardless of how many women wrote detective fiction between the wars, it was still considered to be a masculine form, mainly read by men.[20] Neither gushy nor confessional, the crime story laid a stress on those apparently masculine qualities of reason and logic; its modernist emphasis was upon surface, form and contemplation – the antithesis of romance's depth, substance and emotional involvement. It is an opposition maintained with a superb lack of self-consciousness by some critics today:

> the sort of mind that likes well-made plots is not likely to go in for formless romance and affection as well – murder (in fiction, at least) conforms to disciplines that love does not.[21]

Given the inferiority afforded to 'formless romance', writing detective fiction was, and is, for many women writers not only a way of claiming the 'unfeminine' qualities of orderliness and control, but also of attempting to avoid the 'stigma' of gender altogether. As crime fiction included university dons and 'highbrows' amongst its authors, there was always a meagre portion of cultural *cachet* which writers like Dorothy L. Sayers were only too happy to seize upon. Detective stories (so the argument runs), because of their emphasis upon cerebration, if nothing else, take more 'work' than other popular forms of novel, are closer to 'real novels', and thereby occupy a more elevated position amongst the 'pulp' fictions.[22] Dorothy L. Sayers was the first of many crime writers who sought to 'improve' the detective story, turn it from a mere crossword puzzle into a 'proper' novel: romance writers, on the other hand, were usually content to 'entertain'.

If, as I have argued, women writers helped 'bourgeoisify' crime between the wars, and make it respectable, this 'civilising process'[23] could nevertheless offer the 'well-bred' woman writer an escape from womanliness. Romance was not so easily erased, however. Far from it being the case that as Somerset Maugham argued 'marriage bells have no place in a detective story',[24] Agatha Christie's novels, for example, nearly always have a romantic sub-plot which ends happily once the murderer has been discovered, although part of her skill (unlike a lesser writer like Patricia Wentworth who mimicked Christie in the 1950s) lies in the romantic couple rarely being outside suspicion. In fact women crime writers frequently tried their hand at romance fiction too: Dorothy L. Sayers turned her Peter Wimsey books more and more into love stories and Agatha Christie wrote romances as 'Mary Westmacott'; Georgette Heyer, meanwhile, the creator in the late 1920s of the Regency romance, wrote thrillers throughout the 1930s. Rather than seeing 'masculinity' or 'femininity' confined to discussion within different forms, we need to understand how it is constantly in the process of being revised and discussed across the range of popular genres, to understand the interrelationship of these genres, and their forms of differentiation from each other as well as their specific scope. In some ways these commercial genres, with their formulaic rules and expectations, could be played with by writers quite self-consciously, as forms of *alias*, different social positions from which to write, 'part-egos', as it were.[25]

Du Maurier was one of those young women in the late 1920s whose modernity took the form of dissociating themselves from the wrong kind of romance, from 'formless' femininity, poured 'from the heart' like so much spilt ink.[26] Her work reminds us, however, that the intended rejection of romance by superior women did not mean the disappearance of those out-of-bounds feelings. They could and would return under cover, camouflaged by irony, or treated with a self-consciousness about their lower-class trappings which allowed the reader to establish a distance from all the silliness of romance, whilst enjoying to the full many of its pleasures. Her best-loved romance, *Rebecca*, and her only realist one, is in fact a tale of two genres – a thriller or murder story, as well as a lovestory, in which romance itself comes under scrutiny and is found wanting. For though du Maurier may have 'despised the Barbara Cartland school of romance',[27] she did not ignore it.

It is possible to read the courtship and proposal scenes at the beginning of *Rebecca* as deliberately employing many of the staple ingredients of just that kind of romance: the story of the poor companion (a clergyman's daughter?) 'red-elbowed and lanky haired' (p. 20), meeting a darkly hand-some older man at Monte Carlo, who falls in love with her and snatches her away to a life of wealth and luxury, might have furnished both Barbara Cartland and *Peg's Paper* with a plot: 'I'm asking you to marry me, you little fool' (p. 56).[28] In du Maurier's novel this romantic opening forms the prologue to the story proper, which begins with the girl herself questioning the rapidity and nature of the proposal – is the 'romance' to be trusted or is it all a fantasy on her part?

> Romantic, that was the word. . . . Yes, of course. Romantic. That was what people would say. It was all very sudden and romantic.
>
> (p. 61)

It is her doubts about her own romantic love that set in train the jealous fantasies she has of Rebecca, who must have had, according to her think-ing, a 'real' romance with Maxim.

Rebecca is a romance about respectability in more ways than one – it supports in the end the moral superiority of the girl's way of being, thoughtful, diffident, and conventional, over and against the decadence of Rebecca. Amongst other things, it gives its readers both the pleasures of romance fiction in its narrowest sense and a position from which to feel superior to its foolish idealisms. Du Maurier wrote romances for those readers who imagined they were above that sort of thing, and whose unhappy endings both prolonged the passion and provided a cynical com-ment on the impossibility of romantic love.

Rather than seeing du Maurier as a writer who 'crosses genres', we might see her as one who resists them, and their modern cultural conno-tations, whilst nimbly making the most of the reader's expectations and generic pleasures. Most obviously du Maurier turned to both the romantic appeal of the past and the romantic literature of the past, now claimed as a tradition, in order to write a better class of romance. The romantic writing which du Maurier herself acknowledged was not that which was shaping into a 'genre' between the wars, but that of the nineteenth-century novel. She was the first to admit a lifelong debt to the Brontës and her self-conscious reshaping of their imaginative terrain. She began her career with *The Loving Spirit*, whose title and chapter epigraphs pay homage to Emily Brontë's poetry. Thirty years later she was still revisiting Haworth in her imagination, to produce a scholarly study of *The Infernal World of Branwell Brontë* (1961) and in one of her last books, *Vanishing Cornwall* (1967), she devotes a whole chapter to 'the Brontë heritage' and to establishing the Branwell family's roots in Penzance. *Jamaica Inn* reworks *Wuthering Heights* in its re-imagining of the blasted heaths of the Cornish rather than Yorkshire moors; Jem Merlyn, the roguish hero, is as much a likeable Heathcliff as his brother, Joss, is a more undesirable one. Echoes of *Jane Eyre* abound in her work: Mary Yellan, like the nameless heroine of *Rebecca*, is an orphan sent out to make her living, whilst the Vicar of Altarnun is St John Rivers recast in a sinister mould. Like *Jane Eyre* too, the plain, genteel girl in *Rebecca* falls in love with a gentleman widower and is estranged from her beloved by the discovery of his first wife who casts a shadow over their lives.

We might look to the Brontës too for the fascination with the margins of polite society, the attractive repulsiveness of the outcast and the degenerate (like *The Tenant of Wildfell Hall*), and for the familiar themes of bourgeois transgression – drunkenness, theft, murder, madness – and marital abuse (*Jamaica Inn* has them all). Above all, however, it is in a language of sensibility, the primacy given to her protagonists' thoughts and desires, to the idea of a tumultuous inner life and to a language of a developing selfhood, which sees du Maurier most obviously re-staging a literary romanticism. The heaviest of du Maurier's debts to the Brontës was to a romantic tradition which centred on feeling and which claimed the importance of romantic love as a potentially dangerous place where the individual, and especially the woman, might get taken 'beyond herself', uncover hidden desires and often destructive wants. Du Maurier put romance back into the landscape of individualism; her love-stories are also *Bildungsromane*.

If part of du Maurier's talent as a modern writer lay in taking the reader over the familiar, and the more noticeably *literary* territory of the past, another romantic borrowing reaches back into distinctly male preserves. Most of du Maurier's stories break the bounds of the 'feminine' world of feeling into that of action and incident, answering the call of the wild in another sense. A bold freedom of feeling is matched by a freedom of plot, which makes many of her central characters wanderers and travellers, and many of them male. Her first two novels, *The Loving Spirit* and *I'll Never Be Young Again*, revelled in the uncompromisingly male life of ships and sailing: picaresque in form, these tales of freebooting heroes might have been written with the first line of *Coral Island* uppermost in her mind: 'Roving has always been, and still is, my ruling passion.' Indeed it is to the romantic masculinity of late-nineteenth-century boys' stories, and the historical adventures and 'sea fiction' of the kind which thrilled the readers of the *Boy's Own Paper*, to which we might turn to discover the literary parentage of du Maurier's romantic heroes.[29]

Du Maurier was a devoted Stevensonian, and if *Jamaica Inn* rewrites *Wuthering Heights*, it does so in the buccaneering vein of *Treasure Island*. In her preoccupation with the sea, with sailing, piracy, smuggling and shipwreck, du Maurier draws on a 'tushery' and swashbuckling not to be found in the Brontës, who could hardly have imagined, as she does, a vicar swooping like a black bird from the top of Rough Tor to his death.[30] Du Maurier was of the generation brought up on the adventure story of the late nineteenth century, officially boys' reading, which had become 'children's classics' by the time of the First World War.[31] Perhaps hers was the first generation of girls for whom the prescriptions for a suitably feminine reading were relaxed, allowing them to read the works of Alexandre Dumas, R. M. Ballantyne and Captain Marryat, as well as all the boys' school stories.

If du Maurier was conservative in turning back to a boys' own version of the past, the dilemmas she poses for her characters stem from a modern awareness that such images of masculinity lacked 'intellectual and moral credibility'[32] in the post-war world. Her heroes are by no means simply caught in a time-lag, revivifying, as 'Sapper' or John Buchan might, a kind of 'derring-do' already made distasteful, if not preposterous, by the war. The manliness of her heroes is often as doubtful as the docility of her heroines, and all of the novels provide some kind of commentary on the choices which she sees offered to men and women as forms of sexual freedom. Although the terms in which she couches sexual differences are conservative – maleness is physical strength and emotional inadequacy, femaleness is weakness and emotional strength – the opposition does not satisfy her and her novels try over and again to call such terms in question. It was no doubt both disappointing and reassuring to her readers that they always fail.[33]

ROMANTIC FREEDOMS AND THE PROBLEM OF SEXUAL DESIRE

> What a pity I'm not a vagrant on the face of the earth. Wandering in strange cities, foreign lands, open spaces, fighting, drinking, loving physically. And here I am, only a silly, sheltered girl in a dress, knowing nothing at all – but Nothing.
>
>   (du Maurier in her diary at age 22, *Myself When Young*, p. 123)

The desire to be differently female is central to du Maurier's best-known novels. Mary Yellan imprisoned by family feeling in the hateful Jamaica Inn, the girl in *Rebecca* haunted and paralysed by the idea of a female sexuality more confident than her own, Dona St Columb hemmed in by the tedium of her married life and the dictates of motherhood – all wish to be free of the social expectations of femininity and it is attempted escape which fuels the plots. *The Loving Spirit*, du Maurier's first novel, opens with a scene of female frustration which places discontent firmly inside the mind of the woman about to be *happily* married.

> Janet still stood on the hilltop and watched the sea, and it seemed to her that there were two sides of her; one that wanted to be the wife of a man, and to care for him, and love him tenderly, and one that asked only to be part of a ship, part of the seas and the sky above, with the glad free ways of a gull.
>
>   (*The Loving Spirit*, p. 16)

Janet Coombe is not a Jane Eyre, pacing the battlements at Thornfield, bemoaning her lot as a single woman but finding fulfilment eventually through romantic love and a bourgeois home. She is as Jane Eyre might have been in middle age, after living contentedly with Rochester and producing the requisite number of sons, discovering that, despite a good home and a good man, she is still restless and wanting something more.

When du Maurier starts writing in the late 1920s she takes for granted the idea that the scope given women in their usual social position and their own ideas of 'self-fulfilment' do not tally, and remain incommensurate after, as well as before, marriage. The settled domestic life and romantic notions of individual feminine selfhood are seen as antithetical, and a seed of discontent makes every woman (even a Cornish peasant at the beginning of the nineteenth century) divided, fraught with a modern 'self' consciousness. Gone is the faith in marriage as the healer of all ills, and in the peaceful domestic life as woman's best option: *The Loving Spirit* has absorbed the feminist protest of the late Victorian and Edwardian years and can now offer it to readers as a kind of common sense. No longer the advanced views of quirky or bohemian or free-thinking 'new' women, the idea that a married life, even a happy one, may be a kind of limitation for women, could appear in the popular novel without fear of shocking its readers. And when, as they always do, du Maurier's fictions reassert the unconquerable ties of home and maternity, it is usually at the end of the novel with a sense of resignation and regret, rather than as a cause for celebration.

With youthful enthusiasm, du Maurier solves Janet Coombe's dilemma outside the bounds of realism, by resorting to a supernatural sub-plot and turning her into a ship. No doubt she recognised, however, that such fortunate transfigurations are not the lot of us all, and her fiction tries a variety of means to get beyond what she saw as the limits of being female. Most often it was by placing her female characters at the centre of an historical adventure story in some kind of conflict with its image of freebooting individualism, that du Maurier tried to get to grips with what emancipation might mean. In her historical novels the literature of romantic sensibility in which the self is inward-looking and reflective is yoked to another kind of history which sees the individual as best known in external activity, acting upon the world; in the tension and opposition between these modes of writing du Maurier explores her conception of sexual differences and generates the excitement, as well as the conservatism of her tales.

It was far from being a simple case of transferring the image of masculine 'dash, pluck and lionheartedness'[34] to her tales in the shape either of male or female characters. In bringing together the generic expansiveness of male adventurism and the inward-looking sensibility of the domestic novel, du Maurier worries at the limits of both in the context of a modern consciousness. Both *The Loving Spirit* and her second novel, *I'll Never Be Young Again*, see her trying on the boys' story for size, as it were, and jibbing at the subjective or private implications of its gung-ho version of the past; she is both drawn to, and critical of, the combative and emotionally unencumbered individual. In both novels the reader is distanced from the adventure story by the intrusion of often rather clumsily agonised passages of introspection on the part of the heroine or hero, in which they ponder their feelings after the conventional scenes of 'action'. In the former novel she adopts different narrative voices, first as Janet Coombe, then as Joseph Coombe, her son, a born rover with the rollicking life of a sailor. In old age du Maurier remembered with relish the release which writing as a male character could grant: 'it was fun becoming Joseph madly wanting his silly virgin of eighteen'.[35] The novel, however, clearly condemns Joseph's preoccupation with himself and gives us a man whose emotional inadequacy leaves him at the end of the story half-maddened, and crying for his mother.

The second novel, *I'll Never Be Young Again*, is the story both of the narrator Dick coming to manhood, and of his necessary acceptance that he is a conventional, that is, a domestic, rather than heroic male. It too alternates scenes of intense emotional self-analysis with bouts of drinking, philandering and fighting which give the novel's rather turgid tempo sudden fillips and brief bursts of a 'rattling' pace. It is a realist novel with a contemporary setting but one which begins with a male adventure romance in which Dick is befriended by the older and stronger Jake, and runs away to sea, thus encountering many opportunities for drinking, philandering, etc. A passage in which du Maurier has Dick contemplate his own broadening experience seems like an answer to the prayer she uttered for herself, the 'silly girl', who wanted to be a vagrant on the face of the earth:

I had sailed in a ship and felt the wind in my face, I had wandered in strange cities, I had ridden over the mountains, I had slept under a white sky, I had loved a girl with my body . . . .

(p. 100)

Yet it is just this kind of self-consciousness about being tough and manly which puts her prose closer to Hemingway than to Henty:[36]

I rose to my feet and swung into this man who had thrown the knife and missed, and he was taken unawares, and dropped like a stone, both of my fists smashing into his two eyes. And it was good to know that he was hurt, and it was good to feel his mouth soft and bleeding under my hands, and I heard myself laughing, with the breath shaken from me in sobs, while a pain hammered under my ribs, and this is all right, I thought, this is all right.

(*I'll Never Be Young Again*, p. 116)

Neither Henty's clean-limbed lads, nor Sapper's 'Bulldog Drummond' would bother to examine their feelings in the middle of a scrap. It was the inward as well as the heroic picture of masculinity which was praised:

> Daphne du Maurier's descriptions of riding in Norwegian mountains, of life before the mast and in foreign capitals ring as true as her transportation of a young man's thoughts and talk.[37]

The novel caught the tones of a modern masculinity no longer entirely at ease with itself.

The second half of the novel acts as a commentary on the first. Jake, the quietly heroic older friend, is abruptly drowned and we find ourselves instead in the midst of a contemporary 'sex novel' of the kind that Michael Arlen's *The Green Hat* (1924) made the rage of the late 1920s.[38] Set in the bohemian Paris of the day it is as though Hemingway turns to write as Jean Rhys, and the power of this part of the novel lies in the obssessive love of Dick for Hesta, a music student (with an orange beret rather than green hat) whom he urges into a 'free' sexual relationship which destroys her life. It is a damning portrait of male egotism but also conveys a sense of what du Maurier sees as the emptiness of modern sexual freedoms. Hesta is a modern young woman who is at heart deeply conventional; she tries to live beyond her emotional means, and to express herself sexually, only to be met by a continuing double standard in her male lover, and ultimately with a sense of disgust at herself. Du Maurier's novel was quite 'frank' (a popular word of the day) about Hesta's sexual needs, but is unable to imagine a relationship outside marriage which wouldn't inevitably turn morally sour. Hesta is condemned to a life of 'soul-destroying' sexual liaisons; Dick to discovering, too late, his need for marriage and stability (he ends up with that most humdrum of modern fates, in 'business').

Although these apprentice novels are something of a farrago of styles, they suggest the ambivalence with which du Maurier was to deal with ideas of sexual difference throughout her work. On the one hand there is a revolt in *I'll Never Be Young Again* against post-war 'promiscuity' and a reaction against modernity; on the other, a modern indictment of conservative assumptions about men and women which cannot allow a man to be 'sensitive' or a woman to express sexual desire. The first half of the novel idealises the notion of a freedom outside social conventions, the second half shows it to be egotistical and ultimately destructive. Du Maurier's novels never whole-heartedly approve of the idea of the individual who can somehow shirk all social responsibilities and ties – the image which she culls from the masculine adventurism of the nineteenth century – since she holds fast, too, to the image of home, the need for a resting place, for stability, continuity and connectivity. All the novels are irked by the terms of that conservative vision of sexual difference which would equate sexual pleasure, desirable but irresponsible, with a purely 'masculine' freedom and oppose it to that other kind of desire for the social legitimacy of stable relationships, family and home, seen as a purely 'feminine' domain. In her novels which have male narrators these different desires are shown to conflict within the individual; in the historical novels the pulls of home and away are irreconcilable for the female characters who 'see through' the limitations of masculine freedom: in either case, the one is always at the cost of the other and the pleasures neither of vagrancy nor of shelter can suffice.

For a woman writer in the post-war years the reworking of the heroic-isms of the late-nineteenth-century adventure story could provide new forms of power and ways of portraying fantasies of freedom, but it is an uneasy kind of impersonation, since she writes with a knowledge that such romanticisms are very much a thing of the past. Even in her later historical novels where the exotic settings and outlandish mores ought to allow for 'real heroes', there is no wholly admiring picture of English masculinity such as thrilled the readers before the war. Du Maurier is constantly drawn back in search of an ideal of masculine independence and emotional freedom, a romantic and conservative vision, but her novels are unable to give us such a picture unadulterated. It is not simply that 'freedom' in her novels is masculine and 'limitation' feminine, but rather that the terms of this opposition, inherited from that past, no longer satisfy and are no longer wholly believable. It is the choice itself, between the 'free' life and the home-loving one, which is found wanting, together with the old-fashioned assumptions that masculinity and femininity occupy separate psychological or biological spheres.

What happens in her novels is a psychologising of sexuality which makes the idea of an untrammelled, undivided individual, and with it the notion of the English male as gloriously unselfconscious and at ease with his masculinity, impossible to sustain. Where du Maurier's male characters speak in the first person they cannot by definition be heroic since heroes have no sensibility. Instead they are, like Philip in *My Cousin Rachel*, full of self-doubt, nervy ('neurasthenic' even), and tortured about their own desires, dependent upon their own fantasies of an older, stronger man. Dick has his Jake, Philip has his cousin, Ambrose, John his more confident double, Jean in *The Scapegoat*, Beo, the Italian courtier in *The Flight of the Falcon*, lives in the shadow of his brother Aldo, whilst Richard (in *The House on the Strand*) has Magnus, the superior scientist, as his *alter ego*. They are latter-day Waverleys rather than Rob Roys, Waverleys for whom the question of how to be properly masculine has gone inside as it were, has become a question of sexual being, imagined as the innermost part of self.

Whilst du Maurier's emphasis on a psychology which sees the individual as torn and confused by conflicting desires, was part of that exposure of the myth of an English masculinity as necessarily unexpressive and self-contained, it was quite possible for her nevertheless to see such men as 'lacking', and thereby 'feminine'. The sensitive male is never admirable (unless, like the Frenchman of *Frenchman's Creek*, his foreignness is a special dispensation which allows for tenderness as well as virility); he is not different enough, and therefore not desirable. We might speculate that for some modern young women in the inter-war period the ideal of a strong, emotionally independent masculinity could continue to exercise a powerful imaginative hold precisely because it had been thrown into crisis by the war, and even though the cultural and social institutions which had trumpeted English manhood before the war were severely shaken, if not undermined, such an ideal could remain for many as the benchmark against which all other sexualities were measured and found inadequate.

There is nothing in her historical novels of that 'missionary feeling'[39] which had prompted the imperialist adventurers in fiction, and little of the chivalric motif which ran from Scott (whose entire works she appears to have read by the age of eleven)[40] to Dumas: her men are not latter-day knights, their masculinity is detached from the idea of nationhood or empire which made the historical settings of the stories so often the romantic place where manhood was to be proven. Rather history has become a kind of Never Never Land in which men are still boys who never grow up and where any skirmishing is on the frontiers of sexual relationships with women who question their mode of being.[41] Mary Yellan in *Jamaica Inn*, the girl in *Rebecca*, when she reaches 'maturity', Honor Harris in *The King's General* are all heroines who are finally older and wiser than their men, and come in the end to mother them. 'Real' heroes could only exist in the past, but even there they are subject to the damning psychological judgement of her heroines. Jem Merlyn in *Jamaica Inn* may be a likeable rogue but Mary Yellan makes no bones about his 'insolence and coarseness', analysing him and his callousness toward women:

Mary was silent. The indifference in his voice appalled her.

And when Jem continues with the inimitable line

'Senseless or conscious, women are pretty much the same when you come down to it'

(p. 67)

the reader is meant to find him an object of pity as well as desire. Mary is one of many heroines who no longer believe in the myth of the male protector but who see the male sex as deeply flawed in its aggressive virility. Richard Grenville, the commander of the king's forces in *The King's General*, is another such, whose desirability depends upon his almost brutal sexuality, which makes him an object of compassion to Honor Harris and undermines his sexual mastery.

Whilst there is nothing new in the idea of the cold-hearted hero, the sardonic Darcy or the glowering Rochester are only brutes on the surface; they have soft hearts palpitating beneath their stern exteriors. Du Maurier's heroes (rather than her first-person narrators), on the other hand, must remain ultimately unfathomable men wanting inherently different things from their women in order to be desirable: 'Women think differently to men; they travel separate paths' (*Jamaica Inn*, p. 195). It is the same difference, however, which makes them psychologically and emotionally inadequate. Du Maurier's vision is darker than Austen's or Charlotte Brontë's – there is no promise of bourgeois bliss to come with such a man. Although the girl at the end of *Rebecca* has a Maxim as dependent on her as Rochester is on Jane, his upper lip is as stiff as ever, and she is robbed of the rewards of home and children – her punishment for her complicity in Rebecca's murder. Mary Yellan can either have the man and the sexual pleasure that he offers (which will eventually make her miserable), or return to her peaceful home in Helford – but she can't have both. Du Maurier's view of an essentially different 'maleness' and 'femaleness' is modern in seeing this opposition not as happily complementary but as polarising, a source of explosive conflict and contradiction. Hers is a 'war of the sexes' in which sexuality becomes a beleaguered terrain to be defended under siege conditions if need be, and in which the sexes equal each other only in a kind of deadlock or stalemate.

This is the message she reiterates in her grim short story, 'The Apple Tree' (1952): a man's account of his empty marriage and of his release after his wife's death from her emotional blackmail. Gradually, however, we realise that it was his likeable but careless, even heartless, egotism which helped to precipitate his wife's retreat into martyrish suffering; they have limited and distorted each other, and the destructive force of sexual opposition takes on an almost supernatural form in the image of the perverted fertility of the apple tree which brings about the wife's revenge. Both masculinity and femininity are indicted in this story, and yet there is no way out and no alternative to 'normal' behaviour. In du Maurier's imaginative economy the terms of sexual difference are not inescapably fixed for individuals (Philip is a 'womanish' man) but their valencies always are: sexual desire depends upon an opposition between dominance and subordination, between privilege and deprivation, between authority and obedience. One term must triumph at the expense of the other, and the best a woman can do is to turn the tables and, through whatever means, gain the upper hand.

Even her most playful novels revolve around this fiercely binary sense of sexual opposition. *Jamaica Inn*, the first of her novels to catch the public imagination, is an 'escapade'[42] trying to escape the bounds of gender through historical writing, which can allow for a heroine apparently at a remove from contemporary demands and behaviours. Mary Yellan clearly equates the freedoms she so much desires with masculinity: 'Had she been a man', she says to herself, she would cheerfully tackle all comers and later, when she actually makes a plan to trap her uncle, her lover taunts her, 'if you must be a boy, I can't stop you' (p. 195). In some ways it would seem that Mary is granted her wish, for she is bold and assertive. Even Jane Eyre, romantic rebel though she is, would not have found herself toting pistols as Mary Yellan does when she strikes out across the moors alone. The most powerful image at the heart of *Jamaica Inn*, and the most fantastic one, is not the moment when Mary falls in love with Jem (though this is one of the novel's attractions), but her witnessing of the wreckers on the beach, and her daring attempt to intervene as they pick over the spoils of the men they have murdered. When she is finally cornered by the arch-villain of the piece, he too finds her as mettlesome as any boy:

> Gallant he had called her, and possessed with the spirit of adventure. Well, he should see what distance her courage took her, and that she could gamble with her life as well as he.
>
> (p. 246)

Wish-fulfilment is explicitly built into the plot of *Frenchman's Creek*, where the heroine dresses up as a cabin boy and joins in all the action:

> at last she was playing the part of a boy, which as a child she had so often longed to be, watching her brothers ride off with her father, and she gazing after them with resentful eyes, a doll thrown aside on the floor in disgust.
>
> (p. 116)

Frenchman's Creek, like *Jamaica Inn*, is a novel as much about the sexual meanings of 'escapism' as it is itself 'escapist'.[43]

For du Maurier, trespassing on the territory of adventure romances gives her heroines a claim to a physical existence of the kind which in realist fiction only the most daring or bohemian of authors might have attempted. Historical settings were preferably those which went back before the Victorian period, the period which was still part of intimate family history and saw the formation of those ideas about sexual difference which now seemed so irksome.[44] Yet female bodily experience is always described in the novels in terms of its apparent sufferings and not its pleasures; we are constantly reminded of the vulnerability (as du Maurier sees it) of being female. Physicality is an ordeal for Mary – 'he smashed at her with his clenched fist' (p. 135) – and the female body itself a kind of prison whose walls are ultimately unscalable. Her body is frequently 'in the way'.

Indeed *Jamaica Inn* (itself an image of containment) sees Mary as a kind of escapologist; she is always having to get out of tight places, and constrictions of various kinds. Cooped up and locked into a room of her own in the inn, she is released only to be captured again by her uncle, and eventually she tries to force her body through a coach window:

> She worked and strained at the window, leaning backwards through the gap, the effort made more difficult because of her stiff shoulder and back ... she struggled and pushed through the gap, and then with a sickening squeeze and pressure, her hips were through, the frame of the window scraping the flesh and turning her faint.
>
> (p. 160)

Still later, having narrowly escaped being raped, she is all but unconscious when her uncle claims her again,

> he bent down to her, for she had stumbled to the ground again, and threw her over his shoulder as he would a sack. Her head lolled without support, her arms lifeless, and she felt his hands pressing into her scarred side, bruising it once again, rubbing the numb flesh that had lain upon the shingle.
>
> (p. 168)

It is as though the story needs to drive her to the limits of endurance, and to exhaust the reader, in order to prove that despite her desires, she is not a boy but a tomboy – a cross-dresser, in a kind of masquerade whose femininity, in du Maurier's eyes, like truth, will always out. Being a boy can only be play-acting, the real feminine self is found in that 'weakness of flesh', a curiously biblical turn of phrase, which du Maurier repeats at critical moments in the novel. In acting out the part of a boy, what should be physical release becomes a kind of punishment inflicted on the female body.

If for bourgeois women it was possible, at last, to bring the female body back into print, it must be its pains and not its pleasures that are graphically described. Or rather, and more disturbingly, the only pleasure which is not taboo is the pleasure to be taken in pain. For readers there is the gratification in these imaginary scenes of returning violence with violence, hardness for softness, coldness for warmth, and in adopting in fantasy the masculine position:

> She bit through the palm of his hand, and drove her left fist into his eyes, and now he released her wrist, doubled up beneath her back, so that he could have two hands on her throat, and she felt the pressure of his thumbs on her wind-pipe, choking her. Her right hand struggled for the knife, and suddenly her finger closed upon it, and gripping the cold hasp she drove it upwards, under his arm-pit, and she felt

the horrid yielding of his soft flesh to the blade, surprisingly easy, surprisingly warm with the blood running thick and fast on her hand.

(*Frenchman's Creek*, p. 194)

In imagining this scene of feminine aggression, du Maurier is surely reworking the popular literary language of female submission – the 'yielding of soft flesh' which usually referred to fainting maidens; not surprisingly, when Mary Yellan imagines revenge upon her uncle she simply reverses the roles and sees him 'enslaved' in a degraded, feminine position:

standing as he would with his hands bound behind him, powerless for the first time and for ever, was something that afforded her exquisite pleasure, and she turned the picture over and over in her mind, improving upon it.

(p. 185)

Within such an economy sexual positions are either those of strength or weakness, autonomy or abandonment to the will of the other, and though they are exchangeable, the terms of the dualism are immovable. Erotic pleasure is always annihilating, either romantically so in the complete loss of self which heroines undergo when they fall in love, or in the punitive retribution which such loss of 'self-possession' must bring.

Du Maurier was one of many writers who turned to the popular literature of the nineteenth century, written by men for men (or boys), and to the language of an imperialist and often authoritarian model of sexuality in order to try to find a modern image of female sexual experience. Hers was a far more decorous and self-consciously moralising account, however, than those which took huge numbers of women readers and viewers by storm in the 1920s. Between the wars a whole new market of erotic literature written by women for a female audience had developed, which put the female body at its centre and drew upon 'the ideals of a sexually aggressive culture'[45] in order to imagine female pleasure. E. M. Hull's *The Sheik*, published in 1919, whose sales were to surpass all other bestselling novels in the period put together, was part of a new popular culture of female eroticism which played with the idea of sexual violence.[46] It was considered appallingly 'low' by literary and cultural commentators: Q. D. Leavis typified the class contempt in her judgement of it as 'a typist's day-dream'.[47] Yet what is startling about *The Sheik* is not just its sado-masochistic scenario, which sees its heroine, Diana Mayo, almost continuously raped as the concubine of the Arab chieftain, but her *lack* of punishment either morally or socially: the story's ending sees her released to go back to 'civilisation' but choosing to stay in the desert instead. Whilst marriage with the Sheik is only implied, Diana is neither branded a fallen woman nor given a virtuous death. Clearly the novel was an affront to bourgeois morality and its picture of womanhood and feminine psychology, as well as to those whose model of the new popular literatures and cinematic forms could not see them as the place where desires in excess of the socially acceptable or allowable might come to be explored and represented.[48]

We have yet to map the different forms and meanings of such writing in the inter-war period, but it is clearly a response in the wake of the war to a deep structural crisis over what masculinity and femininity might be.[49] It is in this context of an enormous popular expansion in the visualisation and dramatisation of sexuality that Virginia Woolf's famous plea for the bourgeois woman writer to 'speak the truth about the body' must be read.[50] It seems clear that the question of female emancipation which expressed itself in political languages and campaigns in the period brought with it questions too about the eroticisation of the female body, a troubled, and often quite unconscious sense of the need to find new vocabularies in which it was possible to speak of feminine sexual desires; the startlingly new visibility of the female body, in fashion, in film and advertising, helped to create, but was also part of, this need for reinterpretation. We can start to see that it was not simply prudishness (and prudishness itself needs definition) which made Virginia Woolf write of her own sense of failure at trying to allow physical and sexual experience into writing: the female body was in fact being excessively spoken of by women writers but often in accents which the progressive might find socially as well as sexually distasteful. Such truths as an E. M. Hull or Ethel M. Dell might suggest about contemporary feminine sexual fantasies might well appear better unspoken.

Where du Maurier was a modern was in the place given in her books to sexual desire, which is openly acknowledged as part of the inner life of the bourgeois woman. Du Maurier's treatment of sexual desire is in keeping with a modern and post-Freudian view in so far as it sees sexual desire as an overpowering unconscious force in all humans, but one necessarily repressed by convention. Mary Yellan is in no doubt about her desire which she sees as a natural instinct:

> Men and women were like the animals on the farm at Helford, she supposed; there was a common law of attraction for all living things, some similarity of skin or touch, and they would go to one another. This was no choice made with the mind.
>
> (*Jamaica Inn*, p. 122)

Gone is the idea which had long held cultural sway, and especially in romantic fiction, that women were innocent provokers of passion:

> women are very often like naughty children, putting a lighted match to a train of gun powder, and then surprised and frightened because there is an explosion.[51]

Du Maurier's historical heroines are neither maidenly nor innocent but though they may recognise their desires, they are no more able to 'give in' to them and act upon them than their fictional grandmothers. *Jamaica Inn* is still a kind of conduct book in which the heroine, having realised her feelings for Jem, holds off from staying the night with him with a bourgeois propriety Charlotte Brontë would have been proud of. There remains, for du Maurier, no language in which the respectable woman can describe her own sexual desire positively. It is always felt to be socially degrading, incurring a loss of 'self-respect', because it can only be thought of by imagining oneself as the 'wrong' kind of woman. Thus Dona St Columb feels she must hide her desire else she would appear like 'the women at the Swan' (p. 87). Alone with the man of her dreams at last,

> into her mind suddenly came the thought that he believed her bawdy, promiscuous like the women in the tavern, and considered that her behaviour now, sitting beside him in the open air at night, cross-legged like a gypsy, was but another brief interlude in a series of escapades. . . .
>
> (*Frenchman's Creek*, p. 87)

Sexuality is perceived as an inviolable possession, the innermost and most determining part of one's individuality, 'a thing so personal and so intimate' (p. 113), that the fear of losing one's reputation is a fear of losing a unique and superior selfhood, and of being banished from respectability to join the ranks of those sexual women who must by definition be members of another class.

A woman's capacity to wield her own sexual power is always seen negatively in the novels, and must be used surreptitiously, if at all. Displays of sexuality in a woman are either a sign of decadence, the awful viciousness which made Rebecca 'foul', or 'low', like her cousin Jack Favell, 'the sort of man who invariably goes hatless' (p. 335) and drives an offensively green sports car with a whisky bottle in the glove compartment. When this 'awful bounder' (p. 187) gives the heroine the once-over, she too comments 'I felt like a barmaid' (as though a barmaid thinks of nothing but sex). Favell appeals, she thinks, 'to girls in sweet shops . . . and girls who gave me programmes in the cinema', no doubt the limit, in the mind of the conventionally respectable woman, of debased femininity. How to find sexual pleasure without going beyond the pale – how to be like, and yet not like, those 'other women' is at the heart of the novels.

In *Rebecca* this competitive sense of feminine sexuality, endlessly divided against itself by a perception of social differences, provides the psychological drama which is enacted in the mind of the timid heroine. With her dowdy clothes and down-at-heel niceness, she wants what she believes Rebecca had, complete sexual and social confidence. In the course of the novel the girl constructs this imaginary image out of her own desires and anxieties, producing a series of identifications with an imaginary Rebecca which all but brings about her own suicide. In her fantasies Rebecca is everything the girl is not, and the novel provides a kind of commentary on the instability of women's sense of themselves when everything they do or say needs the approval and imprimatur of men. It is only when she realises that Maxim never loved Rebecca that she can transfer her loyalties away from that image of another, more sexually and socially self-possessed woman, to become the good wife, secure as Mrs de Winter at last. She connives in hushing up Rebecca's murder but because Rebecca represents in the novel the insecurity at the heart of all femininity – there is always another woman the respectable woman would like to be, one whose sexual autonomy would not bring about her social disgrace – the image of Rebecca continues to haunt the mental life of the heroine, even in her calm middle age. In a sense, when the girl believes that she too has destroyed Rebecca ('part of me went with him like a shadow in his tracks. I too had killed Rebecca', p. 297), she has tried to destroy her own sexual desires: like Rebecca, however, they keep on coming back.

In *Rebecca* du Maurier uses a vaguely upper-class setting – Manderley is a 'big house' but is not made much of as a family seat and Maximillian de Winter, with his foreign amalgam of a name, has no title – in order to push her heroine to the limits of her own bourgeois inadequacies.[52] The fictional retribution visited upon Rebecca for her sins is clearly du Maurier's attempt to show her conscious lack of approval for the idea of female sexual licence (we are never told what Rebecca actually did except that it involved making love to workmen and gentlemen alike, and her sexual behaviour was literally 'unspeakable'): not only is the poor woman murdered, she turns out to have been eaten up by cancer, and to have (in a gratuitously cruel touch), 'a certain malformation of the uterus . . . which meant she could never have had a child' (p. 383). This overkill, however, merely testifies to the extraordinary power and fascination which any image of sexual 'anarchy' has in the mind of the conservative.

The circular structure of the novel (which begins with its epilogue and then takes us on a journey back into memory) makes the girl-heroine a kind of Ancient Mariner, destined compulsively to repeat her tale, drawn again and again to that which she fears, because it is also what she desires. The ending of *Rebecca* resists a simple resolution in favour of the middle classes and their 'decent' values, and the triumph of the ordinary girl is suffused with loss. Rebecca's Manderley may be a Tory symbol of an older, grander England, the little Eden from which the new Mrs de Winter and her husband are expelled, but it is also a place in the imagination where a freer and more independent sexuality might have been possible. The novel suggests how cramped was the space in which the well-bred woman was allowed, and allowed herself, a sexuality: caught between barmaids and the decadent upper-classes, she needed constantly to keep a grip on her little patch of difference. Yet the novel's immense popularity suggests that those same readers who approve of a Mrs. Miniver in the daylight hours might secretly imagine themselves a Rebecca de Winter after dark.

It is a 'self-loathing' which propels the heroine of *Frenchman's Creek* into becoming 'another Dona, a strange phantom Dona' who peers at her 'from a dark mirror' (p. 15). Written during the bleakest moments of the Second World War, it is both the flightiest and the most conservative of her novels. It is also the only one which sanctions illicit sexual pleasure – Dona St Columb is (as du Maurier herself was) in her thirties with two children when she slips the net to find love and adventure with a French pirate. Even a reluctant Freudian cannot help reading an image of the female body in the topography of the creek, which Dona explores in order to find a land of private pleasure:

> there, suddenly before her for the first time, was the creek, still and soundless, shrouded by the trees and hidden from the eyes of men. She stared at it in wonder for she had had no knowledge of its existence, this stealthy branch of the parent river creeping into her own property, so concealed by the woods themselves. . . . The creek twisted round a belt of trees, and she began to walk along the bank, happy, fascinated, forgetting her mission, for this discovery was a pleasure quite unexpected, this creek was a source of enchantment, a new escape, better than Navron itself, a place to drowse and sleep, a lotus-land.
>
> (p. 43)

At the same time the novel, in allowing its heroine to eat lotuses, has to be even more outspoken in reiterating that women's best place is not to be a law unto themselves but to be 'cogs in a wheel, and mothers most especially' (p. 59). 'You forget', says Dona's philosophical French pirate (who need not be named since he is everywoman's dream),

> 'that women are more primitive than men. For a time they will wander, yes, and play at love, and play at adventure. And then, like the birds do, they must make their nest. Instinct is too strong for them . . . there is no escape for a woman, only for a night and a day.'

And the heroine agrees with alacrity:

> 'No, you are right', she said, 'there is no escape for a woman.'
>
> (p. 143)

And she eventually returns to become a placid matron, to cry occasionally into her pillow at night and to rail against women and their domestic urges for the curtailment of freedom in the world.

Critics of *Frenchman's Creek* were well aware that despite its protestations, what the novel really warmed to was Dona's escape rather than her return. After all, her only punishment is to remain in her boring marriage. Even disguised as a frolic in the Restoration, the novel's shamelessness provoked *The Sunday Times* reviewer into a half-joking nervous admonition against her 'questionable behaviour':[53] wives having affairs with foreign traitors whilst their husbands were away, even in seventeenth-century Cornwall, was not, especially in wartime, entirely amusing. In the 1940s the idea that respectable women might feel sexual desire after marriage need no longer be alarming; the idea of condoning sexual liaisons was another matter. What was just about permissible in a fanciful historical novel had to be handled much more delicately in the public medium of the cinema whose appeal to verisimilitude was much greater. Alfred Hitchcock, for example, with his far less adventurous views of women, was to bowdlerise du Maurier's novels in his film versions much more unequivocally in favour of upholding English decency.[54]

Whilst du Maurier's novels try to persuade the reader that there is something essentially antagonistic about heterosexuality which creates a conflict of desires in her heroines and which eventually sees them gravitating toward home rather than adventure, the language in which her heroines speak of their desires tells another story. Sexual desire is a problem not simply because it may lead to pregnancy or subordination to a male, but because for women sexual and social place are one, and if they lose one, they lose both. The idea of sexual freedom was for du Maurier, as for many of her generation, too fraught with anxiety about social place to be imaginable, though her novels do recognise that these boundaries are internalised as much as they are actual prohibitions in the world outside. Rebecca, like the Dona seen in a dark mirror, is no longer the madwoman in the attic of the Gothic novel, but inside the mind of bourgeois woman and trying to get out. Yet long after many of their fathers and husbands had stopped locking them indoors, women who wished to be thought part of the middle classes continued to turn the key on themselves. The consolation prize for clipping one's own wings was a considerable one: the power to look down upon and even demonise those other women. What makes du Maurier's romances so compelling is her awareness that the triumph of her heroines over those other selves is ultimately a Pyrrhic victory.

In the end, within this economy of social and sexual containment, no woman can 'go strolling with a knapsack'[55] even in her mind, without risking resemblance to those other 'street walkers'. It is with a depressing kind of irony that du Maurier's final heroine of the war years, Honor Harris, is a camp-follower with impunity: she is crippled from the waist down. *The King's General*, which looks back on the Civil War, might be taken as du Maurier's final abdication from the idea of a female sexual freedom. It is a non-combatant's book, in which the heroine is literally housebound, and its ambiguous message to women at war is to suggest how little freedom and courage need have to do with physical scope.

Honor Harris is resourceful, suffering appalling deprivations and losses, the break-up of her home and family and the continuous absence of the man she loves, and yet she manages, despite a sense of her uselessness and growing demoralisation, to cope. It might seem a heartening and strong view, of course, and it is possible to read in Honor Harris an intensified and displaced version of the experience of being a helpless civilian, a woman on the Home Front, which must have struck many chords. The novel is disfigured though, by a sense of bitterness which makes the vicious cutting down of the heroine seem a fantasy of self-punishment too. Honor Harris's disability is also a brutal kind of release, in du Maurier's eyes, from sexual experience itself – she has no difficulty in protecting her honour. Such memories as Honor Harris is left with are rather wintry compared with those of Dona St Columb, and she can only console herself with an inward courage: the compensations that the novel offers are the virtues of endurance and suffering in silence, the will to survive alone without complaint or reliance on 'handouts' from others. It was an image of Tory stoicism, of 'being brave' in splendid isolation if need be, which du Maurier was to repeat in 'The Birds'.

Only *My Cousin Rachel*, the companion piece to *Rebecca*, raised the spectre of female sexuality directly again, but this time we look through the eyes of a man, whose infatuation with Rachel, the Contessa Sangelletti, signals that our knowledge of her 'true' nature is not to be trusted. The novel leaves the question of Rachel unanswered; we never know whether she is murderess or victim, and the woman, like the crime, is ultimately left an unsolved mystery. It is a position du Maurier is bound to take. The last thing she could do, and the only way out of her social and literary *impasse*, would be to look through Rachel's eyes, to identify with that foreign sexuality once and for all (be it Italian, proletarian or simply 'other'), and give us Rebecca's story from her own point of view.

History in Daphne du Maurier's fiction might seem at first a bolthole for women readers and for fugitives from twentieth-century femininity, but it turns out to be as confined a place as the present. After the second world war, du Maurier seems to have got tired of the conflicts of sexual opposition and sought to find other ways out of the blind alleys into which flights from respectable womanhood seemed to lead. Many of her stories start to look for metaphysical escape routes into a super- or hyper-natural reality, an interest in the 'Fourth Dimension'[56] which seems to have intrigued du Maurier throughout her life, and especially after her husband's death. Being in love becomes only one, though the most common-place, example of the 'altered states' of consciousness which feature in the fiction, which range from the experience of dream and nightmare, to psychological states of obsession, like jealousy or mourning, and to the 'trips' induced by hallucinogenic drugs in *The House on the Strand*. As a romantic she never gave up trying to transcend physical limitations: where else should one go but beyond the body and outside time, in search of another existence altogether, where the weakness of the flesh might be left behind at last?

THE PASSING OF TIME AND THE SPIRIT OF PLACE

> Always the past, just out of reach, waiting to be recaptured. Why did I feel so sad thinking of a past I had never known?
>
> (*Myself When Young*, p. 136)

Daphne du Maurier is obsessed in her fiction with the passing of time. It is not just 'the past' as a discoverable and knowable location, a 'setting', with its implication of time and place fixed together – seventeenth-century Cornwall, France in the 1780s – we encounter in her work, but an intense preoccupation with the idea of time passing, with the temporary, because temporal, nature of things, and with a transience which suffuses every moment with immanent (and imminent) loss. It is that sense of an ending which overshadows all her most popular works – *Rebecca*, *Frenchman's Creek*, *The King's General* and *My Cousin Rachel* – and which contradicts a more romantic view of the past as an idealised place to which we can simply escape in memory and in fiction. The imaginative pull of Manderley in *Rebecca*, which keeps taking the girl-heroine back over old ground in her mind, derives from the knowledge which she shares with the reader from the outset, that this is a place which exists, like 'Manderley', only in fantasy; it is not and never could be somewhere to live.

What gives these novels their pathos is that they evoke failed utopias as well as lost pasts. In a world of perpetual change, futurity is also in doubt, and time, like the hotel existence where the de Winters in *Rebecca* are doomed to stretch out their days, can offer only temporary accommodation:

> This house sheltered us, we spoke, we loved within those walls. That was yesterday. Today we pass on, we see it no more, we are different, changed in some infinitesimal way. We can never be quite the same again.
>
> (p. 49)

History in du Maurier's novels may be a refuge from the present but it is always an unreliable one, since the passing of time is by its very nature unsettling. Her stories frequently manifest a hostile as well as fascinated attitude toward the past; romantically inclined to look for solace there, they evince no little antagonism at being once more disappointed.

At the heart of this paradoxical imagination is du Maurier's sense of memory as a treacherous route back. The act of remembering is her most common narrative device and the most powerful image in her fiction. One of the most insistent of her themes is prefigured in the title of her second book, *I'll Never Be Young Again*: Dick, the disillusioned narrator of this novel, is the prototype of many such to come who tell their tales from an older and wiser present and invite the reader to go back with them into the events of the past, and of their youth. In *Rebecca* it is the desire to go back, to live earlier times again in the imagination, which forms the mainspring of the plot. 'Last night I dreamed I went to Manderley again', that resonant opening line, gives us the novel in miniature, as Manderley is revisited by an older and sadder narrator, remembering, looking back. Both Honor Harris in *The King's General* and Philip Ashley in *My Cousin Rachel* are also narrators in a disenchanted present, returning in memory to tell a tale which is also the story of their growing older.

'Nostalgia', Daphne du Maurier wrote, 'belongs to the middle years' (*Myself When Young*, p. 30), but by her late twenties she already had a fascination with the process of ageing and the sense of loss which to her mind accompanied the 'getting of wisdom'. 'Wait till you come to forty year' are the repeated words of father to son in *Gerald*, du Maurier's portrait of her father, and a warning of the seed of future melancholy which lies waiting to take root. In *Rebecca* Maxim de Winter teases his wife-to-be, young enough to be his daughter, by begging her not to 'wear black satin' and reach the age of 36; she gains her sexual confidence at the price of losing 'that funny, young, lost look' (p. 313). In all du Maurier's writing it is not youth but middle age which forms the core of the individual – the glamour and mystery of 'maturity' which makes growing up as much to be feared as to be desired.

Du Maurier's is not a sentimental imagination, nostalgic, if by that we mean solely a writing whose emotional energy is spent on conjuring up in the reader a bitter-sweet longing for a happier, richer, lost time. There are no lingering scenes of joyful childhood in her fiction: childhood is always already over in her writing, and nostalgia, though present, is a condition taken for granted in many of her characters: it is where they and the reader start from. They already know, and indeed they frequently tell us, that their innocence cannot be regained:

> There is no going back in life. There is no return. No second chance. I cannot call back the spoken word or the accomplished deed.
>
> (*My Cousin Rachel*, p. 10)

> We can never go back again. That much is certain.
>
> (*Rebecca*, p. 8)

If du Maurier is a conservative in nevertheless attempting that journey in many of her novels, she is enough of a modern to see its futility.

The act of remembering in du Maurier's fiction is never a source of simple pleasure. Memory can be a menacing and sinister force as readily as it can be a consoling one: in *Rebecca* it is this dual nature of remembering which makes going back in her imagination a frightening experience for the girl who tells the tale: du Maurier makes memory indelible because it so often appals – its compulsive and repetitive nature depends on just this dialectic. Both *Rebecca* and *My Cousin Rachel* see the reiteration of the past as a kind of exorcism, a calling up of ghosts in order to dispel them, but the protagonists remain haunted by memory, by a past imagined as trauma. Even in a more lighthearted work, *Jamaica Inn*, Mary Yellan's truly nostalgic memories (the longing for the maternal home she has lost) are by no means the strongest emotional pull on the reader; by far the most intensely charged memory is the harrowing scene of destruction which Mary and the reader have to witness and whose memories are irresistible because they horrify. *Jamaica Inn* does not, as so many of her later fictions do, put the psychology of remembering at the centre of the narrative, but the past as it is evoked in that novel is already hedged about with fear.

The act of return is for her narrators as demoralising as it is painful: it is something which they can't help doing but which actually does them no good, revealing as it does truths about themselves and others which they would rather forget. Personal memory, far from being a consoling and comfortable thing, is a creature which will not do the bidding of the rememberer, and for du Maurier memory can as easily destroy as enhance the present, shatter a fragile peace of mind rather than create safe places in fantasy. At the beginning of the girl's story in *Rebecca* nostalgia for the past is the root of all evil: going back to Manderley with her new husband sets in motion an unstoppable train of memories, real and imagined, which poison their life together and make the loss of their home inevitable. In *Frenchman's Creek*, the only novel which makes the past almost entirely benign, the desire to escape to, and luxuriate in, another life comes to an abrupt and bleak end: the heroine goes back to what she was at the beginning of the novel just as the reader, who has also escaped for 'a night and a day', must pick up again the reins of the present.

If du Maurier shares that sense of loss which makes so many moderns yearn for a more vivid and authentic past, her fiction makes the place which the past occupies an unstable one, and the passing of events often a matter of relief, as they are in part for the narrator of *Rebecca*: 'I am glad it cannot happen twice, the fever of first love' (p. 38). Nostalgia is a selective memory and du Maurier's fiction is suspicious of the myth on which it rests: that memory's act of preservation can be solely pleasurable, that we can remember only the good times. When the girl in *Rebecca* wishes she could 'bottle up' her memories, her desire is ironic since it is precisely because memory is inescapable and irresistible that her husband longs to 'blot out the past' (p. 43). Nostalgia, and its limits, are the unspoken subjects treated critically in many of the stories, what it means to have that unsatisfied longing for an idealised place which can never be met, and hers is a modernist imagination in unequivocally evoking a sense of exile as an irremediable condition of subjective life.

The psychology she enters into with the most sympathy is that of the stranger beyond the gates, the outsider who longs for a home but cannot find one, or has lost it, the person shut out from a 'full life'. Mary Yellan at the end of *Jamaica Inn* gives up her dreams of a happy domestic existence by casting her lot with her horse-thief lover to become an itinerant like him. The heroine in *Rebecca*, locked into her shyness and insecurity, feels herself to be 'an interloper' at Manderley (p. 82), her husband's home, begins and ends her life with no fixed abode, excluded from living a conventional home life by the secrets of the past. Honor Harris is another kind of exile, suffering a different kind of paralysis, cut off from the life she would like by her disabled body. It is the person who most has reason to go back into the past – the professor of history in *The Scapegoat* – who endures an even more exaggerated sense of alienation: his study of French history puts him even further from French life and 'the real meaning of history . . . I was an alien. I was not one of them' (p. 8).

This was how du Maurier imagined her own father in *Gerald: A Portrait*, the frank biography with which she made her name as a writer in 1934. Tellingly, she does not describe in detail her own childhood, nor is there one sentence beginning with 'I' or 'my father' inviting us to share in her own sense of loss. She is not present in the account at all except fleetingly as 'Daphne'. Rather, it is a biography which tries out the techniques of fiction and in which we enter the minds of the characters and share their imaginary thoughts: her father is presented to us as the type of person who suffers from nostalgia, and it is his nostalgia that we sympathise with, not his daughter's. The places which gave him happiness and contentment – his childhood home in Hampstead, Wyndham's theatre where he was actor-manager for fifteen years – are not ones to which du Maurier herself wishes to return: they are the staging posts in Gerald's life, just as surely as the writing of this biography, and the placing of her father in history, was one in hers. Gerald in his daughter's eyes becomes a man who imagines the past is lost, yet the reader comes to feel that quite the contrary is the case; du Maurier draws constant parallels between Gerald and his father, and manages to suggest, by a weaving of recurring sentiments and family mannerisms, tags of speech passed down like signet rings, that history actually repeats itself.

Only a very modern daughter could have given such an unsentimental account of such a sentimental father a few months after his death; and only a very modern writer could have so absented herself from authorial comment as to leave his 'inner emptiness and spiritual bankruptcy'[57] so dispassionately exposed. Gerald emerges as a transitional figure, an unhappy mix of late-Victorian inheritance and sentiment, and a nervy modernity:

> the future and the past were at conflict within him, and they dragged him in different ways. He possessed the sentimentality of the one and the cynicism of the other; the moral conventions of the Victorians and the unscrupulous shrug of the twentieth century; the high standards of 1880, and the shallow weakness of 1920.
>
> (*Gerald*, p. 139)

Almost the last of his family to survive, wearied by life and destined to be 'forever unfulfilled' (p. 140), Gerald is pictured by his daughter as seeking comfort in re-enacting the past. Moving house from central London back to Hampstead, where he grew up, Gerald goes in search of peace and is just as unable to find it as his father before him. Though he clings to the rituals of his lost family life, following his father's walks (tapping the end tree with his stick just like Papa) and kissing his family's photographs last thing at night, he is ruled by an inner discontent which remains unappeased by what she calls his 'fetish' of the past (p. 187). The final image of Gerald, surrounded by his reliquary, looking out across the lights of London, is the picture of an exile, 'worshipping the memory'[58] of his family, but irrevocably, in some deeply individual way, alone.

Du Maurier is naturally a partisan in this biography, but she is also writing herself a distance from her father by having, as it were, the last word. She leaves the reader in little doubt as to which side, in the battle of ancients and moderns, she elects to be on: 'standards', she writes with the pomposity of her elders, 'were sinking' (p. 167) after the war, when

> the air was poisoned by the braying of the saxophone, the whine of love songs, and the stamping rhythm of the cottonfields.
>
> (*Gerald*, p. 209)

Her father's modernity exasperates her, his careless morality, his lack of discipline (though a spell as a cadet in 1918 does him good 'as it would any civilian', p. 232), and his over-sensitive, chameleon nature contrast ill with the solidity of his own parents and their 'dignified' way of life. Even so, the opening passages which describe 'Kicky' and 'Pem' (Gerald's parents) and their bower of bliss in Bloomsbury, are the least engaging in the book. They read like an attempt at Thackeray's archness without his satire and the description of the good old days of late Victorian England is flattened into cliché by a conventional form of patrician wishful thinking:

> Prosperity could be counted upon then; there was a certainty that after the lean years came harvest . . . The countryside was not yet desecrated, nor had turmoil come to the streets of London . . . . Not for them the hunger before dawn . . . .
>
> (p. 19)

Those same scenes only gain originality when they become the product of Gerald's mind as he dwells on the past (and, increasingly, in it) rather than as a second-hand attempt on her own part at direct historical commentary. As with *Rebecca* and the later novels, it is the mind of the rememberer as much as the object of memory which becomes the focus of the narrative.

That sense of the past as a constant presence inside the mind, a dimension in which modern people always live, produces the most resonant passages in the book. It is a past become echo, trace and sign, the residue of human personality projected upon the world outside from the mind of the beholder, durable ghosts who constitute the spirit of place. As Gerald was an actor du Maurier writes feelingly of the special ephemerality of his profession: theatre performers become ghosts sooner than most, since voice and gesture leave no vestige of themselves except in the memory. Gerald's voice is heard again in the large number of letters which form the substantial part of the biography but it is Wyndham's theatre which is redolent of Gerald for his daughter, bespeaking him in the ways in which Hampstead expressed his own father. Place becomes the true distillation of a life and the past is best evoked through a sense of attachment:

> Gerald belonged to Wyndham's; he was as much a part of it as the boards, the curtain, the heavy swing door, the row of stalls shrouded in their white and grimy covers, the cat in the dress circle, the backcloth and the false moveable walls that were not walls, the dust in the passage, the intimate, indescribable, musty, fusty smell that was the back of the stage and the dressing-rooms and the front of the house in one.
>
> Much of his personality is embedded in those walls. His laughter is still in the passage, his footstep on the stairs, and his voice calling for Tommy Lovell when the curtain falls. For all their passing away and the coming of other sounds – new voices, new laughter, other men and other memories – something of himself remains for ever amidst the dust and silence of that theatre; a breath, a whisper, the echo of a song.
>
> (p. 156)

These haunted places are as reassuring as, in another register, they can be disturbing. They assert a continuity of human life, that nothing is ever completely destroyed, in the face of evident change and loss. Du Maurier's ghosts are not out there walking the lawns of great houses or riding abroad to meet ill-fated travellers at the crossroads: these are twentieth-century phantoms, walled up inside us – both the best and the worst kind of haunting – called up by ourselves. They are domestic ghosts, the Lares and Penates of the past, sometimes literally attached to old houses, like 'the house on the strand', the home of the narrator who moves between a medieval and twentieth-century life, or summoned up simply by the sight of a 'tumbledown cottage'.

All that remained were the walls, two windows and a hearth. Once, perhaps, two hundred years ago, a woman had bent over that same hearth and stood at the windows watching.

(*Myself When Young*, p. 136)

They are the shadows of past selves, but can also be a portent of selves yet to come. In 'Don't Look Now' a father, who is trying to escape mourning for his child, is haunted not by the past, but by the future after his own death.

Such ghosts are the manifestations of a modern view of history – the past made local, familiar and interior, a continuum of feeling played out in the mind:

we are none of us isolated in time, but are part of what we were once, and of what we are yet to become.

(*Myself When Young*, p. 58)

It is not just that places, and especially houses, are for du Maurier the repositories of the past, where we can best find and read the accumulation of marks of change, but that they house 'us': who we are, and what we imagine ourselves to be, becomes an interior location, the boards and curtains extensions of our 'selves'. 'We' are best discovered in some place to which we belong and our connection with others depends on this sense of identity, a private, individual place, somewhere deep inside, which is then the true subject of history. It is a view which remains remarkably consistent throughout the forty odd years of her writing:

Who can ever affirm, or deny that the houses which have sheltered us as children, or as adults, and our predecessors too, do not have embedded in their walls, one with the dust and the cobwebs, one with the overlay of fresh wallpaper and paint, the imprint of what-has-been, the suffering, the joy? We are all the ghosts of yesterday, and the phantom of tomorrow awaits us alike in sunshine or in shadow, dimly perceived at times, never entirely lost.

(*Myself When Young*, p. 44)

Yet the same message can be a source of consolation or of terror, for if identity is attached to place and places are vulnerable locations in time, identity itself is potentially unstable, always in danger of being uprooted and of needing to be rehoused.

We smile, we choose our lunch, we speak of this and that, but – I say to myself – I am not she who left him five minutes ago. She stayed behind. I am another woman . . . .

(*Rebecca*, p. 49)

Remembering her sensations as a child, when she visited old houses, du

Maurier sees change not in terms of political eventualities or economic determinations but as the dramas of everyday life, an identification with the people of the past which immediately raises questions about the limits of her own sense of self:

> Where had they all gone, the people who lived at Slyfield once? And where was I then? Who was I now?
>
> (ibid., p. 23)

Once the passing of time is perceived as a primarily psychological pheno-menon, and who we are is wholly relative to how things change, what is to stop us being endlessly tossed on the flotsam of the past, the victims of memory as well as its originators?

Something like this happens to the girl in *Rebecca* who has no home and is unable to be at home in Manderley; and when Philip in *My Cousin Rachel* reaches the peak of his infatuation with the mysterious Countess, he gives away his home. That same vagrancy and romantic freedom from 'ties' which in *Jamaica Inn* and *Frenchman's Creek* seem so appealing as fantasies, especially as an escape from femininity, are reinterpreted in her darker 'thrillers' as a condition of psychic vulnerability, a sense of identity without the walls of a stable ego, walls which shelter even as they limit. The girl without a name in *Rebecca* is one of many characters who move backwards and forwards in time, projecting themselves into the place of others, because they are insecure about their own 'self'. It is a capacity which can produce compassion, as when she tries to imagine being old and frail like Maxim's grandmother – 'I thought how little we know about the feelings of old people' (p. 191) – more often it feeds her own self-dislike: always trying to imagine herself differently masks a desire to be someone else, the confident, older woman whom Rebecca represents for her. Her imagination is a truly negative capability which can undo and untether her until she loses all sense of herself:

> I had so identified myself with Rebecca that my own dull self did not exist, had never come to Manderley. I had gone back in thought and in person, to the days that were gone.
>
> (p. 209)

Du Maurier's fiction might be read as part of that popularising of ideas of relativity, as well as theories of psychology after the 1930s which stressed the contingency of the present. Both these and her later interest in extra-sensory perception, in time travel, not through the use of scientific technology (like Wells's time-machine) but through changes in the mind, always stem back to the central role she gives, however, to the imagination, conceived in the modern sense of an unconscious force locked within the individual. Part of the power of *Rebecca* is its recasting of imagination as the private fantasies of a lovesick girl which can alter her behaviour and her future precisely because they remain unexpressed. This is a firmly modern romanticism – an imagination turned wilful, like a sorcerer's apprentice, making desperate magic, out of control. The girl is 'too romantic', projecting herself time and again into an imaginary situation which, far from releasing her into new worlds, turns her back in on herself: she is often shocked by the destructiveness of her own fantasies, imagining her husband killed in an accident, an expression of both fear and desire. She suffers all the time from that confusion and dissolution of boundaries both in time and space which make being in love a kind of madness.

Always in du Maurier's fiction the pressure of the past is felt as a burden on the individual; carried within us it can determine and therefore constrain how we may behave. Those who are most 'insecure', (and the adolescent, middle-class girl is for du Maurier archetypally so), least settled in their sexuality and in their social position, are most hampered by imagination, limited by their great expectations, and hobbled by their constant rehearsals of how they hope their lives might be: 'this is not', says the girl at the beginning of her married life, 'how I had imagined my first morning' (p. 85). The idea of an active and dynamic relationship between past lives, present fantasy and unconscious desires reminds us, of course, of a Freudian scenario: it is no coincidence that *Rebecca* lends itself to the language of psychoanalysis – projection, identification, transference, fixation. *Rebecca*, like *My Cousin Rachel*, is about the power of daydream, those waking fantasies of which Freud wrote, 'past, present and future are strung together, as it were, on the thread of the wish that runs through them'.[59] Such an interior life of fantasy is a kind of modern oracle, seeming to tell us what we want to hear but delivering us unwittingly to more buried, often dangerous desires.

If *Rebecca* is a novel about the perfidious nature of romantic projection, then it is not so much anti-romantic as post-romantic, no longer trusting that the freedom to imagine will bring an escape from self. It does not, however, leave its heroine or its reader in a state of critical disintegration; we know that when she contemplates suicide, all is not lost – the ongoing presence of the older woman narrator tells us so. There is always one coherent ego in the text, the narrative itself, which stays within the safe confines of realism. Du Maurier does not attempt, like Compton Burnett, to stop the flow of time, to freeze the past into an unchanging present. Her stories may push at the limits of realism but they never transgress them, and though their themes are unsettling, the reader always comes back to base. Indeed they often have the satisfaction of completing a circle in their reading: the beginnings of her novels are frequently their epilogues.

Du Maurier's characterisation holds onto the idea of development. Her people do 'mature', grow wiser, if sadder, and find a safer, if duller place. They have arrived at a state of successful repression, not of the past but, magically, of the present, whose day-to-day existence seems to be a matter of comparative peace, a 'complacent armour of aproaching middle age' (*Rebecca*, p. 38) in which all passion's spent. Du Maurier's narratives, for all their obsessive dwelling in unstable, unbounded places, work in the end to reinforce a belief in the succour of four walls. Their voyage out, though it demands most of the story and constitutes two-thirds of the reader's attraction, always becomes a return trip. Du Maurier's writing may take a modern psychological view of human beings as adrift on a sea of memories, but she always leaves the reader on *terra firma*: even 'Don't Look Now', the most unhinging of her short stories, ends with the events, and even her character's clairvoyance, fully understood if not entirely explained. Du Maurier, like Agatha Christie, made entertainment out of modernist anxieties; *Rebecca* is not *Nausea*, though arguably du Maurier's novel shares more than the year of publication with Sartre's, and to suggest that an existential 'anguish' at the instability of subjectivity is at the heart of *Rebecca* is not as preposterous as it might first sound. Certainly du Maurier has as much to say about the social and psychic conditions of the modern bourgeois when 'he' happens to be a woman.

That sense of mutability as the only constant, and of the Janus-faced nature of time, often sounds a mournful note in du Maurier's writing. Her most compelling autobiographical memoir is about the agonies of widowhood; she writes nothing on her own marriage and motherhood. It is the capacity to endure hardship, loneliness, face trauma, that du Maurier admires: personal courage and private fortitude are the only answer to the ravages of time. Her imagination turns an almost religious sense that 'all things must pass' into a state of siege. Her narrators are constantly haunted not just by the past they already know but by knowing that history is voracious, a bottomless pit, into which this moment too will fall. The more convinced a notion of perpetual change, the more tenacious must be the grip on the present:

> for this moment, it is mine, it belongs to me. We know one another. This is the present. There is no past and no future. Here I am, washing my hands, and the cracked mirror shows me myself, suspended, as it were, in time; this me, this moment will not pass.
>
> (*Rebecca*, p. 49)

What is certain is that change can never be for the better, make us more hopeful or freer. It leaves us only a tiny space in the present, soon gone, a temporary haven.

One might be forgiven for imagining Daphne du Maurier living in Hampstead, walking the old walks and tapping the old trees. Yet if places are the best register of the past and of the person, it can be any place that takes on that aura: precisely because attachments are temporary, they are easier to make, and all places aspire to the condition of home. Home for du Maurier was not where she grew up in London but Cornwall, which she made the scene of so much of her writing. Du Maurier was actually a newcomer to Cornwall, moving there in the late 1920s, and her sense of homecoming was built out of very modern disaffections. She was a shining example of that paradoxical modern ability to 'put down roots quickly': she became almost instantaneously attached to this place, felt it was 'home' without having grown up there, worked there, or had connections with the place. It is a sense of belonging which need not depend on actual ownership or possession of land or on being the home of forefathers – a 'family home'. In fact, although du Maurier beat a retreat into a Cornish past in her twenties, she was typical of modern youth in not wanting to live at home. Cornwall was the home du Maurier wanted to have rather than the one she was born with.

FAMILY HISTORY/FAMILY ROMANCE: BEING A DU MAURIER

There is, as yet, no biography of Daphne du Maurier but whoever takes up the commission might do worse than begin by contradicting Virginia Woolf's famous dictum: 'We think back through our mothers if we are women.'[60] For if ever there was a daughter who thought back through her paternal line, Daphne du Maurier seems to have been such a one. Like so many of that generation of English women whose code of honour and feminine reserve eschewed speaking about their own lives, she wrote little about herself. *Growing Pains*, a brief autobiography published in 1977 (when she was seventy), covers just the years of her youth, up to her marriage in 1932, as though only the personal past which was now safely distant were fit material for public consumption. It appears to be a first volume, but although du Maurier lived another twelve years, no second is forthcoming. (It was republished as *Myself When Young: The Shaping of a Writer*.) Given that a sequel would have taken her into the personal experiences of marriage and motherhood and unavoidably have meant commenting on continuing relationships, it is perhaps not surprising that it never appeared. The writing of that autobiography is in keeping, however, not just with a reticence whereby only that family life which concerned dead rather than living presences could be offered to posterity, but with the enormous desire she had throughout her life to talk about her father and his family. Where her own personal history mattered most it was in 'being a du Maurier'.[61]

When she was a girl growing up the du Mauriers were already a well-known family on account of their two famous men: Daphne's grandfather, George du Maurier, had been a much-loved illustrator for *Punch* in its heyday of late-Victorian satire, and had become an overnight sensation with *Trilby*, a novel of the bohemian life written in his sixties; his son, her father, Gerald, was one of London's favourite figures, a matinée idol of the wartime theatre, creator of a number of popular roles, and the most admired of actor-managers. One of a number to revolt against the flamboyance of the late-Victorian theatre he had helped to develop a new naturalistic style of acting or 'underplaying', languid and apparently casual, which was considered daring in its day. The king of London's theatreland throughout Daphne's childhood, he died in 1934, the head of his profession, when Daphne was 27 and he a mere 61.[62]

Artistic achievement was woven into the paternal family past in intimate ways. *Trilby*, published in 1892, is itself nostalgic for the Parisian childhood which George du Maurier had believed to be his happiest years. When he died in 1896 his son Gerald was playing in the stage version of *Trilby* (in a minor part based on his uncle), and though Gerald's apprenticeship to the theatre needed his own talent and dedication to complete it, his daughter was the first to admit that the du Maurier name got him noticed.[63] Growing up with a 'star' for a father, Daphne, the middle one of three daughters, saw herself as repeating the pattern of her own father's life. Making a name for oneself could only mean being a du Maurier, and it was fitting that after her first three, rather unsure novels, it was the tribute to her father, *Gerald*, which launched her as a writer. She carried on her father's name throughout her life, with all the more vigour given that, according to her own accounts, it belonged more and more to the past. No doubt she would have derived a bitter-sweet satisfaction from hearing herself described after death as 'the last of the du Mauriers'.[64]

Certainly a large part of du Maurier's writing was given up to telling stories about her father's family. Since it takes at least two generations to make a tradition, 'the du Mauriers' began with her father, and with her account of his childhood in *Gerald*. *Gerald* was the first in a series of books which became increasingly genealogical, and inevitably more fanciful, as she grew older: biographies shade imperceptibly into novels once the events and persons had passed out of 'living memory'. In 1937 she stepped back a generation further with a book about her grandfather, George du Maurier, in *The Du Mauriers*, which weaves together letters and invented dialogue as *Gerald* had done, and whose cover already hails her as part of a 'lively literary tradition';[65] another step back again, and she writes of her great-grandmother in *Mary Anne* (1954); and finally she establishes the family's bourgeois origins in an historical novel set in revolutionary France, *The Glassblowers* (1963), imagined through the eyes of her paternal great-great-grandmother – Sophie Duval. The fortunes of the family come full circle in that novel with Sophie handing on a glass heirloom to her grandson, 'Kicky' or George du Maurier, thus bringing that distant past of 'the du Mauriers' close to home.

Her family novels, both fiction and non-fiction, were not amongst du Maurier's greatest successes but their significance in terms of her life and work, as a whole, is considerable. It is important that there is no claim to an aristocratic past in the writing, though the name itself might suggest so: in *The Glassblowers*, du Maurier mocks that most obvious version of a family romance in which we secretly believe ourselves to be of noble stock, by disappointing one of her forebears who himself is peeved to discover that the 'Chateau Maurier' turns out to be no more than a barn, and 'du Maurier' an act of bluff on the part of a roguish ancestor. She was more than happy to find her 'roots' in solid bourgeois pride and an entrepreneurial, mercantile family.[66] The romance of family history for du Maurier is not one of social elevation, as it was for Ivy Compton-Burnett; rather it is the very idea of family which appeals, of having a continuous personal history stretching back into the past.

In this imagination every family becomes a kind of lineage and it is not an ancestral home which is threatened with loss but family itself which must be protected as the central way in which individuals make sense of themselves and social changes. Families become the true histories, a connective sense of the past which makes it organic like a 'family tree', with 'roots' and 'branches', where we can place ourselves. The inter-war period saw a boom in the writing of popular 'family sagas', but also of a new kind of historiography which turned to the 'ordinary life' and evinced a new fascination with the domestic past: Daphne du Maurier was one of many moderns who made sense of the losses and ruptures in her own family present by inventing a family past, and who turned to the family as the primary source of historical feeling.[67]

In her own life 'the du Mauriers', as an idea of family, became crucial when they appeared to be almost extinct – a feeling of being orphaned no doubt shared by many after the Great War. If anyone created the legend of the du Mauriers, then it was Daphne herself, an inventive chronicler of a past which took shape only in the retrospect of her writing. For regardless of how many still bore that name, the du Mauriers in Daphne's rendering only began to matter posthumously. It was a lost world of du Mauriers which moved her to write. In 1934 when she begins their chronicle they are nearly all gone: she had never known the grandparents, but her father's siblings, her aunts Trixie and Sylvia, and her uncle Guy, to whom he was very close, and, of course, her father, had all died prematurely. Although Daphne du Maurier's mother lived on for another thirty years, until she was well over 80, she was not a du Maurier as these others were. Her very longevity must have gone against her, for in the romantic imagination it is the discontinuous which makes the stable appealing, the abruptly cut-off which makes for a longing for home. It was the father's family that encompassed this dialectic, and which could embody both a true ancestry and a proper family life.

It was this image of a family, who clung together in London, meeting regularly, eating at each other's houses and holding confabulations, which constituted one desirable image of 'the du Mauriers'. That sense of family as a hold on life, something which endures and is larger than the sum of its members, is one which gains more and more force as it stretches back into the past: 'they were all alike, these du Mauriers' (*Gerald*, p. 142). Family has a 'transcendent value'[68] in the writing. In her first novel, *The Loving Spirit*, it is this theme of transcendence across time and space through shared family characteristics which gives it its title. 'The loving spirit' is passed on from generation to generation; nevertheless the liveliest parts of the novels as of the biographies are concerned with bold individuals and du Maurier has little capacity to evoke settled interiors except as loss (*The Independent Spirit* would have made an apter title).

The image of the family as collective life, duties and bonds (the 'little platoons' as Burke called them, to which we owe allegiance),[69] was one emphasis which only gains weight in opposition to that other term in the equation – the discontented and heroic individual. Du Maurier wrote about the surprising individuals in a family past with far more passion than she was able to put into her evocation of 'home': it is the dialectic between them that makes sense of them both. And it is an opposition which in her account is worked out in the preference of her father's over her mother's family, and repeated in a sexual opposition within the du Mauriers, between its extraordinary men and its conventional women, between France and England, between 'art' and domesticity. Being a 'du Maurier' enabled her to develop a romantic ego as a writer, not because of family *per se* but by claiming that paternity which tied masculinity and artistic ability together, and mingled it with the romance of being French and 'other'.

For it is a family romance she creates in selecting for her 'true' parentage only those elements which spoke best to how she would like to be. Du Maurier showed no signs of wanting to write novels about her mother's family, who appeared to live quietly in Golders Green. Although the du Mauriers were a close-knit family in Daphne's childhood, those other uncharted relatives were probably more so. The du Mauriers, however, were both like and unlike the other people's families; they came with a history of the unsettled and the unconventional, which translated the notion of the family past into something different, and made it seem exotic and exciting, even as it was the routines and conventions of that family life that were praised. Du Maurier's invention of her own heritage suggests how much the discovery of a family history is governed by a modern and rather literary urge, to find a more interesting point of origin for our 'selves' from what otherwise might seem a random, disconnected and heterogeneous past. Family historians believe simultaneously that their own family past is both ordinary and unique (and everyone has relatives living quietly in the suburbs but it is the black sheep amongst the ancestors who often seem the most desirable kin). Without the contrast of the dramatically different, the mundane is not historically interesting.

On the one hand, du Maurier stresses that what bound the du Mauriers together was their love of home and family, and on the other, that they were restless individuals who often best appreciated their family too late. 'The du Mauriers' were as much rootless as rooted people: immigrants on one side, both cosmopolitan and metropolitan – Daphne's grandfather had lived in Paris, Antwerp and Dusseldorf before settling in London, and *Trilby* evokes just that antithesis between a bohemian life and the longing for a settled home. Her childhood, by her own account, could be seen as actually lacking many of the things which her family sagas create: continuity (they were 'a circus family'[70] she says, with an actor as *pater familias* coming home all hours); a long-standing family home (they were renters not owners) and a place from which they had definitely come. Family life for Daphne du Maurier was often a theatrical affair with an entertainer for a father who was temperamental, exasperatingly self-centred, hilarious and lovable at one and the same time. (As we learn in *Gerald*, Daphne's father was quite capable periodically of dragging his family off abroad with waggonloads of his own luggage and then peremptorily ordering their departure after two days of feeling bored, moving them on to pastures new if he took a dislike to the hotel or the weather.[71])

In her family accounts du Maurier seems to offer us a conventional opposition between the sexes: the romantic individuals are the men – 'Kicky', Gerald and his brother Guy – whilst the women, 'Pem' or 'Mummie', her grandmother, and Mo, her own mother, were domestic through and through. For du Maurier then, claiming that male inheritance and seeing herself as the last of the line, was a bold and difficult position for a young woman in the 1920s to take up, and not without its contradictions. In some ways we can see the devotion with which she conjured up a family history in her writing as an antidote to the predominance of these men in her family, a domesticating of them; in other ways it served to heighten their specialness, placing these two remarkable fathers in their domestic *milieux* exaggerated their unique qualities as individuals by contextualising them as family men rather than as lonely artists.

As the writing of *Gerald* might suggest, Daphne's relationship with her father was especially close or even 'uncomfortably close'.[72] As a child, when her sisters and mother went off to church, Daphne would stay at home with her father or go for walks with him; in later years she was his late-night listener and confidante. He saw in her the image of his own father, a compliment which the older Daphne related as a matter of some pride in her autobiography, recalling her adolescence:

he had always hoped that one day I should write, not poems necessarily, but novels. There was plenty of time.

'You remind me so much of Papa,' he said, 'always have done. Same forehead, same eyes. If only you had known him.'

(*Myself When Young*, p. 86)

Yet Daphne du Maurier felt the need, as soon as she was old enough, to put hundreds of miles between herself and this charismatic father, and the family, by making a home in Cornwall. We might see the writing of *Gerald* as a way too of confirming the separation publicly, writing her father into history, as it were. If it was Daphne's way of kissing her father's photograph, there might be another meaning to her symbolic act when, on the day of his death, she let loose two pigeons over Hampstead Heath: she hoped that Gerald felt as free as they were – but why, we might ask with some impertinence, were there two?[73] *Gerald*, to at least some of Daphne's friends, 'smacked of revenge'[74] – but revenge for what? Was it his authority that his daughter was undermining or his lack of it which she was exposing?

Any picture of the daughter's identification with her father has to include a contradictory sense, which runs through the writing, of her dissatisfaction with the kind of man, and father, that he was. That same 'Frenchness' which made them 'artistic', rendered her father and grand-father 'womanish' in their emotions. Gerald would frequently burst into tears; he was not the sort of father who went in for 'rough and tumble' but for dressing up; he was nervy, mildly hypochondriac, given to manic excitement, easily depressed, 'moody', all of which his daughter sees as his 'having a feminine strain':

> he laid too great a stress on woman's values. He had a woman's eager curiosity about other people's private lives, a woman's tortuous and roundabout methods of getting to a certain point, a woman's appreci-ation of gossip, a woman's love of intrigue and drama, a woman's delight and absorption in little mysterious flirtations that last a day.
>
> (p. 234)

He was not 'effeminate', she rapidly assures us, but in some irremediable way these qualities lower him in his daughter's opinion. 'The average male', she airily announces, 'is a little bored with the company of a woman for long' but not Gerald, who boasted a female seraglio of young actresses and female friends whom he would wine and dine. Daphne's mother would frequently make the rendezvous by telephone herself, and Daphne and her sisters called them 'the stable', judiciously backing different win-ners in the race for Gerald's favours.[75]

Du Maurier appears to blame not just the theatre with its promiscuous affections and 'darlings', or a hectic modernity, but an inherent lack of manliness in the unstable and artificial life her father led, which is part and parcel of that metropolitan life. Gerald, she concludes, was 'as incon-sequent in fatherhood as in everything else' (p. 214), sometimes appearing in the role of a 'schoolboy brother' (p. 255), other times turning into a stern patriarch, other times still inviting confidences like a woman, but in none of his parts was he convincing, since he was too good in all of them;

he was too fey, too inconsistent to be a proper figure of authority, too good at play-acting. The enjoyable, lovable Gerald is hardly a man, in her words, at all: he is a 'faun', a 'beachcomber', 'an excitable child'; whilst the father is too emotional, 'capricious', sensitive. Ironically, when Daphne was 14, Gerald's most successful part was that of 'Bulldog Drummond', an upper-class tough whose mindless brawn was about as far from the svelte and insouciant Gerald as could be. It must have seemed that masculinity was merely a piece of theatre for her father, a performance one put on.

One of the most critical passages in *Gerald*, barely concealing her disdain, remarks on how her father would have suffered at the Front. He had 'not enough control' (p. 205). All the time Daphne seems to be measuring him against the image of an heroic masculinity whose archetype was to be found in the soldier, and especially in the dead Guy, the missing older brother, strong and silent, a man of few words where Gerald was weak and voluble. What Gerald needed, according to his daughter, was an older man friend to speak to him 'straight from the shoulder', someone just like Guy. The biography is consonant with a pattern to be repeated in the fiction, that the true hero of the narrative, the manly man, is gone into history, whilst the men one knows, one's contemporaries, are hardly men at all. The power of Gerald du Maurier in the symbolic landscape of his daughter's life lay in his being a dazzling and completely engrossing companion, but his weak spot lay, we can surmise, in making a poor show as a figure of authority.

In *Gerald* Daphne du Maurier's narratorial self is scrupulous in not evincing that feminine sensibility. *Gerald* is remarkable not just for the dry-eyed exposure of her father's foibles – as a spoilt youngest son, a doted-upon husband and an over-indulged father – but for her reticence about her own feelings. Where he was sentimental, even mawkish, she demonstrably is not. *Gerald* is a work of extraordinary self-control: to write a book about one's father six months after he dies, entering into his imaginary feelings and thoughts, but without disclosing one's own, is an exercise in exorcism as well as memorial.[76] She writes of his fecklessness with an airy *panache*, except occasionally when an oddly bitter comment escapes which betrays a buried grievance: this parent left her with 'distorted' values (p. 214), sophisticated beyond her years. Only once in a passage about 'the daughters' does du Maurier analyse a sense of estrangement between her father and herself, which was due, in her words, to his changeability as a father – 'They were never quite sure of him' (p. 255).

Du Maurier's own story of her 'growing pains', written forty years or so after *Gerald*, suggests how much a romantic, more backward-looking image of masculinity provided a place from which she could construct a writing self, and also as a way of achieving a distance from her father. The autobiography takes a conventional form, starting in childhood and

offering the reader the portrait of an artist coming to 'selfhood' by rebellion against an older generation, following the path to maturity through
a forest of adolescent discontents and missed turnings. It is slightly more
adventurous, however, in weaving into the text extracts from the diaries
which she kept from the ages of 12 to 27, to be commented on dryly by
an older and wiser narrator (a technique reminiscent of the novels). The
extracts du Maurier selects present an image of herself as romantic rebel
and are arranged around a recurring theme: protest against being a girl,
against family, parents, but especially the 'confinement' of London
supremely represented by Gerald.

Wanting to be a boy appears to have been Daphne du Maurier's strongest desire in childhood:

Why wasn't I born a boy? They did all the brave things. Fought all
the battles . . . Angela [her older sister] did not mind being a girl.

(p. 22)

A brief passage in *Gerald* already told us that Daphne and her younger
sister, Jeanne, 'dreamed and thought as boys', and that although 'he never
wanted to turn his daughters into boys' (p. 190), Gerald had taught them
to bowl over-arm, had given them boxing gloves as presents, and taken
Daphne to Harrow to see his old school house, regaling her with schoolboy stories. Boys' stories were her 'usual teatime reading' (p. 52), the
historical adventures, the heroic antics of the late Victorian 'bloods', *Tom
Brown's Schooldays*; from an early age, she tells us, she pretended to be
a boy and envied male freedoms, freedoms which she usually depicts in
terms of deeds of adventure, acting out scenes from the stories or from
Lamb's *Tales from Shakespeare*. In play she would always take the male
part, enjoying being the child executioner whilst Jeanne meekly laid her
head on the block.

In the midst of these games comes the war. 'There were soldiers everywhere' and 7-year-old Daphne insists on being a soldier too.

I was given a khaki uniform for Christmas. The leggings, or puttees as
they were called, were hard to put on my legs and I couldn't wrap
them properly, but the soldier's hat was superb.

(p. 26)

For a little girl in an enthusiastically pro-military family, the war was an
exciting drama rather like those in which her father played. In 1917 she
could actually watch him play the part of a beribboned soldier in the
jingoistic *London Pride*, a chirpy Cockney returning on crutches to White-
chapel 'to the frenzied cheers of gallery and stall' (*Gerald*, p. 176).

The family had their own war hero when Guy, the soldier uncle, was
amongst the early victims and was hailed in the newspaper as 'a patriot,
alike with sword and with pen'. Du Maurier was told of his play *An*

Englishman's Home, which had briefly been a popular sensation in 1909 and had pleaded that ordinary people defend their homes and the nation against attack.[77] Daphne remained intensely proud of Guy all her life, and reflecting on the war in *Gerald*, in 1934, she seems completely unaffected by the revulsion which overtook so many of those who had learnt to their horror what the Great War had actually meant. 'He knew', she wrote of her uncle's play, 'what invasion would mean', and maintained with what seems extraordinary ignorance

> that there is some measure of glory in the knowledge that his words must have inspired many of those Englishmen who five years later, laboured amidst carnage and terror in a foreign land to save their precious homes from the disaster he had so fearfully foreseen.
>
> (*Gerald*, p. 129)

The need for national defence outweighed the casualties in her opinion which were simply 'the relentless and necessary drive of the herd to the slaughter'. Perhaps if she had lost her father or a beloved brother as Compton-Burnett did, or been old enough to be a VAD like Christie, grief might have rubbed some of the shine off this image of a just war. But not necessarily. It was perfectly possible, as Vera Brittain's account of her sufferings in *Testament of Youth* makes clear, for those who had lost their loved ones to learn to hate war and yet keep the romantic image of the heroic sacrifice of individuals untarnished: indeed it may have been the only way to cope with the trauma of their loss, as well as offering a felt tribute to the idealism which the war destroyed. Trauma provokes conservative as well as radical responses.[78]

Du Maurier's was the generation who grew up just too young to fight, and who lived to some extent in the shadow of that prematurely aged group, only 8 or 9 years older, who had 'seen it all'. Yet it seems as though Daphne was in mourning just as much as her older female peers, for a lost manhood and the brother whom she never had. Perhaps we might understand the formation of a conservatism in this generation of women, many of whom were the bright young things of the late 1920s, as in some ways taking the place of those lost boys, boys who in a strange way, like Peter Pan, remained immortal in the mind, because they never lived to grow up.[79] It may be that what helped to create a modern femininity was in part this impersonation of boyishness (what in French fashion was called the '*garçon*' look) which was not just a matter of taking over short hair and flat chests, but, for the more conservatively-minded, of sustaining too that romantic image of boyish adventurism which had gone to its grave in the trenches.

Adolescence (as she calls a new chapter in the autobiography) begins for du Maurier with the 'shame and revulsion' at beginning to menstruate and her hoping against hope that 'I would yet turn into a boy' (p. 46).

Having her 'periods' meant lying and subterfuge: being a girl and growing up, the equivalent of a state of deceit. Like her father, pretending to be someone else was often a full-time occupation; round about this time (1919 or so) she invented a companion for herself in fantasy, 'Eric Avon' – very much a first-class chap out of the school stories she loved.[80] This older brother, had he lived, was exactly the kind of sterling fellow who would have volunteered and been amongst the earliest casualties. He was perhaps both a compensation for girlhood and an extension of her resistance to how it had been designated socially and culturally. The older du Maurier narrating the account makes a link at this point with her adoption of the male persona in her fiction by suggesting that always 'there was an Eric Avon struggling to escape from my feminine unconscious' (p. 53). Yet we might say rather that in her unconscious it was always possible to be both masculine and feminine, and that as Freud argued these are concepts of uncertain content, positions whose fixity is never secure.[81] What is sad about du Maurier's account of her past self is not that she had to become a girl, but that no matter how much her own life showed her to be brave or independent, it was never 'the real thing' (war was the ultimately real thing); such qualities (like intelligence itself) were only to be understood as masculine even if she, a woman, exhibited them herself.

As du Maurier grows older she struggles with her femininity by inventing another persona for herself, that of a 'silly, sheltered girl' hemmed in by parental pressure. The diaries of her late 'teens and twenties are written with touches of self-conscious melodrama as she casts herself in the role of an Elizabeth Barrett or Florence Nightingale, the Victorian daughter kept at home by a stern patriarch. She protests that at 22 she is 'treated like a Victorian miss of sixteen' and roundly condemns her parents' narrow-mindedness – 'they might have been born centuries ago' (p. 123). Becoming a writer appears in the diary as a way of escaping from home and girlhood to become 'an individual':

I want to revolt, as an individual, against everything that 'ties'

(p. 126)

The older du Maurier seems content to accept this picture of herself as a romantic rebel, though she mocks the histrionic tone gently. The reader might be struck, however, not by the overbearing paternal control or parental pressure under which she suffered, but by the fact that for their day, her parents were modern and indulgent, and far from disciplinarian.

The du Maurier home hardly appears to be one of pressing filial duties in the Victorian sense, a world in which she is actually made to stay indoors, pour tea, or entertain guests. Rather it is a world of going out, of café society, theatre, first nights, or of being pressed to 'go on the films' as a future actress. (Her first 'serious' boyfriend is Carol Reed, the future film director). Parental pressure to conform to their lives took an unlikely form: 'How about going to a matinée at the Hippodrome? . . . what about the first night of Ivor Novello's new play?' She is given the run of the car at 19 – 'I drive through London, and all over the place. In parks, along tram lines, everywhere' (p. 75). She falls in love with Paris in the late 1920s, where she goes to be 'finished', and makes several trips unaccompanied to go and stay there with friends; in London with Carol she stays out till one or two in the morning, exploring the river or the docks, eating late-night eggs and bacon in the 'Kit-Kat' café, drinking coffee from a pavement stall, driving round town in Carol's battered Morris – hardly the life of a Victorian miss.

Clearly it was possible in fantasy to translate what was a modern youth into a scenario of oppression and rebellion which was as real for Daphne du Maurier as the sense of being imprisoned in their homes was for her Victorian forebears. That rejection of 'the wrong atmosphere' into which she sees herself born ('people to lunch, to tea, to dinner, and endless discussion of plays, of actors, and criticism of everything') was a rejection primarily of her father's world, and of a family life which revolved around him. In a memoir written in 1973 she reminds readers that what might seem glamorous to them was normality for her: 'Other children's fathers, perhaps, went to an office; ours went to the theatre' (*The Rebecca Notebook and Other Memories*, p. 77). It is a parallel, however, which only goes so far. The man in business keeps regular hours and returns to the privacy of home each evening; not only is the theatre disruptive to family life (in the bourgeois sense), matinée idols live in the public eye and ply their trade by being other men. Always du Maurier's memories return to the disturbing quality of Gerald's masculinity, which like the make-up that his daughter thought improved his appearance, was both infinitely appealing and at the same time ought, according to convention, to be rejected. In *Growing Pains*, as in *Gerald*, her filial rebellion is not a rejection of paternal control exercised through brute force, but a reaction against a more unsettling sense of Gerald's compelling difference from other men:

The trouble with D – now that I was becoming adult – was that whenever Angela or I were drawn into a heart-to-heart conversation with him, either walking on the heath, or more usually over his glass of port after Sunday supper, he too easily became emotional, suspicious, even possessive, and this made for reluctance on our part to discuss personal thoughts or our relationships with our friends. M, to her credit, did not pry, though she spoke her mind forcibly when irritated or annoyed, but even now, as in childhood and adolescence, there was little intimacy between us, a mutual reserve.

(p. 92)[82]

The expectations of parental roles within the middle classes seem here to be reversed, father is emotional and mother distant and reserved. Gerald must have seemed to Daphne to belong to 'the weaker sex': left to cope with him one holiday when he 'was going through some kind of personal crisis', 'he kept breaking down and crying' and ended up in bed (*Myself When Young*, p. 104). The young Daphne concluded what a tie married life must be (with all the storms and tantrums of such a partner) and hoped it would never be her lot.

For du Maurier to claim freedom as a young woman in the 1920s was to emulate the right sort of man. In her search for a model of emancipation she modelled herself not on her father but on the masculinity she imagined he lacked, turning back the clock to those images of piracy and vagrancy, soldiers of fortune and soldiers in fact, which had dominated her childhood reading. Smitten with the idea of a seafaring life she studied 'navigation', and thought up stories of boys who ran off to sea. Encouraged to go abroad with friends on a Scandinavian cruise she is propositioned by the elderly host and surprises him with her unconventional requests:

> he offered to buy me a fur coat at a gift shop . . . . This I declined, asking for a dagger instead.
>
> (p. 131)

– a dagger which she kept for years on her desk: 'one never knows when it might come in useful.' But it is only by escaping altogether that she can find a landscape for her desires.

Du Maurier had already discovered a romantic geography with the right kind of literary connotations in the Lake District, whose apparent rural innocence she contrasts to the world-weariness of London: 'There is nothing artificial here, no insincerity, no falseness' (p. 79). Other times she proclaimed that desire for wide, open spaces which took so many out of Britain in search of the remaining 'freedoms' of Empire; she wants to go and live on an African farm, 'away from decadence and modern materialism' (p. 82). (One is reminded, in a different context, of the romanticisation of Africa in the epic landscapes of Isak Dinesen, living out a kind of 'agrarian aristocracy' in Kenya, and speaking of her servants in the language of an officer who loves his men.)[83]

It was Cornwall, however, which provided the right kind of periphery, a place from which she could reject modernity, without having, entirely, to leave home. Cornwall had been the scene of family holidays, often disastrously spoilt by Gerald's loathing of country life. It was for both him and his daughter the antithesis of London and of family commitments there. Gerald, who loved to think of himself as a Cockney, hated the great outdoors and especially 'the elements', couldn't sit still for five minutes, and avoided solitude at all costs. He had a desperate need of people and of the camaraderie which he found in theatre life. His daughter, on the other hand, began to savour and parade a need to be alone; she began to stay on after the family had abandoned their holiday, and eventually to spend as much time as possible away from London. For Daphne the city was empty and pointlessly stimulating; Cornwall offered peace and stillness and 'roots'. Cornwall was the past to London's restless present; space where the other was a 'cage'. And yet the house where she began her first novel was one rented by Gerald, and her being a writer was a way of continuing the male line. Her choice of writing was like, and yet so unlike, her father's form of make-believe in depending as she saw it on a disciplined, almost monastic simplicity of life. As a modern young woman living in the past, she chose a place which turned the family home into 'dreary bloody London' (p. 102) and a landscape where her father would never feel at home.

It was a very different kind of romanticism which this 'fairy princess' took so seriously, roughing it alone in a cold house by the sea, wearing trousers and shorts to the consternation of villagers, chopping wood, camping on the moors in all weathers, riding and learning to sail single-handed: 'the real me is at Fowey in my boat alone' (p. 119). Sailing, swimming and 'exploring' occupied the time left over from writing, as though the psychic terrain of nineteenth-century boyhood was being lived again.[84] Yet four years after her first novel's publication she had a husband and daughter of her own. Perhaps because it seemed to her the least homely, most masculine of places, 'wild' and 'rugged' and 'inhospitable', an unlikely spot for a du Maurier, those creatures of comfort, to bring up a family, it enabled her to take that risk. With a boat moored in the harbour there might seem little danger of being confined to bourgeois routine. And now that family visiting and duties were difficult to maintain, she was free to celebrate the meaning of family in her writings. Du Maurier was, no doubt, 'a great loyalist'[85] but perhaps because she kept her family at a distance.

Nostalgia can be said to take its emotional energy from the opposition of a decadent present to an idealised past, which fuels that longing for a lost home.[86] Yet the meanings of home and modernity, and the particular forms an idealised past may take, are themselves forever shifting in time, and speak in different guises to women and men. By making Cornwall her home, du Maurier was indeed dwelling in an imagined past: the past of smugglers and of legend, of peasants and gentry (her Cornwall never included the middle classes, her own people); yet it was at the same time somewhere from which to protest against a narrow femininity rather than a simple collusion with that nostalgic urge which makes home the embodiment of maternal womanliness. Cornwall could provide a territory of independence and, if need be, of splendid isolation. Like Compton-Burnett's imaginary landed estates, or Christie's Little England villages

dreamt up in Baghdad, du Maurier's Cornwall was a place of contradictions, where uneasy selves could meet.

As her romance with the Cornish past grew, du Maurier liked to
picture Cornwall as a land on the border of Englishness, the last outpost
of the nineteenth century, but also of a rural landscape which she scanned
for the signs of an ancient, even pagan past.[87] She carefully researched her
own homes, Menabilly and Kilmarth, working them into her fiction as
places of the past, to be defended, as they are in *The King's General* and
in her last novel, *Rule Britannia*, against invasions from a levelling future.[88]
In old age, these homes turned out to be tenancies after all: du Maurier
had to leave Menabilly which she had transformed from a ruin and lived
in for twenty years, evicted by her landlord from the old Cornish gentry
as summarily as any peasant. Only Cornwall itself remained on lease to
her and even its 'spirit and history', as her affectionate account of the
county maintained, was 'vanishing'. Unlike many of her contemporaries,
however, she urged not conservationism but a revival of the industrial
centres of Cornwall – the tin and copper trades, alongside china clay. If
her vision of the past trembles on the edge of elegy, it is always held back
by a romantic hope for the future.

This book began with a biography, one whose reading of a life was
contradictory enough to inspire another reading, as the best biographies
should; it is perhaps appropriate that I have finished with a biographical
sketch of my own making, equally intended for revision. The untrustworthiness of biography, however, is exactly why it deserves a place
amongst the highest arts of criticism. Its pitfalls and its pleasures lie in
offering us a romance, as though a life were one story with a united self
at its centre, instead of several, unfinished subjects, ill-matching and ill-
fitting parts. The girl wanting to be a boy, or the married woman with
three children and a husband; the undutiful daughter who disdained her
father's weaknesses but remained devoted to his memory; the anti-sentimental modern who loved the idea of a family past; a Dame of the British
Empire, a general's wife and a 'Lady', or the recluse who hated state
functions and preferred to walk the dog – these are not 'selves' like
theatrical roles, put on at will at different times in our lives, but closer to
the shadowy figures we are divided between in our dreams, where we
think we are playing only one part and yet there is no one else in the
cast.

Biographers must tread carefully amongst these dreams, since we all
make fictions of ourselves in order to live, but it has been one of the
intentions of this work to show that they are neither random nor unique
fabrications, locked away from the world 'outside', the 'private' stuff of
fantasy. What we imagine we are is shaped from the material of the
present, and spoken in the accents of the time, with a history and with

limits we can map, if only temporarily. Even in our most intimate moments of what we need to believe is 'self-expression', we are bound to speak a language larger than ourselves, which testifies to the indissolubility of subjectivity and history.

Daphne du Maurier, writing the story of her own life, could not resist the pleasure of that ultimate romance, the hope that we can find a complete self, and the self's fulfilment in an eternally satisfying present. She chose to end her first volume of autobiography, unlike any of her other stories, without any shadow of a parting or hint of disillusionment to come. Her last scenes are a 'thirties' love-story and we are left, for the one and only time, on an enchanted island from which we need never return. Who else could she fall for but a soldier, the youngest major in the army, who had survived Passchendaele, been decorated for his bravery and leadership, and who literally sailed into her life one morning and invited her aboard his boat?

Hatless, brown leather jerkin, grey flannel trousers thrust into seaboots . . . green eyes and a smile that curled at one corner,[89]

he is still remembered by his widow of 70 as the true romantic hero he must have seemed to her then – 'Boy' Browning, or 'Tommy', his very names seem now so much a part of their times. Such a weight of feeling is attached to that memory it can only be expressed in the undemonstrative slang of her youth. He was, she tells us, 'rather good'. So he gives her a word or two of command – 'I had never had a direct order before and I loved it!' (p. 155) – and they are married in four months. Though her father wept at the prospect ('it's unfair'), he remembered Guy and was content.

Gerald could be exposed to public scrutiny, 'Tommy' never; he appears only vaguely as a 'fellow helmsman'[90] beyond reproach in print. And there is nothing between marriage and widowhood except what we learn from the novels. If her father's death in 1934 had marked the beginning of du Maurier's best writing, her husband's thirty years later put an end, in her own words, to 'faery tales'. She sat wearing his shirts, using his pens to write replies to condolences, observing all their small rituals religiously, with all that special aptitude for mourning she had described in her father. And then there is time for one more memoir to be written of Gerald, that spirit of her past, which she summoned up time and again, and whose image she lovingly restored when it seemed that it might fade.[91] Ironically, despite her efforts, hers may be the du Maurier name that lasts.

Should I end on a note of elegy or romance – those passing bells which du Maurier sounded throughout her work? Perhaps we should leave her where she left us, believing she had 'grown up at last', a soldier husband beside her, sailing off on their honeymoon up the Helford river. 'The past lay behind me', she tells us, looking back. On the contrary, we might say, there was so much of it, in her writing, still to come.

Afterword

In 1945 Laura Jesson leant out of a train window blinking away the tears which pressed into her eyes and waved goodbye to the man who might have become her lover. In *Brief Encounter*'s story of a suburban housewife who refuses to stray from the fold and returns to her safe, dull marriage, post-war Britain saw an image of itself.[1] Celia Johnson, who played the part of Laura against Trevor Howard's tremulous Alec, is remarkable for what she doesn't do and for what she does not say: the film is her imaginary confession to her husband as he sits opposite her on the sofa, all unsuspecting, plying the *Times* crossword, but it is all the more eloquent for being ultimately unspoken. Women pulled out their hankies in the Gaumonts and the Troxys all over Britain as Laura swallowed hard and kept her feelings to herself. It was this quality of reticence which made Celia Johnson a heroine, at times brisk and sensible (even occasionally arch as the mildly repressive wife in *This Happy Breed*), but somehow inconsolably wistful, a life whose still waters ran deep. Her eyes luminous with emotion and her voice brightly cheerful, she was above all a gallant figure, a personification of that class ideal which was the creation of the inter-war period, but which had found its finest hour in 1940. Laura Jesson was the last of the wartime heroines.

It seems that by 1945 there was nothing odd or improbable for cinema audiences around the country to find an icon of Englishness in the sight of a housewife changing her library books and buying a new toothbrush, a notion which would have seemed bizarre in 1914 and inconceivable in 1850. For it was in the domestic situation and the most modest of places, like the railway station and the refreshment room, where Laura's brief encounters take place, rather than on the battlefield or in public life, that the staunchest and most typical expressions of the national character might be discovered. *Brief Encounter* was adventurous in its painstaking portrayal of provincial life, finding cinematic terms for that species of suburban realism which had already evolved a vocabulary of 'ordinariness' in the middlebrow novel between the wars: Laura and Alec are people of a kind whom Agatha Christie would have appreciated. We have to remind ourselves that what may strike us now as entirely 'a vanished scene, a vanished way of life',[2] was nevertheless cinematically bold in picturing the daily lives of middling people.[3]

The film did more than cultivate the ordinary: it made it the stage for romantic melodrama. The lamplit backstreets half-revealed in chiaroscuro translate the scene of documentary into a lovers' lane; those pollarded willows just before the level crossing, which Laura stares at from inside her railway compartment, can as easily dissolve into dreams of romance as they can remind her of mundaneness. If like Mrs. Miniver and Christie's heroines, Laura is a manager and a coper, it is when she is at her most ordinary and least expressive that she takes on the aura of romance: critics praised Johnson's 'under-playing'.[4] the lovers' tight-lipped idiom (of which Noel Coward was past master) could make the everyday and the almost trite seem urgent, even glamorous; an afternoon at the pictures or on the boating lake as exciting and dangerous as the Riviera or the Rialto. The film saw nothing incongruous in Alec Harvey, a local GP, playing the part of a British Count Vronsky, in an 'ordinary mac', snatching moments of illicit pleasure over a fried sole in the Kardomah café (with 'just plain water'), or in his telling Laura how 'awfully nice' she is over a Bath bun in a station buffet to the luscious accompaniment of Rachmaninov's Second Piano Concerto.

Under David Lean's direction *Brief Encounter* became one of the romantic climaxes of that anti-romanticism which signified Englishness between the wars. It was also a kind of swan song. In fact the film is shaped by retrospective, not only in its long flashback to the ill-starred affair, but also in its evocation of a settled life before the war which could now itself take on the appearance of a lost love. Coward set the scene during the winter of 1938–9, basing it on his play *Still Life* which he had written ten years earlier in 1935 as part of the trilogy *Tonight at 8.30.*; together with Lean's moody photography of smoke and steam and rainy streets at night, it has a distinctly autumnal feel. With its sympathy for middle age and affectionate scenes of home comforts, the film is as much an infatuation with a fading image of national life as it is an exposure of its stifling conformity. By 1945 the 1930s had already started to look like 'the long weekend' before the war, and for those of the temper of a Noel Coward what came in the post-war years was to be only a pale shadow of that time. Those rehearsals of national character in the 1930s which gave a command performance during the war, seemed more and more like a second-rate re-run in the 1950s, an Englishness which would rapidly become a has-been.

Brief Encounter was clearly a 'woman's film', making available to a wider audience that centrality afforded to the middle-class woman and her desires which had already achieved a new popularity in novels between the wars.[5] If its conservative morality sent both lovers back to their marriages, it was modern in the equal treatment that it meted out to them, making their fates as well as their dilemmas parallel. Laura, it is true, does not have a career in preventive medicine in which to lose herself, but the film does not suggest that her husband and children should be the sum total of her life, nor does it condemn her for her discontent. It is not out of guilt and shame that (Anna-Karenina-like) she nearly throws herself in front of an express train: it is at the thought of never seeing her lover again. *Brief Encounter* could rely on a complicity in the audience, which writers like du Maurier had already established, that marriage for women no longer necessarily meant sexual fulfilment. Repression might be the familiar keynote of respectability but it could now give femininity heroic proportions. Laura's desires are displayed for all to see in the many close-ups of her suffering silences on the big screen: the message was that women too had to 'master' their passions.

It has been one of the central themes of this book that something happened to middle-class feminity after the Great War which sees it taking on what had formerly been regarded as distinctly masculine qualities: in particular the ethics of a code of self-control and a language of reticence whose many tones can be picked out in the writing and also in the construction of writing selves in the period. The icily peremptory and the forbidding in the syncopated telegraphese of Compton-Burnett, the laconic and the self-effacingly humdrum in Agatha Christie's whodunits, the cheerful literary placebos of a *Mrs. Miniver*, and the timid self-deprecation of the girl in *Rebecca*, are all in their different ways responses to the problem of imagining a femininity whose former *raison d'être* had been primarily to embody and to speak 'romance'. I have argued that something generic and historic rather than simply individual might be read into the out-right denials of autobiography, the silences, understatements, and the 'refusal of interiority' which make up the place of femininity in the work of so many women of the day. Ironic dismissal, worldly wisdom, brisk competence and heroic disavowal could all be part of that reaction to the legacy of representations which had seen ladies as the softer and the frailer sex, the medium of the emotions and of 'higher things'. In a world where the opposing codes of masculinity which might make sense of such ascriptions were in a state of shock or simply blown away, the meanings and the limits of sexual identity were critically unstable.

There is still much work to be done exploring the full cultural meanings of that 'war to end all wars' for British social life, but especially for the female population who became, statistically, and, as I have argued here, in some ways symbolically too, the nation between the wars.[6] For it has never been a matter of just counting heads but of the emergence of a different kind of common sense about the national character in its retreat from more inflationary rhetorics. What might begin in the 1920s as a radical resistance, conscious or unconscious, to previous forms of sexual difference, a refusal, often quite literally, to speak the flowery languages of the past and a desire to find a powerful camouflage in the ironic tones of modernity, could gradually become a mode of settlement, a compromise which identified the national with the private and made the latter speak for the former. I have suggested that as part of the reaction against loss and the ideological rupture which is marked by the Great War, a conservative response might be an increased attachment to the idea of private life, not just as a shell into which the wounded individual might retreat, but as a new locus for the idea of a continuous and stable national history. Whilst the women of the middle classes might be seen to adopt many of the codes of what had been the model of an imperial masculinity, that idiom could at the same time become a new kind of Englishness; it could 'feminise' the idea of the nation as a whole, giving us a private and retiring people, pipe-smoking 'little men' with their quietly competent partners, a nation of gardeners and housewives.

There is clearly much more to be learnt about the recasting of the idea of imperial power itself. What we might call the domestication of the imperial idea between the wars, and the elaboration of imperial fantasies within different kinds of national, private, and indeed feminine contexts, can, however, only be made sense of once we realise how much it was women who represented modernity in the post-war generation. The concept of British nationality can be seen as pre-eminently masculine before the First World War; the female members of the different races were held to share the same feminine qualities to a greater or lesser degree, and whilst Englishwomen could be the guardians of their race, their Englishness, as primarily wives and mothers, derived from the men in their lives.[7] As a result no doubt of their work during the First World War (whatever other political considerations may have played their part), their acquisition of citizenship (in 1919 and then with full suffrage in 1928), suggests a new level of State recognition and of national inclusion. For women themselves it must be seen as an ambiguous advancement: what might be taken as evidence of their forming a self-conscious social and political constituency was ineluctably bound up with their coming into an imperial inheritance. Becoming English, being able to represent one's country, both literally in the judiciary, in parliament, in military uniform, as well as culturally and symbolically, even where it was a condition of emancipation, brought with it insidious modes and histories of privilege. Indeed, if we speculate that the very idea of the Englishwoman is invented between the wars, it would seem that a tying together of empire and understandings of feminine power is expressed not only in the many attacks upon the 'Memsahib' in the literature of the period, but also in the emphasis placed upon the creation of the idea of an imperial subjectivity, fraught and divided within itself, which could now be directly explored: Forster's *Passage to India* gives us imperial rule both at its most ignorant and cruel, and at its most liberal and humane, in the contrast between the figures of Mrs Turton, the Collector's wife, and the elderly Mrs Moore. It is the imperial or colonial experience imagined as an extension of domestic or private life, its internal emotional conflicts and personal dilemmas (like the sad and bitter trials of the sundowner classes in Somerset Maugham's short stories), which seemed to seize the public imagination in Britain between the wars.

There has been an historical narrative of sorts at work in the arrangement of my chapters: Compton-Burnett took us back to a formation brutally modernised by the Great War; Christie into the heart of that compromise which I have called, but not disparagingly, the middlebrow, whilst *Mrs. Miniver* seems the high point and also the turning-point of that accommodation, politically expressed as appeasement. As we have seen from what happened to Jan Struther's columns and the metamorphosis of Mrs. Miniver into a heroine, it was possible by the end of the 1930s for this new vision of the English as a peaceable, tolerant folk to represent the very virtues of a national life worth fighting for. Appeasement offered little resistance to more aggressive kinds of nationalism. In du Maurier's imagination the conciliatory and the reticent are wound up to a higher pitch of stoicism; the insular translates into a splendid isolation.

It is *Mrs. Miniver*, however, despite being the least durable and most historically specific of my texts, which goes right to the heart of that conservatism which has been at the core of this work and its image of the inter-war years. The conservatism of a Mrs. Miniver lies not in her political outlook in the public sense: her praise of family and home is muted and subordinated to a much more powerful sense of privacy; her conservatism does not make her nationalist, it could and did make her pacifist and anti-fascist. Rather it makes the appeal to 'tradition' into the broadest possible sense of the daily and the routine: here are the bare bones of any conservatism, the urge to conserve and maintain what is already there, which, though it can take more dramatic political forms, is their *sine qua non*. It is a minimalist management of emotional and social life which would rather leave things as they are than suffer the pain of disturbance. This is conservatism which depends not in the first place on calls to heredity or birth, on explicit nationalism or a triumphalist rhetoric but manifests itself as 'throttled emotion'. It may have found its apogee in the inter-war middle-class sensibility but it is one which is accessible and available to all.

Throughout the chapters I have come back again and again to conservatism as a matter of temperament as well as particular views on public affairs, a special kind of emotional economy rather than, though it might accompany, specific views on the economy of the State. This is indeed how conservatism likes to see itself – as a politics which eschews politicking; a system of beliefs and values without systematisation; an organic and inevitable way to be: socialists and radicals are those who 'interfere' or tamper with people and their lives. Part of the deep idealism of conservatism lies in its faith in the possibility of unobtrusive government and magically invisible change. This is the quiescent and non-interventionist mode of conservative philosophy which seems to have found new, modern forms between the wars.

Yet as the exclusions and denials in the texts remind us, even at its most apparently effortless, such conservatism does not come easily; it has indeed to be worked at, and strained after, by individuals as by nations; it has a history, vicissitudes and velleities, like any other cultural form or identity. The carefully gay tones which Laura Jesson adopts to talk to her friends and lover are her 'social manner'[8] – an idiom which appears 'natural' but is clearly 'laboured'. And conservatism is always a matter of desire, not just of the repression and denial of feelings; it has its pleasures and its rewards too – as the shift from the harsh universe of Compton-Burnett to the celebratory corner of Jan Struther columns made clear.

It might seem that Daphne du Maurier has played devil's advocate in this discussion, suggesting, in the first place, only those imaginings which a more moderate conservatism works to exclude. If *Mrs. Miniver* offered readers the ideal fiction of a life perfectly at home in the present, du Maurier's *Rebecca* of the same year makes a romance of the past. Where *Mrs. Miniver* evoked an inner life entirely at ease with itself and with femininity, du Maurier's fiction explores personal and marital discontent; her world is as restless as the other's is serene. It would seem that du Maurier has more in common with a grander line of Tory writers and with those preoccupations which have made conservatives on the whole better melancholics than cheer-leaders. Her writing certainly exhibits something of the morbid fascination with time passing, with natural corruption and mortality, which has revealed conservatives to be as much obsessed by change as fearful of it. Du Maurier's writing shows how readily the desire to protect and maintain can shift onto the offensive; a fear of loss become invasion fears.

Yet even in du Maurier's work the dark side of conservatism which dwells on decay and death and reminds us that *pulvus et umbra sumus* (the Latin tag from Horace which Johnson liked to quote) has lost much of its emotional and moral weight. However much she is drawn to ruins and to ghosts, du Maurier's foremost relationship to the past is one of taking pleasure in its invention, finding new settings for enjoyment. In all these writers as noticeable as any continuities with older Tory themes – the resistance to change, the rejection of blueprints for the future – has been their modern reworking. Only by stretching the word to its limits can *Mrs. Miniver* be placed in a tradition of 'consolation' literature or comfortable words. What ought to produce melancholy and despair is turned into entertainment: even Compton-Burnett makes the compulsive mechanism of repetition in her novels into a comedy. Du Maurier's evocation of the great themes of romantic literature is always a self-conscious one, appealing to a modern generation of women which liked to think of itself as sceptical, even cynical about romantic love; her love of strong men is honest enough to see them as a thing of the past.

Whilst each of these chapters has touched in different ways upon the traditional themes of conservative thinking and beliefs, they remind us that conservatism, whatever its shared foundations, finds many different modes and historical forms. The effect of the war may have been not only to produce a conservative reaction but a reaction against older forms of conservatism too. We can readily understand if that part of the conservative imagination which is drawn to charnel-houses and churchyards, and to brooding over the way of all flesh, might well go subterranean in the years after the war. If, as Freud suggested in the theories he evolved in the wake of 1919, a longing for the cessation of life and energy and for a return to an unorganised and inanimate state of rest, is the necessary other half of the dialectic of being human, we might speculate that the most primary conservatism is just this desire for, and fear of, the ultimate equilibrium of non-being.[9] The war had provided, however, a vivid dramatisation of 'entropy' and of the perishability of human matter. 'Thanatos', far from appearing as the bringer of a blessed, inorganic peace, took only the nightmare forms of attrition and inertia which made the trenches and their survivors so many ghastly exemplars of a death-in-life. A sense of dissolution and of moribundity, of wasted life and life as waste, was perhaps too powerful in post-war culture for anything other than the most benign forms of the 'death instinct' to be publicly enjoyed. When modern Englishmen tried to be melancholy – like Nicky in Coward's *Vortex* – they appeared merely hysterical (or neurasthenic); both despair and catharsis were to be blocked by irony, and the lonely and heroic anguish of the nineteenth century took on both a more self-indulgent feel and a more collective form as a twentieth-century blues.

There are naturally other reaches to conservatism in these years which I might have explored but even those more obstinate manifestations of Toryism do not emerge unscathed from what we call modernity. Though a study of Waugh, Wodehouse and Henry Williamson, or of Dorothy L. Sayers, Angela Thirkell, or Georgette Heyer might have given us a different emphasis, their interest would none the less lie as much in their modernity as in their reiteration of well-worked national and political themes. Far from being stuck in the mud of the past, conservatism seems to have improvised rather well in the modern period, making something homely and familiar from the brand new: think of the inventiveness of the spirit which could take that futurist symbol of speed and erotic dynamism – the motor car – and turn it into a Morris Minor! Like the attack on the Victorian family which transferred allegiances to the modern couple and the small family, it could hold on to the mainstays of a conservative frame of mind (like the primacy of the domestic affections), whilst simultaneously updating it. It is this contradictory process of a modernising conservatism which I have seen as central to the period and to its formation, or reformation, of Englishness.

There might seem at first to be nothing new in many of the codes of class reference which help define Englishness in the period. Bourgeois reticence is typically measured against the 'looseness' of speech or behaviour in others – most obviously foreigners, the working classes or the decadent aristocracy. Laura Jesson's 'niceness' is necessarily set off by the casual badinage of the British Rail employees in the film (one of whom has simply upped and left her husband and whose sexuality must be comic in order to defuse its threat). This a familiar kind of comedy. Indeed I have argued that distinctions within the middle classes (as to who might count as people 'like us') were at least as preoccupying as perceptions of easily recognised 'inferiors'. What began as ventriloquy of masculinity and an attempt to emancipate themselves from earlier erotic codes of femininity, locked women into a paralysing and potentially infinite series of social demarcations against their own kind. It might seem that cross-class differences and their markers remained unreconstructed in the period: the comic servants of Compton-Burnett and Christie's adenoidal maids, the loutish mob of *Jamaica Inn* and Mrs. Miniver's garrulous but cheerful char are surely fixed stars in a conservative constellation?

Yet the inter-war period was one in which the English began to see images of themselves and of their cultural behaviour – gestures, bodily movements and facial expressions – at 'the pictures' and in magazine photography as never before. Above all, they got used to hearing their voices reproduced mechanically, on the telephone, the gramophone, at the 'talkies' and on the wireless: for conservatives 'the loudspeaker' was the bane of the times. A buried chapter in this book is the one which would have taken directly as its starting point the significance of those absurd accents, pealing voices and clipped tones, accents which are now so difficult to listen to and seem as dated as bakelite and the cocktail cabinet but which were once the new and distinctive sounds of class between the wars. It is no exaggeration to say that the English middle classes, with their stiff upper lips, seem to have been speaking a kind of Stage English throughout the period. 'BBC English', transmitted and learnt from the wireless was, of course, just that, the voice of trained actors and actresses, enunciating carefully and minding their 'p's' and 'q's'.

There was a revealing paradox in this 'broadcasting' of superior speech. In the adoption of BBC English we can discover not simply the tenacity of forms of English snobbery but also, less obviously, a symptom of the instability of assigning class positions in the period: a voice could be genteel without having any other means of gentility; accent – as Ivy Compton-Burnett herself discovered – was a piece of cultural capital which everyone could borrow; it could be unanchored in older forms of owner-ship or community and was part of that modern shift in which 'class' might only be a matter of appearances, of striking the right note. Rather than seeing 'the middle class' as a fixed and given category in the period it has been more useful to see it as a matter of effects and props, a performance put on for the benefit of others. Both Compton-Burnett and Christie see English cultural life as theatrical: Christie's whodunits revolve around exactly the anxiety that one could so easily play the part of the gentleman. Compton-Burnett's private houses are like stage sets, the dwellings of a gentry without historical place or social networks, disenfran-chised and cut off from notions of tradition, like the imaginary villages where Christie's crimes take place. They are both, in different ways, the class fictions of a radio age in which voice and dialogue must make up for older forms of narrative connection.

If in the 1920s and '30s the representations of Englishness traded in familiar tropes, nevertheless they were increasingly displayed across new forms and modern reproductions, like those of the radio and cinema, but also in the new genres of commercial fiction, which disengaged them from their point of origin and community, offering them rather to hetero-geneous and unpredictable new groups. Loyal rustics and wooden-headed servants might be the stock-in-trade of conservatism; the forms of their reproduction and their new availability to mass audiences most certainly was not. Literature was subject to a new set of cultural determinations and its forms underwent a series of sea-changes, taking risks with older conventions and exploring new markets. The spawning of 'commercial' fiction for the middle classes, like the whodunit, was also part of the increase in forms of domestic consumption which offered new opportunit-ies for opening up the literary to wider and more mixed readerships: there was something in it for everybody. The commodification of literature, which it is so easy to berate, was also a kind of democratisation. Du Maurier's superior romances and Mrs. Miniver's literariness are as much signs of this sense of access to the literary traditions of the past, offered as new sources of entertainment, as they are preservers of old-fashioned images of class differentiation.

Within literary studies we have perhaps suffered from a surfeit of 'mod-ernism' and a dearth of studies of modernity. We don't yet know enough about that modernity which found its way into Beaverbrook's *Express* rather than Pound's *Cantos*; the modernity of the dance craze, the Lyons Corner House, or the wireless programme, all offered new opportunities for relationship and for expression, as did the 'middlebrow' in literature. As I have suggested, new genres like the whodunit make a different kind of sense when we read their concerns as consonant with, rather than opposite to, those of 'high' modernism. Perhaps in literary history we need a concept of the suburban or of modern domestic design like that which has proved so fruitful in studies of the visual arts and architecture. Certainly literary work in Britain with its tight divisions between 'high' and 'low' (often repeated in the opposition between university English and polytechnic 'Humanities') has not been especially adventurous in exploring modernity, preferring to return comfortably to its high priests and sacred texts rather than asking itself about the diffusion of the modern, the creation of modern sensibilities in their most commonplace and common-sense forms.

Much of the study of the inter-war period seems to me to have been obscured by the long shadow cast backwards from the 1950s. Indeed, we might say that the literary imagination of the 1950s was actively engaged in creating the dominant images of those earlier decades: so much writing was, in Elizabeth Bowen's words, inflected by 'the bend back'.[10] It may be that from our own position at the end of the twentieth century we are now better placed to gauge the modernity of those decades after the First World War and should expect new objects to hove into view, as well as finding that those we thought familiar begin to take on a different complexion. At present it seems wise to remain agnostic as to whether in time the kind of journalism offered by a Mrs. Miniver will not turn out to have been as momentous an event in literary history as the modernist's 'stream of consciousness' – either way, the two are clearly related and our understanding is not to be helped by clinging to different 'classes' of writing and keeping them firmly on separate shelves.

Redrawing the map of the 1930s and its relation to what came before and after has many consequences then for feminism and for its analysis of the history of women's lives in Britain. It would be so much easier to see the 1930s as the beginning of the bad times for women, a trough after the peak of suffragism, sinking towards the nadir of the 1950s, in its turn a kind of slough of despond from which women were gratefully led on to the new heights of the Women's Movement after 1969. Instead the queasiness I felt at reading Mrs. Miniver (of all the texts surely the most remote from feminism?) seemed to me to suggest as many continuities as breaks across these generations, continuities which raised awkward questions about 'domesticity' and its place in women's lives. Rather than seeing the feminists of the 1970s as rejecting the terms in which their mothers saw their lives, it seems to me that their preoccupations were remarkably similar; that it is in the debates about home and the 'wifely life' in the 1930s that we might look for the seeds of that later discontent, as well as for some of the limitations of the agenda which another generation of feminists were to set themselves.

Central to any discussion of the inter-war years must be the ambiguous place of home and private life in the period, and the problematic and contradictory ways in which it signalled the feminine. Ambiguous because, on the one hand, these were the decades, as historians remind us, of home-ownership and of house-building and, as I have argued, of an identification of the nation with the increasing privatisation of social life; yet, on the other hand, the 1920s and '30s saw blistering attacks upon older versions of domestic life and made questions of the conduct of home life public property as never before. Older and more elaborate forms of bourgeois comfort (those which depended on a household of servants, for example) were decried, efficiency and management increasingly became the new watchwords of women who no longer saw themselves as simply wives at home but 'housewives', something altogether more professional. Feminists and non-feminists alike could agree on rejecting the domestic culture of the past, but the values given to domesticity and the place of domestic labour remained a source of intense division between women within, and across, the classes.

Not surprisingly it is the 'suburban' woman who is inveighed against most violently by conservatives and progressives alike, earning the scorn of both a Jan Struther and a Vera Brittain. Here was a new breed of woman who merely enjoyed her 'labour-saving' home, who got respectability on a mortgage, social status and its rewards on the never-never. For the conservative she was the person who had broken ranks and no longer knew her place, thereby unsettling everyone; for the feminist she was a modern woman but not an emancipated one, a woman more bent on material pleasures than intellectual ones; on home- rather than on self-improvement. Faced with those women who seemed only to want 'baths and money', Mrs. Miniver would have agreed with Virginia Woolf's assertion (though without Woolf's ironic self-awareness) that

> it is much better to be a lady; ladies desire Mozart and Einstein – that is, they desire things that are ends, not things that are means.

They are, she maintained, able to 'fly free at the end of a short length of capital' and avoid the horror of being tied down to a 'narrow plot of acquisitiveness and desire'.[11]

Woolf was writing about the women of the respectable working classes but these women were, after all, the future residents of the suburbs. Yet it ought to be a matter of some disturbance rather than approval to present-day feminists to recognise how consistently a part of what makes a 'middle-class' identity has been the assumption that there is something essentially stultifying and degrading in domesticity. Re-reading Mrs. Miniver one is struck by how much, despite her praise of the quiet life, she shares with the feminism of the 1930s and indeed of the 1970s the view that the domestic is something one rises above in order to get on with the real business of life and explore a 'richer' sense of self. What Q. D. Leavis called 'the complacency of enlightenment'[12] amongst progressive women was at its most glaringly obvious when those who sneered at dusting or shopping actually depended for their own comfort on other women doing the dirty work, but it is equally worrying when it is not just housework but 'home-making' and the acquiring of 'things' that comes under automatic fire: these too have played a different part in the dreams as well as in the 'oppression' of different women. The carpet and the three-piece suite, the hoover and the new gas-oven are icons of hope and dignity as well as of pride and envy.[13]

We have still to write the histories of the emotional and affective relations which women have with home-making as part of the histories of what we call 'class'. The idea of comfort, and the attitudes toward domestic labour, the whole panoply of relations which is covered by the word 'home' has formed a symbolic as well as literal interior which women inhabit: 'domesticity' is a complex knot of feelings, ideas and activities which have structured a sense of the feminine self. This history of the 'private sphere' is one fraught with conflict between women, as well as between the sexes, and given Britain's history of domestic service, no history of feminism here can fail to confront the schism between women which separated them in the very heart of 'private life'. Whilst we have begun as feminists to subject to historical scrutiny woman's place in the home, we have more to discover about the place of home in the woman. If the 'language of class-formation is gendered',[14] we also have much to learn about the social divisions which continue to make women see themselves as superior to, or lesser than, each other.

The writings by women in the inter-war years played a crucial part in bringing buried anxieties and desires about older forms of domesticity to the surface and in voicing just how much the women of the middle classes had suffered from being identified with, and shut up in, the home. A revolt against their own mothers and the femininity of the 1890s is as clearly signalled in Compton-Burnett as in Christie; in Struther as in Woolf. Such a reaction could take progressive or conservative forms; it could lead to new and modern notions of privacy even as it resisted the domestic ideologies of the past. But we do not yet know what sense that revolt made to their women servants, nor how crucial the 'lower class' of woman was to the imaginative energy of that revolt. It is interesting, if somewhat disquieting, that it is not until the 1950s, when the servant class is finally a disappearing species, that the next generation of women begin to write of privacy itself as form of oppression. Brought up to expect help in the home, these daughters of educated men are actually the first generation of the reasonably well-off actually faced with the prospect of doing all the housework themselves (without even a 'daily' to do 'the rough'). We might wonder how much this resentment at not having servants was itself an unconscious drive to proto-feminist protest. When Elizabeth Taylor's housebound heroine asks herself whether making 'a really spongy sponge-cake' is to be the whole of her existence, part of her anguish is born of not having a cook.[15]

'Mrs. Miniver' was in her forties in 1938; her daughter a young mother in the 1950s. How could the granddaughter, escaping to college in the 1960s, have failed to put the horrors of housework at the centre of her feminism, taking questions about 'the interior' of women's lives even further indoors and making the most intimate places inside the woman the subject for collective 'consciousness-raising'.[16] In the proper attempt to condemn the 'incarceration' of women in the home, there was perhaps a reiteration of unconsciously bourgeois assumptions, and a necessary but unfortunate foreclosing of any discussion of domestic pleasures. An insufficient openness to the huge investment which members of this culture make in domesticity, and the skills which women learn (whose competences we take for granted until we see a man put on a pillow-slip), as well as to the history of domestic labour itself, may have done its own fair share in the silencing of some women. Lamenting the deadening and demoralising effects of being at home can make little sense to those who are longing to put their feet up, especially when they may have inherited from their own mothers 'standards' of comfort and housework which were learnt under duress in those other women's homes. The animus which was directed by the Women's Movement against the 'housewife syndrome' may have been one of the reasons why it failed to become a truly 'mass' movement, involving women from all walks of life.

Another account of the inter-war years might press harder on these divisions than I have done. For myself, writing this book has meant a battle of a more intimate kind, one which, were I to confront it explicitly, would need quite another, braver kind of writing. I come from exactly those people who, in the 1930s and still today, feature as the icons of suffering and the objects of uneasy fears within much political discourse. For many years even the sound of an educated woman's voice would make me wince and squirm. It was the voice of the employer and the landlady, of 'madam' or 'her ladyship' (both terms of abuse applied half-jokingly to little working-class girls to bring them down a peg or two), of the girls I encountered at college who didn't know the right end of a broom, and of the friends and colleagues who, when they want to be funny, put on working-class accents. Hearing a 'posh' voice I can still experience in reverse what many 'lady writers' complain of in the 1930's about the 'lower orders' – a sense of their offensive anonymity, that they all sound the same, look the same: it is a response I now see as no less de-humanising for being understandable.

It has taken me far longer than the eight years of writing this book to accept that the middle classes are a mixed bunch. Their voices and their forms are legion, their manifestations contradictory and confused. It is both a relief and a sadness to me to be more generous, for it still goes against the grain to acknowledge what these chapters have made me realise: that even the most privileged have had their deprivations. None of this means that their worst conceits cannot be satirised, nor their injustices attacked, but that the coherence of a political polemic comes best out of a specific and historical understanding of those differences within class formations as well as outside them; from a gauging of their instabilities rather than an assumption that they are forever fixed in place. If our own identities fit us ill, it makes poor sense always to imagine that others wear their own more comfortably. And since political allegiances cannot finally be predicated upon forms of social belonging – being a woman does not make you a feminist, any more than being 'working-class' has meant espousing socialism – they too have to be seen as historically shifting territories, temporary, nomadic dwellings, however much we want to make them places where we can settle down.

Such an unsettling of the reassuring categories of class has meant a farewell to some my own pieties, though no doubt it will be a long goodbye. But it has opened up too, new possibilities of writing about that 'working-class' past without the righteous anger which always threatens to make the daughters of uneducated men into martyrs or saints. Ironically the chapter that I most wanted to write – one which would examine the complex literary strategies by which writers evoked 'that other tribe' – the working classes – never got written. In the process of what has emerged in these pages, however, I have begun to realise that any such account will need to let go of the consoling fiction that whatever challenged or was 'other' to an idea of the middle classes in the period was essentially more honest, more authentic. If this book begs another, a history of that other subjectivity, of what it meant to be 'working-class' in the inter-war years, and of its modern remaking, it will need to accommodate all the interiorisations of social difference, the corrosive and the deforming feelings which lead to deference and belligerence, as well as the powerful creations of belonging that can lead to co-operation. The writing of that account will not be served by hagiography but it might begin by attending to the part played in 'class consciousness' by those conservatisms which both limit and give form to the imagination of any person, culture or nation.

Appendix: Mrs. Miniver writes to *The Times*

To the editor of *The Times*

Sir, Since the last time I appeared in your columns, on November 29, I have had so many letters from those of your readers who are good enough to take an interest in this family chronicle that I venture to ask whether you will let me send them, through you, a reply and a request.

All the writers of these letters share my feelings about the Jewish tragedy, but some of them question the truth of the sentence, 'to shrink from direct pain was bad enough, but to shrink from vicarious pain was the ultimate cowardice.' If one reads everything that is written about such horrors, they suggest, one may find oneself 'haunted almost beyond endurance'. 'And what is the use of that,' they add beseechingly, 'if there is nothing whatever one can do about it?'

I am afraid I still think that it is a great deal of use. The only force which can be brought to bear upon those who are responsible for such an outrage is the tide of public opinion. But what is this tide, except the aggregate of a million small drops of private opinion? A paragraph in a letter to a friend, a remark passed on the telephone or at the dinner-table, may seem to do little good; but in reality every word, spoken or written, helps to swell the tide. In such a cause, surely, one should be willing to accept the burden of being haunted?

Besides, is there really 'nothing whatever one can do about it'? I feel sure that the writers of these letters have already turned out their pockets on behalf of the refugees. But have they, I wonder, turned out their cupboards as well? And if not, will they join with me in doing so? I am not suggesting a raid upon their current wardrobe, though if there is anything to spare from that, too, so much the better. What I am talking about is the 'put-away cupboard' – that time-honoured institution which is one of the glories of English family life: the cupboard which contains the spare blankets; and the brown cardigan suit which one bought in a hurry and never really liked; and those flannel shirts of one's husband's which have shrunk in the wash but are still too big for Vin: and a whole collection of Vin's clothes which will probably have the moth in them before Toby can wear them; and Judy's and Toby's last year's winter coats, kept on the off-chance that they would be able to get into them again this year (which they can't); and a rabble of stockings and sweaters and woollen underclothes of various shapes and sizes, all carefully, if rather vaguely, hoarded against a rainy day.

Well, our own rainy day may never actually arrive; but for other people, at this moment, it is raining very hard indeed. There is a desperate need for clothes – especially children's clothes – for the refugees. I feel sure that a concerted raid upon all the 'put-away cupboards' of this country would go far towards meeting the need. And while my fellow 'Mrs. Minivers' (this very week-end, perhaps) are engaged upon that could the Judys and Tobys be persuaded to have yet another go at their toy-cupboards? Probably they have just combed them out for the sake of the hospitals or the unemployed; but if they could manage to spare even one more toy apiece it would help to make the refugee children's Christmas a less forlorn one. Books would be welcome, too, for many of the children already speak English and the rest are eager to learn.

Parcels should be addressed to:–

Lord Baldwin's Appeal Fund (Clothing Dept.), Westbourne Terrace, W.2.

May I take the opportunity of wishing all my unknown friends, on behalf of this family, a very happy Christmas?

I am, Sir, yours faithfully,

CAROLINE MINIVER

(*The Times*, Saturday, 17 December 1938)

Notes

PREFACE

1 Raymond Williams, *The English Novel from Dickens to Lawrence* (Chatto & Windus, London, 1970), Chapter V.
2 Publicity material on the cover of the Virago edition (London, 1981).
3 ibid.; for the weevils and rats, see section 5 of Part One of the novel.

INTRODUCTION

1 Salman Rushdie, 'Is Nothing Sacred?', the Herbert Read Memorial Lecture, February 6 1990; printed in *Granta*, no. 31 (Spring 1990) (Penguin, Harmondsworth).
2 The few literary studies of the inter-war period have tended to concentrate upon its second decade as being more historically and politically identifiable: for example, Samuel Hynes, *The Auden Generation: Literature and Politics in England in the 1930s* (Bodley Head, London, 1976); Bernard Bergonzi's *Reading the Thirties: Texts and Contexts* (Macmillan, London, 1978) and Richard Johnstone, *The Will to Believe: Novelists of the Nineteen Thirties* (Oxford University Press, Oxford, 1984), all of which seem content to limit themselves to – as one of Bergonzi's chapter headings puts it – 'Men among boys, boys among men'. On the other hand, *Class, Culture and Social Change: A New View of the 1930s*, ed. Frank Gloversmith (Harvester, Brighton, 1980), offers a more adventurous, interdisciplinary account of the era, and yet the anlaysis (again with its stress upon the 1930s) gives us the familiar literary landmarks, whilst 'women' (with the usual honorary exception of Virginia Woolf) are simply added on in a separate chapter, not as part of a literary culture but as the material base of social history (housing, nutrition, birth-control, etc.); more remarkably, the one essay on popular fiction ignores the question of writing by women or the possibility of new female readerships altogether. Valentine Cunningham's more ambitiously titled *British Writers of the 1930s* (Oxford University Press, Oxford, 1988) seemed to promise a more generous account, but whilst it makes mention of 'women writers' in the period, this is little more than lip-service and the book as a whole reinstates 'the Auden generation' as canonical (indeed the all-male gallery of photographs of Auden, Isherwood, Spender and Co. on the cover speaks for itself). Naturally, the introduction of writing by women is not a question of mere addition to footnotes or the inclusion of the odd chapter but asks for a revaluation of the idea of literary

culture between the wars as a whole, as well as calling in question our political and historical definitions of the period.

The only literary historical account of writing by women in Britain between the wars to date is Nicola Beauman's affectionate survey, *A Very Great Profession: The Woman's Novel 1914–39* (Virago, London, 1983). I have gratefully drawn upon Beauman's research but would argue that it suffers from too close an identification with her authors' social and literary positions.

3 Paul Fussell, *Abroad: British Literary Travelling between the Wars* (Oxford University Press, Oxford, 1980), p. 23. The phrase is A. J. P. Taylor's.

4 'Nottingham and the mining countryside', in *Phoenix: The Posthumous Papers of D. H. Lawrence* (Heinemann, London, 1936; reprinted 1961), p. 140. Lawrence is quite clear who is responsible for the 'ugliness' of England: 'Anyhow, it's only the woman who idolizes "her own little home" – and it's always the woman at her worst, her most greedy, most possessive, most mean' (pp. 138–9).

5 Evelyn Waugh went to Abyssinia as correspondent for the *Daily Mail* in 1935 to cover the war. *Waugh in Abyssinia* (1936) ends with a twelve-page epilogue in praise of Italian colonial efficiency and splendour.

6 Kate Caffrey, *'37–'39: The Last Look Round* (Gordon & Cremonesi, London, 1978); Robert Graves and Alan Hodge, *The Long Weekend: A Social History of Great Britain 1918–1939* (Faber & Faber, London, 1940).

7 The phrase is Deidre Beddoe's in *Back to Home and Duty: Women between the Wars* (Pandora, London, 1989), p. 3, whose title suggests her overall view of the period. It echoes a similar view taken in Gail Braybon and Penny Summerfield, *Out of the Cage: Women's Experiences in Two World Wars* (Pandora, London 1987), which sees the inter-war years largely as a regression. Otherwise feminist historians have been comparatively silent about the inter-war years although Jane Lewis's *Women in England, 1870–1950* (Harvester, Brighton, 1984) offers some thoughtful demographic and statistical analyses of social changes and an excellent bibliography; there is also useful, though piecemeal, social historical discussion of domestic life of the period in her edition of *Labour and Love: Women's Experience of Home and Family 1850–1940* (Blackwell, Oxford, 1986); see also Carol Dyhouse, *Feminism and the Family in England 1880–1939* (Blackwell, Oxford, 1989).

Feminist literary critics have also generally been at a loss to include the inter-war period in their accounts: Elaine Showalter's pioneering work, for example, *A Literature of Their Own: British Women Novelists from Brontë to Lessing* (Virago, London, 1978) neatly put what she saw as the doldrums of the 1930s, '40s and early '50s between chapters, leapt nimbly from the experimental modernism of Woolf and her lesser acolytes to arrive rather breathlessly in the late 1950s and early 1960s when the true note of a feminism (in writers like Lessing and Drabble) could be heard again, heralding even better things to come.

8 There are hopeful signs of new kinds of historical interest in these years and in women's experience of modernity: see, for example, Billie Melman, *Women and the Popular Imagination in the Twenties: Flappers and Nymphs* (Macmillan, London, 1988); Sally Alexander's nuanced discussion of the cultural denigration of femininity and of the dreams and desires of working women, 'Becoming a woman in the 1920s and 1930s' in David Feldman and Gareth Stedman Jones (eds), *Metropolis. London: Histories and Representations since 1800* (Routledge, London, 1989), and Jill Matthews's riveting account of the cultural meanings and pleasures of physical activity for women, 'They had such a lot of fun: the

Women's League of Health and Beauty', *History Workshop Journal*, no. 30 (Autumn 1990).

9 Beatrix Campbell's prescient and bold *Iron Ladies: Why Do Women Vote Tory?* (Virago, London, 1987) broke the silence on the part of British feminists about conservatism; there have since been a number of studies concentrating upon Mrs Thatcher and her politics. Tellingly, the only earlier discussion of 'right-wing women' was the American Andrea Dworkin's radical feminist account, *Right-wing Women: The Politics of Domesticated Females* (Women's Press, London, 1983), emanating from what many British feminists would see as feminism's most conservative branch.

10 Marilyn Butler, *Jane Austen and the War of Ideas* (Oxford University Press, Oxford, 1987), p. xxiii.

11 For the sake of convenience here I have adopted the usual distinction between Conservatism as a party politics and conservatism as a state of mind or generalised set of attitudes and needs. As will become clear, this distinction is itself far from unproblematic.

12 Martin Pugh, *The Tories and the People 1880–1935* (Blackwell, Oxford, 1985), p. 2.

13 Quintin Hogg, *The Case for Conservatism* (Penguin, London, 1947), p. 11.

14 Lord Hugh Cecil, *Conservatism* (Williams & Norgate, London, 1912), p. 8.

15 Stuart Ball, *Baldwin and the Conservative Party* (Yale University Press, London, 1988), p. xi. He argues that the history of the Conservative Party after 1914 is 'one of the darkest areas of modern historiography' (p. xii).

16 See, for example, Lord Blake's history, *The Conservative Party from Peel to Churchill* (Eyre & Spottiswoode, London, 1970).

17 For this kind of intellectual and political history, see Russell Kirk, *The Conservative Mind: from Burke to Santayana* (H. Regnery Co., New York, 1953); Noel O'Sullivan, *Conservatism* (Dent, London, 1976); Frank O'Gorman, *British Conservatism: Conservative Thought from Burke to Thatcher* (Longman, London, 1986); and Robert Nisbet, *Conservatism: Dream and Reality* (Open University Press, Milton Keynes, 1986).

18 Bill Schwarz's essay, 'The language of constitutionalism: Baldwinite Conservatism' in *Formations of Nation and People* (Routledge, London, 1984), argues, for example, that the very idea of politics, and the language of its appeal to voters, was transformed between the wars; Stuart Ball, *Baldwin*, makes a similar argument, though in very different terms, for the inter-war years as a key moment in the modernisation of the party system and its organisation.

19 Cecil, *Conservatism*, p. 14.

20 Hogg, *The Case for Conservatism*, p. 29.

21 Burke is cited by Hogg, ibid., p. 25.

22 Cecil, *Conservatism*, p. 13; Hogg, ibid.

1 THE DEMON IN THE HOUSE: THE NOVELS OF I. COMPTON-BURNETT

1 To avoid the proliferation of notes, references to novels are given where possible in the main body of the text and the full details of original editions, together with the editions used, can be found in the bibliography.

2 Hilary Spurling, *Secrets of a Woman's Heart: The Later Life of Ivy Compton-Burnett 1920–1969* (Hodder & Stoughton, London, 1984; Penguin, Harmondsworth, 1985), p. 222.

3 ibid., p. 174.

4 Cited by Hilary Spurling, 'The Last and the First' in *The New Statesman*, 5 February 1971; reprinted in Charles Burkhart, *The Art of I. Compton-Burnett* (Gollancz, London, 1972), p. 76.

5 ibid., p. 155.

6 See, for example, the discussion of this divorce in Raymond Williams, *The English Novel from Dickens to Lawrence* (Chatto & Windus, London, 1970).

7 Perhaps Angus Wilson's obituary (*Observer*, 31 August 1969; reprinted in Burkhart, *Art of I. Compton-Burnett*) gives the best sense of how unplaced her work is: 'too eccentric to be among the very great, but far too profound to be among the minor' (p. 194); in his early volume, *I. Compton-Burnett* (Gollancz, London, 1965), Charles Burkhart headed a chapter 'Towards a definition of the eccentric novel'.

8 Ifor Evans, *A Short History of English Literature* (Penguin, Harmondsworth, 1969), p. 215.

9 Elizabeth Sprigge, *The Life of Ivy Compton-Burnett* (Gollancz, London, 1973), p. 45.

10 Nathalie Sarraute, *L'Ere du Soupcon* (Gallimard, Paris, 1959); translated by Maria Jolas in *Tropisms and the Age of Suspicion* (Calder & Boyars, London, 1963); Studs Terkel, *Talking to Myself* (Pantheon, New York, 1973).

11 See for example Walter Allen, *The English Novel* (Penguin, Harmondsworth, 1973); Evans, *Short History*; Boris Ford, *The Pelican Guide to English Literature* (Penguin, Harmondsworth, 1963); Randall Stevenson, *The British Novel since the Thirties* (Batsford, London, 1986).

12 Nicola Beauman, *A Very Great Profession: The Woman's Novel 1914–39* (Virago, London, 1983), p. 253.

13 Ellen Moers, *Literary Women* (Women's Press, London, 1978), p. 45; see also Mary Ellman, *Thinking About Women* (Macmillan, London, 1969). A helpful though brief discussion of Compton-Burnett's writing is to be found in Jane Rule, *Lesbian Images* (Doubleday, New York, 1975)), who makes much of her marginality as a single woman and a potential sexual outsider.

14 Margaret Crosland, *Beyond the Lighthouse: English Women Novelists in the Twentieth Century* (Constable, London, 1981), p. 78. Crosland launches an extremely normative and moralising diatribe against Compton-Burnett as a kind of sick mind. Crosland, who makes no bones about not 'writing feminist propaganda', betrays a deep suspicion that all women writers are somehow lacking as rounded human beings, and in her account no one is more lacking than Compton-Burnett: 'the saddest aspect of it is that she cannot have been a happy person, let alone a happy woman, until she had the second-class success of being a successful novelist'.

15 'Fact or fiction', *Times Literary Supplement*, 7 October 1960.

16 Spurling, *Secrets*, and *Ivy When Young: The Early Life of I. Compton-Burnett 1884–1919* (Gollancz, London, 1974; rev. edn Allison & Busby, London, 1983); I have drawn upon her work a great deal, especially in the first part of this chapter, and although I certainly do not share many of her loyalties I am very grateful for her scholarship.

17 'the private house, with its nullity, its immorality, its hypocrisy', Virginia Woolf, *Three Guineas* (Penguin, Harmondsworth, 1977), p. 86. Writing in 1938, Woolf argues for a connection between 'the tyrannies and servilities' (p. 162) of the private world and the more public political systems of fascism: both in her view are patriarchies.

18 James Lees-Milne, *Caves of Ice* (Chatto & Windus, London, 1983), p. 215.

19 This is from the standard form of the biographical details given on the Penguin (Harmondsworth) editions of her fiction.

20 Spurling, *Ivy When Young*, p. 44. See pp. 15–17 for a detailed account of Ivy's ancestry.

21 Kay Dick, *Ivy and Stevie: Conversations and Reflections* (Duckworth, London, 1971; Allison & Busby, London, 1983), p. 49.

22 Spurling, *Secrets*, p. 148.

23 Spurling, *Ivy When Young*, p. 54.

24 The Comptons and the Burnetts were two branches of the family who had intermarried; James Burnett's paternal grandmother was a Compton which was his middle Christian name. See Spurling, *Ivy When Young*.

25 *Pike's Directory of Brighton and Hove*, quoted by Spurling, *Ivy When Young*, pp. 53–4.

26 See J. M. Richards, *Castles on the Ground: The Anatomy of Suburbia* (John Murray, London, 1973).

27 Spurling, *Ivy When Young*, p. 45.

28 Richards, *Castles*, p. 3.

29 See Leonore Davidoff, *The Best Circles: Society, Etiquette and the Season* (Croom Helm, London, 1973).

30 Sprigge, *Life*, p. 26.

31 'Vital mess' is a description used by the postmodernist architect and writer Robert Venturi *et al.* in *Learning from Las Vegas* (MIT Press, London, 1972).

32 See Davidoff, *Best Circles*.

33 'A conversation between I. Compton-Burnett and Margaret Jourdain', *Orion* I, 1945', reprinted in Burkhart, *Art of I. Compton-Burnett*, p. 29.

34 ibid., p. 28. Virginia Woolf gives a passionate description in 'Old Bloomsbury' of a similar sense of claustrophobic intensity in her own childhood home in Hyde Park Gate in the 1890s:

> When I look back upon that house it seems to me so crowded with scenes of family life, grotesque, comic and tragic; . . . that I feel suffocated by the recollection. The place seemed tangled and matted with emotion. I could write the history of every mark and scratch in my room, I wrote later. The walls and the rooms had in sober truth been built to our shape. We had permeated the whole vast fabric – it has since been made into an hotel – with our family history.
>
> (*Moments of Being*, Hogarth Press, London, 1985, p. 183)

35 Spurling, *Ivy When Young*, p. 120.

36 ibid., p. 121.

37 ibid.

38 Royal Holloway, in Egham, whose new Gothic façade aimed to make it like a French château but whose frontage hid the most modern central heating and comforts, was a *nouveau riche* alternative to Oxbridge. Established in 1886, its founder was a maker of patent pills. Like her brothers' sham public school, Brighton College, Royal Holloway wasn't quite the real thing. Indeed having an education was in itself a sign of slight bohemianism – it was not yet desirable in smarter or more aristocratic circles. Like the daughters of many a free-thinking businessman Compton-Burnett went to college before it held any fashionable overtones.

39 Olive Compton Burnett had waged an unstinting war against her stepmother who treated her husband's first family as second-class citizens; she left home

shortly after her father's death to try to make her living as a journalist. See Spurling, *Ivy When Young*, pp. 130ff.

40 ibid., p. 164.

41 ibid., p. 177.

42 The two oldest of Ivy's younger sisters, Vera and Juliet, whose circles consisted mainly of 'mystics and musicians', remained in part bohemians and free-thinkers all their lives; before and after the war they took a keen interest in spiritualism and theories of reincarnation, Anthroposophy and the teachings of Rudolf Steiner. Their excursus into the unknown is as fascinating as a possible revolt against the strictures of villadom, as is Ivy's consequent career as a writer.

43 Spurling, *Secrets*, p. 26.

44 Spurling, *Ivy When Young*, p. 273.

45 'A conversation', p. 27.

46 'Mr Bennett and Mrs Brown', in *The Captain's Death Bed and Other Essays* (Hogarth Press, London, 1950).

47 *Brothers and Sisters* was rejected by the Hogarth Press; according to Richard Kennedy who was *A Boy at the Hogarth Press* (Penguin, Harmondsworth, 1972) at the time, Leonard Woolf found the book tedious – 'she can't even write', he said. (p. 82). After its enormous success, however, the press asked for first refusal on the next book, and Compton-Burnett had the pleasure of turning them down: Spurling, *Secrets*, p. 24.

48 John Middleton Murry (ed.), *Letters of Katherine Mansfield to John Middleton Murry 1913–1922* (Constable, London, 1951), p. 380.

49 Raymond Mortimer, review of *A House and Its Head*, New Statesman and Nation, 13 July 1935 (reprinted in Burkhart, *Art of I. Compton-Burnett*).

50 An established writer and scholar by the time she met Compton-Burnett, Margaret Jourdain came from a family who, though not lustrous, were, in one of those agonising caste distinctions upon which the middle classes depend, slightly superior stock. The daughter of a country vicar who had been 'dangerously high' church, penniless but a 'gentleman', with a sister who was Principal of St Hugh's, Oxford and a brother who was a brilliant mathematician and friend of Bertrand Russell, there was nevertheless much in her own childhood which resembled Ivy's: it had also, in the words of a friend, 'tended to be centrifugal', emotionally repressive and overly intense: Spurling, *Secrets*, p. 71.

51 Jourdain had worked for the decorator Francis Lenygon, cataloguing and promoting the idea of English Palladian, wrote extensively on Regency furniture and contributed to journals like *Country Life, The Conoisseur* and *Architectural Review*; her major work was a rehabilitation of William Kent, the landscape gardener and architect. Her enthusiastic articles promoting eighteenth-century 'style' were early trumpetings of a taste for the period which found further expression in the Neo-Georgian designs of architects like Edwin Lutyens. The furniture field was itself deeply conservative, an inbred circle of those in the know, operating as a latter-day system of patronage and preferment and covering a multitude of shady dealings and private collecting as well as a more orthodox trade in the rapidly growing auction houses.

52 Leonard Woolf, *An Autobiography* (Oxford University Press, Oxford, 1980), vol. 2, p. 19. In the first volume of his autobiography, Woolf (himself a child of villadom) describes the 'battle' of his generation against Victorianism, their exhilarating emancipation from the nineteenth century and their belief that 'We were out to construct something new; we were in the van of the builders

of a new society which should be free, rational, civilised, pursuing truth and beauty' (vol. 1, p. 102). Woolf remained committed to 'the Georgian': writing of an earlier home – Hogarth House in Richmond – built in 1720, he was sure that this was 'the best moment for English architecture' (vol. 2, p. 192). Interestingly, 'the Woolves' only once lived in a house built after 1830 – Little Talland – a Victorian villa which they hated.

53 Virginia Woolf, '22 Hyde Park Gate', in *Moments of Being* (Hogarth Press, London, 1985), p. 164; 'Old Bloomsbury', ibid. p. 184.

54 'Old Bloomsbury'.

55 A. B. Connor, *Highways and Byways* (London, 1908, publisher unknown), p. 21.

56 G. L. Gomme, *London in the Reign of Victoria* (Blackie, London, 1898), p. 136.

57 Jourdain's circle included James Lees-Milne, who became one of Ivy's greatest admirers. Lees-Milne was secretary of the National Trust's new Country House scheme launched in 1937 with a view to protecting the houses and easing the financial burden upon those who lived there (in exchange for often rather minimal demands), and was a founding member of the Georgian Group also set up that year as a focal point for the revival of interest in the architecture of 1714–1830.

Patrick Wright, *On Living in an Old Country* (Verso, London, 1985), provides an account of connected issues, and see also Robert Hewison, *The Heritage Industry* (Methuen, London, 1987), for a brief history of the part played by the National Trust, in particular, in promoting a taste for the Georgian. I am also grateful to Raphael Samuel for insights into the creation of the 'Georgian': see *Theatres of Memory* (Verso, London, forthcoming).

58 Walter Runciman, cited by Spurling, *Secrets*, p. 90. A shared link between these right-wing aesthetes and the liberal intelligentsia was Vita Sackville-West; a friend of both Margaret Jourdain and Virginia and Leonard Woolf, both she and her home, Knowle, in Sussex exercised considerable fascination as exemplars of aristocratic taste.

59 Spurling, *Ivy When Young*, p. 52; *Secrets*, p. 148.

60 Spurling, *Secrets*, pp. 15–20 *passim*.

61 Even Margaret Jourdain seems not to have been entirely taken into her confidence: 'She said she knew little of Ivy's antecedents, but thought her family had lived in a *substantial* house' (James Lees-Milne, *Caves of Ice*, p. 47); elsewhere Lees-Milne's diaries reveal him to be slightly suspicious of Compton-Burnett's 'memories' of life in great houses: see *Prophesying Peace* (Chatto & Windus, London, 1977), p. 216.

62 James Lees-Milne, *Ancestral Voices* (Chatto & Windus, London, 1975), p. 62. A later entry reads: 'I asked her at luncheon to which county she belonged. She said "Wilt-sheer", for her father had a house there when she was a child' (p. 64). Hilary Spurling omits this reference.

63 Freud offered some reflections on the child's self-elevation in fantasy in 'Family romances', in *On Sexuality: Three Essays on the Theory of Sexuality and Other Works*, vol. 7, Pelican Freud Library, ed. Angela Richards (Penguin, Harmondsworth, 1977) though he does not discuss the structuring of the fantasies specifically in class terms.

64 From a radio interview with John Bowen in 1960, cited in Spurling, *Secrets*, p. 174.

65 Dick, *Ivy and Stevie*, p. 33.

66 Spurling reads this novel as Compton-Burnett's final attempt to 'make peace'

with her own tyrannical mother, though the unfinished manuscript has a scene, written in huge, dramatic scrawl, of Eliza 'hounded and brought down to the horror of her pursuers before staggering, damaged and in pain, to her feet again, (*Secrets*, p. 294). This scene, which suggests sadistic as well as expiatory desires, was tactfully omitted from publication.

67 Burkhart, *Art of I. Compton-Burnett*, p. 35.
68 Crosland, *Beyond the Lighthouse*, p. 86.
69 Spurling, *Secrets*, p. 173.
70 ibid., p. 64.
71 Robert Liddell, 'The novels of I. Compton-Burnett', in Burkhart, *Art of I. Compton-Burnett,*, p. 99.
72 Spurling, *Secrets*, p. 214.
73 'One world and its way', *Twentieth Century*, CLVII (August 1955), p. 173.
74 Robert Liddell is one of many critics who thought her a kind of 'Sibyl'; Ivy prided herself on believing: 'I know everything about everything.' Spurling, *Secrets*, pp. 128, 153.
75 *Public Secrets* (British Film Institute, London, 1988) by David Buckingham looks at some of the pleasures of candidly probing other people's business as they are dramatised within contemporary television soap operas. Though she would not welcome the comparison, we might look for a historical link between the melodramas and sensation novels which Compton-Burnett so enjoyed in her youth, her own writing, and soap operas via the radio play – a form which admirably suited Compton-Burnett's novels. See also Tania Modleski, *Loving with a Vengeance* (Methuen, London, 1984).
76 *Jokes and Their Relation to the Unconscious*, vol. 6, Pelican Freud Library, ed. Angela Richards (Penguin, Harmondsworth, 1976), p. 77.
77 Sprigge, *Life*, p. 125.
78 The other humorist who continued to make novel after novel from just this ill-at-ease inwardness of the middle classes, but in a far more generous spirit, and who captured the desire to rag one's betters but not seriously offend them, was P. G. Wodehouse. It is interesting that critics have consistently summoned up the ghosts of Congreve and Racine in their attempts to place Compton-Burnett's 'wit'. Whilst these are certainly impressive credentials, a more apt comparison might be with Wodehouse, a contemporary much the nearest to her in class origin. A scion of well-to-do villadom in Dulwich (in fact a slightly superior locale to Ivy's), only three years her senior, Wodehouse had already begun publishing his Jeeves novels by the 1920s, in which he is both more relaxed and more blatant in his social snobberies: 'I have always been a suburbanite at heart, and it is when I get a plot calling for a suburban setting that I really roll up my sleeves and give of my best' (Michael Davie, 'Sir Plum of Dulwich', *Observer*, 5 June 1988).

Robert Liddell in *The Novels of Ivy Compton-Burnett* (Gollancz, London, 1955) passes over the resemblance quickly for fear of lowering the tone, merely suggesting that it is probably due to the fact that 'both authors are true to a kind of life which the reader, in later and more uncomfortable days can no longer distinctly remember' (p. 84). Both Compton-Burnett and Wodehouse might be said to be ventriloquising the anxieties of the middle rather than the working classes in their 'great tradition of comic servants': Robert Liddell, *Elizabeth and Ivy* (Peter Owen, London, 1986), p. 43.

79 Dick, *Ivy and Stevie*, p. 31.
80 The delight which readers took in her verbal fencing produced a veritable armoury of critical terms all of which stressed the combative and violent force

of the domestic inquisitions. As Elizabeth Taylor noted, 'rapiers, axes, stilettos, knives, grenades', are ways of describing communication reduced to sniping, family life as a kind of warfare: Spurling, *Secrets*, p. 213. It was no doubt, too, a particularly appropriate vocabulary for readers in the 1940s.

81 V. S. Pritchett, writing a review in 1949 of Elizabeth Taylor's *A Wreath of Roses*; cited Spurling, *Secrets*, p. 228.

82 'The Last and the First', in Burkhart, *Art of I. Compton-Burnett*, p. 80.

83 Noel Coward was another contemporary who frequently exposed the comfortable and hypocritical verities of domestic life – the role-playing theatricality of the 'Bliss' family in *Hay Fever*, and the smug and heartless self-righteousness of the Whittakers in *Easy Virtue* – yet his heroines and heroes are mostly those who refuse to play their part and manage to make some escape.

84 Spurling, *Secrets*, p. 265.

85 Walter Pater, review of *The Picture of Dorian Gray*, cited by Isobel Murray (ed.), *Oscar Wilde* (Oxford University Press, Oxford, 1989), p. xi.

86 For example, Elizabeth Bibesco, Asquith's daughter, reviewing *More Women Than Men* in 1933, maintained that 'Oscar Wilde is not so much borrowed from as contributed to': see Spurling *Secrets*, p. 110. Also Wilson, obituary.

87 Richard Ellmann, *Oscar Wilde* (Hamish Hamilton, London, 1987), p. xiv.

88 ibid., p. 474.

89 Spurling, *Secrets*, p. 170.

90 ibid.

91 ibid., p. 171.

92 Edward Sackville-West (Vita's cousin), in a study of Compton-Burnett and Elizabeth Bowen in 1949, 'Ladies whose bright pens . . .' (reprinted in Burkhart, *Art of I. Compton-Burnett*), gives an extreme example of this recoil, preferring her 'high degree of abstraction' to 'the hysteria of fashion and the blight of political theory' (p. 122).

93 'Parents and children' (1941) in Hermione Lee (ed.), *The Mulberry Tree: Writings of Elizabeth Bowen* (Virago, London, 1986), p. 162.

94 Review of *Elders and Betters* in 1944, cited by Spurling, *Secrets*, p. 171.

95 Edwin Muir, cited on the cover of *A Family and a Fortune* (Penguin, Harmondsworth, 1962).

96 E. Sackville-West, 'Ladies whose bright pens . . .', p. 108.

97 Wilson, Obituary, p. 65.

98 Two recent encomia taken from Penguin books.

99 Spurling, *Secrets*, p. 144.

100 E. Sackville-West, 'Ladies whose bright pens . . .', p. 113.

101 Robert Liddell, 'Novels of I. Compton-Burnett', refers to Fowler's *Modern English Usage* to show that Compton-Burnett is right in assuming that 'faults' of speech 'are not merely faults of expression, but generally spring from real faults in feeling and character; they are not merely due to faulty taste, but to moral faults – insincerity, vanity, cowardice, and more' (p. 87). The widespread desire at this time to purify English, (of which Fowler's is itself a product), and the fears of its 'bastardisation' and invasion from outside as well as corruption from within, would make an interesting chapter in itself. Nor was it limited to right-wing aesthetics, as Orwell's celebrated essay 'Politics and the English language', written in 1946, reminds us.

102 Burkhart, *I. Compton-Burnett*, p. 43; Cicely Greig, *Ivy Compton-Burnett: A Memoir* (Garnstone Press, London, 1972), p. 71.

103 28 August 1969.

104 Liddell, *Novels of Ivy Compton-Burnett* pp. 14–15.

105 One might instance the distinctions which Sir John Betjeman makes in his poetry and prose, and especially in *Metroland* (1973), between older, 'more traditional' suburbs, namely the Victorian (which he treats with affection) and more recent developments in towns like Bournemouth, or Slough (which he treats with contempt).

106 Spurling, *Secrets*, p. 9.

107 Greig, *Memoir*, p. 18.

108 Spurling, *Secrets*, cites an old friend, Raisley Moorsom, who had known both Compton-Burnett and Jourdain in the days before they met, and who recognised the patterns of Margaret's speech in the writing: 'Ivy couldn't do it then. In the end she learnt to talk like one of her own characters' (p. 102).

109 Obituary, *Spectator*, 6 September 1969; reprinted in Burkhart, *Art of I. Compton-Burnett*, p. 187.

110 Sprigge, *Life*, p. 14.

111 Greig, *Memoir*, p. 49.

112 ibid., p. 116.

113 ibid., p. 36.

114 Spurling, *Secrets*, p. 282.

115 ibid., p. 295.

116 Robert Liddell is a good case in point. Describing himself as 'a refugee from a concentration camp', a survivor of a repressive South Kensington home, he recounts how in 1935, when Compton-Burnett was already 51 and he was at Oxford, he recognised immediately that her novels were 'about us' and 'the horror that can lurk behind the façade of the respectable upper-middle-class English home' ('Notes on Ivy Compton-Burnett', *Twentieth Century Literature*, Ivy Compton-Burnett Issue, guest ed. Charles Burkhart, vol. 25, no. 2 (Summer 1979), p. 135).

Despite his historical awareness of the specific social location of his childhood experience, Liddell is equally convinced that this is human nature and as such 'will go on until the consummation of Time' (*Novels of Ivy Compton-Burnett*, p. 23). Nor do the cruelties of that past prevent him from closely identifying Compton-Burnett with a lost civilisation.

Other critics make a far simpler confusion of the text with history: Blake Nevius, for example, sees her style as 'deriving from that essentially ordered and complacent period before World War I', *Ivy Compton-Burnett* (Columbia University Press, New York, 1970), p. 12.

117 Dick, *Ivy and Stevie*, 'Foreword'. Interviewing Compton-Burnett in 1963, Kay Dick was told that 'we had a house in Hove for a time' and naturally accepted the idea created that this was a passing interlude (p. 37).

118 ibid., p. 49.

119 Spurling, *Secrets*, p. 246.

120 ibid., p. 244.

121 ibid., p. 272.

122 Greig, *Memoir*, p. 109.

123 James Lees-Milne, *Midway on the Waves* (Faber & Faber, London, 1985), p. 199.

124 'From Our Special Correspondent', *Times*, 21 November 1963, p. 18; Greig, *Memoir*, p. 113.

125 'From Our Special Correspondent'.

126 Dick, *Ivy and Stevie*, p. 35.

127 Spurling, *Secrets*, pp. 277–8 and *passim*.

128 Greig, *Memoir*, p. 113. 'Beatniks' were amongst those excluded from her

world: 'she was quite unable, she said, to take any interest in people of that kind, and she was sure none of her friends could know about them, or want to know about them (ibid., p. 61).

129 Spurling, *Secrets*, p. 245.
130 ibid., pp. 35; 262.
131 'Thatcher claims Wesley as ally', *Guardian*, 26 May 1988.
132 ibid.
133 'The inventions of I. Compton-Burnett', in *The Writing on the Wall and Other Literary Essays* (Weidenfeld & Nicolson, London, 1970).
134 ibid., p. 112.

2 AGATHA CHRISTIE AND CONSERVATIVE MODERNITY

1 Brigid Brophy, 'Sir Hereward', *New Statesman*, 6 December 1963; 'Fact or fiction', *Times Literary Supplement*, 7 October 1960.
2 'The mighty and their fall', *Times Literary Supplement*, 22 September 1961; Hilary Spurling, *Secrets of a Woman's Heart: The Later Life of Ivy Compton-Burnett 1920–1969* (Hodder & Stoughton, London, 1984; Penguin, Harmondsworth, 1985), p. 20.
3 Spurling, *Secrets*, p. 133: Compton-Burnett never 'entirely got over her hankering to write a bestseller'. She also envied Daphne du Maurier that capacity.
4 Robert Liddell, *The Novels of Ivy Compton-Burnett* (Gollancz, London, 1955), p. 47.
5 Dennis Sanders and Len Lovallo, *The Agatha Christie Companion* (W. H. Allen, London, 1985), p. xviii.
6 Namely, *Murder She Said* (1962); *Murder at the Gallop* (1963); *Murder Most Foul* (1963); *Murder Ahoy!* (1964). Christie had constant disagreements with MGM who turned the novels into 'rollicking farces', and she found Rutherford's portrayal, though enjoyable, ludicrously unlike Miss Marple. See Janet Morgan, *Agatha Christie* (Fontana, London, 1985), p. 334.
7 Peter Porter, 'On-screen authors', *Times Literary Supplement*, 9 December 1988; Julian Symons, *Critical Observations* (Faber & Faber, London, 1981), asserts that Christie's novels look back to 'that time when social life was settled and people knew their places in it' (p. 142); Colin Watson in *Snobbery with Violence: English Crime Stories and their Audience* (Eyre Methuen, London, 1979) sees the novels as 'a museum of nostalgia' (p. 171); Gwen Robyns, *The Mystery of Agatha Christie* (Penguin, Harmondsworth, 1978), takes for granted their 'nostalgia for a middle-class way of life that will never return to England' (p. 219).
8 Peter Saunders, programme notes for *The Mousetrap*, 1984. (Saunders was its first producer in 1952).
9 Apart from the periodic screening of the box-office hits of the 1970s – *Murder on the Orient Express* (1974) and *Death on the Nile* (1978) – and the less successful feature films, *The Mirror Crack'd* (1980), *Evil under the Sun* (1982) and *Ordeal by Innocence* (1985), a multitude of new adaptations and series made specifically for television have flitted across British screens. London Weekend Television (distributed by Mobil Showcase which sponsored the films in the US) dramatised *The Seven Dials Mystery* and *Why Didn't They Ask Evans?* in 1981; in 1982 Thames Television launched 'The Agatha Christie Hour'; versions of *The Secret Adversary* and *Partners in Crime* followed a year later. In 1984 the BBC retaliated with the first of their full-length 'Miss

Marple' mysteries, *The Body in the Library*, leading to versions (so far) of *The Moving Finger, A Murder is Announced, A Pocket Full of Rye, Sleeping Murder, Nemesis,* and *A Caribbean Mystery*; in 1989 the first television 'Poirot' series appeared (made by Thames) which the BBC answered with *Campion*, based on Margery Allingham's detective stories, a 'series destined to fill the Miss Marple slot. The flavour and period and style like Agatha Christie – pure golden age' (*Radio Times*, 21–7 January 1989). See Sanders and Lovallo, *The Agatha Christie Companion*, for more details.

10 Watson, *Snobbery with Violence*, p. 169.

11 Television also brought the boorish Slack into *The Body in the Library* where the original Inspector (called Harper) is described as 'a decent, kindly man' (p. 112).

12 Perhaps the 1980s version of *Nemesis* had special resonance for a Britain where classicism underwent a revival amongst conservative asethetes and architects, the National Trust became the country's biggest landowner and the Prime Minister lived in a new 'Georgian' mansion.

13 A number of 'fan' appreciations have appeared, though usually from American writers: Robert Barnard, *A Talent to Deceive: An Appreciation of Agatha Christie* (Dodd, Mead & Co., New York, 1980); G. C. Ramsey, *Agatha Christie: Mistress of Mystery* (Collins, London, 1968); Charles Osbourne, *The Life and Crimes of Agatha Christie* (Collins, London, 1982). See also H. R. F. Keating (ed.), *Agatha Christie, First Lady of Crime* (Holt, Rinehart & Winston, New York, 1977).

14 John G. Cawelti offers a stimulating study of the meanings and scope of literary 'formulas', including those of crime fiction, in *Adventure, Mystery and Romance* (University of Chicago Press, Chicago, 1976); also Robert Winks (ed.), *Detective Fiction: A Collection of Critical Essays* (The Foul Play Press, Vermont, 1988) contains literary analyses of the form; David Glover gives a critical account of such approaches in 'The stuff that dreams are made of: masculinity, femininity and the thriller', in Derek Longhurst (ed.), *Gender, Genre and Narrative Pleasure* (Unwin Hyman, London, 1989).

15 See, for example, Julian Symons's popular survey, *Bloody Murder* (Penguin, Harmondsworth, 1985); Ernest Mandel, *Delightful Murder: A Social History of the Crime Story* (Pluto, London, 1984) and Ken Worpole, *Dockers and Detectives* (Verso, London, 1983) offer a more historically located overview but not in any depth: they also group Christie with other 'golden age' writers.

16 Mandel, *Delightful Murder*, p. 26; Worpole, *Dockers and Detectives*, p. 33.

17 Cora Kaplan was the first to raise the question of the conservatism of the 'queens of crime' in 'An unsuitable genre for a feminist?', *Women's Review*, no. 8 (June 1986), pp. 18–19. Like her, Rosalind Coward and Linda Semple (who mistakenly place Josephine Tey in the 'golden age' of crime) are primarily interested in what Christie shares with other writers in the period: see 'Tracking down the past: women and detective fiction', in Helen Carr (ed.), *From My Guy to Sci-Fi: Genre and Women's Writing in the Postmodern World* (Pandora, London, 1989). Coward and Semple aim to uncover a specifically 'feminine' relation to the law and to crime writing; this is also the project of Alison Hennegan's introduction to Jen Green (ed.), *Reader, I Murdered Him* (Women's Press, London, 1989).

18 Miss Marple first appeared in some magazine stories of 1928 which formed the first half of *The Thirteen Problems* (1932), and then briefly in *Murder at the Vicarage* (1930). Christie dropped her for the next twelve years (until *The Body in the Library*), in favour of Poirot, on whom her reputation was built.

19 Mary Cadogan and Patricia Craig, *The Lady Investigates: Women Detectives and Spies in Fiction* (Oxford University Press, Oxford, 1986), typically assert that 'Christie was not so much a novelist as the inventor of a novelty, a peculiarly intricate and entertaining type of puzzle' (p. 166); Julian Symons, *Bloody Murder*, sees her as the exponent of 'the puzzle, pure and complex' (p. 92). More recently, P. D. James has damned Christie with similar faint praise, seeing her as 'pre-eminently a literary conjuror who places her pasteboard characters face-down and shuffles them with practised cunning' ('A universal aspirin and the talent to deceive', *Daily Telegraph*, 8 September 1990).

20 Peter Dunn, 'Morse, codes and crosswords', *Independent*, 28 January 1989. For discussion of sales, see Watson, *Snobbery with Violence*, p. 31. who bases his figures on the W. H. Smith lists for popular fiction, and Symons, *Bloody Murder*, who maintains that 'it is safe to say that . . . the number of crime stories published had multiplied by five in 1926 and by ten in 1939' (p. 108).

21 The OED gives the first usage of 'whodunit' as an Americanism from the *News of Books* in 1930 but it does not seem to enter popular English currency until after 1945 when, like the 'Golden Age of Crime', it is applied retrospectively and nostalgically.

22 Richard Usborne, *Clubland Heroes* (Barrie & Jenkins, London, 1953; rev. edn. 1974), p. 31. Usborne offers an affectionate and sometimes critical account of Dornford Yates, 'Sapper', John Buchan and their heroes. Yates created 'Berry and Co.', an aristocratic fivesome with a country seat in Hampshire who were much given to chasing crooks across the Continent. Although their lifestyle was already dated when they first appeared in 1911, they remained popular until the early 1930s. For the aggressive reassertion of late-Victorian values after the war, see also Jenni Calder, *Heroes* (Hamish Hamilton, London, 1977) and Martin Green, *Dreams of Adventure, Deeds of Empire* (Routledge, London, 1980).

23 Watson, *Snobbery with Violence*, p. 152.

24 Symons, *Bloody Murder*, p. 105.

25 Raymond Chandler, 'The simple art of murder', in *Pearls are a Nuisance* (Penguin, Harmondsworth, 1964), p. 193. Compare Mary Cadogan and Patricia Craig's assumption that Christie 'is not capable of evocative prose', *The Lady Investigates*, p. 14.

26 Edmund Wilson, 'Who cares who killed Roger Ackroyd?', reprinted in Winks, *Detective Fiction*, p. 37. In seeing detective stories as 'lax' and addictive, he is, of course, following in the footsteps of Q. D. Leavis's famous broadside against the corrupting and debased nature of the modern bestseller in *Fiction and the Reading Public* (Chatto & Windus, London, 1932). Leavis's attack on such fiction as morally and linguistically inadequate set the terms for much later discussion of commercial fiction. Even Raymond Williams, for example, in *The Long Revolution* (Chatto & Windus, London, 1961) warns against the effects of the 'easy drug' of 'blotterature' (p. 171) and cites Leavis in support of his views.

27 See Harvey Curtis Webster, *After the Trauma: Representative British Novelists since 1920* (University Press of Kentucky, Lexington, 1970).

28 Christie was 'well-steeped in the Sherlock Holmes tradition': *An Autobiography* (Fontana, London, 1978), p. 261.

29 ibid., p. 262.

30 Poor Hastings began rapidly to stick out like a sore thumb; Christie married

him off in the second Poirot novel, *Murder on the Links* (1923) and shipped him to the Argentine, though she was later required to bring him back.

31 *Murder on the Links* is similarly poised between the old and the new. Moving between France and Britain (like many a modern novel it opens on a train), it combines a melodramatic inheritance drama worthy of the nineteenth-century stage with new images of bourgeois ceremony like that of the golf links. (Christie's first husband, Archie, had become such a devotee of this new sport that they moved to Sunningdale in 1924 so that he could be near the excellent golf course there.).

32 *The Big Four* invents 'Achille' Poirot, who is apparently, like Mycroft Holmes, the detective's brilliant brother. *Partners in Crime* (1929) is an equally heavy-handed play with conventions in which each short story is told in the manner of another popular writer of detective fiction.

33 One of Edmund Wilson's complaints against detective novels is an irritation with their 'faked-up English county people' ('Who cares', p. 37).

34 Christie, *An Autobiography*, p. 200. Philpotts also wrote detective stories under the name 'Harrington Hext' which, according to Julian Symons, were 'among the most ridiculous of the time' (*Bloody Murder*, p. 106).

35 John Lahr, *Coward: The Playwright* (Methuen, London, 1982), p. 7; Lahr suggests that it was 'not the situations of English life' which interested Coward 'but the sound of it' (p. 8).

36 *Murder on the Links* begins with a linguistic disturbance, the uttering of an expletive by a 17-year-old flapper (a privilege which Christie notes is usually given to duchesses), flirtatiously ragging Hastings with American slang. She is 'the prototype of the modern neurotic girl who jazzes from morning to night, smokes like a chimney and uses language which would make a Billings-gate fishwoman blush' (p. 5), and she is Hastings's future wife. So much for Mrs Watson, the angel of the hearth, whose appearances in Conan Doyle's stories were purely offstage: 'Bella' is a circus performer whose daredevil acrobatics save the day.

37 Much of the new slang of the day seemed to play with the idea of age – like 'egg' and 'old thing' as terms of endearment.

38 Or the description of Dr Percy Trevelyan in 'The Resident Patient', whose neck, dangling from a hook, 'was drawn out like a plucked chicken's, making the rest of him seem the more obese and unnatural by the contrast', *The Complete Sherlock Holmes* (Penguin, Harmondsworth, 1986), p. 431.

39 Cadogan and Craig, *The Lady Investigates*, p. 38.

40 Edmund Wilson, 'Who cares', p. 37.

41 C. H. B. Kitchin, *Death of His Uncle* (Constable, London, 1939; reprinted Hogarth Press, London, 1986), p. 35.

42 'Preaematuri', in Catherine Reillly (ed.), *Scars upon My Heart: Women's Poetry and Verse of the First World War* (Virago, London, 1981), p. 22.

43 E. F. Benson, *As We Are: A Modern Review* (Longman, London, 1932; reprinted Hogarth Press, London, 1985), p. 190. W. Somerset Maugham saw detective fiction as ideal reading for the sanatorium (which was where he had spent part of the war) and for convalescence generally: 'The decline and fall of the detective story', in *The Vagrant Mood* (Heinemann, London, 1952), p. 94.

44 On the crossword craze which began in 1924, see Robert Graves and Alan Hodge, *The Long Weekend: A Social History of Great Britain 1918–1939* (Faber & Faber, London, 1940), p. 131, and Charles Loch Mowat, *Britain Between the Wars 1918–1940* (Methuen, London, 1956), who comments 'It

was more than a pastime. It took time and it took ingenuity (as clues became more "literary" and allusive), diverting energy from more serious matters, distracting the mind from the questions of the day. In a sense the crossword puzzle was the symbol of the age: an inexpensive and ostensibly harmless amusement, leading – nowhere. Utopia in seven letters' (p. 202).

Q. D. Leavis, *Fiction and the Reading Public*, groups detective stories with 'the passion for solving crossword puzzles' under the heading of 'mental relaxation', a notion which appals her (p. 50).

45 Indeed *The Baffle Book*, put together in 1930 by two Americans, Lassiter Wren and Randle McKay (and edited in Britain by F. Tennyson Jesse), offered a collection of detective story puzzles complete with score sheets and answers as a form of parlour game – a forerunner, perhaps, of Waddingtons' 'Cluedo'.

46 Paul Fussell, *The Great War and Modern Memory* (Oxford University Press, Oxford, 1977), p. 33.

47 ibid., p. 109. Fussell's account only acknowledges the 'bright young men' of the period.

48 *1066 And All That* (Methuen, London, 1930; reprinted Penguin, Harmondsworth, 1960), p. 121.

49 'The Lament of the Demobilised', in Reilly, *Scars Upon My Heart*, p. 14.

50 The patriotic side of Holmes was much to the fore when he took 'His Last Bow' in 1917 (he was to make another comeback). With an England faced at home by 'a devil's brew of Irish civil war, window-breaking Furies, and God knows what', Holmes looks forward to the invigorating stiff east wind of war: 'It will be cold and bitter, Watson, and a good many of us may wither before its blast. But it's God's own wind none the less, and a cleaner, better, stronger land will lie in the sunshine when the storm has cleared.' (*The Complete Sherlock Holmes*, p. 980) In old age, with these hopes foundering, Conan Doyle turned to spiritualism and to campaigning against the 'filth' of modern art: see H. R. F. Keating, *Sherlock Holmes: The Man and His World* (Thames & Hudson, London, 1979).

51 Wimsey makes a brief appearance in Elaine Showalter's *The Female Malady: Women, Madness and English Culture* (Virago, London, 1987). She argues for an understanding of shell-shock as 'male hysteria' and suggests that neurasthenia was both a response to, and an effect of, a masculinity traumatised by the experience of war. See also her essay 'Rivers and Sassoon: the inscription of male gender anxieties', in Margaret Randolph Higonnet *et al.* (eds), *Behind the Lines: Gender and the Two World Wars* (Yale University Press, New Haven, 1987), and Sandra M. Gilbert and Susan Gubar, *No-Man's Land*, vol. 2: *Sex Changes* (Yale University Press, New Haven, 1989) who also argue for a crisis in the meanings given to sexual difference in the period through an examination of literary modernism. That such anxieties about virility after the war went deep can be seen across the culture: James Hilton's curious whodunit, *Murder at School* (1931), has fears about masculinity as its buried subtext with the prime suspect a neurasthenic master. Hilton's story is eventually reassuringly conservative in making an adulterous young woman the murderess but our emotional interest centres on the idle amateur detective, 'Revell', who learns in the course of the story to grow up and become a wiser man. Hilton is better known for his other school story, *Good-bye, Mr Chips*.

52 See the fictional entry for *Debrett* which Sayers appended to the novels.

53 This is a comparison brought home by *The Labours of Hercules* in which twelve cases of mental agility on Poirot's part are compared to the Greek hero's physical exploits.

54 *Styles*, p. 21.

55 Watson, *Snobbery with Violence*, p. 166.

56 Anthony Berkeley (A. B. Cox), for example, author of *The Poisoned Chocolates Case* (1929), announced the end of puzzle writing in 1930 in favour of the 'novel with detective or crime interest' (Symons, *Bloody Murder*, p. 107). He went on to write one of the first psychological thrillers *Malice Aforethought* (1931), as 'Francis Iles', but continued to pose detective conundra in the old style, as with *Jumping Jenny* in 1933.

57 Only Harley Quin in *The Mysterious Mr. Quin* (1930) borders on romance but this supernatural sleuth never caught on.

58 Poirot did, however, get an obituary after the publication of *Curtain* in America, in the *New York Times*, 6 August 1975.

59 By far the most popular anti-hero to have emerged from the 1920s, and one who could appeal to both girls and boys, is Richmal Crompton's creation in the 'Just William' stories, the scapegrace schoolboy. (Crompton was a contemporary of Compton-Burnett at Royal Holloway, a huge admirer of her work, and would herself bear investigation as a species of conservative modernist.) See Mary Cadogan, *Richmal Crompton: The Woman behind William* (Allen & Unwin, London, 1986) and Kay Williams, *Just Richmal: The Life and Work of Richmal Crompton Lamburn* (Genesis, Guildford, 1986). The same urge toward the anti-heroic, though celebrating a far gentler kind of anarchy, can be found in the pacifist A. A. Milne's *Winnie the Pooh* (1926) and in the popularity of Kenneth Grahame's Toad in *Wind in the Willows*. Although originally written in 1908, the story was reprinted in 1931, partly as a result of Milne's play version in 1929, *Toad of Toad Hall*, which has remained a favourite of the English stage. Even 'Toy Town's' 'Mr Plod' offered a self-effacing version of the masculine, whilst the middlebrow paper with the largest circulation between the wars, the *Daily Express*, had a 'Little Lost Bear' as its popular anti-hero: Rupert, created by Mary Tourtel.

60 Symons, *Bloody Murder*, p. 132. Dorothy L. Sayers's comment that 'one gets tired of a literature without bowels' is equally revealing of her more full-blooded Toryism (ibid., p. 120).

61 H. R. F. Keating, *Whodunit?: A Guide to Crime, Suspense and Spy Fiction* (Windward, London, 1982), p. 9; Watson, *Snobbery with Violence*, p. 107.

62 Chandler, 'Simple art of murder', pp. 7; 194; 196. Masculine feeling also runs high in Ken Worpole's aptly named *Dockers and Detectives* which argues for the appeal of the hard-boiled style to a British working-class audience as part of the making of a new demotic. Yet whilst Worpole acknowledges the misogyny of writers like Chandler, this does not seem to disturb his view of such writing as a kind of democratisation of the form, nor move him to consider the position of female readers (or writers). David Glover, 'The stuff that dreams are made of', on the other hand, begins with a consideration of the 'sexual politics' of the genre.

63 Q. D. Leavis, *Fiction and the Reading Public*, p. 210. Leavis puts such fiction on a par with 'kill-time interests like listening to the radio and gramophone, looking through newspapers and magazines, watching films and commercial football, and the activities connected with motor cars and bicycles', as the modern degraded version of the truly 'creative' interests of the past – country arts, traditional crafts and games and singing' (ibid., p. 209).

64 Gladys Mitchell even has an Inspector Boring in *Speedy Death* (1929) to offset the brilliance of her detective, Mrs Adela Lestrange Bradley.

65 Lahr, *Coward*, p. 7.

66 From the portrait of Wimsey given by his uncle 'Paul Austin Delgardie' and attached as an afterword to the novels.

67 Albert Campion, for example, Margery Allingham's detective, is an aristocrat and possibly even a minor member of royalty. See T. J. Binyon, *Murder Will Out: The Detective in Fiction* (Oxford University Press, Oxford, 1989) for a descriptive account of the different detectives.

68 C. H. B. Kitchin's stockbroker detective, Malcolm Warren, is another such case in point. He may have the humdrum air of the commuter on the train (which is how he is introduced to us in *Death of My Aunt* in 1929), but he is an Oxford graduate, knowledgeable about Pirandello and modern art and deeply mocking of the new garden suburbs. In *Death of His Uncle* Kitchin lays claim to finding 'middle-class manners delightful' (p. 36), but he nevertheless made sure that his own hero came from the 'right' social bracket.

69 As, for example, J. C. Masterman, *An Oxford Tragedy* (1933); C. Day-Lewis, *A Question of Proof* (1935); Dorothy L. Sayers, *Gaudy Night* (1935).

70 Edgar Wallace's J. G. Reeder is another little, dumpy man in late middle-age; unlike Poirot, however, he carries a revolver and a walking-stick disguising a blade.

71 This description appears all the more generous when one realises that this is Christie's own part of the world and that in 1930, through lack of funds, she was forced to sell her childhood home, Ashfield, only to see it replaced by a new development.

72 E. F. Benson's 'Lucia' books, for example, begun in 1920, acquired a cult following for sending up the doings of a 'social climber'.

73 *The Sittaford Mystery, Crooked House, Hercule Poirot's Christmas, Murder is Easy, 4.50 from Paddington*, all provide examples of 'new money'.

74 *An Autobiography*, p. 538.

75 Chandler, 'Simple art of murder', p. 191. None of Christie's plots are bound up with the kind of mysticism which Margery Allingham frequently attaches to the idea of the English aristocracy – in *Look to the Lady* (1931), for example, where an 'ancient' family protects a holy chalice.

76 One can only boggle at Jack Adrian's comment in John M. Reilly (ed.), *Twentieth Century Crime and Mystery Writers* (St James' Press, London, 1985) that Wallace had 'an instinctive feel for such low-life characters as garrulous charwomen and small-time burglars' (p. 877).

77 Alma Rattenbury, a respectable married woman, lived in a Bournemouth villa and took as her lover their 18-year-old chauffeur, who was later convicted of murdering her husband. Although she was cleared of the charge, Alma Rattenbury was convicted, unofficially but quite overtly, in the press and in the dock, for her 'disgusting' sexuality. She took her own life after the verdict. (Terence Rattigan wrote a stage version of the case, *Cause Célèbre*). The earlier case of 'Thompson and Bywaters' in 1923 had also revolved around passion in the suburbs and, arguably, Edith Thompson (whom the press hailed as 'the Messalina of Ilford') was hanged as much for her adulterous liaison with a younger man as for her part in her husband's murder.

78 Cited by Usborne, *Clubland Heroes*, p. 163.

79 After *The Seven Dials Mystery* (1929), Christie waited until 1940 to write *One, Two, Buckle My Shoe*, followed by a 'fifth column' thriller *N or M* in 1941.

80 Watson, *Snobbery with Violence*, p. 174.

81 The other 'Mary Westmacott' novels were *Unfinished Portrait* (1934), *Absent in the Spring* (1944), *The Rose and the Yew Tree* (1947), *A Daughter's a*

Daughter (1952), and *The Burden* (1956). They were often clearly autobiographical: *Giant's Bread* is, amongst other things, a memoir of the Great War, suffused with a sense of loss and giving a thinly disguised account of Christie's gruelling work as a VAD.

82 *An Autobiography*, p. 482. Christie describes meeting the Director of Antiquities at Baghdad, a dedicated Nazi, in 1932 and being stunned by the violent extent of his anti-Semitism. Her biographer, Janet Morgan, recounting the incident, points out that most of the complaints about Christie's own use of Jewish stereotypes were made after 1945 (Morgan, *Agatha Christie*, p. 264).

83 The year 1930 saw the first British Empire Games, an event which signalled some shift, however ambiguous, in the perception of 'foreigners'.

84 Lady Una Troubridge, *Etiquette and Entertaining: To Help You on Your Social Way* (Amalgamated Press, London), p. 11. The volume is undated but a reference to 'anything goes' puts it later than Cole Porter's 1930 musical.

85 *An Autobiography*, pp. 36; 54. Freudians will no doubt relish the gun.

86 It was this unnerving return of the familiar in a strange guise which Freud identified as producing a sense of the 'uncanny' or the *'unheimlich'* (literally, 'unhomely'): see 'The "uncanny" ' in *Art and Literature*, vol. 14, Pelican Freud Library (Harmondsworth, 1985).

87 Many critics would want to place the formulaic whodunit in the realm of folk and faery tale as a ritualised exorcism of primary fears about the world in a form whose safe rules return the individual reader to a collectivity of shared experience. The make-believe of popular fictions can be seen as one of the last outposts (however mediated by commodity capitalism) of the folkloric, performing a therapeutic process. See Cawelti, *Adventure*; George Grella, 'The formal detective novel' in Winks, *Detective Fiction*. W. H. Auden in 'The guilty vicarage', in *The Dyer's Hand* (Faber & Faber, London, 1963), interprets such fiction in a Christian-cum-Freudian light as the expiation of individual guilt which is both communally restorative and personally reassuring. Such universalist readings, however, can seem to ignore the socially and historically limited ways in which such material is chosen, structured and read. Those who place a premium on achieving adulthood will in any case find such magic solutions unnecessary, even stale; Elizabeth Bowen no doubt spoke for many when she called detective fiction 'the only above-board grown-up children's stories', appealing to that 'great malleable bulk' of readers who 'read without the brain': 'Out of a book' (1946), in Hermione Lee (ed.) *The Mulberry Tree: Writings of Elizabeth Bowen* (Virago, London, 1986), p. 50.

88 For details see Sanders and Lovallo, *The Agatha Christie Companion*.

89 See, for example, *The Regatta Mystery and Other Stories* (1939).

90 Paul Fussell's *Abroad: British Literary Travelling between the Wars* (Oxford University Press, Oxford, 1980), makes a convincing case for the inter-war passion for travel but deals only with the *literati*; despite attempts at broadmindedness he certainly sees some forms of travelling as more authentic than others – *viz.* travel as an individual rather than a collective activity.

91 An advertisement in *The Times*, 21 January 1938, invited readers to 'Winter Amidst The Palms and Sub-Tropical Foliage At Torquay', assuring them that 'Fog, Frost and Snow Are Virtually Unknown'. A history of travel journalism would be a helpful extension of Fussell's account; it might point to the recasting of Britain itself as a species of 'abroad', which even included a re-imagining of the weather.

92 In 1939 Christie wrote her own travel book, *Come, Tell Me How You Live*

(Hamlyn, London, 1985), an account of the years spent with her second husband, Max Mallowan, the archaeologist. It begins with the purchase of unwanted 'Empire kit' from Debenhams which provokes Max later into snorting: 'You look like the most offensive kind of memsahib' (p. 86). Christie herself tried to avoid 'ex-pats' when she was travelling, and seems like many of her class to be in mild revulsion from the idea of Empire.

93 Morgan, *Agatha Christie*, p. 170. Christie had an especial love of trains.

94 It is not too far-fetched here to read in the pleasures of the whodunit an enjoyable reworking of those same themes of nightmarish isolation and alienation which made the train journey across borders and the idea of foreign travel and tourism an image of the disaggregation of Europe in high cultural texts. (One thinks, for example, of Mann's *Death In Venice* in which tourism is literally deadly.)

95 See Binyon, *Murder Will Out*, p. 32, for a discussion of these differences which, incidentally, match the major distinctions between British and American crime fiction between the wars: the private detective belongs to the 'closed circle' crime; the 'private eye' to a world in which the number of suspects is infinite.

96 'Murder, I have often noticed, is a great matchmaker', *The ABC Murders*, p. 107.

97 Ramsey, *Agatha Christie*, p. 69.

98 In the view ('unfair perhaps') of Max Mallowan, Christie's husband, 'the analytical critic of detective fiction is either a knave or a fool', *Mallowan's Memoirs* (Collins, London, 1977), since the critic is bound – reader, be warned – to give the game away.

99 Though she frequently varied her choice of favourites amongst her books, Christie liked best those which, like *Crooked House* and *Ordeal by Innocence*, depended on 'a family and the interplay of their lives' (*An Autobiography*, p. 538).

100 We might contrast this with Dorothy L. Sayers's view of the village in *Busman's Honeymoon* as 'an ordered society' in which 'they were all immutably themselves: parson, organist, sweep, duke's son, doctor's daughter, moving like chessmen on their allotted squares'. Peter Wimsey was the embodiment of 'tradition': 'I have married England' sighs his wife, Harriet, blissfully (p. 98).

101 Herbert Read, 'Blood wet and dry', review of *Death on the Nile* in *Night and Day*, 23 December 1937, p. 269. Interestingly, Read finds nothing old-fashioned about Christie but sees her as 'energetic, decisive and slightly catty'.

102 See Morgan, *Agatha Christie*, p. 122; Osborne, *Life and Crimes*, p. 34.

103 Tynan attacked 'Loamshire' in the *Observer*, 31 October 1954.

104 Jacquetta Hawkes, in her introduction to *Come, Tell Me How You Live*, suggests that Christie can be said 'to have taken characters out of a box' (p. 11).

105 Mallowan, *Memoirs*, p. 223.

106 Christie dedicated *Hallowe'en Party* (1969) to Wodehouse, 'whose books and stories have brightened my life for many years. Also to show my pleasure in his having been kind enough to tell me that he enjoys *my* books.'

107 Christie's first play *Alibi* (a version of *Roger Ackroyd*) was produced in 1928 by Gerald du Maurier; she wrote twenty-one plays including stage versions of her novels.

108 René Cutforth, *Later Than We Thought* (David & Charles, Newton Abbot, 1976), p. 34.

109 James Fenton, cited by Sanders and Lovallo, *The Agatha Christie Companion*, p. 349.

110 Cutforth, *Later Than We Thought*, p. 39.

111 Any interpretation of the period depends on the relative weight we might give either to the staying power of older conservatisms or to the impact of forms of modernity which surfaces as the main tension in the inter-war years. See, for example, John Stevenson's discussion of radio as both a potentially revolutionary medium and also, paradoxically, a means for creating a 'more effective national cohesion' in Britain, in *British Society 1914–45* (Penguin, Harmondsworth, 1984), p. 410.

112 Christie took her title from a children's rhyme based on a popular Victorian 'nigger' minstrel show song whose lyrics were written by Frank Green for the Christy minstrels and published in England in 1869. Green's lyrics were themselves an adaptation of an American comic song and chorus, *Ten Little Indians*, by the Philadelphia songwriter Septimus Winner, published the year before. When the American edition of Christie's story was published in 1940, Dodd, Mead & Co. judged the original title to be racially offensive; it subsequently appeared as *And Then There Were None* (the title given also to René Clair's film version of 1945). American editions have also been titled *Ten Little Indians* and *The Nursery Rhyme Murders*.

But the plot thickens. Textual changes in the American editions usually involved merely substituting Indian for nigger, although the exchange which runs 'Nigger Island, eh? There's a nigger in the woodpile' simply becomes 'Indian Island, eh? There's a nigger in the woodpile', suggesting some confusion about the issue. See Sanders and Lovallo, *The Agatha Christie Companion*, pp. 178–84 for a fuller discussion. They make no mention of the fact, however, that what was considered racist as far as American Blacks were concerned was acceptable when changed to native Americans. (British editions now appear as *And Then There Were None*.)

113 *Lord Edgware Dies*, for example, was written in Rhodes and Nineveh; *Three Act Tragedy*, *The ABC Murders* and *Cards on the Table*, all on the digs in Syria (See Morgan, *Agatha Christie* for details).

114 Mallowan, *Memoirs*, p. 200.

115 Keating, *Whodunit?* p. 16.

116 Mallowan, *Memoirs* p. 222.

117 Christie was fascinated by parental possessiveness all her life, and especially in the mother-daughter relationship, which she explored (as Mary Westmacott) in *A Daughter's a Daughter* (1952). Its story, in which an attractive widow decides against remarriage for the sake of her 19-year-old daughter, seems like a replay of her own dilemma on meeting Max Mallowan, and perhaps a retrospective justification of her own choice: in the novel, the self-sacrifice turns out to be a bad mistake. Christie's daughter, Rosalind, had, of course, only been 11 years old when her mother remarried, and must have spent a great deal of her childhood separated from her.

118 Critics have noted the similar terrains of the process of detection in fiction and of psychoanalytic treatment: see Cawelti, *Adventure*; Franco Moretti, 'Clues', in *Signs Taken for Wonders* (Verso, London, 1983); and Carlo Ginzburg, 'Morelli, Freud and Sherlock Holmes: clues and the scientific method', *History Workshop Journal*, no. 9 (Spring 1980).

119 'Common sense' is the term used by the Italian Marxist, Antonio Gramsci, to describe the set of assumptions about people and ways of understanding the world which, though they are in fact subject to constant change, come to

seem unquestionable and indispensable to our thinking. 'Every social class has its own "common sense" . . . enriched with scientific notions and philosophical opinions that have entered into common circulation. "Common sense" is the folklore of philosophy,' *Selections from Cultural Writings*, ed. David Forgacs and Geoffrey Nowell-Smith (Lawrence & Wishart, London, 1985), p. 420.

120 Morgan, *Agatha Christie*, p. 373.

121 Feminists would surely be mistaken to set too much store by Miss Marple. Although intended originally as a mild debunking of the Victorian past, and a reversal, to some extent, of the assumption that women are 'inexperienced' or unable to deal with the seamy side of life, Miss Marple's 'specialised knowledge' – like reading character and relying on her 'intuition' – does little to challenge the conservative view of femininity as an extension of domestic life.

Not that Poirot is immune to a hardening of views. In *Hallowe'en Party* (1962), for example, there is little of the sympathy for psychologising which we find in the earlier novels. Instead we are offered a firm belief in genetic inheritance which predetermines social deviancy:

'One must accept facts', said Poirot, 'and a fact that is expressed by modern biologists . . . seems to suggest very strongly that the root of a person's actions lies in his genetic make-up. That a murderer of twenty-four was a murderer in potential at two or three years old.'

(p. 117)

122 F. E. Gordon, organiser of the 1937 *Daily Mail* 'Ideal Home Exhibition', cited by Tom Jeffrey and Keith McClelland, 'A world fit to live in: the *Daily Mail* and the middle classes 1918–1939' in James Curran *et al.* (eds), *Impacts and Influences* (Methuen, London, 1987), p. 50.

123 Graves and Hodge, *The Long Weekend*, p. 320.

124 Privy to the rich but against the stuffy, the *Daily Express* cultivated an agreeable attitude to life and politics, with an emphasis on leisure and consumption. Its mood was determinedly optimistic and upbeat (as caught in its slogan 'There Will Be No War') as opposed to the more grandiose and gloomy tone of the *Daily Mail*. Its circulation rose from under half a million in 1910 to almost two and a half million in 1939. See Jeffrey and McClelland, 'A world fit to live in', for detailed figures; Stevenson, *British Society 1914–45* and A. J. P. Taylor *English History 1914–45* (Penguin, Harmondsworth, 1975) for discussion of the press as a whole. Raymond Williams, *The Long Revolution*, also looks at changes in the layout and style of the press.

125 John Betjeman evokes a similar marriage of old and new in 'Death of King George Vth', with his image of the next king arriving for the coronation,

the new suburb stretched beyond the run-way,
Where a young man lands hatless from the air.

126 Hilary Spurling, 'Happy ever after' (review of Morgan's biography), *Observer*, 23 September 1984.

127 Mallowan, *Memoirs*, p. 208.

128 ibid., p. 211.

129 This is the view put forward tentatively by Carolyn Steedman in her very thoughtful discussion of the difficulties of writing biography, 'Women's biography and autobiography', in Carr, *From My Guy to Sci-Fi*.

130 *An Autobiography*, p. 133.

131 *Come, Tell Me How You Live*, p. 68.
132 Steedman, 'Women's biography and autobiography', p. 106.
133 T. J. Binyon, review of *An Autobiography*, cited in Sanders and Lovallo, *The Agatha Christie Companion*, p. 393.
134 *An Autobiography*, p. 516.
135 Jacquetta Hawkes's description of Christie in the introduction to *Come, Tell Me How You Live*, p. 10.

3 'PEACE IN OUR TIME': *MRS. MINIVER*

1 ' "Mrs. Miniver" in the war', *Times*, 6 June 1942. For fascinating material giving the responses of the British public to the film, see *Mass-Observation at the Movies*, ed. Jeffrey Richards and Dorothy Sheridan (Routledge & Kegan Paul, London, 1987).
2 Valerie Grove, Introduction to *Mrs. Miniver* (Virago, London, 1989), p. xi. Jan Struther was the pen-name of Joyce Maxtone Graham.
3 ' "Mrs. Miniver" ', *Times*, 8 July 1942.
4 'Great success in U.S. of "Mrs. Miniver" ', *Times*, 17 August 1942. *The Times* also carried strategically hopeful accounts of the film's reception in Switzerland and Sweden plus the report of an 'incident' in Argentina at the film's showing there: the foreign minister applauded it enthusiastically. (See *The Times*, 23 November and 3 December 1942; 1 January 1943.).
5 Maureen Turim, 'Fashion shapes: film, the fashion industry and the image of women', *Socialist Review*, no. 71 (vol. 13, no. 5, 1983).
6 The 'Mrs. Miniver' columns were collected together in book form in 1939 and published by Chatto & Windus. Virago Press (London) reprinted this edition in 1989 with the inclusion of four wartime letters. All future page references in the text are to this edition.
7 Prime Minister Neville Chamberlain's actual words to the crowd outside Downing Street on 1 October 1938, after the signing of the Munich agreement, were 'I believe it is peace for our time.' These words, repeated later in parliament, were misreported by *The Times* on 7 October in a column headed 'Peace in our time'. See Charles Loch Mowat, *Britain between the Wars 1918–1940* (Methuen, London, 1956), p. 619.
8 An article of my own, 'That blithe English spirit', *Guardian*, 7 September 1989, was guilty of this.
9 The first column, 'Mrs. Miniver comes home', appeared on 6 October 1937; the last on 28 December 1939.
10 The two fourth leaders in *The Times* were: 'Meet Mrs. Miniver', 19 May 1938, and 'Concerning Clem', 7 July 1938; the letters appeared on 27 July, 1 August and 5 August 1938.
11 'Miniver Fans', *Times*, 28 September 1939.
12 Readers should turn to *The Times*, 21 January 1938, to pursue these topics.
13 Grove, Introduction to *Mrs. Miniver*, p. x.
14 Jan Struther lived at 16 Wellington Square in Chelsea. She was married to a Lloyds broker.
15 E. M. Delafield, a successful novelist, was a director of *Time and Tide* when she was asked to contribute something light to it in 1929. So successful was the diary that she went on to publish four more volumes. (Page references are to the Macmillan collected edition of 1947.) See also Violet Powell, *The Life of a Provincial Lady* (Heinemann, London, 1988).
16 For a preliminary discussion of this journal and a selection of some of its key

pieces, see Dale Spender (ed.), *Time and Tide Wait for No Man* (Pandora, London, 1984).

17 Anita Brookner, 'Good husbandry', *Observer*, 25 September 1988.

18 ibid.; Jilly Cooper, introducing the Folio Society edition (1979) of the diary, wonders (without any trace of irony) how it is 'that anyone living a comparatively sheltered upper-class life of forty years ago could think and behave so exactly like me' (p. 5). Perhaps there is an element of wishful thinking here. (Naturally Cooper makes no reference to Delafield's feminism or to *Time and Tide*.)

19 The 1930s saw an enormous expansion of the readership of the daily press, as well as a growth in the number of dailies read. The broad band of middle-class readers now took morning papers and it was no longer surprising or shocking to see a woman reading a paper – or even reporting for them. Indeed, women readers were a new and booming market and an interesting study has still to be written examining the changes in style and content (without merely reading these as the effects of advertising and American influence) which ackowledge these shifts in the home market. One innovation was the increased space given to the 'columnist', whose reflective and often personal commentary on events or everyday life became a popular feature of many of the papers.

20 I would therefore take issue with the analysis of the period offered by Deirdre Beddoe, *Back to Home and Duty* (Pandora, London, 1989), whose welcome emphasis on the power of images in advertising, magazines and fiction nevertheless construes them as almost entirely coercive and manipulative, and comes close to seeing women as either innocent victims or willing dupes. Yet the effects of the new focus on home were contradictory: the new emphasis which many magazines placed upon home-making, for example, and the growing market for consumer goods connected with the home, made the world of housework visible as domestic labour in ways which were impossible with a servant class. Once such work had been called 'drudgery' by the advertisers (which the purchase of a new hoover or toaster would magically eliminate), there was also a more legitimate language of complaint. See Cynthia White, *Women's Magazines 1693–1968* (Michael Joseph, London, 1970) for a more nuanced, though equally pessimistic, discussion of the 'professionalisation' of housewifery in the period.

21 Lady Una Troubridge, *Etiquette and Entertaining: To Help You on Your Social Way* (Amalgamated Press, London, n.d.), p. 247.

22 According to Lady Una 'bromides' were phrases which were meant to be witty but 'have a sedative effect' (p. 194).

23 This is not to say that there was any kind of dramatic decrease in the number of women employed in domestic service in the inter-war period. The female servant population actually increased by 16 per cent between 1920 and 1931; it seems, however, that the number of resident servants declined, and that the war had left many women with a desire for any kind of employment other than domestic service. See Jane Lewis, *Women in England 1870–1950*, for a discussion of employment patterns in the period; also Beddoe, *Back to Home and Duty*, ch. 4. Pam Taylor, 'Daughters and mothers – maids and mistresses: domestic service between the wars' in John Clarke *et al.* (eds), *Working Class Culture*, (Hutchinson, London, 1979), also provides some useful and moving oral testimony.

24 *Woman's Leader*, 1 April 1920, cited in Beddoe, *Back to Home and Duty*, p. 61.

25 Lady Una Troubridge, *Etiquette*, p. 246.

26 Woolf used this egalitarian image of the cook in her famous essay 'Mr. Bennett
    and Mrs. Brown' to mark the nature of modernity and the change in human
    character which, slightly whimsically, she dated from the year 1910. Her own
    fraught relations with Nellie Boxall, the live-in domestic at Monk's House in
    Rodmell, suggest how much longer social and psychic expectations take to
    change than their outward trappings. On 13 April 1929 she writes: 'I am
    sordidly debating within myself the question of Nellie; the perennial question.
    It is an absurdity, how much time L & I have wasted in talking about servants.
    And it can never be done with because the fault lies in the system.' It is not
    until 18 May 1934 that she is able to be free of 'the grumbling Nellie', and
    declare in triumph 'Yes, we do without a Char!': we must add, however, that
    Mabel Haskins was employed in London as the new living-in cook and servant
    within the month. See *The Diary of Virginia Woolf*, vols. 3 and 4, ed. Ann
    Olivier Bell (Penguin, Harmondsworth, 1983). See also Carol Dyhouse, *Femin-
    ism and the Family in England 1880–1939* (Blackwell, Oxford, 1986), especially
    her conclusion, for a discussion of the conflictual relations between middle-
    class feminists, their view of independence and their employment of domestics.
27 Penelope Mortimer, *About Time* (Allen Lane, London, 1979), p. 170.
28 *Thank Heaven Fasting* (Virago, London, 1988), p. 62. The title is an ironic
    reference to Rosalind's speech in Act III of *As You Like It*, when she upbraids
    the proud shepherdess thus: 'Thank heaven, fasting, for a good man's love,
    For I must tell you friendly in your ear, Sell when you can.' Rosalind is
    passing herself off as a man at the time.
29 *Thank Heaven Fasting*, p. 123.
30 Nicola Beauman, *A Very Great Profession: The Woman's Novel 1914–1939*
    (Virago, London, 1983), p. 65.
31 'Married Love' had, of course, been the subject (and title) of one of the biggest
    post-war bestsellers. Marie Stopes's book had sold half a million copies by the
    mid–1920s. Almost as successful was Helena Wright's *The Sex Factor in Mar-
    riage*, published in 1930 and reprinted eleven times over the next twelve years.
    Though debates about birth-control and erotic pleasure were no doubt beyond
    the pale for many upper-middle-class women, the idea of the 'companionate'
    marriage seems to become the common-sense thinking of the 1930s, and in
    particular the notion of the 'double standard' which countenanced adultery for
    men but not for women was increasingly discredited; women's magazines
    showed a new readiness to discuss marital and sexual problems, the staple of
    the new advice columns, and to offer readers pamphlets on subjects like family
    planning. See Jeffrey Weeks, *Sex, Politics and Society* (Longman, London, 1981)
    for an overview of thinking about sexuality in the period and White, *Women's
    Magazines*, ch. 3.
32 Dr Truby King's baby and childcare manuals were a charter for scientific
    motherhood and hugely influential in their day. A Truby King baby was
    breast-fed until the ninth month, learnt to take its feeds at regular four-hour
    intervals (with no night feeds), spent much of its time out in the fresh air (in
    all weathers), and was brought up hygenically and without any 'pampering'.
33 Jan Struther was perhaps prompted by a distaste for nationalism to edit an
    edition of *The Modern Struwwelpeter* (Methuen, London, 1936) with illus-
    trations by E. H. Sheppard, friend of the pacifist A. A. Milne.
34 'Meet Mrs. Miniver', *Times*, 19 May 1938.
35 'Concerning Clem', *Times*, 7 July 1938.
36 The popularisation of psychoanalysis and its theories of infantile trauma was
    particularly influential amongst women writers of all varieties and is to date

an unwritten history. See Beauman, *A Very Great Profession*, ch. 6. for a brief discussion of the work of May Sinclair. Cynthia White, *Women's Magazines*, pp. 107–9, gives evidence of the widespread take-up of Freud's work in the pages of *Good Housekeeping* for 1938.

37 Grove, Introduction to *Mrs. Miniver*, p. ix.
38 Raphael Samuel stresses the importance of this distinction and of the 'embattled sense of caste' which set up all kinds of pecking orders within the middle classes in 'Middle class between the wars', *New Socialist*, January/February (part 1) and June/July (part 2), 1983.
39 Ysenda Maxtone Graham, 'Wit and Mrs Miniver', *Observer*, 13 August 1989.
40 'Meet Mrs. Miniver', *Times*, 19 May 1938.
41 Letter from M. F. Savory, *Times*, 12 October 1939.
42 'Mrs. Miniver', dated 1939, reprinted in *Two Cheers for Democracy* (Edward Arnold, London, 1951), p. 306.
43 Jan Struther was herself an agnostic but when asked to compose a hymn by her friend, Canon Percy Dearmer of Westminster Abbey, she wrote several, including the cheerful school favourite 'When a Knight Won his Spurs in the Stories of Old' – and the consoling 'Lord of All Hopefulness, Lord of All Joy', an optimistic prayer for peace (Grove, Introduction to *Mrs. Miniver*, p. xii).
44 *Betsinda Dances* (Methuen, London, 1931); *Sycamore Square* (Methuen, London, 1932); *When Grandmamma Was Small* (Methuen, London, 1937); *Try Anything Twice* (Chatto & Windus, London, 1938).
45 *The Essays of Elia* (Oxford University Press, Oxford, 1912), p. v. These essays were first published in the years between 1820 and 1833.
46 *Times*, 19 May 1938.
47 *Times*, 8 July 1938; 25 May 1938.
48 Grove, Introduction to *Mrs. Miniver*, p. v.
49 ibid., p. xviii.
50 A similar enthusiasm was taken up by the magazine *Reader's Digest* in the 1940s which advised readers on 'How To Increase Your Wordpower'.
51 A study of working-class speech as it is represented and invented in inter-war novels would be welcome; the lengthy 'monologues' often given to proletarian characters suggest as much a fascination with, as a distaste for, the 'excessive' nature of their speech.
52 Richard Usborne, *Clubland Heroes* (Barrie & Jenkins, London, 1953; rev. edn 1974), pp. 40–3, describes the careful choice of 'appropriate' names which authors, like Dornford Yates, found for the different social orders: 'when the landed gentry come on it's as though a poet had been taken on as assistant editor of Debrett'. Mrs. Miniver's friends ('Lelia Havelock' and 'Teresa Frant') are not as aristocratically euphonious as 'Sarah Cust Vulliamy' or 'Madrigal Chicele' but her 'Downce' and 'Burchett' are clearly related to the bathetically named 'Erny Balch', 'Douglas Bladder' and 'Herbert Bason'. Mrs. Miniver's own name (miniver is a fur used in ceremonies and heraldry) was so thoroughly *comme il faut* as to provoke even *The Times* (19 May 1938) into the rather heavy jest that her first name might be 'Minnie'. (It turned out to be a queenly 'Caroline'.)
53 The feminist movement from the 1920s found itself divided, roughly speaking, between the older suffragists demanding parity with men (the 'equalitarians' as Winifred Holtby, one of their number, called them), and women like Eleanor Rathbone who were campaigning for reforms around what they saw as specifically female issues like family allowances and birth-control, and who sought

protective legislation which would recognise 'the woman's point of view'. See 'Feminism divided' by Winifred Holtby, in Paul Berry and Alan Hislop (eds), *Testament of a Generation* (Virago, London, 1985) for an 'Old Feminism' manifesto; Eleanor Rathbone, 'Changes in public life', in Ray Strachey (ed.), *Our Freedom and its Results* (Hogarth Press, London, 1936), for the alternative position; Spender, *Time and Tide Wait for No Man*, for some of the contemporary debate in *Time and Tide* and Lewis, *Women in England 1870–1950*, Dyhouse, *Feminism and the Family*, and Beddoe, *Back to Home and Duty* for recent feminist reassessment. Marion Shaw's 'Feminism and fiction between the wars' in Moira Monteith (ed.), *Women's Writing: A Challenge to Theory* (Harvester, Brighton 1986) offers a thought-provoking parallel with the arguments amongst novelists over the desirability of a 'feminine aesthetic' in the period.

54 Naomi Michison deals with contraceptives in *We Have Been Warned* (1935); Enid Bagnold's *The Squire* (1938) with breast-feeding and childbirth. Nicola Beauman claims E. Arnot Robertson's *Four Frightened People* (1931) as the first mention of 'the curse' in English fiction (*A Very Great Profession*, p. 143).

55 Letter from Katherine Mansfield to John Middleton Murry, cited by Tillie Olsen in *Silences*, (Virago, London, 1980), p. 18.

56 Nancy Armstrong, *Desire and Domestic Fiction: A Political History of the Novel* (Oxford University Press, Oxford, 1987), p. 289.

57 One of the first British 'soap operas' was, of course, 'Mrs Dale's Diary', daily episodes of the life of a doctor's wife in a London suburb, which began its BBC radio career in 1948 and ran for twenty-one years. (It is perhaps worth adding that 'Woman's Hour' went on the air in 1944.)

58 May Sinclair first coined the phrase 'stream of consciousness' in her review of the novels of Dorothy Richardson (*The Egoist*, April 1918) and Virginia Woolf meditated further on the idea of a 'woman's sentence', as an alternative to the realist style associated with predominantly male Edwardian novelists, in several of her critical essays. See Michèle Barrett (ed.), *Virginia Woolf: Women and Writing* (Women's Press, London, 1979); Gillian E. Hanscombe, *The Art of Dorothy Richardson and the Development of Feminist Consciousness* (Peter Owen, London, 1982); and Jean Radford, *Dorothy Richardson* (Harvester, Brighton, forthcoming). Within feminist literary criticism an attack on Woolf and the experimental modernist writers from a position of privileging social realism which sees their project (and indeed the authors) as 'closed' and 'sterile' can be found in Elaine Showalter, *A Literature of Their Own: British Women Novelists from Brontë to Lessing* (Virago, London, 1978); for a rejection of Showalter's reading and the feminist literary critical approach employed, see Toril Moi, *Sexual/Textual Politics* (Methuen, London, 1985), and Janet Todd, *Feminist Literary History* (Blackwell, Oxford, 1988) for a polemical discussion of the divisions between Anglo-American and recent French critical theories which comes to the defence of the former. Rachel Bowlby, *Virginia Woolf: Feminist Destinations* (Blackwell, Oxford, 1988), on the other hand, aims to provide a reading of the work which avoids the trap of invoking Woolf to support 'any and every position' as an exemplary 'woman writer'.

59 Witold Rybczynski, *Home: A Short History of an Idea*, (Heinemann, London, 1988), pp. 75 and 223. Rybczynski's account aims to celebrate women's work in creating the space of home. It does so, however, without any sense of the constraints and limitations which the maintenance of domestic privacy might involve, especially for women. Leonore Davidoff and Catherine Hall's *Family Fortunes: Men and Women of the English Middle Class 1780–1850* (Hutchinson,

London, 1987) gives an historically rich and sensitive account of the emergence of the middle-class home and its creation as a 'separate sphere' for women.

60 Bowlby, *Virginia Woolf*, p. 118.

61 Beauman, *A Very Great Profession*, p. 5.

62 E. M. Delafield, *The Way Things Are* (Virago, London, 1988), p. 336.

63 The erotic image is a revealing one. Spending, with its momentary gift of autonomy and power, has a long history as a sexual metaphor, and was coming to be thought of more and more as a feminine activity in this period. Perhaps the culture of 'the sales' at big department stores and the frantic crushes which such shopping involved, provided a female equivalent to the homo-erotic pleasures of the football match?

64 Beaumann, *A Very Great Profession*, p. 114.

65 Katherine Burdekin's little-known but extraordinarily prescient novel, *Swastika Night* (1937; reprinted by Lawrence & Wishart in 1985), is one such attempt to connect the patriarchal dominance of the private sphere with the psychology and sexual politics of fascism. It takes more explicitly feminist form in Virginia Woolf's *Three Guineas*, published in 1938. See Q. D. Leavis, however, for an attack on Woolf's class-blindness and separatism, in her scathing review, 'Caterpillars of the commonwealth unite!', *Scrutiny*, vol. 7, no. 2 (1938–9), pp. 203–14.

66 An over-ripe Lawrentian mixture of maternal mysticism, nature worship, and deference to privilege, *The Squire* (reprinted Virago, London, 1986) now makes uncomfortable reading. Bagnold's heroine (referred to throughout with self-conscious and archaic reverence simply as 'the squire') is about to give birth to her fifth child and welcomes the obliteration of self: 'I am a pipe through which the generations pass' (p. 155). Much the strongest character in the novel is the midwife who summons up a kind of primeval knowledge in the 'mystery' of motherhood: the squire finds completion in surrendering to the discipline of giving birth, imagined as a sensuous ecstasy of pain. The heroine's feudal soul leads to some contemptuous views of the serfs – a potential cook is 'a born lavatory attendant if ever there was one' (p. 73) – whilst the ancient ceremony of the 'squire's' confinement confirms her fitness for a ruling place in society. It comes as no surprise to learn of Bagnold's own admiration for Nazism in its early days: 'I love to see things born', she wrote naïvely of Hitler's Germany. The novel is a salutory reminder of how far a celebration of maternity cannot be assumed to be progressive, even when it is written by a woman.

There is a whole volume still to be written on English letters and fascism: Bagnold should be read alongside Henry Williamson, for example. See also Patrick Wright, *On Living in an Old Country* (Verso, London, 1985), for an illuminating discussion of connected themes in Mary Butt's *The Crystal Cabinet*, also published in 1938. Ann Sebba, *Enid Bagnold* (Weidenfeld & Nicolson, London, 1986), gives a fascinating account of Bagnold's life and views.

67 Entry for Sunday, 8 March 1941, *A Writer's Diary* (Hogarth Press, London, 1953), p. 365.

68 These are the terms in which Bevis Hillier contrasts the difference in the 'look' of the 1920s and '30s woman, in *The Style of the Century 1900–1980* (E. P. Dutton, New York, 1983), p. 94.

69 *Quiet Thoughts* (Frederick Muller, London, 1937). *Quiet Corner*, 2 vols (Frederick Muller, London 1936) was the first of many volumes written by Winifred May under the pseudonym of Patience Strong which were to earn her a devoted public for over thirty years. Her titles in the late 1930s and '40s – *The Sunny*

Side (1938), *Wings of the Morning* (1938), *Paths of Peace* (1939), *Silver Linings* (1939), *Windows of Hope* (1940), suggest the tenor of her message to the nation. No doubt there is a story to be told, too, about the life of Winifred May.

70 *Night and Day*, 4 November 1937. *Night and Day* was launched 1 July 1937 under the editorship of Graham Greene and John Marks. It was modelled on the lively *New Yorker*, carrying fiction, poetry, cartoons and political commentary as well as film, book and theatre reviews. Present-day journalism might learn something from its adventurous choice of contributors, amongst whom were Walter Allen, the literary critic, who wrote a football column; Herbert Read, the art historian, who wrote on crime fiction; Elizabeth Bowen, the novelist, on theatre, and Graham Greene himself on cinema. The latter's review of a Shirley Temple film, suggesting that the child-star was a sexual tease, led to an expensive libel suit; the magazine's financial condition was already fragile, however, and it folded in December of the same year.

71 Grove, Introduction to *Mrs. Miniver*, p. xiii.

72 ibid., p. xv.

73 Ysenda Maxtone Graham, 'Wit and Mrs. Miniver'.

74 'Prime Minister's Optimism', *Times*, 27 July 1938.

75 *Times*, 15 September 1938. The editorial was so strongly anti-war that it was able to dismiss the fate of Czechoslovakia with the opinion that there was no point in the nations of the most densely populated continent of the world bombing one another 'on account of the troubles of some three and a half million folk in the pleasant land of Bohemia'.

76 A 'National Tribute Fund' was the suggestion of the Bishop of Coventry, who wrote effusively to *The Times* (1 October 1938) of his 'profound sense of deliverance, gratitude and joy' which he was sure the nation shared.

77 'I am convinced that this is the beginning of World peace and the end of wars. I am looking forward to a better and brighter world, as a result of Mr Chamberlain's wonderful work', was the view of one 52-year-old builder interviewed by 'Mass-Observation', the independent organisation founded in 1937 by Charles Madge and Tom Harrison to canvas public opinion on a range of issues: cited by Frank Simkins, '1938: The Munich crisis and public opinion' (Ruskin College, Oxford, unpublished dissertation), p. 29. For a vigorous, if at times dogmatic, attack upon 'leading appeasers', see Martin Gilbert and Richard Gott, *The Appeasers* (Weidenfeld & Nicolson, London, 1963): their main concern is, however, with 'the men who supported and opposed' appeasement (p. 11), *viz.* diplomats and politicians: an intriguing suggestion that 'appeasement was a mood less alien to women than to men' (p. 45) is not followed up.

78 'Vigil for peace', *Times*, 1 October 1938.

79 Tom Hopkinson (ed.), *Picture Post*, (Penguin, London, 1970), p. 10. *Picture Post* began under the editorship of Stefan Lorant, an Hungarian refugee who had been imprisoned by the Nazis in Munich. The 'Back to the Middle Ages' feature was largely his idea.

80 See Appendix (p. 222) for Jan Struther's letter to *The Times*. This was the only Mrs. Miniver contribution omitted from both the original collection and the Virago reprinted edition, presumably because its topical nature interfered with the 'literary' tone. Under the wide umbrella of conservatism very different shades of opinion took shelter: Struther's well-meaning letter should be read against Enid Bagnold's piece on Hitler's Germany in the same month, which had hailed the vigour and energy of the new regime and archly dismissed the

'problem' of the Jews thus: 'Hitler had decided that the Jews were to be no more than the touch of yeast in the bread. The proportion of yeast in the continental loaf is too old and too strange a problem for English minds.' ('In Germany today – Hitler's new form of democracy', *Sunday Times*, 6 November 1938). Sebba, *Enid Bagnold*, gives the full text in an appendix.

81 She wrote one other piece in the old style – 'Mrs. Miniver makes a list', Christmas 1939, which was published in *The Queen's Book of the Red Cross* and can be found in the Virago edition, p. 124.

82 Jan Struther's own life was to be changed out of all recognition by the war which separated her from her husband for five years after his capture as a prisoner of Rommel. The marriage broke down and they were divorced in 1947. The following year Struther married Adolf Placzek, an Austrian refugee whom she had first met in 1938. He was 'the love of her life' (Grove, Introduction to *Mrs. Miniver*, p. xiv). The couple then went to live in America. Hardly the model of womanly stability which Greer Garson was to project. Sadly though, Struther, at the age of 52, was to die of cancer, like MGM's heroine; she had sued the company for killing off her character only the year before.

83 Only someone constitutionally heedless of the future could have penned such a blithe epitaph for herself as Struther did:

> One day my life will end; and lest
> Some whim should prompt you to review it,
> Let her who knows the subject best
> Tell you the shortest way to do it:
> Then say, 'Here lies one doubly blest.'
> Say, 'She was happy.' Say, 'She knew it.'
>   (Grove, Introduction to *Mrs. Miniver*, p. xx)

84 Andrea S. Walsh, *Women's Film and Female Experience* (Praeger, New York, 1984), p. 93. Unfortunately, Walsh takes the film's depiction of Englishness at face value.

85 British cinema-goers varied hugely in their response to the film. Some praised it for being 'true to life' and showing 'so well and unaffectedly the English spirit' and 'ordinary, natural people'; others scorned it as a 'smooth Hollywood faerytale' and disparaged its 'loathsome family'; one woman respondent (a secretary) found it so 'deplorable' she 'could hardly sit through it'. See the discussion of the 1943 Mass-Observation directive on favourite films of the previous year in Richards and Sheridan, *Mass-Observation at the Movies*, ch. 13.

86 Raphael Samuel, 'Continuous national history', in *Patriotism: The Making and Unmaking of British National Identity*, vol. 1: *History and Politics* (Routledge, London, 1989), p. 15. See also his introduction 'Exciting to be English' in the same volume, for further discussion of the ways in which a mood of 'splendid isolation' characterised English life between the wars.

4 DAPHNE DU MAURIER'S ROMANCE WITH THE PAST

1 General Frederick or 'Boy' Browning was wartime commander of the Airborne Forces, Chief of Staff to Earl Mountbatten, Treasurer to the Duke of Edinburgh and Deputy Lieutenant of Cornwall.

2 'Dame Daphne du Maurier' (obituary), *Independent*, 21 April 1989.

3 'Romantic storyteller. in the grand manner', *Daily Telegraph*, 20 April 1989.

4 Sheila Holland (better known amongst romance readers as 'Charlotte Lamb'), quoted in 'Rebecca author du Maurier dies', Guardian, 20 April 1989.

5 'Last of the du Mauriers' (obituary), Guardian, 20 April 1989.

6 Entry for du Maurier by Jane S. Bakerman, in James Vinson (ed.), Twentieth Century Romance and Gothic Writers (Macmillan, London, 1982), p. 220.

7 Guardian, 20 April 1989; see also Michael Thornton, 'Secret jealousy of the real Rebecca', Observer, 23 April 1989, who claims that 'Daphne was anything but a romantic, either in her writing or in her life.'

8 From Miracle, 1938, cited by Cynthia White, Women's Magazines 1693–1968 (Michael Joseph, 1970), p. 98.

9 White, Women's Magazines, discusses some of these shifts. Kirsten Drotner, More Next Week! English Children and Their Magazines 1751–1945 (Aarhus University, Aarhus, 1985) offers a thoughtful analysis of the growth of new markets for women's fiction; Asa Briggs, Mass Entertainment (Griffin, London, 1960) and W. H. Fraser, The Coming of the Mass Market 1850–1914 (Macmillan, London, 1981) provide an overview and some statistics. There is as yet no critical history of the development of forms of romance fiction in the late nineteenth and early twentieth century, or indeed a study of the reading of working women on a par with Louis James's Fiction for the Working Man 1830–1850 (Oxford University Press, Oxford, 1963); Rachel Anderson, The Purple Heart Throbs: The Sub-literature of Love (Hodder & Stoughton, London, 1974) is a mainly descriptive account of popular writers like Marie Corelli and Elinor Glyn; Mirabel Cecil, Heroines in Love 1750–1974 (Michael Joseph, London, 1974) and Nicola Beauman, A Very Great Profession: The Woman's Novel 1914–39 (Virago, London, 1983) are also helpful; Helen Taylor also provides a helpful retrospective on contemporary feminist debates about popular romance in 'Romantic readers', in H. Carr (ed.), From My Guy to Sci-Fi: Genre and Women's Writing in the Postmodern World (Pandora, London, 1989).

10 See Billie Melman, Women and the Popular Imagination: Flappers and Nymphs (Macmillan, London, 1988); A. Huyssen, 'Mass culture as woman: modernism's Other', in T. Modleski (ed.), Studies in Entertainment – Critical Approaches to Mass Culture (Indiana University, Bloomington, 1986). Film-going does not seem to have been seen as respectable until the late 1930s, and then it might be pilloried as 'suburban'.

11 Storm Jameson, 'Novels and novelists' and 'Apology for my life', in Civil Journey (Cassell, London, 1939), p. 83 and p. 19.

12 F. R. Leavis, Mass Civilisation and Minority Culture (Minority Press, Cambridge, 1930), p. 10. For Leavis the 'industrialisation' of literature is at once a 'levelling down' in class terms and a hybridisation: a kind of anarchy which de-centres all systems of discrimination. This is 'the plight of culture': 'The landmarks have shifted, multiplied and crowded upon one another, the distinctions and dividing lines have blurred away, the boundaries are gone and the arts and literatures of different countries and periods have flowed together' (p. 19). Fears about modernity as a cultural miscegenation – the threat to 'the Anglo-Saxon race' – surface in the singling out of jazz ('negro' music) by many critics. Storm Jameson, for example, maintains that bestsellers left audiences 'where they found them, confused by the noise of saxophones' (Civil Journey, p. 82).

13 'The Tosh Horse', in The Strange Necessity (Virago, London, 1987), p. 321.

14 ibid., p. 323.

15 Jameson, Civil Journey, pp. 18; 82; 84.

16 'Women and fiction' first appeared in *The Forum*, March 1929 and then in *Granite and Rainbow* (Hogarth Press, London, 1958); reprinted in Michèle Barrett (ed.), *Virginia Woolf: Women and Writing* (Women's Press, London, 1979), p. 51.

17 See Steedman, 'Women's biography and autobiography: forms of history, histories of forms' in Carr, *From My Guy to Sci-Fi*.

18 Even *Eve*, a high-society magazine for women, declared after the war that 'there has been a slump in sentimentalism' and 'misty-eyed emotionality' was dead: Cecil, *Heroines in Love*, p. 151. Of course romance came back, but differently.

19 Beauman, *A Very Great Profession*, p. 183.

20 See, for example, George Orwell's assumptions in 'Bookshop memories' (November 1936), in *The Collected Essays, Journalism and Letters of George Orwell*, vol. 1 (Penguin, Harmondsworth, 1970), p. 275.

21 G. C. Ramsey, *Agatha Christie: Mistress of Mystery* (Collins, London, 1968), p. 52.

22 The same divisions between 'high' and 'low' operate within the genre too: P. D. James, now published in large paperback format by Faber & Faber, appears more literary and more respectable than the other bestselling British 'queen of crime', Ruth Rendell. Their relation is rather like that which obtained between Sayers and Christie.

23 Glover, 'The stuff that dreams are made of', p. 72.

24 Somerset Maugham, 'The decline and fall of the detective story', in *The Vagrant Mood* (Heinemann, London, 1952), p. 107.

25 This is the term used by Sigmund Freud to argue that a splitting of the author's ego takes place in the process of writing and fantasising: see 'Creative writers and day-dreaming', in Sigmund Freud, *Art and Literature*, vol. 14, Pelican Freud Library (Penguin, Harmondsworth, 1985), p. 138.

26 Woolf, in Barrett, *Virginia Woolf*, p. 51.

27 Thornton, 'Secret jealousy of the real Rebecca'.

28 'Then one sunny morning, Romance stepped right across Peggy's path . . . it led her right away from the hat-shop and the drabness which had made up her life, and introduced her to an absolutely new world, where wealth made life easy and love paved the way to happiness.' (Synopsis of story in *My Weekly*, 17 January 1920, p. 44, cited by White, *Women's Magazines*, p. 98) Du Maurier's novel transposes romance into a bourgeois key. Her heroine is more respectable than a milliner (though milliners were themselves 'superior' to mill girls) but she is not a socialite. In fact, like her, Max de Winter dislikes 'Monte' (the conventional setting for a high-society romance) and the true love story is not with abroad but with England. His proposal, nevertheless, is in keeping with a modern sangfroid which saw sentiment as 'shy-making' or 'hush-making' (Cecil, *Heroines in Love*, p. 151).

29 The *Boy's Own Paper*, begun in 1879 under the auspices of the Religious Tract Society, published fiction by clergymen as well as writers like Ballantyne, Henty and Jules Verne and was intended as 'respectable' boy's reading, though it would seem bloodthirsty enough by today's standards. Its emphasis fell on historical fiction which was seen to be mildly educative and 'improving', unlike the 'penny dreadfuls' or 'bloods' which had previously formed the main entertainment for boy readers and had little (however faint) didactic purpose. See E. S. Turner, *Boys Will Be Boys* (Michael Joseph, London, 1957); Martin Green, *Dreams of Adventure, Deeds of Empire* (Routledge, London, 1980). (One might also see a similar pattern of elevation and 'bourgeoisification' in

the enormous growth of historical novels written by and for women between the wars; by raiding history, fiction could be both popular and respectable.)

30 'Tushery' was coined by R. L. Stevenson to describe the often spurious use of 'local colour', like archaic dialect, employed by novelists to create an historical effect. There are innumerable references to Stevenson in du Maurier's autobiography, *Myself When Young – The Shaping of a Writer* (Pan, London, 1978), whose works she appears to have read as a child several times over.

31 For historical accounts of children's reading see F. J. Harvey Darton, *Children's Books in England* (Cambridge University Press, Cambridge, 1932); Amy Cruse, *The Victorians and Their Books* (Allen & Unwin, London, 1935); and Humphrey Carpenter, *Secret Gardens* (Allen & Unwin, London, 1985). Margaret and Michael Rustin, *Narratives of Love and Loss: Studies in Modern Children's Fiction* (Verso, London, 1987) sees the rise of children's fiction as part of that 'emergence of childhood as a distinctive and internally-differentiated life-stage in the latter half of the nineteenth century for a small, privileged minority and increasingly, in this century, for nearly all' – a thesis which Drotner, *More Next Week!* also supports.

32 Green, *Dreams of Adventure*, p. 323.

33 It is interesting to find du Maurier at 22 reading Robert Graves's *Goodbye to All That* when it first came out in 1929 (*Myself When Young*, p. 142).

34 Green, *Dreams of Adventure*, p. 220.

35 *Myself When Young*, p. 139.

36 G. A. Henty wrote nearly eighty immensely popular boys' adventure books, mainly exploits of the British army in colonial settings, urging a strict ethic of self-control, patriotic duty and the condemnation of 'milksops'. Paul Fussell, *The Great War and Modern Memory* (Oxford University Press, Oxford, 1977), places Henty as one of the masters of the romantic dictum of manliness and Christian self-abnegation who formed the childhood reading and emotional universe of those who died in the Great War (p. 21).

37 From *Punch*, quoted as publicity material for the Pan edition of *I'll Never Be Young Again* (1975).

38 See Melman, *Women and the Popular Imagination*, for discussion of the sex novels of the time and of the *The Green Hat*, which is also the subject of a chapter in Claud Cockburn, *Bestsellers: The Books that Everyone Read 1900–1939* (Sidgwick & Jackson, London, 1972). The term was used in the 1920s to describe the new fiction which set out to explore feminine sexuality and was seen either as a decadent symptom of the post-war malaise or as a sign of modern emancipation from the past.

39 Green, *Dreams of Adventure*, p. 272.

40 Angela du Maurier, *Old Maids Remember* (Peter Davies, London, 1966), p. 19.

41 The Never Land is, of course, the place where Peter Pan lives with his 'lost boys'. It is by no means an arbitrary choice of image in connection with du Maurier's writing. James Barrie, the author of the play, was a great friend of the family and had written it for Daphne's cousins, the sons of Sylvia Llewellyn Davies (her father's sister) whose guardian he became after the death of their father. Daphne's own father, Gerald, played Captain Hook (and Mr Darling) in the first performances and immortalised the role, whilst the character 'Wendy Moira Angela Darling' was named after her sister who later came to play the part in the theatre alongside her father. *Peter Pan* was endlessly performed in the children's nursery and the trip to the theatre was the great event of their year. Its influence on Daphne's imaginative and emotional formation can hardly

be overestimated. (I shall return to this image of the 'lost boys' later in the chapter).

Barrie was in his own way revising the masculine adventure story, bringing it together with the domestic novel and the fairy tale and locating its landscape of fears and desires within the confines of Edwardian family life: as he wrote in his introduction to *Coral Island*, 'To be born is to be wrecked on an island.' See Jacqueline Rose's fascinating and rigorous analysis of the play as 'a little history of children's fiction in itself', *The Case of Peter Pan or the Impossibility of Children's Fiction* (Macmillan, London, 1984).

42 This was also the term which Virginia Woolf used to describe her own 'historical novel', *Orlando*, published in 1928. Whereas Woolf transgresses the bounds of realism in order to offer the reader different positions from which to understand the 'sexing' of Orlando's subjectivity – first as a man, then as a woman – du Maurier works within the limits of a realism which even when it goes back into a fantastical past cannot afford to disturb the reader's expectations too far.

43 It appears to be between the wars that 'escapism', in the sense of the 'tendency to, or practice of seeking distraction from what normally has to be endured' (according to *The Oxford English Dictionary*'s somewhat puritanical definition), comes into common currency. The OED gives no entry for its application to books and films etc. before 1933: like the bestseller and the cinema it belongs to modernity.

44 An enormous number of women historical novelists began writing in this period: Margaret Irwin, Norah Lofts, Georgette Heyer, amongst the best known. For many writers the uses of the historical were primarily a kind of licence – thus Naomi Michison's *The Delicate Fire* (1933) escaped censorship whilst including a scene in which a man expresses a woman's breast-milk because they were wearing 'wolfskins and togas' (see Beauman, *A Very Great Profession*, p. 141). For a discussion of the transgressive, though not always progressive, possibilities of historical fiction, see Helen Taylor, *Scarlett's Women: 'Gone with the Wind' and Its Female Fans* (Virago, London, 1989); Cora Kaplan, '*The Thorn Birds*: fiction, fantasy and femininity', in *Sea Changes* (Verso, London, 1986), and my own '*Young Bess:* historical novels and growing up', *Feminist Review*, no. 33 (Autumn 1989). Carolyn Steedman reflects on why it might be the most conservative of historical fictions which appeal to children in school in 'True romances', in Raphael Samuel (ed.), *Patriotism: The Making and Unmaking of British National Identity*, vol. 1, *History and Politics* (Routledge, London, 1989).

Taking this fiction into account one would have to disagree with Martin Green's view that 'the moral and social basis of adventure narrowed' between the wars (*Dreams of Adventure*, p. 321); it is more accurate to say that the ground shifted and many of the sites of adventure were taken over by women's and girls' fiction in the period. Green's categorical statement, that 'at least in the world of literature one can flatly say that England after 1918 was unadventurous' is only true if England does not include the female population. For a female readership England became a hugely adventurous place, though we must see battlefields and warfare (claimed by an author like Irwin, for example) as ambiguous territories for the woman writer and reader to lay siege to, and we need to analyse how they were differently occupied.

45 Melman, *Women and the Popular Imagination*, p. 104.

46 *The Sheik* ran into 108 editions in Britain alone between 1919 and 1923. First

published at 3s 6d, cut to 2s 6d, and finally to a one-shilling edition, nevertheless 'the demand for cheap editions could not be met' (ibid., p. 46).

47 ibid., p. 90.

48 The first film version in 1926 with Rudolph Valentino was seen by 125 million
viewers, the majority of them women. Billie Melman, *Women and the Popular
Imagination*, sees this as signalling the rise of a new kind of cult hero – the
male film star or sex symbol (p. 90).

49 See Sandra M. Gilbert and Susan Gubar, *No-Man's Land: The Place of the
Woman Writer in the Twentieth Century*, vol. 2, *Sex Changes* (Yale University
Press, New Haven, 1989), for some reflections on this crisis in expressivity,
although they are almost exclusively interested in 'high culture'.

50 In 'Professions for women' Woolf put forward her now famous view that the
woman writer has two adventures to face in her professional life, the first that
of killing 'the Angel in the House' who constantly seeks male approval, which
she believes she has managed, and the other, that of 'telling the truth about
my experiences as a body', which she admits 'I do not think I have solved.'
She reasons that this repression is due to the fear of shocking men (surely a
resurrection of the Angel after all?); we might also look to unconscious taboos
which made the expression of sexuality 'lower class'. (The essay, based on a
speech given to the London/National Society for Women's Service in 1931,
was first published in *The Death of the Moth* (Hogarth Press, London, 1942),
and is reprinted in Barrett, *Virginia Woolf*.) Katherine Mansfield also shared
this bourgeois distaste for those female writers who were writing erotic fiction
and – in her view – revealing themselves as 'sex maniacs': 'it's a very horrible
exposure', she wrote to John Middleton Murry in 1920: cited by Kate
Fullbrook, *Katherine Mansfield* (Harvester, Brighton, 1986), p. 95.

51 Rhoda Broughton, *Red As a Rose Is She* (1870), quoted by Anderson, *The
Purple Heart Throbs*, p. 56.

52 I was, therefore, in error to argue as I did in an earlier piece, ' "Returning to
Manderley": romance fiction, female sexuality and class', *Feminist Review*, no.
16 (Summer 1984), that Manderley is 'the site of feudal freedom' (p. 20). Max
is clearly not an aristocrat and Manderley is not offered to the reader as an
aesthetic or moral education in the manner of a *Brideshead Revisited*. The
novel is far more about anxieties within the middle classes and if Manderley
is a stately home then it is valued by the girl only for its more bourgeois
rooms – the comfortable library and chintzy bedroom – and for the grounds
outside the house. Manderley is like a house visited on a guided tour, an
experience which reminds us – as it does the heroine – of our exclusion from
that other, grander existence as much as it gives us temporary admission to it.
In fact Maxim is, of course, punished as well as admired for his feelings
about property. See also Roger Bromley, 'The gentry, bourgeois hegemony and
popular fiction: *Rebecca* and *Rogue Male*', in Peter Humm *et al.* (eds), *Popular
Fictions*, (Methuen, London, 1986).

53 From the publicity material on the cover of the 1962 Penguin edition.

54 The film of *Jamaica Inn* made in 1939 robbed the heroine (played by Maureen
O'Hara with a genteel Irish accent and in various states of undress) of her
autonomy and of her love affair with an outlaw; she falls in love instead with
an officer of the law who is in disguise as a peasant. There is enough fear of
the mob in du Maurier's novel to justify this invention (Jem does turn King's
evidence in the original, after all), but not to sanction the removal entirely of
the true villain, the vicar of Altarnun, who was obviously felt to be too
disturbing to British decorum. The film is hardly about female desire at all,

but rather becomes a costume drama with a decadent squire (another invention) played by Charles Laughton, centre stage.

What Hitchcock seems most to owe to du Maurier's novels are the haunting and heightened landscapes, both exterior, as dramatised in her choice of Cornwall, and interior. The Gothic elements in du Maurier's work are far more present in Hitchcock's *Rebecca* (1940), made explicitly as a 'woman's film' and clearly troubled by the question of female sexuality. It is also more straightforwardly moralising – Hitchcock makes Rebecca die by accident, for example, thus removing the main shock of the narrative, Maxim's deliberate joy in her death: 'I'm glad I killed Rebecca. I shall never have any remorse for that, never, never' (p. 313). For psychoanalytic readings of Hitchcock's *Rebecca* as an Oedipal drama from the feminine point of view, see Tania Modleski, *The Women Who Knew Too Much* (Methuen, London, 1988) and Mary Ann Doane, *The Desire to Desire* (Macmillan, London, 1989). A further reading of the film might also attempt an analysis of the versions of Britishness which it offered and aim to historicise the question of femininity as it is articulated in both film and novel. See also Light, ' "Returning to Manderley" '.

55 R. L. Stevenson, *An Inland Voyage* (Dent, London, 1984), p. 86.

56 See her discussion of 'the sixth sense' in 'This I believe', *The Rebecca Notebook and Other Memories* (Gollancz, London, 1981).

57 Obituary, *Times*, 20 April 1989.

58 Gerald du Maurier, Preface to the Everyman Library edition of *Trilby* (Dent, London, 1931), p. vii.

59 Freud, 'Creative writers and day-dreaming', p. 135.

60 *A Room of One's Own* (Hogarth Press, London, 1929; Granada, London, 1977), p. 72.

61 In her last published work in 1981 du Maurier apologised for not having 'as yet, written about my own children and my seven grandchildren' (*The Rebecca Notebook*, p. 55); she never did.

62 Amongst the many roles, including Captain Hook, were 'Raffles', the gentle-man burglar, 'Bulldog Drummond', and 'Will Dearth', the happy-go-lucky artist father, in Barrie's *Dear Brutus*.

63 *Gerald: A Portrait* (Gollancz, London, 1934), pp. 58; 63.

64 Obituary, *Guardian*, 20 April 1989.

65 She also edited in 1951 *The Young George du Maurier: A Selection of his Letters 1860–1867* (Peter Davies, London).

66 Such is the power of names that I assumed her to be 'a displaced aristocrat' in my article of 1984, ' "Returning to Manderley" '. Her father was knighted for his services to the theatre in 1922 ('Why was Daddy knighted?' Daphne asked her mother when making notes for *Gerald*. 'I don't think we ever knew', came the reply: *The Rebecca Notebook*, p. 83); Daphne's own title as Lady Browning came, of course, from her husband.

67 The first three volumes of John Galsworthy's *The Forsyte Saga* were published together in 1922, the second trilogy in 1929, and the third posthumously in 1934. They provided in some sort an attempt to span the disjuncture of the war and offered a model for many other family sagas. One thinks, too, of the chronologies offered in projects as different as Virginia Woolf's *The Years* (1937) and Naomi Jacob's *Gollancz* saga, whose first volume appeared in 1935, both of which are trying to make sense of the present as 'times out of joint' by charting a continuous history of family life. Peter Widdowson takes up this theme in 'Between the acts? English fiction in the thirties', in Jon Clark *et al.* (eds), *Culture and Crisis in Britain in the '30s* (Lawrence & Wishart, London,

1979). See also Raphael Samuel's discussion of shifts in British historiography between the wars in 'Continuous national history', in Samuel, *Patriotism*, vol. 1, *History and Politics*.

68 Patrick Wright, *On Living in an Old Country* (Verso, London, 1985), p. 96.
69 See Raphael Samuel, 'The little platoons', introduction to *Patriotism*, vol. 2, *Minorities and Outsiders*.
70 'My name in lights', in *The Rebecca Notebook*, p. 97.
71 The du Maurier family resemble the 'Sangers' in that bestseller of 1924, Margaret Kennedy's *The Constant Nymph*; du Maurier echoes the novel in the book she herself wrote about a theatrical family life overshadowed by a charismatic father, *The Parasites* (1939).
72 Chris Cook, interview with du Maurier in 'Scenes from the life of Dame Daphne du Maurier', broadcast on BBC Radio 4, on 7 January 1990. Richard Kelly in his obituary for *The Independent* (21 April 1989) described du Maurier as 'an author overwhelmed by the memory of her father's commanding presence'.
73 ibid.
74 ibid.
75 Tactfully she draws a veil across the extent to which these were sexual relationships, though a later memoir reveals her mother's occasional jealousy and that Gerald had been known to stay for the afternoon at the house of a young actress in St John's Wood ('The matinée idol', in *The Rebecca Notebook*, p. 80).
76 It may be that this book had been partly anticipated and feelings rehearsed in the novel she published two years earlier, *I'll Never Be Young Again*. 'Dick's' story of the getting of wisdom reaches its climax with the death of his father, a famous poet and national figure, which leaves him free to be 'himself'. It is tempting to read a disguised expression of her own negative feelings about having a famous father in the raw outbursts of resentment which du Maurier gives to her character:

> My father was a legend, and he had created his legend, his life, his atmosphere. . . . And I grew to loathe my father, loathe his genius which made such a mockery of his son; and my spirit rebelled against all the things he stood for, it struggled to resist his power, it fought to escape from the net that bound me imprisoned in his atmosphere.
>
> (p. 23)

Dick particularly wishes he had had a more 'manly' father.
77 According to Viscount Esher, du Maurier's play (which he wrongly ascribes to Gerald and not Guy) initiated a 'revivalist fortnight' of patriotic fervour. See Anne Summers, *Angels and Citizens: British Women as Military Nurses 1854–1914* (Routledge & Kegan Paul, London, 1988), p. 252, who cites the play as the inspiration for thousands of young men joining the Territorial Force in that year.
78 Invasion fears and the need for discipline both nationally and privately are reiterated in the pamphlet du Maurier wrote for 'Moral Rearmament' in 1940, *Come Wind, Come Weather*, appealing in ringingly Churchillian tones to patriotic duty and personal sacrifice.
79 In 'Sylvia's Boys' du Maurier describes her joy at visiting her cousins, the Llewellyn Davies's five sons: 'The Davies boys are *boys*. Hurrah! for them!' (*The Rebecca Notebook*, p. 89). The eldest, George, was killed in the war and imagining her childish reactions to this death she writes, 'Angela, Jeanne and

I have no brother. Why? I shall pretend to be a boy, then. Like the lady who acts Peter Pan. . . .' (ibid., p. 91). And it is 'the boys' who fascinate her in her biographical writings, as she commented on her life of Branwell Brontë, 'everybody always seemed to know about the girls and nobody cared much about the brother' (Cook, interview with du Maurier; see note 72 above). In 1975 she wrote *Golden Lads*, the lives of Sir Francis and Anthony Bacon.

80 Du Maurier observes that although she also read girls' school stories, especially those of Angela Brazil, she felt no desire to create a 'Peggy' Avon (*Myself When Young*, p. 52).

81 See Freud, 'Some psychical consequences of the anatomical distinction between the sexes' (1925), reprinted in *On Sexuality*, Pelican Freud Library, vol. 7, (Penguin, Harmondsworth, 1977), p. 342.

82 'M' and 'D' are what she calls her parents throughout *Myself When Young* on the strange grounds of avoiding the constant repetition of 'Mummy' and 'Daddy', names 'seldom used today' (p. 14). In fact she merely draws more attention to her adult distance from them by doing so.

83 See Green, *Dreams of Adventure*, p. 328. Dinesen's *Out of Africa* was published in 1938.

84 She remembers, for example, 'reading *Treasure Island* over a peat fire at night' (*Myself When Young*, p. 153). *Jamaica Inn* was also the result of an escapade with a friend riding across the moors, which found them lost, cut off by darkness, and arriving by chance at the inn. The friend was Foy Quiller-Couch, the daughter of Sir Arthur, or 'Q', who lived in Fowey and was one of Daphne's first friends there. He provides an interesting link back to the pre-war world of seafaring romances and national pride (his two-volume *Story of the Sea* in 1895–6 included the myth of the Protestant wind that helped defeat the Armada and save England in 1588), and Paul Fussell, *The Great War and Modern Memory*, sees his anthology, the *Oxford Book of English Verse*, which went through seventeen reprints between 1900 and 1930, as 'the book which presides over the Great War' (p. 159). As King Edward VIIth Professor of English at Cambridge from 1912, 'Q' was also an important figure in the turn away from more 'belligerently chauvinistic' nationalism toward an idea of the English as a 'common folk' in the literary studies of the period. See Peter Brooker and Peter Widdowson, 'A literature for England', in Robert Colls and Philip Dodd (eds), *Englishness: Politics and Culture 1880–1920* (Croom Helm, London, 1986), and Green, *Dreams of Adventure*, p. 322. He was also a prolific writer about Cornwall, and in 1929 we find du Maurier reading all his novels (*Myself When Young*, p. 138). So close did she become to the family that in 1962 she completed his novel *Castle Dor*. By one of those coincidences which delight researchers, 'Q' himself had completed *St Ives* by R. L. Stevenson in 1898. Perhaps wheels do come full circle.

85 Obituary, *Guardian*, 20 April 1989.

86 This is the view put forward by Janice Doane and Devon Hodges, *Nostalgia and Sexual Difference* (Methuen, London, 1987), p. 128.

87 She was obviously not the first to do this. There is a story still to be told about the imaginative construction of Cornwall as a Celtic periphery which would include Stevenson and 'Q', but also the artistic 'colonies' established in the 1880s and '90s, at Newlyn and eventually St Ives, and which 'fixed the identity of the Cornish as that of ancient communities closer to nature than was metropolitan England' (Philip Dodd, 'Englishness and the national culture', in Colls and Dodd, *Englishness*, p. 14).

88 Du Maurier's roundheads in *The King's General* (1946) are an army of prolet-

arian vandals (remarkably like Nazis with their brownshirts and cropped hair), speaking like Cockney barrow-boys and setting up a totalitarian State. (One is reminded of Evelyn Waugh's army of 'Hoopers' in *Brideshead Revisited*). In *Rule Britannia* an 80-year-old widow fights an invasion of American troops aiming to take over Britain.
89 *Myself when Young*, p. 155.
90 'Death and widowhood', *The Rebecca Notebook*, p. 129.
91 'The matinée idol', ibid.

AFTERWORD

1 *Brief Encounter*, written and produced by Noel Coward, directed by David Lean, was their fourth collaboration after *In Which We Serve* (1942), *This Happy Breed* (1944) and *Blithe Spirit* (1945).
2 John Russell Taylor, Introduction to the screenplay of *Brief Encounter* (Classic Film Scripts, Lorrimer, London, 1984), p. 6.
3 A recent discussion of Lean's contribution to the development to British social realism is Andrew Higson's assessment, ' "Britain's outstanding contribution to the film": the documentary-realist tradition', in Charles Barr (ed.), *All Our Yesterdays: 90 Years of British Cinema* (British Film Institute, London, 1986).
4 Roger Manvell, for example, admires the absence of 'false intonations' in Johnson's acting: *The Film and the Public* (Penguin, Harmondsworth, 1955), cited in Taylor, Introduction to screenplay of *Brief Encounter* p. 8.
5 See Sue Aspinall, 'Women, realism and reality in British films, 1943–53', in James Curran and Vincent Porter (eds), *British Cinema History* (Weidenfeld, London, 1983), for an overview of the representations of femininity and class in British films in the period.
6 For a recent addition to the literature of war, see Claire Tylee, *The Great War and Women's Consciousness: Images of Militarism and Womanhood in Women's Writings, 1914–64* (University of Iowa Press, Iowa, 1990).
7 See Jane Mackay and Pat Thane's discussion, 'The Englishwoman', in R. Colls and P. Dodd (eds), *Englishness: Politics and Culture 1880–1920* (Croom Helm, London, 1986).
8 'Still Life', *Tonight at 8.30* (I) (Heinemann, 1936); in *Plays: Three* (Methuen, London, 1983), p. 351.
9 Freud explicitly introduced his idea of the 'death instinct' or 'death drive' in *Beyond the Pleasure Principle* (1920) as a development of his thoughts on the 'compulsion to repeat' which suggested to him the inherently conservative nature of living substances. Interestingly he was working at this time on the 'war neuroses' and also 'the traumatic neuroses of peace': *On Metapsychology: The Theory of Psychoanalysis*, vol. 11, Pelican Freud Library (Penguin, Harmondsworth, 1984), p. 281.
10 'Nostalgia', she writes, 'is not a literary concoction, it is a prevailing mood. . . . That day-before yesterday represents at once the last and the best of the old order', 'The bend back' written in 1950; reprinted in Hermione Lee (ed.), *The Mulberry Tree: Writings of Elizabeth Bowen* (Virago, London, 1986), p. 57.
11 Virginia Woolf, introductory letter to Margaret Llewelyn Davies (ed.), *Life As We Have Known It: by Co-operative Working Women* (Hogarth Press, London, 1931; reprinted Virago, London, 1977), pp. 27–8.
12 'Lady novelists and the lower orders', *Scrutiny*, vol. 4, no. 2 (September 1935), p. 113.
13 I am indebted in these closing thoughts to Carolyn Steedman's remarkable and

provocative explorations of the meaning of class and its relation to domesticity and ideas of female interiority: *The Tidy House* (Virago, London, 1982) and *Landscape for a Good Woman* (Virago, London, 1986).

14 Leonore Davidoff and Catherine Hall, *Family Fortunes: Men and Women of the English Middle Class 1780–1850* (Hutchinson, London, 1987), p. 450; see also Cora Kaplan, 'Pandora's box: subjectivity, class and sexuality in socialist feminist criticism', in *Sea Changes: Culture and Feminism* (Verso, London, 1986).

15 Elizabeth Taylor, *A Game of Hide and Seek* (Peter Davies, London, 1951), p. 50.

16 Amongst the earliest precursors of the modern Women's Movement were two books which reflected on the housewife's lot: in America Betty Friedan's *The Feminine Mystique* (1963) and in Britain the sociologist Hannah Gavron's *The Captive Wife* (1966) prefigured later, more overtly feminist accounts like those of Sheila Rowbotham, *Woman's Consciousness, Man's World* (1973) and Ann Oakley, *Housewife* (1974). Oakley firmly maintains that 'housework is work directly opposed to the possibility of human self-actualisation' (Penguin edn, Harmondsworth, 1976, p. 222); those women who believe that they enjoy housewifery merely suffer from false consciousness.

Bibliography

The place of publication is London unless otherwise stated.

FICTION, POETRY AND DRAMA

Only works from which quotation has been made in the text are given in full here, with both details of the original publication and, where relevant, additional details of editions used.

Bagnold, Enid, *The Squire* (Heinemann, 1938; Virago, 1986).
Christie, Agatha, *The Mysterious Affair at Styles* (Bodley Head, 1920; Granada, 1982).
——*The Secret Adversary* (Bodley Head, 1922; Pan, 1960).
——*Murder on the Links* (Bodley Head, 1923; Granada 1982).
——*The Murder of Roger Ackroyd* (Collins, 1926; Fontana, 1957).
——*Peril at End House* (Collins, 1932; Fontana, 1988).
——*Murder on the Orient Express* (Collins, 1934; Fontana, 1974).
——*Three Act Tragedy* (Collins, 1935; Fontana, 1971).
——*Death in the Clouds* (Collins, 1935).
——*The ABC Murders* (Collins, 1936; Fontana, 1962).
——*Murder in Mesopotamia* (Collins, 1936; Fontana, 1973).
——*Cards on the Table* (Collins, 1936; Fontana, 1969).
——*Appointment with Death* (Collins, 1938; Fontana, 1972).
——*Murder is Easy* (Collins, 1939; Fontana, 1968).
——*Ten Little Niggers* (Collins, 1939; Fontana, 1966).
——*The Body in the Library* (Collins, 1942; Fontana, 1968).
——*Towards Zero* (Collins, 1944; Fontana, 1972).
——*Death Comes as the End* (Collins, 1945; Fontana, 1981).
——*They Came to Baghdad* (Collins, 1951; Fontana, 1960).
——*Mrs McGinty's Dead* (Collins, 1952; Fontana, 1988).
——*The Mirror Crack'd from Side to Side* (Collins, 1962).
——*At Bertram's Hotel* (Collins, 1965).
——*By the Pricking of My Thumbs* (Collins, 1968; Fontana, 1971).
——*Hallowe'en Party* (Collins, 1969; Fontana, 1976).
Compton-Burnett, Ivy, *Pastors and Masters* (Gollancz, 1925; Allison & Busby, 1984).
——*Brothers and Sisters* (Gollancz, 1929; Allison & Busby, 1984).
——*Men and Wives* (Gollancz, 1931; Allison & Busby, 1984).
——*More Women Than Men* (Gollancz, 1933; Allison & Busby, 1983).

——— *A House and Its Head* (Gollancz, 1935; Penguin, Harmondsworth, 1982).
——— *Daughters and Sons* (Gollancz, 1937; Allison & Busby, 1984).
——— *A Family and a Fortune* (Gollancz, 1939; Penguin, Harmondsworth, 1962).
——— *Elders and Betters* (Gollancz, 1944; Allison & Busby, 1983).
——— *Manservant and Maidservant* (Gollancz, 1947; Oxford University Press, Oxford, 1983).
——— *Two Worlds and Their Ways* (Gollancz, 1949).
——— *Mother and Son* (Gollancz, 1955).
——— *A God and His Gifts* (Gollancz, 1963; Penguin, Harmondsworth, 1983).
——— *The Last and the First* (Gollancz, 1971; Penguin, Harmondsworth, 1986).
Conan Doyle, Arthur, *The Complete Sherlock Holmes* (Doubleday, 1930; Penguin, Harmondsworth, 1986).
Coward, Noel, *Design for Living* (Heinemann, 1933); in *Plays: Three* (Methuen, 1983).
——— 'Still Life', *Tonight at 8.30* (I) (Heinemann, 1936); in *Plays: Three* (Methuen, 1983).
Delafield, E. M., *The Way Things Are* (Hutchinson, 1927; Virago, 1988).
——— *The Diary of a Provincial Lady* (Macmillan, 1930; collected edition, Macmillan 1947).
——— *Thank Heaven Fasting* (Macmillan, 1932; Virago, 1988).
Du Maurier, Daphne, *The Loving Spirit* (Heinemann, 1931; Pan, 1975).
——— *Jamaica Inn* (Gollancz, 1936; Pan, 1976).
——— *Rebecca* (Gollancz, 1938; Pan, 1975).
——— *Frenchman's Creek* (Gollancz, 1941; Penguin, Harmondsworth, 1962).
——— *The King's General* (Gollancz, 1946; Pan, 1974).
——— *My Cousin Rachel* (Gollancz, 1951; Penguin, Harmondsworth 1962).
——— *The Scapegoat* (Gollancz, 1957; Pan, 1975).
Kitchin, C. H. B., *Death of His Uncle* (Constable, 1939; Hogarth Press, 1986).
Marsh, Ngaio, *Death in a White Tie* (Collins, 1938; Fontana, 1960).
Murray, Isobel (ed.), *Oscar Wilde* (Oxford University Press, Oxford, 1989).
Osborne, John, *Look Back in Anger* (Faber & Faber, 1960).
Reilly, Catherine (ed.), *Scars upon My Heart: Women's Poetry and Verse of the First World War* (Virago, 1981).
'Sapper', *The Black Gang* (Hodder & Stoughton, 1922).
Sayers, Dorothy L., *Clouds of Witness* (Gollancz, 1926; New English Library, 1970).
——— *Gaudy Night* (Gollancz, 1935; first cheap edition, 1936).
——— *Busman's Honeymoon* (Gollancz, 1937; New English Library 1977).
Sellar, W. C. and Yeatman, R. J., *1066 And All That* (Methuen, 1930; Penguin, Harmondsworth 1960).
Stevenson, R. L., *An Inland Voyage* (1878; Dent, 1984).
Strong, Patience, *Quiet Thoughts* (Frederick Muller, 1937).
Struther, Jan, *Try Anything Twice* (Chatto & Windus, 1938).
——— *Mrs. Miniver* (Chatto & Windus, 1939; Virago, 1989).
Taylor, Elizabeth, *A Game of Hide and Seek* (Peter Davies, 1951).
Wallace, Edgar, *The Coat of Arms* (Hutchinson, 1931).
Westmacott, Mary, *Giant's Bread* (Collins, 1930; Fontana 1973).

AUTOBIOGRAPHICAL AND BIOGRAPHICAL MATERIAL: DIARIES, MEMOIRS, ETC.

Bell, Ann Olivier (ed.), *The Diary of Virginia Woolf*, vols 3 and 4 (Penguin, Harmondsworth, 1983).

Benson, E. F., *As We Are: A Modern Review* (Longman, 1932; Hogarth Press, 1985).

Cadogan, Mary, *Richmal Crompton: The Woman behind William* (Allen & Unwin, 1986).

Christie, Agatha, *An Autobiography* (Collins, 1977; Fontana, 1978).

Christie, Agatha Mallowan, *Come, Tell Me How You Live* (Hamlyn, 1985).

Cook, Christopher, interview with du Maurier, 'Scenes from the life of Dame Daphne du Maurier', BBC Radio 4, 7 January 1990.

Davie, Michael, 'Sir Plum of Dulwich', *Observer*, 5 June, 1988.

Davies, Margaret Llewelyn (ed.), *Life As We Have Known It: by Co-operative Working Women* (Hogarth Press, 1931; Virago, 1977).

Dick, Kay, *Ivy and Stevie: Conversations and Reflections* (Duckworth, 1971; Allison & Busby, 1983).

du Maurier, Angela, *Old Maids Remember* (Peter Davies, 1966).

du Maurier, Daphne, *Gerald: A Portrait* (Gollancz, 1934).

——*Vanishing Cornwall* (Gollancz, 1967).

——*Myself When Young – the Shaping of a Writer* (published as *Growing Pains*, Gollancz, 1977; Pan, 1978).

——*The Rebecca Notebook and Other Memories* (Gollancz, 1981).

du Maurier, Gerald, Preface to *Trilby* by George du Maurier (Dent, 1931).

Ellmann, Richard, *Oscar Wilde* (Hamish Hamilton, 1987).

Greig, Cicely, *Ivy Compton-Burnett: A Memoir* (Garnstone Press, 1972).

Kennedy, Richard, *A Boy at the Hogarth Press* (Penguin, Harmondsworth, 1972).

Lees-Milne, James, *Ancestral Voices* (Chatto & Windus, 1975).

——*Prophesying Peace* (Chatto & Windus, 1977).

——*Caves of Ice* (Chatto & Windus, 1983).

——*Midway on the Waves* (Faber & Faber, 1985).

Liddell, Robert, *Elizabeth and Ivy* (Peter Owen, 1986).

Mallowan, Max, *Mallowan's Memoirs* (Collins, 1977).

Middleton Murry, John (ed.), *Letters of Katherine Mansfield to John Middleton Murry 1913–1922* (Constable, 1951).

Morgan, Janet, *Agatha Christie* (Fontana, 1985).

Mortimer, Penelope, *About Time* (Allen Lane, 1979).

Powell, Anthony, Obituary, 'Ivy Compton-Burnett', *Spectator*, 6 September 1969; reprinted in Charles Burkhart (ed.), *The Art of I. Compton-Burnett* (Gollancz, 1972).

Powell, Violet, *The Life of a Provincial Lady* (Heinemann, 1988).

Robyns, Gwen, *The Mystery of Agatha Christie* (Penguin, Harmondsworth 1979).

Sebba, Ann, *Enid Bagnold* (Weidenfeld & Nicolson, 1986).

Sprigge, Elizabeth, *The Life of Ivy Compton-Burnett* (Gollancz, 1973).

Spurling, Hilary, *Ivy When Young: the Early Life of I. Compton-Burnett 1884–1919* (Gollancz, 1974; Allison & Busby, 1983).

——*Secrets of a Woman's Heart: The Later Life of Ivy Compton-Burnett 1920–1969* (Hodder & Stoughton, 1984; Penguin, Harmondsworth 1985).

Terkel, Studs, *Talking to Myself* (Pantheon, New York, 1973).

Thornton, Michael, 'Secret jealousy of the real Rebecca', *Observer*, 23 April 1989.

Williams, Kay, *Just Richmal: The Life and Work of Richmal Crompton Lamburn* (Genesis, Guildford 1986).
Wilson, Angus, Obituary, 'Ivy Compton-Burnett', *Observer*, 31 August 1969; reprinted in Charles Burkhart (ed.), *The Art of I. Compton-Burnett* (Gollancz, 1972).
Woolf, Leonard, *An Autobiography*, 2 vols, (Oxford University Press, Oxford, 1980).
Woolf, Virgina, *Moments of Being* (Hogarth Press, 1985).
——*A Writer's Diary* (Hogarth Press, London, 1953).

LITERARY CRITICISM, ESSAYS AND JOURNALISM BEFORE 1950

Bagnold, Enid, 'In Germany today – Hitler's new form of democracy', *Sunday Times*, 6 November 1938.
Bowen, Elizabeth, 'Parents and children' (1941); 'Out of a book' (1946), 'The bend back' (1950), reprinted in Hermione Lee (ed.), *The Mulberry Tree: Writings of Elizabeth Bowen* (Virago, 1986).
Forster, E. M., 'Mrs Miniver' (1939) in *Two Cheers for Democracy* (Edward Arnold, 1951).
Holtby, Winifred, 'Feminism Divided', *Yorkshire Post*, 26 July 1926; reprinted in P. Berry and A. Bishop (eds), *Testament of a Generation: The Journalism of Vera Brittain and Winifred Holtby* (Virago, 1985).
Jameson, Storm, *Civil Journey* (Cassell, 1939).
Lamb, Charles, *The Essays of Elia* (Oxford University Press, Oxford, 1912).
Lawrence, D. H., 'Nottingham and the mining countryside', in *Phoenix: The Posthumous Papers of D. H. Lawrence* (Heinemann, 1936; reprinted 1961).
Leavis, F. R., *Mass Civilisation and Minority Culture* (Minority Press, Cambridge, 1930).
Leavis, Q. D., *Fiction and the Reading Public* (Chatto & Windus, 1932).
——'Lady novelists and the lower orders', *Scrutiny*, vol. 4, no. 2 (September 1935).
——'Caterpillars of the commonwealth unite!', *Scrutiny*, vol. 7, no. 2 (1938–9).
Liddell, Robert, 'The novels of I. Compton-Burnett', Appendix III in *A Treatise on the Novel* (Cape, 1947); reprinted in Charles Burkhart (ed.), *The Art of I. Compton-Burnett* (Gollancz, 1972).
Mortimer, Raymond, 'A House and Its Head', *New Statesman and Nation*, 13 July 1935; reprinted in Charles Burkhart (ed.), *The Art of I. Compton-Burnett* (Gollancz, 1972).
Orwell, George, 'Bookshop memories', in *The Collected Essays, Journalism and Letters of George Orwell*, vol. 1. (Penguin, Harmondsworth 1970).
Rathbone, Eleanor, 'Changes in public life', in Ray Strachey, *Our Freedom and Its Results* ((Hogarth Press, 1936).
Read, Herbert, 'Blood wet and dry', *Night and Day*, 23 December 1937).
Sackville-West, Edward, 'Ladies whose bright pens . . .', in *Inclinations* (Secker & Warburg, 1949); reprinted in Charles Burkhart (ed.), *The Art of I. Compton-Burnett* (Gollancz, 1972).
Strachey, Ray, *Our Freedom and Its Results* (Hogarth Press, 1936).
Troubridge, Lady Una, *Etiquette and Entertaining: To Help You on Your Social Way* (Amalgamated Press, n.d.)
West, Rebecca, *The Strange Necessity* (Cape, 1928; Virago, 1987).
Wilson, Edmund, 'Who cares who killed Roger Ackroyd?' (1945), in Robert

Winks (ed.), *Detective Fiction: A Collection of Critical Essays* (Foul Play Press, Vermont, 1988).

———Woolf, Virginia, *A Room of One's Own* (Hogarth Press, 1929; Granada, 1975).

———Introductory letter to Margaret Llewelyn Davies (ed.), *Life As We Have Known It: by Co-operative Working Women* (Hogarth Press, 1931; Virago, 1977).

———'Mr. Bennett and Mrs. Brown' in *The Captain's Death Bed and Other Essays* (Hogarth Press, 1950).

———'Women and fiction', in *Granite and Rainbow* (Hogarth Press, 1958); reprinted in Michèle Barrett (ed.), *Virginia Woolf: Women and Writing* (Women's Press, 1979).

———'Professions for Women', in *The Death of the Moth* (Hogarth Press, 1942); reprinted in Michèle Barrett (ed.), *Virginia Woolf: Women and Writing* (Women's Press, 1979).

———*Three Guineas* (Hogarth Press, 1938; Penguin, Harmondsworth, 1977).

LITERARY CRITICISM, ESSAYS AND JOURNALISM POST–1950

Allen, Walter, *The English Novel* (Phoenix House, 1954; Penguin, 1973).

Amis, Kingsley, 'One world and its way', *Twentieth Century* CLVIII (August 1955).

Anderson, Rachel, *The Purple Heart Throbs: The Sub-literature of Love* (Hodder & Stoughton, 1974).

Armstrong, Nancy, *Desire and Domestic Fiction: A Political History of the Novel* (Oxford University Press, Oxford 1987).

Auden, W. H., 'The guilty vicarage', in *The Dyer's Hand and Other Essays* (Faber & Faber, 1963).

Barnard, Robert, *A Talent to Deceive – An Appreciation of Agatha Christie* (Dodd, Mead & Co., New York, 1980).

Barrett, Michèle (ed.), *Virginia Woolf: Women and Writing* (Women's Press, 1979).

Beauman, Nicola, *A Very Great Profession: The Woman's Novel 1914–39* (Virago, 1983).

Bergonzi, Bernard, *Reading the Thirties: Texts and Contexts* (Macmillan, 1978).

Berry, P. and Bishop, A. (eds), *Testament of a Generation: The Journalism of Vera Brittain and Winifred Holtby* (Virago, 1985).

Binyon, T. J., *Murder Will Out: The Detective in Fiction* (Oxford University Press, Oxford, 1989).

Bowlby, Rachel, *Virginia Woolf: Feminist Destinations* (Blackwell, Oxford, 1988).

Brooker, Peter and Widdowson, Peter, 'A literature for England' in R. Colls and P. Dodd (eds), *Englishness: Politics and Culture 1880–1920* (Croom Helm, 1986).

Brookner, Anita, 'Good husbandry', *Observer*, 25 September 1988.

Bromley, Roger, 'The gentry, bourgeois hegemony and popular fiction: *Rebecca* and *Rogue Male*', in P. Humm, P. Stigant and P. Widdowson (eds), *Popular Fictions: Essays in Literature and History* (Methuen, 1986).

Brophy, Brigid, 'Sir Hereward', *New Statesman*, 6 December 1963.

Burkhart, Charles, *I. Compton-Burnett* (Gollancz, 1965).

———(ed.), *The Art of I. Compton-Burnett* (Gollancz, 1972).

———(guest ed.), Ivy Compton-Burnett Issue, *Twentieth Century Literature*, vol. 25, no. 2 (Summer 1979).

Butler, Marilyn, *Jane Austen and the War of Ideas* (Oxford University Press, Oxford, 1987).

Cadogan, Mary and Craig, Patricia, *The Lady Investigates: Women Detectives and Spies in Fiction* (Oxford University Press, Oxford, 1986).

Calder, Jenni, *Heroes: From Byron to Guevara* (Hamish Hamilton, 1977).

Carr, Helen (ed.), *From My Guy to Sci-Fi: Genre and Women's Writing in the Postmodern World* (Pandora, 1989).

Cawelti, John G., *Adventure, Mystery and Romance* (University of Chicago Press, Chicago, 1976).

Chandler, Raymond, 'The simple art of murder', in *Pearls Are a Nuisance* (Hamish Hamilton, 1950; Penguin, Harmondsworth, 1964).

Cecil, Mirabel, *Heroines in Love 1750–1974* (Michael Joseph, 1974).

Cockburn, Claud, *Bestsellers: The Books That Everyone Read 1900–1939* (Sidgwick & Jackson, 1972).

Cooper, Jilly, Introduction to *Diary of a Provincial Lady* by E. M. Delafield (Folio Society edition, 1979).

Coward, Rosalind and Semple, Linda, 'Tracking down the past: women and detective fiction', in Helen Carr (ed.), *From My Guy to Sci-Fi: Genre and Women's Writing in the Postmodern World* (Pandora, 1989).

Crosland, Margaret, *Beyond the Lighthouse: English Women Novelists in the Twentieth Century* (Constable, 1981).

Cunningham, Valentine, *British Writers of the 1930s* (Oxford University Press, Oxford, 1988).

Drotner, Kirsten, *More Next Week! English Children and their Magazines 1751–1945* (Aarhus University Press, Aarhus, 1985).

Dunn, Peter, 'Morse, codes and crosswords', *Independent*, 28 January 1989.

Ellmann, Mary, *Thinking About Women* (Macmillan, 1969).

Evans, Ifor, *A Short History of English Literature* (Penguin, Harmondsworth, 1963).

Ford, Boris, *The Penguin Guide to English Literature*, vol. 7, (Penguin, Harmondsworth, 1961; 1972).

Fullbrook, Kate, *Katherine Mansfield* (Harvester, Brighton, 1986).

Gilbert, Sandra M. and Gubar, Susan, *No-Man's Land; The Place of the Woman Writer in the Twentieth Century*, vol. 2, *Sex Changes* (Yale University Press, New Haven, 1989).

Glover, David, 'The stuff that dreams are made of: masculinity, femininity and the thriller' in Derek Longhurst (ed.), *Gender, Genre and Narrative Pleasure* (Unwin Hyman, 1989).

Green, Martin, *Dreams of Adventure, Deeds of Empire* (Routledge, 1980).

Grella, George, 'The formal detective novel', in Robert Winks (ed.), *Detective Fiction: A Collection of Criticial Essays* (Foul Play Press, Vermont, 1988).

Grove, Valerie, Introduction to *Mrs. Miniver* (Virago, 1989).

Hanscombe, Gillian E., *The Art of Dorothy Richardson and the Development of Feminist Consciousness* (Peter Owen, 1982).

Humm, P., Stigant, P. and Widdowson, P. (eds), *Popular Fictions: Essays in Literature and History* (Methuen, 1986).

Hynes, Samuel, *The Auden Generation: Literature and Politics in England in the 1930s* (Bodley Head, 1976).

James, Louis, *Fiction for the Working Man 1830–1850* (Oxford University Press, Oxford, 1963).

James, P. D., 'A universal aspirin and the talent to deceive', *Daily Telegraph*, 8 September 1990.

Johnstone, Richard, *The Will to Believe: Novelists of the Nineteen Thirties* (Oxford University Press, Oxford, 1984).

Keating, H. R. F., *Agatha Christie, First Lady of Crime* (Holt, Rinehart & Winston, New York 1977).
——*Sherlock Holmes: The Man and His World* (Thames & Hudson, 1979).
——*Whodunit?: A Guide to Crime, Suspense and Spy Fiction* (Windward, 1982).
Lahr, John, *Coward: The Playwright* (Methuen, 1982).
Lee, Hermione (ed.), *The Mulberry Tree: Writings of Elizabeth Bowen* (Virago, 1986).
Liddell, Robert, *The Novels of Ivy Compton-Burnett* (Gollancz, 1955).
Light, Alison, ' "Returning to Manderley": romance fiction, female sexuality and class', *Feminist Review*, no. 16 (Summer 1984).
——'*Young Bess*: historical novels and growing up', *Feminist Review*, no. 33, (Autumn 1989).
——'That blithe English spirit', *Guardian*, 7 September 1989.
Longhurst, Derek (ed.), *Gender, Genre and Narrative Pleasure* (Unwin Hyman, 1989).
Lovallo, Len and Sanders, Dennis, *The Agatha Christie Companion* (W. H. Allen, 1985).
Mandel, Ernest, *Delightful Murder: A Social History of the Crime Story* (Pluto, 1984).
Maugham, W. Somerset, *The Vagrant Mood: Six Essays* (Heinemann, 1952).
Maxtone Graham, Ysenda, 'Wit and Mrs Miniver', *Observer*, 13 August 1989.
McCarthy, Mary, *The Writing on the Wall and Other Literary Essays* (Weidenfeld & Nicolson, 1970).
Melman, Billie, *Women and the Popular Imagination in the Twenties: Flappers and Nymphs* (Macmillan, 1988).
Modleski, Tania, *Loving with a Vengeance: Mass-produced Fantasies for Women* (Methuen, 1984).
Moers, Ellen, *Literary Women* (Women's Press, 1978).
Moi, Toril, *Sexual/Textual Politics* (Methuen, 1985).
Monteith, Moira (ed.), *Women's Writing: A Challenge to Theory* (Harvester, Brighton, 1986).
Moretti, Franco, *Signs Taken for Wonders: Essays in the Sociology of Literary Forms* (Verso, 1983).
Nevius, Blake, *Ivy Compton-Burnett* (Columbia University Press, New York, 1970).
Olsen, Tillie, *Silences* (Virago, 1980).
Osbourne, Charles, *The Life and Crimes of Agatha Christie* (Collins, 1982).
Porter, Peter, 'On-screen authors', *Times Literary Supplement*, 9 December 1988.
Ramsey, G. C., *Agatha Christie: Mistress of Mystery* (Collins, 1968).
Reilly, John M. (ed.), *Twentieth Century Crime and Mystery Writers* (St James' Press, 1985).
Rose, Jacqueline, *The Case of Peter Pan or the Impossibility of Children's Fiction* (Macmillan, 1984).
Rule, Jane, *Lesbian Images* (Doubleday, New York, 1975).
Rushdie, Salman, 'Is Nothing Sacred?', the Herbert Read Memorial Lecture, 6 February 1990; printed in *Granta*, no. 31 (Spring 1990) (Penguin, Harmondsworth).
Rustin, Margaret and Rustin, Michael, *Narratives of Love and Loss: Studies in Modern Children's Fiction* (Verso, 1987).
Sarraute, Nathalie, *L'Ere du Soupçon* (Gallimard, Paris, 1959); translated by Maria Jolas in *Tropisms and the Age of Suspicion* (Calder & Boyars, 1963).
Shaw, Marion, 'Feminism and fiction between the wars: Winifred Holtby and

Virginia Woolf', in Moira Monteith (ed.), *Women's Writing: A Challenge to Theory* (Harvester, Brighton, 1986).

Showalter, Elaine, *A Literature of Their Own: British Women Novelists from Brontë to Lessing* (Virago, 1978).

Spurling, Hilary, 'The Last and the First', *New Statesman*, 5 February 1971; reprinted in Charles Burkhart (ed.), *The Art of I. Compton-Burnett* (Gollancz, 1972).

——'Happy ever after', *Observer*, 23 September 1984.

Stevenson, Randall, *The British Novel since the Thirties* (Batsford, 1986).

Symons, Julian, *Bloody Murder* (Penguin, Harmondsworth, 1974).

——*Critical Observations* (Faber & Faber, 1981).

Taylor, Helen, *Scarlett's Women: 'Gone with the Wind' and its Female Fans* (Virago, 1989).

——'Romantic readers', in Helen Carr (ed.), *From My Guy to Sci-Fi: Genre and Women's Writing in the Postmodern World* (Pandora, 1989).

Todd, Janet, *Feminist Literary History* (Blackwell, Oxford, 1988).

Turner, E. S., *Boys Will Be Boys* (Michael Joseph, 1948; revised 1957).

Usborne, Richard, *Clubland Heroes* (Barrie & Jenkins, 1953; revised 1974).

Watson, Colin, *Snobbery with Violence: English Crime Stories and Their Audience* (Eyre Methuen, 1971; revised 1979).

Webster, Harvey Curtis, *After the Trauma: Representative British Novelists since 1920* (University Press of Kentucky, Lexington, 1970).

White, Cynthia, *Women's Magazines 1693–1968* (Michael Joseph, 1970).

Widdowson, Peter, 'Between the acts? English fiction in the thirties', in J. Clark, M. Heinemann, D. Margolies and C. Snee (eds), *Culture and Crisis in Britain in the '30s* (Lawrence & Wishart, 1979).

Williams, Raymond, *The English Novel from Dickens to Lawrence* (Chatto & Windus, 1970).

Winks, Robert, (ed.), *Detective Fiction: A Collection of Critical Essays* (Foul Play Press, Vermont, 1988).

Worpole, Ken, *Dockers and Detectives* (Verso, 1983).

HISTORICAL, POLITICAL AND CULTURAL COMMENTARIES

Alexander, Sally, 'Becoming a woman in the 1920s and 1930s', in David Feldman and Gareth Stedman Jones (eds), *Metropolis. London: Histories and Representations since 1800* (Routledge, 1989).

Aspinall, Sue, 'Women, realism and reality in British films, 1943–53', in James Curran and Vincent Porter (eds), *British Cinema History* (Weidenfeld, 1983).

Ball, Stuart, *Baldwin and the Conservative Party* (Yale University Press, New Haven, 1988).

Barr, Charles (ed.), *All Our Yesterdays: 90 Years of British Cinema* (British Film Institute, 1986).

Blake, Robert, *The Conservative Party from Peel to Churchill* (Eyre & Spottiswoode, 1970).

Beddoe, Deirdre, *Back to Home and Duty* (Pandora, 1989).

Braybon, Gail and Summerfield, Penny, *Out of the Cage: Women's Experiences in Two World Wars* (Pandora, 1987).

Briggs, Asa, *Mass Entertainment* (Griffin, 1960).

Buckingham, David, *Public Secrets: Eastenders and its Audience* (British Film Institute, 1988).

Caffrey, Kate, *'37-'39: The Last Look Round* (Gordon & Cremonesi, 1978).

Campbell, Beatrix, *Iron Ladies: Why do Women Vote Tory?* (Virago, 1987).

Cecil, Hugh, *Conservatism* (Williams & Norgate, 1912).

Clark, J., Heinemann, M., Margolies, D. and Snee, C. (eds), *Culture and Crisis in Britain in the '30s* (Lawrence & Wishart, 1979).

Clarke, J., Critcher, C. and Johnson, R. (eds), *Working Class Culture* (Hutchinson, 1979).

Colls, R. and Dodd, P. (eds), *Englishness: Politics and Culture 1880–1920* (Croom Helm, 1986).

Connor, A. B., *Highways and Byways* (1908; publisher not given).

Cruse, Amy, *The Victorians and Their Books* (Allen & Unwin, 1935).

Curran, James and Porter, Vincent (eds), *British Cinema History* (Weidenfeld, 1983).

Curran, J., Smith, A. and Wingate, P. (eds), *Impacts and Influences: Essays on Media Power* (Methuen, 1987).

Cutforth, René, *Later Than We Thought: A Portrait of the Thirties* (David & Charles, Newton Abbot, 1976).

Darton, F. J. Harvey, *Children's Books in England* (Cambridge University Press, Cambridge, 1932).

Davidoff, Leonore, *The Best Circles* (Croom Helm, 1973).

Davidoff, Leonore, and Hall, Catherine, *Family Fortunes: Men and Women of the English Middle Class 1780–1850* (Hutchinson, 1987).

Doane, Janice and Hodges, Devon, *Nostalgia and Sexual Difference: The Resistance to Contemporary Feminism* (Methuen, 1987).

Doane, Mary Ann, *The Desire to Desire* (Macmillan, 1989).

Dodd, Philip, 'Englishness and the national culture', in R. Colls and P. Dodd (eds), *Englishness: Politics and Culture 1880–1920* (Croom Helm, 1986).

Dworkin, Andrea, *Right-wing Women: The Politics of Domesticated Females* (Women's Press, 1983).

Dyhouse, Carol, *Feminism and the Family in England 1880–1939* (Blackwell, Oxford, 1989).

Feldman, David and Stedman Jones, Gareth (eds), *Metropolis. London: Histories and Representations since 1800* (Routledge, 1989).

Fraser, W. H., *The Coming of the Mass Market 1850–1914* (Macmillan, 1981).

Freud, Sigmund, *Jokes and Their Relation to the Unconscious*, vol. 6, Pelican Freud Library (Penguin, Harmondsworth, 1976).

————*On Sexuality: Three Essays on the Theory of Sexuality and Other Works*, vol. 7, Pelican Freud Library (Penguin, Harmondsworth, 1977).

————*On Metapsychology: The Theory of Psychoanalysis*, vol. 11, Pelican Freud Library (Penguin, Harmondsworth, 1984).

————*Art and Literature*, vol. 14, Pelican Freud Library (Penguin, Harmondsworth, 1985).

Fussell, Paul, *The Great War and Modern Memory* (Oxford University Press, Oxford, 1977).

————*Abroad: British Literary Travelling between the Wars* (Oxford University Press, Oxford, 1980).

Gilbert, Martin and Gott, Richard, *The Appeasers* (Weidenfeld & Nicolson, 1963).

Ginzburg, Carlo, 'Morelli, Freud and Sherlock Holmes: clues and the scientific method', *History Workshop Journal*, no. 9 (Spring 1980).

Gloversmith, Frank (ed.), *Class, Culture and Social Change: A New View of the 1930s* (Harvester, Brighton, 1980).

Gomme, G. L., *London in the Reign of Victoria* (Blackie, 1898).

Gramsci, Antonio, *Selections from Cultural Writings*, ed. David Forgacs and Geoffrey Nowell-Smith (Lawrence & Wishart, 1985).

Graves, Robert and Hodge, Alan, *The Long Week-End: A Social History of Great Britain 1918–1939* (Faber & Faber, 1940).

Hewison, Robert, *The Heritage Industry* (Methuen, 1987).

Higonnet, M. R., Jenson, J., Michel, S. and Weitz, M. C. (eds), *Behind the Lines: Gender and the Two World Wars* (Yale University Press, New Haven, 1987).

Higson, Andrew, ' "Britain's outstanding contribution to the film": the documentary-realist tradition', in Charles Barr (ed.), *All Our Yesterdays: 90 Years of British Cinema* (British Film Institute, 1986).

Hillier, Bevis, *The Style of the Century 1900–1980* (E. P. Dutton, New York, 1983).

Hogg, Quintin, *The Case for Conservatism* (Penguin, 1947).

Hopkinson, Tom (ed.), *Picture Post* (Penguin, Harmondsworth, 1970).

Huyssen, A., 'Mass culture as woman: modernism's Other', in Tania Modleski (ed.), *Studies in Entertainment – Critical Approaches to Mass Culture* (Indiana University Press, Bloomington, 1986).

Jeffrey, Tom and McClelland, Keith, 'A world fit to live in: the *Daily Mail* and the middle classes 1918–1939', in J. Curran, A. Smith and P. Wingate (eds), *Impacts and Influences: Essays on Media Power* (Methuen, 1987).

Kaplan, Cora, *Sea Changes: Culture and Feminism* (Verso, 1986).

Kirk, Russell, *The Conservative Mind: from Burke to Santayana* (H. Regnery Co., New York, 1953).

Lewis, Jane, *Women in England 1870–1950: Sexual Divisions and Social Change* (Wheatsheaf, Brighton, 1984).

——(ed.), *Labour and Love: Women's Experience of Home and Family 1850–1940* (Blackwell, Oxford, 1986).

Mackay, Jane and Thane, Pat, 'The Englishwoman', in R. Colls and P. Dodd (eds), *Englishness: Politics and Culture 1880–1920* (Croom Helm, 1986).

Matthews, Jill, 'They had such a lot of fun: the Women's League of Health and Beauty', *History Workshop Journal*, no. 30 (Autumn 1990).

Modleski, Tania (ed.), *Studies in Entertainment – Critical Approaches to Mass Culture* (Indiana University Press, Bloomington, 1986).

——*The Women Who Knew Too Much: Hitchcock and Feminist Theory* (Methuen, 1988).

Mowat, Charles Loch, *Britain between the Wars 1918–1940* (Methuen, 1956).

Nisbet, Robert, *Conservatism* (Open University Press, Milton Keynes, 1986).

O'Gorman, Frank, *British Conservatism: Conservative Thought from Burke to Thatcher* (Longman, 1986).

O'Sullivan, Noel, *Conservatism* (Dent, 1976).

Pugh, Martin, *The Tories and the People 1880–1935* (Blackwell, Oxford, 1985).

Richards, J. M., *The Castles on the Ground: The Anatomy of Suburbia* (John Murray, 1946; reprinted 1973).

Richards, Jeffrey and Sheridan, Dorothy, *Mass-Observation at the Movies* (Routledge & Kegan Paul, 1987).

Rybczysnki, Witold, *Home: A Short History of an Idea* (Heinemann, 1988).

Samuel, Raphael, 'Middle class between the wars', *New Socialist*, January/February (part 1); June/July (part 2), 1983.

——(ed.), *Patriotism: The Making and Unmaking of British National Identity*, vol. 1, *History and Politics*; vol. 2, *Minorities and Outsiders* (Routledge, 1989).

——*Theatres of Memory* (Verso, forthcoming).

Schwarz, Bill, 'The language of constitutionalism: Baldwinite Conservatism', in *Formations of Nation and People* (Routledge, 1984).

Showalter, Elaine, 'Rivers and Sassoon: the inscription of male gender anxieties' in M. R. Higonnet, J. Jenson, S. Michel and M. C. Weitz (eds), *Behind the Lines: Gender and the Two World Wars* (Yale University Press, New Haven, 1987).

——*The Female Malady: Women, Madness and English Culture* (Virago, 1987).

Simkins, Frank, '1938: the Munich crisis and public opinion' (Ruskin College Oxford, unpublished dissertation).

Spender, Dale (ed.), *Time and Tide Wait for No Man* (Pandora, 1984).

Steedman, Carolyn, *The Tidy House* (Virago, 1982).

——*Landscape for a Good Woman: A Story of Two Lives* (Virago, 1986).

——'True romances', in Raphael Samuel (ed.), *Patriotism: The Making and Unmaking of British National Identity*, vol. 1, *History and Politics* (Routledge, 1989).

——'Women's biography and autobiography: forms of history, histories of forms', in Helen Carr (ed.), *From My Guy to Sci-Fi: Genre and Women's Writing in the Postmodern World* (Pandora, 1989).

Stevenson, John, *British Society 1914–45* (Penguin, Harmondsworth, 1984).

Summers, Anne, *Angels and Citizens: British Women as Military Nurses 1854–1914* (Routledge & Kegan Paul, 1988).

Taylor, A. J. P., *English History 1914–45* (Penguin, Harmondsworth, 1975).

Taylor, John Russell, Introduction to *Brief Encounter* (Classic Film Scripts, Lorrimer, 1984).

Taylor, Pam, 'Daughters and mothers – maids and mistresses: domestic service between the wars', in J. Clarke, C. Critcher and R. Johnson (eds), *Working Class Culture* (Hutchinson, 1979).

Tylee, Claire, *The Great War and Women's Consciousness: Images of Militarism and Womanhood in Women's Writings, 1914–64* (University of Iowa Press, Iowa, 1990).

Turim, Maureen, 'Fashion shapes: film, the fashion industry and the image of women', *Socialist Review*, no. 71 (vol. 13, no. 5, 1983).

Venturi, Robert, Brown, Denise Scott and Izenour, Steven, *Learning from Las Vegas* (MIT Press, 1972).

Walsh, Andrea A., *Women's Film and Female Experience* (Praeger, New York, 1984).

Weeks, Jeffrey, *Sex, Politics and Society* (Longman, 1981).

Williams, Raymond, *The Long Revolution* (Chatto & Windus, 1961).

Wright, Patrick, *On Living in an Old Country* (Verso, 1985).

Index